Economics, Ethics, Ecology:
Roots of Productive Conservation

Economics, Ethics, Ecology:
Roots of Productive Conservation

Edited by Walter E. Jeske

Based on material presented at the
35th annual meeting of the
Soil Conservation Society of America,
August 3-6, 1980,
Dearborn, Michigan

Published by the
Soil Conservation Society of America
Ankeny, Iowa 50021

Library of Congress Catalog Card Number 81-5325

ISBN 0-935734-07-4

$10.00

Library of Congress Cataloging in Publication Data

Economics, ethics, ecology.

1. Conservation of natural resources—Congresses.
I. Jeske, Walter E., 1929-   . II. Soil Conservation
Society of America.
S912.E28   333.7'2   81-5325
ISBN 0-935734-07-4   AACR2

Soil Conservation Society of America
7515 N.E. Ankeny Road
Ankeny, Iowa 50021

President: Jesse L. Hicks

President Elect: Robert C. Baum

Vice President: Chris J. Johannsen

Second Vice President: Floyd E. Heft

Treasurer: H. Lynn Horak

Council: Elmer E. Offerman, Maurice G. Cook, Carl V. Thompson, Donald E. Van Meter, Howard M. Hughes, Norris P. Swanson, Earl Burnett, Richard F. Sanders, David R. Cressman, John R. Henry, Andy I. Tucker

Staff: Larry D. Davis, Executive Vice President (acting); Tim Kautza, Program Assistant; Max Schnepf, Editor; James L. Sanders and John R. Walter, Assistant Editors

The Soil Conservation Society of America, founded in 1945, is a nonprofit scientific and educational association dedicated to advancing the science and art of good land use. Its 14,000 members worldwide include researchers, administrators, educators, planners, technicians, legislators, farmers and ranchers, and others with a profound interest in the wise use of land and related natural resources. Most academic disciplines concerned with the management of land and related natural resources are represented.

This book is based on material presented at the 35th annual meeting of the Soil Conservation Society of America, held August 3-6, 1980, at Dearborn, Michigan. The following members of the Society served on the annual meeting program core committee: Walter E. Jeske (chairman), Washington, D.C.; Raymond Vlasin (vice-chairman), East Lansing, Michigan; Anson R. Bertrand, Washington, D.C.; Alyson C. Deans, Downsview, Ontario; Laurence R. Jahn, Washington, D.C.; Jerry L. Keller, East Lansing, Michigan; Phyllis Marcuccio, Washington, D.C.; Charles McLaughlin, Britt, Iowa; and Louis E. Reid, Jr., Washington, D.C. Other members of the program committee included chairpersons of the Society's resource conservation divisions: Gerald J. Post (Soil Resources), Lincoln, Nebraska; Wayne O. Willis (Water Resources), Fort Collins, Colorado; Mason C. Cloud (Air Resources), Bryan, Texas; Sheridan Dronen (Plant Resources), Huron, South Dakota; L. Dean Marriage (Fish and Wildlife Resources), Portland, Oregon; Robert M. Craig (Environmental Conservation Education), Gainesville, Florida; Russell L. Shultz (Land Use Planning), Lincoln, Nebraska; Raymond Allmaras (Erosion and Sedimentation), Pendleton, Oregon; Richard L. Phillips (Waste Management), Lanham, Maryland; Norman Smola (Outdoor Recreation), Stillwater, Oklahoma; and Orus L. Bennett (Surface Mine Reclamation), Morgantown, West Virginia.

Contents

I. Economics, Ethics, Ecology: An Overview

II. The Land Planning Urgency

III. The Water Management Crunch

IV. The Energy Squeeze on Land and Water Management

V. Assessing the Future

VI. Resource Conservation Technology for the Future

VII. Education for Productive Conservation

VIII. Restoring and Maintaining Living Space

IX. Energy Challenges to Natural Resource Values

X. Protecting a Finite Land Base

XI. Water Quantity and Quality: Trends and Issues

Preface

In 1980, recession gripped the economies of both the United States and Canada; unemployment remained a national problem in both countries; and inflation continued its upward spiral. About the same time, public concern for environmental quality seemingly peaked as individuals and governments sought to deal with more pressing social needs; scarce energy supplies continued to divert financial resources away from North America; and the interdependencies among the world's nations increased amid cries for national self-sufficiency.

This setting brought about immense pressures to trade off investment in land and water conservation for other needs thought to be more immediate. It also emphasized the importance of looking at conservation in North America as an economic issue as well as an ethical and ecological one. With these realities in mind, the Soil Conservation Society of America selected the theme "Economics, Ethics, Ecology: Roots of Productive Conservation" for its thirty-fifth annual meeting, August 3-6, 1980, in Dearborn, Michigan.

To get at the roots—not just the symbols—of the critical issues in land and water conservation, the program committee for the meeting attempted to meld the facts and values from economics, ethics, and ecology. The thought was that much more than mere recognition of each discipline's domain and grudging acceptance of a few compromises are needed, that people, especially professionals in natural resources, need to be able to think about and consider economic, ethical, and ecological perspectives at the same time. No less is necessary if the United States and Canada are to move boldly ahead with resource conservation efforts that respond efficiently and equitably to people's needs.

The program committee sought to establish economic, ethical, and ecological threads throughout the program. This book contains most of the papers presented, beginning in Part I with discussions of economic realities by L. L. Boger, ethical perspectives by James Bruce, and sustained use of natural resources by Eugene Odum.

A number of prominent natural resource leaders then look closely at three issues confronting North American nations—land planning (Part II), water management (Part III), and the implications of energy development for land and water (Part IV). Each part includes the summary of a roundtable discussion that involved meeting registrants.

Part V of the book looks to the future of natural resources use. Reports on five major resource-oriented assessments sponsored by the U.S. government are followed by Futurist Robert Theobald's ideas about what natural resource professionals can do to influence the course of political events and thereby create a future that harmonizes economic, ethical, and ecological values.

Parts VI through XI consist of papers presented in a series of concurrent, thematic sessions. The point of these papers is to discuss a number of current resource issues in the context of economic realities, ethical values, and ecological principles, with at least some thought given to how potential conflicts might be reconciled. There is considerable emphasis on technology transfer also.

Professionals in natural resources are at least partly responsible for getting Americans and Canadians alike to think about the future and what facts and values should enter into decisions about how both nations use their bountiful but limited natural resources. It is SCSA's hope that publication of these papers will encourage natural resource professionals, and others for that matter, to exercise this responsibility and thereby bring about more productive conservation efforts in the decade ahead.

Walter E. Jeske
Program Chairman
Thirty-fifth Annual Meeting

1981

I. Economics, Ethics, Ecology: An Overview

1

Fitting Conservation into Economic Realities

L. L. Boger
President, Oklahoma State University, Stillwater

Although they have honed their theories and improved their abilities to test their theories, economists today approach the subject of the economics of conservation much as they did several decades ago. This is not to say that the science of economics should be reindicted as dismal. Instead, economists may be credited for explaining such phenomena as the conflicts between private and public goals and between short-run and long-run goals.

The role of economics in conservation is apparent in that national conservation programs, projects, and practices have been sold as a result of cost-benefit budgets and ratios based upon the results of economic analysis. Furthermore, the waves of technology associated with soil and water together with the economic realities of our expanding population and trade in agricultural products have demanded new and updated analysis—conservation or environmental impact studies, if you will.

This context prompts a number of questions: What is conservation? What are the problems? How does economics solve these problems?

A brief history

Quite a long time ago, Americans began to realize that something was wrong in the way land was being used. In 1928 Congress took the first step in the fight against soil erosion when it established erosion control research stations. This was followed in 1933 by creation of the Soil Erosion Service, the forerunner of the Soil Conservation Service (SCS), which became a permanent agency in the U.S. Department of Agriculture in 1935.

In 1937 many states passed laws to permit locally organized soil conservation districts. In 1944 Congress authorized a number of flood prevention projects, followed by pilot watershed projects in 1953. In 1954 Congress passed Public Law 566, the Watershed Protection and Flood Prevention Act. In 1956 Congress approved the Great Plains Program, liberalized the Watershed Protection and Flood Prevention Act, and approved the Soil Bank Act. SCS activities were broadened by the Food and Agriculture Act in 1962.

A successful partnership grew out of this history. SCS exists at the federal level; conservation commissions and similar agencies operate under state jurisdiction; and conservation districts function at the local level.

Toward a definition of conservation

As people began to view conservation as not only desirable but necessary, they also had began to define it. In 1908, President Taft, quoting Van Hise of the University of Wisconsin, defined conservation as "the greatest good to the greatest number, and that for the longest time."

Van Hise said in 1908 that "conservation is meant that [resources]... should remain as nearly undiminished as possible in order that this heritage of natural wealth may pass in full measure to succeeding generations."

In 1930, John Hammond added another dimension—recovery. He said, "While conservation in its primary meaning implies saving rather than outlay or deliberate development, the word has come to be closely allied with reclamation."

Raleigh Barlowe of Michigan State University defines conservation in an economic sense as "the wise use of resources over time." "Conservation is a concept of many meanings," he says. "Some people visualize it as a moral issue tied up with man's responsibility to safeguard certain resources for the use of future generations." Barlowe further notes that conservation involves orderly and efficient resource use, elimination of waste, and the maximization of social net returns over time.

Roland Renne, the former president of Montana State University and first executive director of the federal Office of Water Resources Research, says conservation is "protecting land resources against wasteful exploitation." "In the restricted sense of 'preservation'," Renne says, "conservation means the reduction of the rate of resource disappearance."

A paradise gained

Many of the early immigrants were motivated by the portrayal of America as a land of abundance, a veritable paradise. This was in sharp contrast to the situation in their homelands.

Thomas Inge (*4*) wrote of early America: "To the mind of the European during the age of discovery, America suggested a virgin land, an unspoiled and undefiled Garden of Eden, a new Arcadia. Sir Thomas More used the Americas as a setting for his *Utopia* for this reason.

"The extent to which preconception overrode reality is indicated by the English explorers' description of the Indian girls of Roanoke Island as nymphs, or the insistence of Christopher Columbus that he heard nightingales singing throughout the night in this country, where they never existed.

"Captain Arthur Barlow in 1584 described Virginia as a lush garden of 'incredible abundance,' overladen with fragrant flowers, fruits and succulent grapes, and blessed with soil—'the most plentifull, sweete, fruitfull and wholesome of all the worlde'."

But as people settled in the new land and migrated westward, they found that natural resources were not boundless and that problems were created by poor stewardship of these resources.

It is easy to see why Americans fell into bad conservation habits—land frontiers were boundless. We were careless with, and wasteful of, natural resources because they were so plentiful. We plowed up the prairies. We cut down the forests.

If those responsible had only practiced the conservation methods of their parents and grandparents, we could have reduced the tragedies of the dust bowl era.

Are we doing any better today? A couple of years ago this statement appeared in a publication that crossed my desk: "Although the dust storms of the fifties were not as spectacular as those of the thirties, more land was actually damaged annually by wind erosion in the Great Plains. Soil loss in the mid-seventies was on a scale comparable to the thirties."

Current pressures on the land

We've learned lessons from our wasteful, careless practices of the past and have overcome some of our mistakes. By generating and adopting new technology we have put together the most economically powerful nation on earth, a nation that provides its citizens unparalleled material wealth. We have accomplished this by combining our science and imagination with the use of our natural resources, enhanced by the creation and efforts of facilitating institutions, organizations, societies, and agencies.

We are hearing a lot about our nonrenewable resources today in the face of a worldwide energy crisis. However, many people are not convinced that we have to be careful with those resources that can be renewed. Good stewardship—conservation—is using everything we have prudently, frugally, with close attention to conserving our resources and replenishing them so that others will benefit in the future. My father used to say that his objective on the home farm was to provide a living for the family, then leave the farm in better shape than he found it for the next generation. He, like many in his generation, never heard the term "productive conservation," but he believed in it. The philosophy of productive conservation is well-stated in each issue of the *Journal of Soil and Water Conservation*:

"...the development and the advancement of the science and art of good land use and the promotion of the conservation of soil, water, air and related renewable natural resources including, without limitation, trees, grass, fish, wildlife and all forms of beneficial plant and animal life. For these purposes we employ education of the people and other appropriate means to the end that mankind may have the use and enjoyment of these resources forever."

The National Wildlife Federation puts the same thought well in its creed:

"I pledge myself, as a responsible human, to assume *my share* of man's stewardship of our natural resources.

"I will use my share with gratitude, without greed or waste.

"I will respect the rights of others and abide by the law.

"I will support the sound management of the resources we use, the restoration of the resources we have despoiled, and the safe keeping of significant resources for posterity.

"I will never forget that life and beauty, wealth and progress, depend on how wisely man uses these gifts...the soil, the water, the air, the minerals, the plant life and the wildlife. This is my pledge!"

Both of the above statements of purpose reflect productive conservation.

Problems of growth

In occupying new land areas and expanding our population, we have brought virgin land under cultivation. We created obvious problems, such as the dust bowl, stark erosion in once-productive fields, and sedimentation of our waters. With these problems we began to realize the finite nature of the land base, and we launched conservation policies, programs, and practices intended to reduce the impact of losses and the amount of that loss as these developments occur.

But the land base is finite as we now appreciate. It takes ages to form soil. Soil forms directly from the very slow decay and disintegration of the strata from which it is derived, which means a gain of only about nine-thousandths of an inch every 100 years (7). That is virtually a zero soil renewable factor.

The quality and condition of the soil is of concern to at least three groups—those now farming the land, those downstream or downhill from them, and those who will use the land 20 or 50 or 100 years from now.

How each farmer or rancher uses his land is determined by a set of circumstances that varies from one to the other. These include mortgage commitments, labor constraints, livestock requirements, liquidity needs, the owner's planning horizon, and others. Thus, each farmer will use his or her resources uniquely.

Current soil conservation programs are walking a narrow line between farmers' freedom and the overall interests of society. Conservation programs offer incentives to lower the individual's costs of conservation while attempting to maintain and improve the social capital embodied in the resource.

A productive agriculture and a strong national economy depend to a large degree on cropland retention and soil conservation (6).

The best arable land in the United States is already in agricultural production. Highway construction, urbanization, and other special uses claim more than 2.5 million acres of arable cropland each year. Soil erosion steadily reduces the productivity potential of our cropland. Increased energy is needed in the form of fertilizer and mechanical application to offset the decline in productivity potential that soil loses through degradation.

About 25 percent of our nation's land—470 million acres—is arable. And about 81 percent of our arable land in the United States is under cultivation. This does not include about 740 million acres in pasture and rangeland and another 470 million acres in forest. An estimated 75 million acres are potentially arable, but much energy and many dollars would be required to drain swamps, irrigate deserts, and grade land. Therefore, bringing new land into production to increase food production is not economically feasible.

We see an obligation, however, to provide increasing amounts of food and fiber for a rapidly growing world population. The world's population, now some four billion, is projected to reach 6 to 7 billion by the year 2000. Fortunately, food and agricultural commodities enjoy a positive balance of trade—we can export more than we import, thanks to our fertile cropland and our ability to get production from it.

Past conservation efforts and practices have enhanced this situation, but future demands on our agricultural production will call for greater diligence and attention to good conservation practices. About half of the land converted to urban use in this country formerly had been cropland. And our surface transportation systems in the United States require a minimum area of nearly 700,000 acres just for parking. The passenger car system alone accounts for one-half of the total loss to highways, urbanization, and other special uses. Strip mining takes a toll, disturbing at least 153,000 acres a year, and the affected area can be three to five times greater because of mining acids and soil erosion, which pollute 12,000 miles of streams. Urbanization is more likely to take cropland than noncropland. Cities spring up in areas of the best farmlands; and when cities expand, the sprawl devours that rich land. Also, highways and railroads within and between urban areas generally follow the flat river basins that contain some of the best agricultural land. There clearly is a need for intensive long-term land use planning.

The global situation

Worldwide environmental degradation is an even more serious problem. Soil erosion is the biggest culprit. Demand for more housing and enlarged highway systems because of rising population and affluence puts more pressure on us.

To help alleviate world food shortages, the United States cannot afford to degrade and eliminate from production another several million acres of cropland, as it did in the past. We are obligated to protect and preserve our vital land resources and environment—for ourselves and the world and for future generations.

Growing demands from the rest of the world for our agricultural products and increased production to fill those demands has taken a toll through soil erosion and sedimentation of water courses. We are, in effect, exporting our soil and water quality in the form of food and feed grains exports (9). When we increase our agricultural production, there are predictable and positive economic results. Increased production means higher income.

There can be negative results, too, as an Iowa State University study dramatically illustrates (1). The study sketched two future scenarios and examined the estimated soil erosion losses resulting from increased agricultural production between a base period—1969 to 1971—and projections to the year 1985 in 12 corn belt states. These scenarios included alternative sets of export demands, land management and erosion control practices, product prices, and farm policies.

Scenario I, which assumed a continuation of historical trends, resulted in a 17 percent increase in planted crop acres and a 39 percent increase in soil losses. These losses varied from 68 percent in Iowa to 8 percent in Kansas.

Scenario II, which featured expanded production because of increased exports, resulted in a 29 percent increase in planted crop acres and a 72 percent increase in soil losses. The soil losses varied from 102 percent in Iowa to 40 percent in Illinois.

If we expand this thinking to encompass most agricultural productivity, then we must conclude that soil erosion problems may well increase as export sales expand. Also, we may assume that rising demands will result in use of increased amounts of fragile land on which erosion is more severe. Consequently, we can safely say that to control soil losses effectively we need to encourage extensive use of conservation technologies.

We have already looked at how we step up production as export demand increases and how along with this increased demand come higher prices. The incentive to exploit land resources in the short term thus increases. Practices may be used that are damaging to the soil in the long run. We have seen how the best farmland is likely to be urbanized first, going to roads, cities, railroads, and the like; and we can recall the old saying that "they aren't making any more land," though we are talking about productive soil, not just acreage.

Structure of agriculture

For more than a century we have encouraged a family farm structure for American agriculture. Today this structure is threatened by many of the same forces that encourage expanded production—rising product prices and rising land prices.

The price of farmland has been growing at a rate of two and a half times that of inflation (5). Farmland is an attractive, sheltered investment for urban-industrial wealth. The flow of investment dollars into farmland is stimulated by favorable tax laws and the search for something to help hedge against inflation. As a result, farmland is being priced out of the market for farm use. As prices skyrocket, some farmers become millionaires on paper. Others have mortgagable value to borrow against to buy high-cost machinery. But the nonestablished farmer is precluded from full participation in agriculture because the price of farmland is just too high.

We have seen that increased productivity results in a corresponding increase in soil erosion. Historically, increased productivity reflected a major change in the technologies employed by American farmers, principally in the form of massive substitution of capital for labor. Also, the amount of irrigated land rose by more than 50 percent, even though the total amount of cropland declined (2).

To illustrate these dramatic changes, the number of man-hours used each year in crop production from the 1946-1950 period to the 1970-1972 period dropped from 26.4 per acre to 9.6 per acre, a reduction of 64 percent. In contrast, fertilizer applications rose from 21.4 pounds of nutrients per acre to 143.4 pounds for the same period, an increase of 570 percent. This was truly a technological revolution; but as in all progress, there were some prices to pay. One of these was increased soil erosion.

We have not heard much about windbreaks for a number of years. At one time they were popular, particularly in areas of the country where significant wind erosion occurs. Windbreaks are becoming popular again in some areas, particularly parts of Oklahoma, Kansas, Texas, and New Mexico. Wind-whipped farmers in those states are fighting back with the help of their local conservation agencies.

In 1978, according to *Progressive Farmer*, Oklahoma farmers planted more than one-half million trees, twice the number planted just five years before. In Kansas, farmers planted one and one-third million trees, an increase of more than 200,000 in just five years.

Another economic benefit is possible for farmers who take advantage of cost-sharing conservation payments from certain federal and state conservation programs, according to *Progressive Farmer*. Some of these need not be reported as income. Another option is to deduct soil and water conservation expenses as a current expense instead of adding it to the cost or basis of the land. Also exempt are payments under any small watershed program administered by the secretary of agriculture and approved by the secretary of the treasury. State program payments for conservation, environmental protection, forest improvement, or wildlife are also exempt.

Best Management Practices (BMPs) have emerged that involve the most practical and effective measure or combination of measures that prevent or reduce the generation of pollutants in water to a level compatible with water quality goals. BMPs are being used today by more than a million and a half farmers and ranchers who are cooperating with the nation's 3,000 soil and water conservation districts (3).

Policy guidelines

BMPs and other policy instruments require good information (8). Those information requirements that appear to be and are especially applicable to the joint problems of soil erosion and water quality include the following:

1. The immediate and long-run physical and economic consequences, on the farm, of adopting alternative cropping systems, practices, and technologies.

2. The physical relationships between levels of the generation of on-farm pollutants and the various parameters of water quality at the locations of interest.

3. The functional relationships between these parameters and damage to the environment, including human health.

4. The costs of policy implementation, such as those for information programs, tax or subsidy administration, enforcement, monitoring, and litigation.

5. The response of individuals in the system, in particular the manner in which agricultural producers respond to such actions as economic incentives, appeals to adopt practices to meet social goals, and regulatory devices.

Pursuing these information needs, we can more systematically propose solutions to the problems at hand. These solutions can be divided into two categories—private and public. From the standpoint of the private sector, the individual farmer and rancher, there is a need first for education—education to provide pertinent information needed to appreciate that there are situations calling for conservation measures. Education must also inform individuals as to what conservation measures are available.

Second, most private operators will need all the financial help they can get to carry out those conservation practices—incentives to conserve.

From the public point of view, we need consistent agricultural, foreign, reclamation, and conservation policies. What kinds of laws or programs should we have when the costs are borne by society as a whole? Should the programs be voluntary or mandatory? Should there be cross-compliance with other programs? Farm managers can adopt some limited practices, but the costs of many good conservation programs are going to have to be borne by society.

The point here is that if you are farming, and prices are rising, you have an incentive to put your land under the plow. In so doing, you probably will use practices that lead to water and wind erosion and thereby reduce present and future quality of land and water. You can exploit a farm to the extent that you leave it in ruin, to be somebody else's problem. That is one of our major problems, and that is why we must have public policy to discourage such exploitation. That is why we have had cost-sharing programs in the past. That is why we have encouraged conservation on set-aside acreages. And that is why we have had restrictions on reclaimed land.

These and other similar programs will be needed in the future, and society as a whole must bear the lion's share of the costs.

REFERENCES

1. Cory, Dennis C., and John F. Timmons. 1978. *Responsiveness of soil erosion losses in the Corn Belt to increased demands for agricultural products.* Journal of Soil and Water Conservation 33(5): 221-226.
2. Crosson, Pierre. 1979. *Agricultural land use: A technological and energy perspective.* In Max Schnepf [ed.] *Farmland, Food and the Future.* Soil Conservation Society of America, Ankeny, Iowa.
3. Dodson, Max H. 1978. *Goals and objectives of Section 208 of Public Law 92-500.* Publication No. 86. Great Plains Agricultural Council, Lincoln, Nebraska.
4. Inge, M. Thomas. 1969. *Agrarianism in American literature.* Odyssey Press, New York, New York.
5. Little, Charles E. 1979. *Farmland and the future.* In Max Schnepf [ed.] *Farmland, Food and the Future.* Soil Conservation Society of America, Ankeny, Iowa.
6. Pimental, David, Elinor C. Terhune, Rada Dyson-Hudson, Stephen Rochereau, Robert Samis, Eric A. Smith, Daniel Denman, David Riefschneider, and Michael Shepard. 1976. *Land degradation: Effects on food and energy resources.* Science 194: 149-155.
7. Sharp, Basil M. H., and Daniel W. Bromley. 1979. *Soils as an economic resource.* Economic Issues (October). University of Wisconsin, Madison.
8. Swanson, Earl R. 1977. *Economic evaluation of soil erosion: Productivity losses and off-site damages.* Publication No. 86. Great Plains Agricultural Council, Lincoln, Nebraska.
9. Timmons, John F. 1979. *Agriculture's natural resource base: Demand and supply interactions, problems and remedies.* In *Soil Conservation Policies: An Assessment.* Soil Conservation Society of America, Ankeny, Iowa.

2

Choices in Resource Use: Ethical Perspectives

J. P. Bruce
Assistant Deputy Minister
Environmental Management Service, Environment Canada
Ottawa, Ontario.

Because people are taught to be so pragmatic, ethics is a subject of which we are likely to be wary. We worry that a discussion of ethics will expose us to a sermon, rather than practical talk. My view of the subject, however, is that ethics reflects the accumulated wisdom of experience. Ethical precepts may force us to do some things that we do not want to do because they may not be profitable in the short-run; but the important and sound ethical principles are those that give proper weight to long-run concerns, such as surviving on this planet, providing for our grandchildren, and making sure that the productive capacity of our most basic resources—air, soil, and water—is not impaired.

In terms of resource use, we need to apply a set of conservation ethics—principles of resource management—that enable us to use the productivity of the biosphere in a fashion that meets the needs of present and future generations. So the ethics on which I believe we should base our considerations of resource use can be thought of as rules that enable us to live in harmony one with another and to live together in harmony with nature. What makes these ethical rules difficult to accept in our well-managed, logical age is that they are not provable. This is true of all ethical precepts. They tend to be stated as self-evident, like the Declaration of Independence. I recall a cynical observation I once heard that it was a good thing that those truths were self-evident because you would have a hell of a time trying to prove them.

My area of concern is resource use and environmental ethics. Some people claim that the market will sort out ethical problems and that we need no other ethic except the one: "Let the market decide." What happens, though, with pollution. If we start, as most nations have, with the right to pollute, then we have to use the market to buy off polluters, which takes a lot of effort and money, as well as a sufficiently high degree of pollution to worry people into action. Generally, the market operates politically, but the costs are the same. If we start with the assumption that pollution rights have to be bought, or if we had some other way of charging the external costs to the polluter, then the market leads to a lower pollution level. Whether polluting is an industrial right or an imposition on society is a political question, the answer to which depends very much upon our ethical position.

The same analysis applies to resources. If we begin with the right of landowners to deplete their resources, then the rate of exhaustion of these resources will be higher than if the resource user has to pay for depletion. In Canada and the United States we have a bit of both: Governments charge royalties, but they also offer tax breaks, depletion allowances, and a host of special subsidies for resource exploitation. On balance, we likely subsidize resource depletion. The result is wastefulness of resources and a rate of consumption that from another ethical perspective, that of the gap between rich and poor nations, is verging on the criminal.

A historical perspective

In general, our societies have started from an ethical position that favors rapid resource exploitation and use of the environment, what Kenneth Boulding (3) calls the "cowboy economy." We have largely stuck with this position, even though from time to time we have proposed and supported alternative ethics. It is interesting to examine four major attempts to introduce an alternative ethic, which is somewhat closer to what I have referred to as a conservation ethic.

The first attempt was presented in the mid-nineteenth century by Thomas Malthus. Malthus is best known for his pronouncements on population growth, but his basic message was that population would, over time, tend to grow faster than production, especially food production. Since his time, we have experienced a few green revolutions. We have mechanized and modernized agriculture. And we now produce food in quantities undreamed of by the Reverend Thomas. But his ghost still mocks us, because in many countries his depressing arithmetic is clearly true, and because many people argue that this fantastic growth in productivity cannot be maintained. In general, however, technological progress has refuted Malthus.

Second, almost 50 years later came the conservation movement, led by Gifford Pinchot and Theodore Roosevelt. They argued that the world would run out of resources, and accordingly, they formulated a series of rules or principles to avoid waste. These may be summarized as follows:

1. The regenerative capacity or potential of renewable resources, such as forest, grazing land, cropland, and water, should not be physically damaged or destroyed.

2. Insofar as physically possible, renewable resources should be used in place of minerals.

3. Plentiful mineral resources should be used before less plentiful ones, insofar as physically possible (2).

To this list, Talbot Page added a fourth, more modern rule:

4. Nonrenewable resources should be recycled as much as possible.

These views were influential at the turn of the century and led directly to the founding of the U.S. national park system and the U.S. Forest Service, and to similar developments in Canada. However, the movement suffered from the "cry wolf" and "Chicken Little" syndromes. The movements claimed that we were running out of resources, that we had only 20 years of timber supply and 50 years of anthracite coal remaining. Like Malthus, they were confounded by the progress of technology and by the discovery of new resources. The sky did not fall.

The third wave of alternative ethics came in the 1960s. A remarkable book, Rachel Carson's *Silent Spring* (4), signalled the beginning and marked the growing strength of the environmental conservation movement, which has spawned a wide range of actions from bans on toxic substances to automobile emission standards. *Silent Spring* demonstrates that even if technology can solve the resource supply problem, the environmental side-effects will push too hard at the carrying capacity of the natural environment, resulting in local or even global catastrophe. These arguments have proved to be most powerful and, unlike those of previous revisionists, have not been swiftly disproved by events. Rachel Carson was concerned primarily with DDT. Since that time, a veritable multitude of world threats have emerged, from PCBs to radiation, from microwaves to ozone depletion, from carbon dioxide and melting ice caps to mercury poisoning. It is useful to note that technology is seen by some as more a part of the problem than a part of the solution, at least in the short-run. This has led to a widespread distrust of technology, which in turn could have widespread implications for the rate and direction of future technological innovation. When pollution is obvious in the forms of soot, smoke, sewage, and terribly unsanitary dumps, we can see the threat approaching and act to stop it. But by the time the problems become visible, they may be too far gone. By the time the canary stops singing, our lungs may already be damaged beyond repair. By the time the fish die in the lakes, the soil may have lost its productivity.

The fourth thrust can be traced to the Club of Rome and the book *The Limits to Growth* (5). This book is largely neo-Malthusian, but it has had a major impact, because it has coincided with a general slowdown of economic activity, with a resource shortage imposed on the world by OPEC and by spiralling consumption of nonrenewables. The book also coincides with a heavy dose of guilt in western nations regarding the Third World and those nations' lack of access to resources. Many of the limits described in *The Limits to Growth* and related literature can be overcome, I believe. But the concept of limits is now firmly established and the concept of infinite growth is broadly viewed as inane. Given the evolution of this outlook, I believe that we can now accept the concept of resource and environmental limits as truly existing, and that we must now apply an appropriate set of ethics to our decision-making.

Conservation principles

To follow along these lines, I suggest four conservation principles based on economic considerations:

1. The economy and the natural environment should provide for a flow of goods and services sufficient to meet societal needs in perpetuity.

2. The fundamental stability and productivity of the biosphere should not be risked.

3. The value of goods and services is in the use that is made of them in satisfying wants and needs, not in the goods themselves.

4. Environmental degradation reduces the value that people get from their lives and from the use of goods and services.

If we apply these principles in our economic decision making, they should lead to economic policies that (a) substitute plentiful resources for scarce ones, (b) substitute renewables for nonrenewables, (c) minimize waste, (d) increase recycling and product durability, and (e) minimize environmental impact by working in cooperation with, rather than against, natural processes.

We would, I hope, develop national economies that care for the future and care about the impact of economic activities on people and on the environment. These principles can be thought of as stewardship economies.

Recently, Richard Barnet (*1*) wrote in *The New Yorker*: "Stewardship implies a rational system of sharing not only *across distance* but also *across time*. When people were tied to particular plots of land, it was easier for them to feel that they were part of the rhythm of generations. The son, the grandson, and the great-grandson would till the same land in the same way. But with those ties broken, where are the roots of obligation to posterity? There is a weakening of the sense of tradition, of participation in a chain of being.... The lack of connectedness to the future (and to the past as well) reveals itself in the special restlessness that permeates the industrial culture. If we do not see ourselves as trustees of the natural order for something beyond ourselves, there is no answer to the inescapable human question, Why are we here? (*11*).

An ethical view of current problems

Thus far, I have examined largely the philosophical level of conservation ethics. Perhaps it would be helpful to review a few of the current problems that we can see from this sort of ethical perspective.

An almost classic example of the issues I have been discussing is the problem of acid rain or, more generically, the long-range transport of airborne pollutants. The two dimensions of Barnet's view of stewardship—the effects on the future and the effects on distant neighbors—are dominant features.

First, let me summarize the facts of the case as we now know them. Sulfur dioxide emissions, mainly from thermal power plants and nonferrous smelting operations, and nitrogen oxides, mainly from cars and trucks, are transported and transformed in the atmosphere. The residence times of sulfur compounds in the atmosphere are typically one to five days in North America. During the first 24 hours, the sulfur is gradually changed to a dilute sulfuric acid. Because particles and gases are typically transported some 1,000 kilometers (621 miles) per day at mid-levels of the atmosphere, the dilute sulfuric acid tends to fall on land and lakes far from its sources. We are already seeing the long-term effects of emissions from the Ohio Valley and Ontario on the northeastern parts of the continent.

Nearly the entire eastern half of the continent is now subject to rain with a pH less than 4.6, 10 times the acidity of "clean" rain. In some areas the average is as low as 4.0. Falling over several decades, acid rain has eliminated the buffering capacity and turned acidic all the approximately 100 Adirondack lakes with an altitude of more than 610 meters (2,000 feet) and 140 or more lakes in Ontario, wiping out previously flourishing sports fishery populations and the complete aquatic ecosystems on which they depended. Thousands of other lakes and rivers in eastern North America are heading in the same direction. They have only a decade or two left as healthy aquatic systems if present deposition rates continue (6). When lakes become more acidic, and headwater lakes generally go first, toxic trace metals, such as mercury and cadmium, are leached more rapidly from the rocks and sediments, and may affect drinking water supplies as well as the remaining biota. Rusting of water pipes, corrosion of buildings, and impacts on soils, forests, and agriculture are also of concern.

While effects on vegetation are not easily demonstrated because of the many other variables at work, long-term effects on soils must make us extremely concerned about the continued productivity of our lands. The extensive soil sampling program in Sweden, where the pH of the precipitation is about the same as in much of eastern North America, shows losses of up to 30 percent of calcium and some other nutrients, like magnesium and potassium, in the lower soil horizons. The loss of nutrients *is* occurring. At the same time in the same area, groundwater has become more acidic and aluminum concentrations have increased. The complex chemistry of the soils and the fact that the rain is not only acidic but contains other chemical contaminants makes this work difficult to interpret. It requires a huge number of samples to obtain statistical reliability and we have yet to mount the kind of soil monitoring program needed in North America.

Now who is doing what to whom in North America? The wind respects no provincial, state, or international borders. Some of the acid rain in the Adirondacks and in Quebec is caused by sulfur emissions in Ontario, and some of the problems in Ontario, Quebec, and the Atlantic provinces result from emissions from the midwestern United States. The best estimates are that in a typical summer month sulfur depositions in Canada from the United States are more than three times the Canadian depositions in the United States. But in a winter month, U.S. contributions to Canada exceed those going the other way by only 30 percent (6). If depositions continue at present rates, thousands more lakes will die in the next decade, and changes in soil chemistry and groundwater will continue.

This situation has two features characteristic of the ethical perspectives discussed earlier: The adverse effects of the actions in one location are felt most severely hundreds or thousands of miles away, and the effects take a long time to manifest themselves. At present rates of deposition, it will take several decades of acid rain to use up the alkalinity or buffering capacity in natural lakes and rivers. Our present pollution control legislation in both countries is neither designed nor suited to cope with pollution problems with impacts so distant in time and space.

There is a further dimension to the problem. Whether acid rain in eastern North America gets better or worse is inextricably linked with choices of energy sources. Many Canadians and New Englanders are alarmed over the potential effects of the proposed program to convert oil-fired thermal generating plants to coal, a plan announced by President Carter on March 6, 1980, and recently passed by the U.S. Senate. These proposals have been made in the midst of ongoing discussions between the two governments on the objective of reducing transboundary air pollution. The fundamental concern is that the conversion program presents a unique opportunity to begin reducing emissions of acid-causing pollutants. The application of best available control technology could reduce sulfur dioxide emissions from the converted sources by one-half million tons. Instead, in the absence of stringent emission control requirements, increased emissions will inevitably aggravate an already serious situation. Moreover, the converted plants will have their useful lives extended for some years—extending for decades the duration of precipitation of high acidity.

The prediction of thousands of more lakes becoming devoid of life over the next decade or two is based on present levels of sulfur and nitrogen emissions. If these increase, rather than decrease, effects on aquatic ecosystems in eastern North America will be disastrous. The productivity of our lands could be seriously affected. U.S. figures indicate there will be substantial increases in the emissions of sulfur dioxide, nitrogen oxides, and fine particulate matter from the energy sector in the next decade or so. In addition, the Environmental Protection Agency (EPA) is currently considering adjustments to the manner in which control requirements are calculated in state implementation plans. This could further increase emissions.[1]

[1]Roberts, John. 1980. *Address to Air Pollution Control Association annual meeting.* Montreal, June 23, 1980.

We must find a way of incorporating ethical concerns into our selection of policy options. We must consider alternative fuels for electric power generation but do it in a way that builds in the cost of pollution controls so that full costs and benefits can be weighed. An initial analysis shows that in the case of the U.S. fuel conversion program application of the EPA's new source performance standards would result in reduced emissions from the converted sources. And the savings in costs in going from oil to coal would more than offset the emission control cost.

Ethical action and hope for the future

The acid rain example illustrates the complexity of resource and economic choices required for stewardship of the environment when it involves states, another country, or future generations. These concerns have spurred Canada and the United States to try to deal more effectively with transboundary transport of airborne pollutants. But these current issues do not have anything like the history of what one might call "water diplomacy."

North Americans can proudly claim that water negotiations have played a prime role in developing a written pattern of international ethics and principles of law to govern conduct between our nations. One of the most important achievements of our diplomacy has been the Great Lakes Water Quality Agreement of 1972 and its updated 1978 version. These agreements follow from the simple principle of the 1909 Boundary Waters Treaty that says that each country shall not pollute the other's waters "to the injury of health or property." The concept of "injury of health or property" is made specific by defining numerical water quality objectives for bacteria, dissolved oxygen, phenols, iron, toxic metals, etc., beyond which uses of the waters would be impaired, including uses to support healthy aquatic ecosystems. The two nations then committed themselves to control programs to achieve those objectives.

How has it worked out? In spite of early problems and continuing difficulties in completing major municipal waste treatment plants in Detroit and Cleveland, the cooperative effort has worked well. The two countries have committed $6 to $7 billion for wastewater treatment, and the evidence of improvement in lake waters is accumulating.

In 1978 herring gull eggs from islands in Lake Ontario showed reductions of 48 percent in DDT and PCBs and 75 percent in Mirex from 1974. These reductions have been associated with increased breeding success of the gulls. Spring phosphorus concentrations in nearshore areas and in the main body of Lake Ontario have shown substantial declines since the mid-1970s, accompanied by reductions in excess algal growths in the lake. There are similar indications in the other lakes. In short, we are well on our way to one of the most remarkable environmental success stories ever.[2]

[2]Bruce, J. P. 1980. *Water quality issues in boundary and transboundary waters.* Address to "Inland Waters '80" Conference of American Society of Civil Engineers, Green Bay, Wisconsin, July 30, 1980.

What are some of the ethical ingredients of this ongoing effort of reversing the trend toward serious environmental degradation of the Great Lakes? First, the establishment of the specific water quality objectives was based on the precept that we must jointly protect the "highest" use of the Great Lakes waters, and we recognized as a legitimate use the protection of aquatic ecosystems. "Highest" use in this case meant the use, whether for drinking, swimming, or protection of aquatic life, that required the most stringent water quality conditions. Second, when the countries came to consider largely unspoiled Lakes Superior and Huron, they decided that water quality objectives less stringent than present water quality would not be acceptable and agreed that no further degradation of the quality of these lakes should be permitted.

The third and most important ethical aspect has been the willingness of citizens, their governments, and the industries in both countries to pay for the clean-up. On a straightforward economic analysis, it would be difficult or impossible to justify clean-up expenditures of the size spent and committed. However, it is clear that we are willingly paying the costs for two main reasons: so that we don't continue to pollute our neighbor's waters and so that we do not go down in history as the generation that hopelessly fouled the Great Lakes for all future generations. In short, for ethical reasons.

Our collective experience concerning the Great Lakes gives me great hope for the future and in particular for solving the problems associated with acid precipitation. The sums of money required are not much different, and the impact of acid rain is even more widespread than are the effects of Great Lakes' pollution.

And these hopes are based on the clear demonstration that our peoples and our countries in North America can be and are motivated by ethical concerns. Stewardship of our vital natural resources does give purpose to the lives of many conservationists. It is also just possible that the concerns for future generations, for protection of endangered species, and for ensuring the sustained productivity of our natural resources may just provide the kind of shared ethical concept needed to sustain North American society in the 1980s.

REFERENCES

1. Barnet, R. 1980. *Human energy*. The New Yorker (April 7).
2. Barnett, H., and C. Morse. 1963. *Scarcity and growth*. Johns Hopkins, Baltimore, Maryland.
3. Boulding, K. 1966. *The economics of the coming spaceship earth*. In H. Jarret (ed.) *Environmental Quality in a Growing Economy*. Johns Hopkins, Baltimore, Maryland
4. Carson, R. 1962. *Silent spring*. Houghton-Misslin, Greenwick, Connecticut.
5. Meadows, D., et al. 1974. *The limits to growth*. 2nd edition. Universe Books, New York, New York.
6. U.S.-Canada Research Consultation Group on Long Range Transport of Air Pollutants. 1979. *The LRTAP problem in North America: A preliminary overview*. 31 pp.

3

Alternatives for Sustained Use of Resources

Eugene P. Odum
Director, Institute of Ecology
University of Georgia, Athens

It would seem, at least to the ecologist, that we have no alternative but to change our basic approach to environment and resources. A break from the past is necessary to avoid the slow, worldwide downhill slide caused by a status quo that continues to depend upon declining and increasingly expensive energy sources and once-through flows of recyclable resources. Well-documented studies, such as the federal government's interagency Global 2000 Report (2) make the situation crystal clear: There is no time to lose in making a transition from a wasteful society to a much more efficient one. Fortunately, because there are a number of good choices for making the transition we can be optimistic about our chances for success.

Supplanting short-term economic goals

Accordingly, ideas such as conservation and land-use planning, which have largely been external to economic practices, must now come to the forefront and become part of cost and benefit computations. Nearly everyone agrees that conserving and planning are worthwhile, but until recently both had generally taken a back seat to short-term economic goals. To win the support of the public and political leaders for a reordering of priorities, however, it may be necessary to change traditional conservation rhetoric in

20

order to obtain a more positive response and provide a more realistic basis for Aldo Leopold's environmental ethic.

Let's now examine some possibilities.

Harnessing new terminology

In a recent book, *The Unsteady State,* Ken Watt and co-authors express the basic problem of the transition we require. The need is to move from haphazard or undifferentiated development to differentiated or organic development. In many ways "differentiated growth and development," as seen in the orderly growth of an individual organism, for example, might appear to be synonymous with "land-use planning," but there is a difference. Differentiated, organic growth implies following natural laws; in contrast, the term land-use planning implies government control of how we use the environment. *The Unsteady State* spotlights an optimum quality of life as the key index to replace the present short-term economic indices that increasingly reflect the well-being of the affluent minority exclusively. And because the phrase "land-use planning" causes excessive heartburn among political and corporate leaders, it might even be a good idea to present our case for better planning under the heading of "differentiated organic development." At least it is worth a try!

Likewise, the phrase "energy conservation" gets a lukewarm response from the public and often a negative response from politicians. To conservation professionals, "conservation" means wise use of resources, but to the layman it means doing without things. The case for energy conservation could be much better sold, I believe, in terms of efficiency, or energy thrift.

A recent Council on Environmental Quality report (*1, 3*) points out that if we could increase the efficiency of energy use, that is, get more useful work out of each unit transformed, we could reduce consumption by one-half and not deprive ourselves of economic growth. In so doing we would greatly reduce the need for imported oil, and we would not have to rush into hasty "crash" programs for the development of synfuels and atomic power, which are bound to be extremely wasteful of capital and tax monies. Conserving through efficiency would also create time to plan new energy developments for maximum efficiency at the lowest cost and with minimal environmental damage. Following this scenario, our goal for the rest of the century could be put in terms of "getting more bucks out of a BTU" to buy time for orderly development of new sources of energy.

The role of ecology in planning

Equally important to making better planning more politically and economically palatable is the need to develop a more holistic philosophy in the minds of the public and its managers. Here ecosystem ecology and the more formal science of systems ecology have a great role. The emerging concept of the ecosystem can be likened to a box that represents a given unit or area and two big funnels that represent the input and output environments necessary for the system inside the box to function (Figure 1).

To develop order and new structures, ecosystems as well as organisms must operate, in the words of Nobel laureate Ilya Prigogine (*4, 5*), as open, far-from-equilibrium, thermodynamic systems. There must be a large flow of energy and materials at all times. Otherwise the system rapidly degrades into disorder. Accordingly, by definition an ecosystem must include the input environment, especially energy sources, and the output environment. To understand and to deal with a tract of forest, a crop field, or a metropolitan district, we must go beyond the forest, field edge, or city limits. We need to consider what must enter the system to sustain it and what goes out that impacts systems downstream or downwind, so to speak. In the real world the ecosystem consists of the three parts—input, system, output (Figure 1). Furthermore, agroecosystems and urban ecosystems have much more extensive input and output environments than do natural systems, such as forests. This is to say that man-made systems are less self-sufficient and more dependent on the surrounding environment.

To illustrate the great urgency for going from piece-meal (one-problem/one-solution) approaches, which no longer work, to more comprehensive ecosystem approaches, let's look at the impact of urbanization and the al-

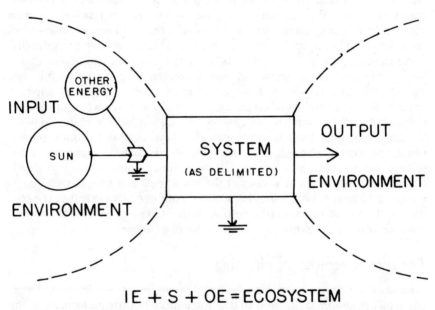

$$IE + S + OE = ECOSYSTEM$$

Figure 1. A complete ecosystem must include the input environment (IE) and the output environment (OE) as well as the unit or area under consideraton (S). Systems must function as open, far-from-equilibrium thermodynamic entities if complex structures are to develop and be maintained.

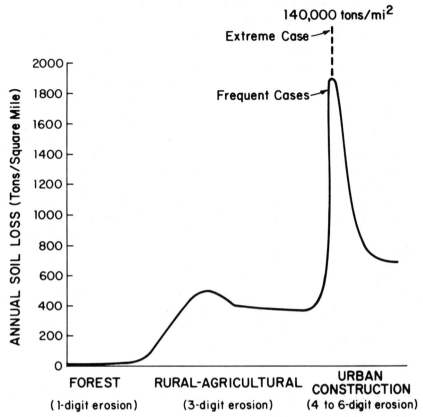

Figure 2. Comparison of soil losses as forests are replaced by agriculture and then by urban and suburban development (Source: Geographical Perspectives and Urban Problems. National Academy of Science Report 1973).

most painfully obvious need to deal with city and country as an integrated system.

The rapid urbanization and growth of cities that has occurred during the past half-century is changing the face of the earth probably more than any human activity in recorded history. The urban influence extends into the far reaches of America, creating demands on distant resources and discharging pollutants, such as acid rain, that reach far downwind and downstream from sources in the cities.

Urban construction has become the leading cause of soil erosion in the United States, threatening to cancel all the hard-earned soil conservation gains achieved in rural areas. We worry about double-digit inflation, yet we should also be worrying about four- to six-digit erosion (tons of soil lost annually per square mile) that results from haphazard and poorly planned urban and suburban construction (Figure 2). Literally hundreds of county agents and other dedicated professionals are helping the farmer avoid soil losses, but there is no organized effort in or out of government that helps developers avoid soil erosion. Even on the farm we are beginning literally to lose ground again as the pressure to produce food for export to pay for oil imports is causing farmers to abandon such practices as crop rotating, fallowing, and cover crop planting. Again, if we would commit ourselves to energy thrift in a big way, the pressure to overwork the land would be reduced and the holistic approach would have its way.

That an urban-industrial ecosystem includes extensive input and output environments is a concept only very slowly perceived by agencies and professionals. Partly, this is because science, economics, and politics are so fragmented into specialized disciplines and departments. As a result, soil conservation wisdom and practices are still largely rural. And urban impacts and problems are approached piecemeal with tragically inadequate results. Federal agencies such as the Soil Conservation Service and Housing and Urban Development, for example, stick so tightly to their "territories" that real problems involving the interaction between cities, agriculture, and the natural environment are neglected. We do not need a Department of Ecosystems, but existing agencies must adopt the ecosystem perspective. Likewise, land grant universities and other research institutions need to unite efforts. In this way we can sustain our use of the nation's resources by reducing waste, increasing efficiency of energy use, and raising management to the ecosystem level.

REFERENCES

1. Council for Environmental Quality. 1979. *The good news about energy.* Washington, D.C.
2. Council for Environmental Quality. 1980. *The global 2000 report to the president: Entering the twenty-first century.* G. O. Barney, study director, Washington, D.C.
3. Odum, E. P. 1979. *There is some good news about energy.* USA Today (September).
4. Prigogine, Ilya. 1977. *Self-organization in non-equilibrium systems.* John Wiley & Sons, New York, New York.
5. Prigogine, Ilya. 1980. *From being to becoming: Time and complexity in the physical sciences.* W. H. Freeman, San Francisco, California.

II. The Land Planning Urgency

4

An Economic Perspective of Land Use

Melvin L. Cotner, Nelson L. Bills, and Robert F. Boxley
Natural Resources Economics Division,
Economics and Statistics Service,
U.S. Department of Agriculture, Washington, D.C.

People and land resources combine in complex relationships, influenced by law, custom, economic factors, and prevailing social values. These complex features create persistent patterns of land use; conditions created in one generation are often passed on to succeeding generations.

Federal policies and programs long ago transferred most of the public domain to private ownership. Accordingly, rights to the use of many of the nation's land resources in the United States have been conferred through ownership. The bulk of the nation's intensively cultivated land is privately owned. Subsequently, private control of farmland has been a dominant force in the economic and social development of the United States. This situation sets the background for an exploration of the public policy implications of decisions made by private owners of agricultural land.

Growth and development in the United States occurred when land resources were thought to be boundless. Settlement of the western frontier and expansion of agricultural production fueled economic progress throughout the 19th century. Over time the ratio of population to land has greatly increased. Technological innovation has accompanied population growth and shaped the productivity of land resources.

The American frontier—virgin land resources that could be quickly converted to agricultural uses—was largely settled by 1890. Widely held perceptions of a boundless natural resource base gave way to concerns over the nation's capacity to meet future requirements for raw materials. These concerns were clearly manifested in resource conservation efforts in the late 1800s (2). Congressional action reserved timber and mineral lands for public management. The nation also augmented its capacity to produce food and fiber commodities with publicly sponsored investments in irrigation development. Supplemental water made crop production feasible on millions of acres in arid portions of the United States.

More recently, the debate over scarcity and resource depletion has been matched in intensity by dialogue and debate over degradation of the natural environment (19). In the past 20 years, the public has turned more attention to the environmental side-effects of natural resource use. Some take the view that man's technical capacity to manipulate the natural environment has advanced to the point that the natural processes and systems that support all human and biological life are jeopardized or at least vulnerable to irreversible damage.

Public concerns of this breadth and magnitude place considerable demands upon the analytical capacity of all branches of the physical and social sciences. They raise fundamental questions about man's relationship with the natural environment and how the relationship is to be structured in the future. Will new and more stringent balances need to be struck between supplies of material goods and the capacity of the environment to support all biotic systems?

Economics, ethics, and ecology

Economics is commonly defined as a discipline that deals with choice under conditions of resource scarcity. Economic theory holds that in a private market system, individuals act to maximize monetary profits as well as nonmonetary services from scarce resources. Whether it be farm income, wage earnings, recreational experiences, or aesthetic qualities, available resources will generally be applied or used to obtain the greatest benefits over the costs of attaining these products and services. The theory also holds that producers and consumers, acting collectively in their economic self-interest, will use resources in the best interest of society.

These economic concepts are central to the theory of capitalism, the economic system of most western countries. The literature is replete with examinations of these concepts. Space does not permit a review of the literature. In general, however, the economics profession agrees that economics, as expressed in private markets, does not deal directly with questions about the distribution of income and who should own and benefit from resource ownership. Further, the private market economic system does not say who in society should benefit from economic activity and when products should be produced and consumed.

Questions of who should benefit, distribution of benefits, and when resources should be used depend upon value judgments. Therefore, they are matters relating to ethics. Ethics involves moral judgments and determinations of equity. Ethics provides the basis for establishing the social time preferences for resource use. In other words, interpersonal and intergenerational questions relating to resource ownership and benefits are the proper subjects of ethics. Economic studies, however, can aid in analyzing ethical questions by estimating benefit levels, income distribution effects, and resource use patterns of past and proposed policies.

Both economics and ethics deal with man's interaction with the physical environment, especially decisions about the use of scarce resources. Scarcity primarily is a natural phenomenon, although man can greatly influence the supply of stock and flow resources by the way resources are organized and managed. The interaction of natural and social systems is the subject of ecology. Ecology can be viewed as the broad study of man in his physical and social environment.

Economics and ethics are sister disciplines within the social sciences. Economics suggests how resources should be organized and used given certain objectives. Ethics indicates whether resource patterns are just and timely. Ecology deals with the total system within which economics and ethical systems work. The nation and world are facing a range of resource use and allocation issues that cannot be addressed fruitfully without economic analysis and moral judgment. The subject of this paper has ecological, ethical, and economic implications. The three perspectives cannot be separated.

Historical trends in farmland use

The current status of the nation's farmland base reflects the effect of economic, social, and political factors that have been at work for several decades. Since 1900, the American agricultural scene has been dominated by two central trends: continual increases in food and fiber production and modest changes in the total volume of land resources committed to the production of food and fiber commodities. The general trend in food and fiber

Table 1. Indexes of farm output by major enterprise groups for the United States, selected years, 1910-1977 (1967 = 100) (6).

Year	Total	All Livestock and Livestock Products	All Crops
1910	43	42	54
1920	50	44	65
1930	52	54	59
1940	60	60	67
1950	74	75	76
1960	91	87	93
1970	101	105	100
1977*	121	106	129

*Preliminary.

production can be demonstrated by referring to indices of total farm output (Table 1). The nation realized almost a four-fold increase in crop and livestock production between 1910 and 1977.

Uses of crops and livestock products have also changed abruptly since 1900. In 1910, slightly more than 10 percent of all harvested crop acreage was used to produce farm commodities for export markets (Table 2). The production of feed for work animals accounted for much domestic use, and other domestic uses absorbed the production from 62 percent of harvested crop acreage.

In recent decades, applications of the internal combustion engine have

Table 2. Distribution of crops harvested and used for specified purposes for the United States, selected years, 1910-1977 (6).

Year	Total	Exports	Domestic Uses	
			Feed for Workstock	All Other Uses
			Percent of acres harvested	
1910	100.0	11.4	27.1	61.5
1920	100.0	16.7	25.0	58.3
1930	100.0	10.6	17.6	71.8
1940	100.0	2.3	12.6	86.0
1950	100.0	14.1	5.3	77.9
1960	100.0	19.7	1.5	78.7
1970	100.0	24.6	†	75.4
1977*	100.0	31.2	†	68.8

*Preliminary.
†Data for horses and mules were not tabulated after 1964.

Table 3. Trends in major uses of land for the United States, selected years, 1900-1974 (9).

Major Land Use	1900	1920	1940	1950	1959	1969	1974
				million acres			
Cropland*	319	402	400	409	392	384	383
Available grassland pasture and range†	832	731	719	701	699	692	681
Forest and woodland‡	719	721	727	721	728	723	718
Other land§	400	416	426	442	452	465	483
Special-use area	-	-	-	(134)	(146)	(172)	(182)
Unclassified-area	-	-	-	(308)	(306)	(293)	(301)
Total‖	2,270	2,270	2,272	2,273	2,271	2,264	2,264

* Exludes cropland used only for pasture.
† Grassland pasture and other nonforested grazing land plus cropland used only for pasture.
‡ Exclusive of reserved forest land in parks, wildlife refuges, and other special-use areas.
§ Includes special land uses such as urban areas, highways and roads, farmsteads, parks, and military reservations, and also land having slight surface-use value.
‖Changes in total land area are attributable to changes in methods and materials used in occasional remeasurements, and to increase in the area of artificial reservoirs.

Table 4. Major uses of cropland for the United States, selected years, 1949-1974 (9).

Use of Cropland	1949	1959	1969	1974
	million acres			
Cropland harvested	352	317	289	322
Cropland failure	9	10	6	8
Cultivated summer fallow	26	31	39	31
Total used for crops	387	358	334	361
Soil improvement and idle	22	33	51	21
Cropland used for pasture	69	66	88	83
Total cropland	478	457	473	465

virtually eliminated feed requirements for workstock. Widespread use of the automobile, trucks, and power machinery released millions of acres of cropland for alternate uses over the 1910-1970 period. Cropland used for this purpose amounted to 88 million acres in 1910 (6). Conversely, export markets have accounted for an increasing fraction of all acreage used for crop and livestock production. Currently, almost one-third of all harvested crop acreage is used for products that move to export markets (Table 2).

Major categories of farmland use, on the other hand, have been relatively stable since 1900 (Table 3). The nation's total cropland base increased from 1900 to 1920, reflecting additional entries under homestead legislation designed to transfer the public domain to private ownership. New owners put the land to an agricultural use. Land in farms reportedly, increased from 841 to 958 million acres between 1900 and 1920 (30). The increase mainly was due to increased use of land for farming in the north central and western United States. The nation's total cropland base ranged between 402 and 409 million acres between 1920 and 1950. In 1974 an estimated 383 million acres fell within the cropland category, a decrease of 26 million acres over the 1949-1974 span.

Post-World War II reductions in total cropland are far less abrupt, however, if increases in the use of cropland for pasture are taken into account (Table 4). The nation's total cropland base stood at an estimated 465 million acres in 1974.

Increases in farm output after 1900 have been enabled primarily by technological developments and production adjustments in the farm sector. These developments and adjustments have generally enhanced the productivity of U.S. farmland. The nation realized more than a two-fold increase in average crop production per acre from 1910-1977 (6). Increases in cropland productivity have come from several sources: improvements in machinery; increased utilization of commercial fertilizers, pesticides and herbicides; developments in plant and animal breeding; expanded use of irrigation water; and adjustments in the location of crop production (25).

Many, if not all, of these developments have made American farmers increasingly more dependent on purchased factors of production (Table 5).

Because these factors have been available at favorable prices, farmers have substituted these inputs for both land and farm labor to augment the nation's capacity to produce food and fiber (28).

In some regions of the nation, irrigation has materially affected land productivity. In 1958, 37 million acres of cropland were irrigated. By 1967 this acreage had increased to 44 million. In 1977 almost 58 million acres were irrigated, an average annual increase of slightly more than 1 million acres for the period 1958-1977.

Some 48 million acres of the irrigated land is in the 17 western states where irrigation water enables high-valued crops to be grown on land that would otherwise be used for extensive crops, such as wheat, or for range. Both the western states and the humid eastern states have shared in the expansion of irrigated acreage. In 1977 about 9.5 million acres received supplemental water in the eastern United States.

Regional adjustments in the use of cropland have also had a significant impact on cropland productivity. From 1944 to 1964, a period of moderate decline in total cropland, 868 counties gained a total of 27 million acres of cropland, while 2,204 counties lost a total of 54 million cropland acres (Figure 1).

Cropland increases over this period are fairly well defined (25). Increases in Florida were associated with drainage and reclamation projects; in the Mississippi Delta with clearing and drainage; and in the Texas High Plains, California, and Washington with expanded irrigation facilities. Improved dryland farming techniques and new investments in such land improvements as drainage, clearing, contouring, and leveling led to cropland expansion in northern Montana and throughout the Corn Belt.

Table 5. Indexes of total farm input and selected input subgroups for the United States, selected years, 1910-1977 (1967 = 100) (6).

Year	All Inputs†	Farm Labor‡	Farm Real Estate§	Mechanical Power and Machinery‖	Agricultural Chemicals#	Feed, Seed, and Livestock Purchases**
1910	86	321	98	20	5	19
1920	98	341	102	31	7	25
1930	101	326	101	39	10	30
1940	100	293	103	42	13	42
1950	104	217	105	84	29	63
1960	101	145	100	97	49	84
1970	100	89	101	100	115	104
1977*	103	71	97	116	151	110

* Preliminary.
† Measured in constant dollars.
‡ Includes hired, operator, and unpaid family labor.
§ Includes all lands in farms, service buildings, grazing fees, and repairs on service buildings.
‖Includes interest and depreciation on mechanical power and machinery, repairs, licenses, and fuel.
Includes fertilizer, lime, and pesticides.
**Includes nonfarm value of feed, seed, and livestock purchases.

Cropland declines have resulted from cropland abandonment and conversion to new uses. Abandonment has occurred on a large scale in the southern and northeastern states. Low soil fertility and a topography that has proved to be ill-suited to the use of modern farm machinery have contributed to farmland abandonment in those areas. In extensive areas of Oklahoma and Texas, cropland has reverted to grass.

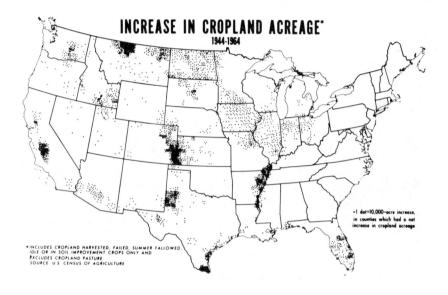

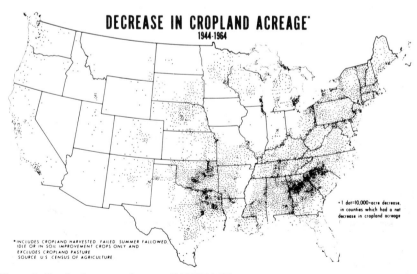

Figure 1. Cropland acreage changes, 1944-1964 (25).

New land uses compete for cropland too. Population growth has expanded land requirements for residential, commercial, industrial, and transportation uses. Some of these requirements have been met by using land formerly in crops.

All of these broad trends have been accompanied by important adjustments in the structure of farm businesses. Farm consolidation has been one of the more striking features of American agriculture since the mid-1930s (Figure 2). More than 6.8 million farms were counted in the 1935 census.

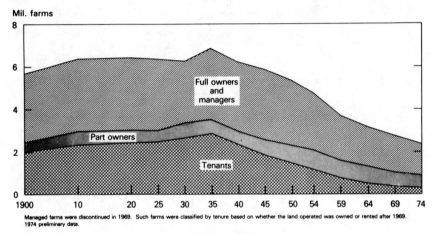

Managed farms were discontinued in 1969. Such farms were classified by tenure based on whether the land operated was owned or rented after 1969. 1974 preliminary data.

Figure 2. Number of farms, by tenure of operator (21).

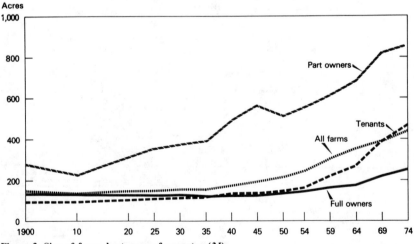

Figure 3. Size of farm, by tenure of operator (21).

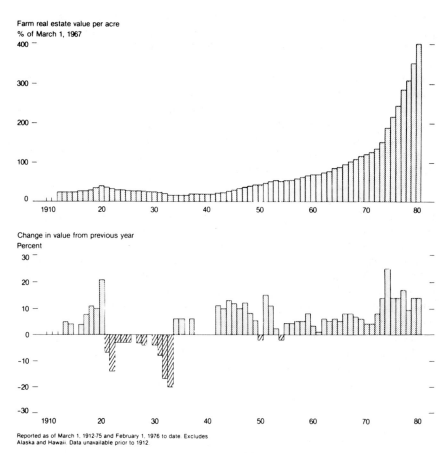

Figure 4. Change in U.S. farm real estate values (24).

Slightly more than 2.3 million farms were reported in 1974.

Changes in farm numbers have not been uniform for all tenure groups. Farms operated by tenants increased between 1900 and 1935, accounting for about 70 percent of the 2.8-million increase in all farms during this span. Similarly, tenant farms accounted for 58 percent of the 4.5-million decline in farm numbers between 1935 and 1974.

Large, absolute declines in farms operated by tenants greatly boosted the proportion of owner-operated farms. Only 11 percent of all farms were operated by tenants in 1974 while 1.4 million or 61 percent of all farms were operated by owners. After 1935, part owners (farm owner-operators who depend upon some rented land) emerged as a prominent feature of tenure in American agriculture. Twenty-seven percent of all farms are currently operated by part owners. They operate 53 percent of the nation's farmland.

Traditionally, part owners have operated larger farms (Figure 3). The average size of farms increased from 147 to 440 acres during the 1900-1974 period. Farms operated by part owners increased from 277 to 852 acres between 1900 and 1974. Growth in farm size has been closely associated with increases in mechanization, the availability of financial resources to expand farm operations, and the efforts of farm operators to increase net farm income by increasing the scale of their farming operations.

Farm size expansion has been accompanied by increases in farm real estate values. Estimates of the prevailing market value per acre of farm real estate have, with few exceptions, increased yearly since the late 1930s (Figure 4). Increases since 1973 have been particularly abrupt, and in 1978 the average per acre value of U.S. farmland stood at $490 (26). Growth in both value and farm size have worked in concert to lever up the real estate component of total farm assets. The average farm has real estate valued at more than $196,000. The majority of all farm real estate sales—an estimated 64 percent—are voluntary transfers between buyers and sellers (26). The remaining one-third stems from estate settlements, foreclosures, tax sales, inheritances, and gift transfers. Based upon national estimates, it would appear that active farmers are a major component of the effective demand for farm real estate. In 1978, 58 percent of all purchases involved situations in which the buyer intended to operate the purchased estate in conjunction with other land already owned or leased (26).

These trends provide a useful perspective on topical issues of agricultural land policy. These issues are related to the effective demand for food and fiber products and the ability of the American agricultural sector to supply commodities in sufficient quantities in the near and longer term.

Demand-related trends

Exports. In the past, U.S. agriculture was oriented toward production for domestic consumption. Although the dollar value of agricultural exports ran a comfortable margin over agricultural imports, the net agricultural contribution to foreign trade accounts was small (20). These relationships changed drastically in 1972-1973 with the failure of the Russian wheat crop and worldwide drought conditions. Between 1967 and 1977, exports of agricultural products increased about 77 percent. In carrying out the 1977 Resource Conservation Act (RCA), the U.S. Department of Agriculture (USDA) projected that exports would grow at an annual rate of 2.3 percent between 1975-1977 and 2000 (29).

In fact, exports have been growing at an even faster rate than has been estimated for the RCA. Starting from an export index of 169 in 1975 (1967 = 100), the index was 184 in 1977, 196 in 1978, and 228 in 1979, nearly halfway toward the projected index of 290 for the year 2000. The partial embargo of grain sales to Russia in early 1980 created uncertainty in export markets, but U.S. agricultural exports have recovered. Increases amounting to 34 percent in the first two quarters of fiscal 1980 over the comparable period of a year ago have been recorded. If the present rate of exports continues, U.S. agricultural exports could exceed $40 billion for fiscal 1980 (22).

There are several notable points about our export situation. First, considerations related to production for export markets are pivotal in assessing future agricultural land requirements. The nation can satisfy its domestic food requirements. Farm production geared to domestic needs would require less cropland and fewer purchased inputs (29). The nation currently exports 55 percent of its wheat, nearly 40 percent of its soybeans, and 28 percent of its feed grains. Projections to the year 2000 suggest that the nation will be exporting at least two-thirds of its wheat and over half its soybean production by that time (29).[1,2]

A second key point about the export situation is that growth in export demand has largely been for wheat, feedgrains, and soybeans. Furthermore, the largest portion of U.S. grain and soybean exports in recent years has gone to developed countries, such as Western Europe, Russia, Poland, and Japan.

These commodities have been mainly used by importing countries to support dietary shifts to animal protein. Most of the projections of increased demand for U.S. feed grains are predicated on continuing dietary shifts in developed countries and the development of livestock economies in some developing countries. Although there is still a humanitarian component in U.S. food export policies, most production in excess of domestic needs is apparently being used to improve the diet of already prosperous consumers. In fact, one may ask how much priority should be given to the use of U.S. land to produce commodities for affluent consumers in other developed countries as opposed to making land available to U.S. citizens for nonfarm purposes or to produce food for aid to developing countries.[3]

Finally, another basic export consideration is that world trade markets are more volatile and unpredictable than the domestic market. Projections of future demand for U.S. exports depend critically on assumptions about our balance of trade with other nations and the purchasing power of the U.S. dollar. These factors, along with possible shifts in agricultural policies of other countries (especially agricultural price support and tariff policies of the European economic community), will determine whether the United States can maintain its share of world agricultural trade.

There is some evidence that the current U.S. position in agricultural export markets may not continue on course. A recent study of world food prospects by the Organization for Economic Cooperation and Development

---

[1]Abel, Martin. 1980. "Growth in Demand for U.S. Crop and Animal Production by 2000s." Paper prepared for the Adequacy of Agricultural Lands Conference, sponsored by Resources for the Future (RFF), June 19-20, Washington, D.C.

[2]Crosson, Pierre, and Sterling Brubaker. "Resource and Environmental Issues of Agriculture in the United States: An Interim Report." Manuscript in process, RFF, Washington, D.C.

[3]Heady, Earl O. 1980. "Technical Change and the Demand for Land." Paper prepared for the RFF Conference on the Adequacy of Agricultural Lands.

reaches a basically positive conclusion about the ability of the world to feed itself to the year 2000 and beyond (*18*). There is still a reservoir of untapped technology and land reserves in the rest of the world that may eventually reduce foreign dependence on U.S. agricultural exports.

Ironically, since oil prices began their upward spiral in 1973, the 13 member nations of OPEC have become one of the fastest growing markets for agricultural products. U.S. farmers have captured a large share of this increased trade. In 1978 U.S. sales of farm goods to OPEC reached a record $2.4 billion—up from $1.7 billion in 1977 and more than five times the value at the start of the decade (*23*).

One of the concerns raised about the relationship between our exports of agricultural products and our imports of oil is that we may be trading "soil for oil." This concern is based upon the argument that projections of export demand are premised upon the competitiveness of American agriculture in world markets. However, programs that subsidize agriculture and the environmental costs of agricultural production often are not reflected in the market price for food and fiber,[4] nor does the nation have a good estimate of what these subsidies and environmental costs might total. Any distortions caused by the failure of export prices to reflect the full costs of production (on farms and increased costs to consumers and taxpayers) reverberates back to the domestic economy. Thus, the nation may be underpricing renewable land resources and using them beyond their sustainable capacity in exchange for current trade objectives and consumer gratification.

Demographic trends. Three population trends during the 1970s contribute to the current interest in agricultural land use and its conversion to nonfarm uses: (a) renewed growth and vitality of rural communities beyond the suburban fringe, (b) continued suburbanization, and (c) a population shift from the North to the South and West. All three trends move population and economic activities into less densely settled areas. Consequently, all three trends bear potential relationships to the use of land[5] (*3*).

The concentration of population into and on the fringe of large cities has been one of the most consistent population trends of the twentieth century. Migration from rural to urban areas outnumbered the reverse flow in every decade from 1900 to 1970.

Changes in the structure of agriculture underlie the cityward migration. Mechanization of farming and the resulting migration of farm people to cities reduced the population in hundreds of counties in the United States. From 1940 to 1970, about 900 of the nation's 3,100 counties dropped in population in each successive decade. The vast majority of the decline

---

[4]Brubaker, Sterling. 1980. "Agricultural Land: Policy Issues and Alternatives." Paper prepared for the RFF Conference on the Adequacy of Agricultural Lands.

[5]Brown, David L., and Calvin L. Beale. 1980. "The Sociodemographic Context of Land Use Change in Nonmetropolitan America in the 1970s." Paper presented at the Conference on Land Use Issues of Nonmetropolitan America. College Park, Maryland, June 24-25.

stemmed from reduction in farm employment.

Nonmetropolitan population loss through out-migration accelerated sharply following World War II. From 1950 to 1960, 2.6 million people left nonmetropolitan counties for metropolitan destinations. This loss continued from 1960 to 1970, although the rate diminished to a net loss of 2.2 million persons for the decade.

The seemingly inexorable trend of rural decline was suddenly reversed in the 1970s. For the first time in the twentieth century, the rate of population growth in nonmetropolitan America (1.21 percent per year) exceeded that in metropolitan counties (.72 percent per year). This renewed growth affects remote and completely rural areas as well as those that are partly urbanized and dominated by large metropolitan cities. Nearly three-fourths of all nonmetropolitan counties in the United States have gained population in the 1970s. Although more than 500 counties are still losing population, many of these show a reduced rate of loss. Hence, past notions of metropolitan concentration and decline or abandonment of small towns and rural areas can no longer serve as guides for understanding population distribution in the United States.

The reasons for this turnaround are complex, but economic decentralization, preferences for rural living, and modernization of rural life appear to be at the root. There has been a decentralization of economic opportunities from metro to nonmetro areas.[6] Between 1970 and 1977, nonfarm wage and salary employment grew by 22 percent in nonmetro areas. In addition, the character of nonmetro employment has changed, with service-performing jobs taking the lead in recent growth. Mining and energy extraction are new sources of employment growth in some areas, such as the Northern Great Plains. Also, people are no longer being displaced from rural areas by diminishing employment in extractive industries, as they were during the 1950s and 1960s. Commuting from nonmetro to metro areas brings additional jobs within the reach of rural residents, although recent increases in petroleum prices have generated higher commuting costs.

National surveys have repeatedly found a decided preference for living in the country and in small towns, particularly in locations that are within commuting range of a metropolitan central city. This preference for rural living is increasingly important as the constraints that employment opportunities previously placed upon living in rural areas are reduced. Also, longer life expectancy and extended retirements influence residential choices made by some segments of the population.[7]

All-weather roads, controlled-access highways, cable television, telephone service, and centralized water and sewer systems have helped modernize rural living. Such advances in transportation, communication, and

---

[6]Ibid.

[7]One can argue that the current predisposition toward rural living may not be as widespread for future generations. It may well be that the residential preferences of future citizens will be more closely aligned with the environment provided in urban locations.

public facilities make increasingly inappropriate the stereotype that rural areas are isolated and backward.[8]

These changes appear to have a number of implications for rural land use. Most obviously, a growing population requires more economic establishments and supporting infrastructure, which, in turn, require land for their construction and operation. The available data on how much land is actually converted to accommodate economic growth are not definitive, but collectively these conversions are probably not large.

The indirect effects of growth and development are probably much more substantial. An improving economic climate is one of the contributing factors in the resurgence of rural population growth. Economic opportunities not only attract migrants from other areas, they also help to retain lifelong residents who otherwise might have been forced to move to another community. Hence, economic development may have an indirect effect on forcing up the demand for housing and subdivision development.

There is reason to believe that the availability of nonagricultural jobs tends to stabilize the agricultural structure of many rural areas. Opportunities to supplement their income off-farm helps farmers (especially small farmers) stay in business and maintain ownership of their land. Consolidation of farmland parcels owned by smaller operators with larger farm businesses or its conversion to nonagricultural uses may be avoided.

Hence, while rural population growth and economic development appear to be somewhat competitive with agricultural and other open space uses of the land, there are reasons to suspect that it is also a stabilizing force. Vigorous nonfarm growth in rural communities may promote maintenance of farm structure and a healthy farm economy. This may differ from location to location because farmland is more vulnerable to conversion in suburban fringe areas than in small towns and the open country.

Domestic consumption patterns.   Most forecasts imply rather stable domestic demand for agricultural products in the United States. The annual rate of population growth has been declining since the 1960s and stood at 0.7 percent in 1976; the immediate prospects are for only moderate population growth (*29*). As disposable personal income increases, the demand for such commodities as beef, veal, chicken, fruits, and vegetables will continue to grow. Meanwhile, the demand for eggs, milk, dry beans and peas, and cereal products will decline. Because the possibilities for substitution of foods within a diet are limited by the need for variety and nutritional balance, shifts in consumption caused by changes in income possibly will decline over time.

---

[8]Often times, modern public services come at a relatively high dollar cost in less densely settled rural areas. This occurs because many public agencies, like private businesses, realize lower average costs if services (water and sewer facilities, for example) are provided on a larger scale. These higher costs per unit of service must be borne by the taxpayer. Also, all rural residents can incur new costs through regulations, building codes, ordinances, etc., as local jurisdictions coping with new population growth seek to maintain public health and environmental standards.

Changes in domestic red meat consumption may be on the horizon.[9] There is increasing concern in the United States that meat consumption on the present scale is wasteful compared with other methods of meeting nutritional requirements. This belief, whether justified or not, could slow meat consumption. Beef consumption in particular may slacken. Beef production is the most profligate converter of grain to meat. At the same time, fibers and starches are increasingly thought of as natural foods. They may compete for a larger share of the diet of a health-conscious public. If this occurs, some of the pressure that feed grain production now places on agricultural land will be relieved in the future.

Biomass and ethanol production. The oil embargo and rapidly rising energy prices in the 1970s have precipitated interest in alternative energy sources. Alcohol fuels, ethanol and methanol, have been proposed as alternative energy resources that use domestic renewable resources or coal to extend supplies of high-quality liquid fuels. Ethanol (as a component of gasohol) is currently available commercially. The Report of the Alcohol Fuels Policy Review concludes that methanol can be made from coal using commercially available technology and that this fuel could be produced in quantity by the mid-to-late 1980s (*31*).

The contribution of alcohol fuels is expected to be modest through 1985. Production over this span will be limited by the capacity to convert agricultural and waste materials into alcohol, although in agricultural states alcohol fuels may become a significant local supply source. The Report of the Alcohol Fuels Policy Review foresees larger potential for alcohol fuels beyond 1985, although the report emphasizes that no one energy source can solve our national energy problems (*31*).

The economic and energy balance feasibility of ethanol production is still subject to controversy. According to a recent report (*32*), some argue that the ethanol currently available for blending comes from manufacturing processes that consume as much or more energy in the form of petroleum or natural gas than ethanol yields as a fuel. On the other hand, a technical study by the U.S. Office of Technology Assessment concluded that an efficient distillery fired by oil or natural gas could save the equivalent of one-third gallon of gasoline for every gallon of ethanol produced. The policy review report presents energy balance budgets for ethanol production that yield net energy gains ranging from 5 percent (corn) and 16 percent (cassava) to 89 to 100 percent for sweet sorghum and 143 percent for sugarcane (*31*). *Science* magazine, however, reported that the energy balance for sugarcane ranged between minus 10 percent and plus 80 percent, depending upon whether crop residues or fossil fuels were used for the manufacturing process (*11*). Partially offsetting the low net energy yield from corn conversion, its proponents argue, are the process's yields of distillery by-products that provide high protein animal feed.

[9]Brubaker, Sterling. 1980. "Agricultural Land: Policy Issues and Alternatives." Paper prepared for the RFF Conference on the Adequacy of Agricultural Lands.

The alcohol policy review also examined the question of grain availability and concluded that, because of the major unpredictability of world weather and geopolitics, "the cyclic nature of grain availability dictates that any large national gasohol program cannot be based only on grains" (31).

Crop residues offer an alternative source of biomass for energy conversion. A trade-off, however, exists between energy production, maintenance of soil productivity, and erosion control. A team of USDA scientists has examined this question in considerable detail (13). If the criterion is that crop residues should be removed only if calculated erosion rates do not exceed the soil tolerance limit, then the total crop residues available for energy use are considerably limited.

An examination (34) of the land requirements for biomass farms concluded that satisfying 1 percent of U.S. energy needs from biomass farming would require at least 10 million acres of good to very good quality land. If biomass crops are relegated to lower quality land, the estimate would be nearer to 30 to 40 million acres. The study estimates that, with careful management, much of the 470 million acres of cropland in the 48 conterminous states might be suitable for growing biomass but that biomass farming is more likely to be economically competitive with lower valued pasture, range, and forestry uses. While the study sheds some light on land requirements, the economic feasibility of producing biomass on farms and converting it to useable energy is yet to be fully understood. Under current cost-price relationships, the cost of energy contained in biomass grown on farms is greater than the cost of energy contained in crude oil and coal. Substantial reductions in production, assembly, and processing costs will have to be realized before biomass can compete for land that is currently devoted to crop or forest production.

Supply-related trends

Energy and agricultural land supply. The oil embargo and the search for substitutes for imported oil potentially impact agricultural land use through higher on-farm production costs, competition between agriculture and domestic energy development for land and water, and competition in the production of agricultural products for food versus energy feedstocks. We have discussed production of farm products for energy feedstocks. But the other possible impacts need elaboration.

Many analysts initially thought that the oil price "shocks" of 1972-1973 would induce farmers to restrict their use of fuel and such inputs as nitrogen fertilizer and petroleum-based chemicals while switching to more extensive land-using production technologies. The response of farmers to the energy price shocks in the years following the oil embargo was never clear, because energy use on farms was affected by several other factors. These included fluctuations in weather (especially the unfavorable weather for crop production in 1974), shortages of fertilizers, temporary disruption of supplies of some other inputs, and the fact that farmers did bring additional, less-productive land into production. However, after faltering in the mid-1970s, fertilizer use reached record levels at the end of the decade in response to higher crop prices and, in effect, was still being substituted for land.[10]

The energy used in agricultural production is a small proportion of total energy use in the United States, about 3 percent in 1974. Furthermore, the direct cost of energy is a small proportion of the value of agricultural production, and the amount of energy that farmers use is relatively insensitive to the price of energy in the short run. Crosson reported that the price elasticity of demand for energy by farmers is about -0.5 percent (5). In other words, a 100 percent increase in energy prices (all other prices constant) reduces demand for energy only 5 percent. This suggests that in the short run substantially higher energy prices have little effect in shifting farmers to less energy-intensive technologies. Over the longer run, however, we can expect farmers to adjust their operations to higher energy prices. The effect on energy use in production in the longer term may be significant.

Higher energy prices would first affect irrigated agriculture by increasing pumping costs. However, several other economic factors influence irrigated agriculture in the United States. On the one hand, groundwater supplies and/or increasing competition for water from urban and energy developments threaten not only the expansion of irrigation but also the continuation of irrigation at current levels in parts of the West. Irrigated acreage in the southern High Plains of Texas has declined since 1964 because of falling water tables. In other states urban growth already has brought the transfer of water rights from agricultural to urban uses. Because continued urban growth seems certain and the marginal value of water in urban uses is considerably higher than in agriculture, additional transfers can be expected (5). On the other hand, we also might expect that increased pumping efficiency, improved water distribution systems, and more efficient irrigation scheduling may temper these impacts to an extent. These developments would allow producers to enhance production with supplemental water at a more favorable cost.

The major conflict, if any, between agriculture and energy development is likely to be with strip mining for coal—strip mining can have a number of undesirable effects on land and water quality. Direct disturbance comes from excavation of the land itself and from bulldozing and/or filling additional acres for haul roads, storage, and other mining-related facilities. Stripping may also disrupt drainage on adjoining land, degrade surface water quality, and disturb underground hydrology.

In the long run, effects on water quality are probably more serious than those on the land itself. In many instances land reclamation is now technically possible, if not economically feasible. To date, though, no effective method has been developed to abate serious water quality problems.

---

[10]Heady, Earl O. 1980. "Technical Change and the Demand for Land." Paper prepared for the RFF Conference on the Adequacy of Agricultural Lands.

Currently, about 1.5 million acres of land are disturbed by coal surface mining (8). Increased dependence on coal for electricity generation and other fuel-related uses will increase strip mining. It is estimated that about 1 million additional acres will be disturbed by 2000. Another 800,000 acres will be needed for new coal and nuclear plants (1).

The proportion of coal strip mining on cropland varies by region. For example, in Illinois 52 percent of the land on which permits were granted for strip mining was in cropland, 27 percent in forest, and 21 percent in pasture (8). Large acreages of cropland are also underlain with strippable coal in Indiana, Kentucky, and North Dakota. In contrast, much less cropland is disturbed by strip mining in Appalachia, Wyoming, or Montana.

Transportation. A quirk of U.S. geography is that the basic transcontinental railroad orientation is east-west, while that of the major navigable river systems of the central United States is north-south. Thus, differences between rail and barge freight rates create regional economic consequences. For example, cities along the Mississippi River have grown into major shipping points for grain exports. Favorable barge rates for the shipment of grain encouraged the growth of livestock and poultry production in the South. The number of cattle and calves increased 74 percent between 1950 and 1977 in the region while broiler numbers increased 864 percent. This growth in livestock numbers, in turn, contributed to the 684 percent increase in soybean acreage for the same period (17).

The growth of agriculture in the South has some far-reaching land use implications. Slightly less than half of the 127 million acres of land with high or medium potental for conversion to cropland as enumerated in the 1977 National Resource Inventory is located in southern states (Appalachia through Southern Plains). Of this potential cropland, one-third is now in forest use. One potential land use conflict here is that the Forest Service is looking to the private forests of the South for an increasing proportion of the nation's softwood timber supply.[11]

Energy developments in western states, particularly rapid increases in the strip mining of coal, raises a variety of issues with implications for agriculture. Moving coal to eastern markets in increasing quantities may challenge the capacity of existing railroad facilities (10). Farmers and ranchers are highly dependent upon this means to move agricultural commodities, and a recent study sees problems. By 1985 the study forecasts that several major rail links to the West will be used to capacity (7). Moreover, no new rail facilities to help meet these rapidly increasing transport requirements are expected in the near future (10).

Land ownership. Throughout U.S history, few restrictions have been placed upon the timing or manner in which privately owned land changes

---

[11]Hair, Dwight. 1979. "Future Timber Requirements—Expectations for Private Lands." Paper presented to the Private Nonindustrial Forestry Conference, Washington, D.C.

hands. Individuals and corporations for the most part have freely participated in land markets. Similarly, individuals make their own arrangements for transferring landed property to younger generations.

The cumulative result is a highly heterogeneous pattern of land ownership. Forty percent of all land in the United States is held by federal, state, and local governments (9). In terms of acreage, public ownership is concentrated in land with extensive range, pasture, forest, and other uses. Accounting for almost 60 percent of all land, private owners hold virtually all of the nation's cropland and about two-thirds of all pasture and rangeland.

Few regularly published data sources provide information on private landowners. But a 1978 USDA survey describes the characteristics of 33.7 million ownership units (14), which accounted for more than 1.3 billion acres of privately owned land.

About 69 percent (938 million acres) was reported as land in farms and was in the hands of 6.9 million ownership units. Farmers are the largest single group of farmland owners. They make up 25 percent of all owners and own 56 percent of all farm and ranch land. About 25 percent of all owners are retired; the retirees own 17 percent of all farmland. Farmland owners employed in nonfarm professions are relatively large in number—white and blue collar workers make up 42 percent of all noncorporate owners—but own less than one-quarter of all farm acreage.

Over time, market sales and intergenerational transfers have afforded owners opportunities to consolidate or subdivide their interests in farmland. A 1946 study of farmland owners showed that the ownership of U.S. farmland was not widely distributed (12). Although the trend toward fewer but larger farms has accelerated greatly since World War II, comparisons of the 1946 data with the 1978 data suggest that concentration in farmland ownership has not substantially increased over the 30-year span. In the United States in 1978, 1 percent of all farmland owners held 32 percent of all farmland. In 1946, 1 percent of all owners held 28 percent of the nation's total farmland base; 3 percent held 41 percent.

Owners ultimately make land use decisions. Therefore, an understanding of their characteristics enhances current discussions about public land use policies and programs. Persistent concerns have been the extent of absentee ownership, foreign ownership, and recent trends in corporate ownership (27). The 1978 USDA survey shows that about 10 percent of all landowners are absentee in the sense that they reside outside the county where their land is located. This group owns 20 percent of the land (14). Only 0.2 percent of U.S. land was reported as being controlled by foreign citizens; 6 percent of all owners contacted in the 1978 USDA study were unwilling to identify their citizenship.

Corporate ownership of farm and ranch land is only slightly more prominent now than just after World War II. Despite recurring concern over corporate ownership, the corporate share of all privately owned farmland has only increased from 6 percent to slightly more than 10 percent between 1946 and 1978 (*12, 14*), and the bulk of all corporate-owned farmland is held by family corporations.

Most private landowners contacted in the 1978 USDA survey were white, male, and high school educated; the average owner was 52 years of age. Altogether, 31 percent of privately owned, noncorporate land was owned by persons 65 years of age or older (*14*).

Productivity trends. In a paper prepared for a National Research Council workshop in 1979 on the "Long Range Environmental Outlook," Sylvan Wittwer (*13*) noted:

"During the last 20 years, there have been vacillations of progress and catastrophe in meeting world food needs. In the mid-1960s there was a cloud of doom projected from the two-year drought in India and Pakistan. In the late 1960s there arose a happy euphoria from the progress of the green revolution. The poor harvests of 1972-74 brought new predictions of doomsday. More recently, complacency from world food grain surpluses once again abounds, the set-aside acreage program again flourished in the USA, and record harvests for corn, soybeans, and wheat are projected for 1979. The current view will not prevail. There will be further crises because of the precarious balance between people, climate, and food."

Charles Little (*15*), writing about the failure of the Agricultural Land Protection Act in the 96th Congress, made a similar point about the volatility of public opinion on agricultural abundance or scarcity:

"The idea of a limit to the amount of land necessary for agriculture would have seemed laughable during the 1950s and 1960s when genetic breakthroughs, reclamation projects, and large-scale mechanization led to such increases in yields as to make the land base almost beside the point. Today, as yield increases begin to level off, even while export demands burgeon (and the need for the income exports produce to affect oil imports grows), the land base concept has reasserted itself."

In 1971 the National Academy of Science organized a Committee on Agricultural Producton Efficiency to "evaluate the adequacy of this nation's policies, knowledge, and technology relative to agricultural research and education efforts" (*4*). The 1975 report is frequently cited by proponents of the view that agricultural productivity has plateaued. Yet the report itself acknowledged that the committee reached "no simple direct unequivocal answers" to the questions it has posed for itself and that the "records of agricultural production during the past few decades presents conflicting evidence, as far as its implications for future output are concerned."

The hypothesis that productivity has leveled off or plateaued focuses attention on recent yields and productivity trends through the mid-1970s. When 1978 and 1979 yield data are added, the arguments for a productivity plateau are, at first appearance, reduced. Heady[12] concluded that the available data provide no firm evidence of yield plateaus and that several more years of observations will be required to determine statistically whether yields will continue to increase or whether they will taper off. Heady also examined measures of total agricultural productivity and found no hard statistical evidence of a decline in productivity growth during the period 1970-1979.[13]

An examination (16) of the relationship between public and private sector investments in research and education (R&E) and rates of growth in productivity revealed that a 1 percent increase in R&E in a specific year will increase productivity over a 13-year period by 0.037 percent, while a 1 percent increase in education and weather indexes will increase productivity 0.78 and .2 percent, respectively. Given these coefficients and an assumed rate of investment in R&E, we can attempt to predict expected rates of productivity growth. For example, we can expect an annual increase in R&E investment of 3 percent per year to yield a 1.1 percent annual increase in agricultural productivity (this is the compounded growth rate for agriculture since the beginning of World War II).

Reported productivity coefficients (16) are based on historical investment levels and technological advances. Use of these relationships to predict future rates of growth must assume either a reservoir of unexploited but currently available technology or the possibility of technological breakthroughs. An indication of the existence of a pool of currently unexploited technology is the difference between average or current and ultimate crop yields. Currently the top 10 percent of U.S. farmers routinely achieve yields 50 to 80 percent greater than the average; biological limits have not been achieved for the productivity of any of the major food crops, and the record yields for nine major crops are about one-half of the potential estimated maximum yields (33).

Beyond yields obtainable with known technologies, there is the possibility of the development of new technologies. Researchers (16) identified 12 emerging technologies that they view as having significant potential for future growth in agricultural productivity. They range from the introduction of new crop varieties and reduced tillage practices to improvement of photosynthetic efficiency in plants.

Heady[14] summarized the arguments for technological growth:

"While we can be optimistic, we cannot be complacent.... Attainment of yields which only approach biological potential will require vigorous research programs and a favorable pricing environment for the capital goods which represent the resulting technologies. Important bottlenecks are still to be broken through if the rate of agricultural productivity growth of recent decades is to be maintained, the potentials in transforming solar energy to food are attained, and biological innovations which are economic substitutes for fossil energy are developed for doing so.... Some persons maintain that the easy and more obvious technologies to increase yields and create land substitutes have already been attained and the road ahead is more com-

---

[12]Heady, Earl O. 1980. "Technical Change and the Demand for Land." Paper prepared for the RFF Conference on the Adequacy of Agricultural Lands.
[13]Ibid.
[14]Ibid.

plex and difficult. Offsetting, however, is the presence of a higher level and more sophisticated agricultural research profession than in the past."

Implications for shaping future policies

I have devoted attention to an economic perspective on agricultural land use, stressing that the economic view is often confined to land as a factor in food and fiber production. The economic approach to land use dwells upon the monetary costs and returns that accrue when land is used in production. Consequently, economics provides insights into the incentives that confront private owners when they make land use choices. Furthermore, economic analyses often provide a basis for measuring the trade-off between economic considerations and broader social and environmental objectives involving land use. These results can be helpful in deliberations over the design and implementation of public land use policies and programs.

Current policy concerns and issues in agricultural land use involve the structure of American agriculture, competing demands for land resources, and forces that impinge upon agriculture's ability to supply food and fiber products in the future. Should Americans encourage a structure of agriculture that results in fewer but more productive farms? Should production for export markets assume a pivotal role in future assessments of future agricultural land requirements?

Production sufficient to meet domestic food and fiber requirements is assured. Exports take a substantial share of the cropland base and production for international markets is heavily oriented toward food grains, feed grains and oil crops. A large fraction of these products go to developed countries. Should more humanitarian aid to consumers in less developed countries be encouraged? Will concerted efforts to use food and fiber products to maintain favorable trade balances promote long-term effects on the productivity of the nation's land and water base? These matters must be incorporated into the current debate over public land use policy for U.S. agriculture.

At the same time, future needs for alternate uses of the farmland should be considered. Population growth generates land requirements for a variety of purposes, but overall, these requirements do not appear to pose an immediate threat to the production capacity of American agriculture. Population growth in connection with farmland use took on greater importance in the 1970s because the long-term trend of concentration of the population in metropolitan areas was apparently reversed. Population growth beyond the urban-suburban fringe generates land requirements for a variety of nonfarm uses. Direct land requirements for these purposes are small collectively, but the indirect effects upon commercial agriculture may be more substantial. Similarly, efforts to secure alternate sources of energy—energy from biomass, for example—may have some impact on the nation's farm production capacity. Direct use of substantial quantities of cropland to produce energy products, however, seems unlikely in the near term.

On the supply side, the general issue of land productivity appears to be pivotal in deliberations over public policy related to agricultural land use. Increases in land productivity, as pointed out, have historically been the source of expansion in the nation's capacity to produce food and fiber. Now, as in the past, these matters deserve the strict attention of those concerned with public policy for U.S. agriculture. Movements in productivity are not very predictible because a key factor is the rate and composition of technological development. Adaptation of new production technology is a principal route to expansions in land productivity.

Production adjustments to incorporate new technologies and management techniques can produce unintended and undesirable side effects on the natural environment. Future conflicts and eventual trade-offs seem inevitable between the opportunity to adopt agricultural technology and broad social concerns over the quality of the natural environment.

Comprehensive analyses needed

Economics is but one of the disciplines to be used in the debate and the search for public policy remedies regarding the use of land resources. Ethics and ecology as well as other disciplines must be brought to bear on these issues.

On the other hand, economic considerations cannot be dismissed from the social concern about land use. Economic incentives and disincentives are influential, if not overriding, in decisions private owners make in land use. The economic ramifications of alternative policy options—who stands to gain or lose and by what amounts—need to be ascertained to guide public decisions in the management of one of the nation's most important assets. A challenge for our professions is to fashion more sophisticated, timely, and comprehensive sets of information to encourage wise decision making.

REFERENCES

1. Barse, Joseph R. 1977. *Agriculture and energy use in the year 2000: Discussion from a natural resource perspective.* American Journal of Agricultural Economics 59(5).
2. Bills, Nelson L., and Raymond I. Dideriksen. 1980. *Land and water base: Historical overview and current inventory.* In *Farm Structure—A Historical Perspective on Changes in the Number and Size of Farms.* U.S. Senate Committee on Agriculture, Nutrition, and Forestry, 96th Congress, 2nd Session. Washington, D.C.
3. Brown, David L. 1979. *Agricultural land use: A population perspective.* In Max Schnepf [editor] *Farmland, Food and the Future.* Soil Conservation Society of America, Ankeny, Iowa.
4. Committee on Agricultural Production Efficiency. 1975. *Agricultural production efficiency.* National Academy of Sciences, Washington, D.C.
5. Crosson, Pierre. 1979. *Agricultural land use: A technological and energy perspective.* In Max Schnepf [editor] *Farmland, Food and the Future.* Soil Conservation Society of America, Ankeny, Iowa.
6. Durost, Donald D., and Evelyn T. Black. 1978. *Changes in farm production and efficiency.* Statistics Bulletin 612. Economics, Statistics, and Cooperatives Service, U.S. Department of Agriculture, Washington, D.C.
7. Ebeling, K. A., and N. A. Dalsted. 1978. *Assessment of costs of various interregional energy transportation systems—final report, phases I and II.* Engineering and Agricultural Experiment Station, North Dakota State University, Fargo.
8. Esseks, J. Dixon. 1979. *Nonurban competition for farmland.* In Max Schnepf [editor] *Farmland, Food and the Future.* Soil Conservation Society of America, Ankeny, Iowa.
9. Frey, H. Thomas. 1979. *Major uses of land in the United States: 1974.* Agricultural

Economics Report 440. Economics, Statistics and Cooperatives Service. U.S. Department of Agriculture, Washington, D.C.

10. Green, John. 1980. *Western energy: The interregional coal analysis model.* Technical Bulletin 1627. Economics, Statistics, and Cooperatives Service, U.S. Department of Agriculture, Washington, D.C.
11. Hopkinson, C. S., Jr., and J. W. Day, Jr. 1980. *Net energy analysis of alcohol production from sugarcane.* Science 207(4428): 302-304.
12. Inman, Buis T., and William H. Fippen. 1949. *Farm land ownership in the United States.* Miscellaneous Publication 699. Bureau of Agricultural Economics, U.S. Department of Agriculture, Washington, D.C.
13. Larson, W. E. 1979. *Crop residues: Energy production or erosion control.* Journal of Soil and Water Conservation 34(2): 74-76.
14. Lewis, James A. 1980. *Landownership in the United States, 1978.* Agricultural Information Bulletin 435. Economics, Statistics and Cooperatives Service, U.S. Department of Agriculture, Washington, D.C.
15. Little, Charles E. 1980. *Demise of the Agricultural Land Protection Act: Some optimism in defeat.* Journal of Soil and Water Conservation 35(2): 99-100.
16. Lu, Yao chi, Philip Cline, and Leroy Quance. 1979. *Prospects for productivity growth in U.S. agriculture.* AER 435. Economics, Statistics, and Cooperatives Service, U.S. Department of Agriculture, Washington, D.C.
17. McArthur, W. C. 1979. *The South: Another revolution in U.S. farming?* Agricultural Economics Report 441. Economics, Statistics, and Cooperative Service, U.S. Department of Agriculture, Washington, D.C.
18. Organization for Economic Cooperation and Development. 1979. *Interfutures: Facing the future.* Paris, France.
19. Page, Talbot. 1977. *Conservation and economic efficiency—an approach to materials policy.* The Johns Hopkins University Press, Baltimore, Maryland.
20. U.S. Department of Agriculture. 1978. *Agricultural statistics.* Washington, D.C.
21. U.S. Department of Agriculture. 1979. *1978 handbook of agricultural charts.* Agriculture Handbook 561, Washington, D.C.
22. U.S. Department of Agriculture. 1980. *Agricultural outlook.* A0-54(May). Washington, D.C.
23. U.S. Department of Agriculture. 1980. *Farmline.* Number 1. Washington, D.C.
24. U.S. Department of Agriculture. 1980. *1980 handbook of agricultural charts.* Agricultural Handbook 574. Washington, D.C.
25. U.S. Department of Agriculture, Economic Research Service. 1974. *Our land and water resources—current and perspective supplies and uses.* Miscellaneous Publication 1290. Washington, D.C.
26. U.S. Department of Agriculture, Economics, Statistics, and Cooperatives Service. 1978. *Farm and real estate market developments.* C083, Washington, D.C.
27. U.S. Department of Agriculture, Economics, Statistics and Cooperatives Service. 1980. *Foreign ownership of U.S. agricultural land.* Agricultural Economics Report 447. Washington, D.C.
28. U.S. Department of Agriculture, Soil Conservation Service. 1978. *1977 national resource inventories.* Washington, D.C.
29. U.S. Department of Agriculture, Soil Conservation Service. 1980. *RCA summary of appraisal, Parts I and II and program report.* Review draft. Washington, D.C.
30. U.S. Department of Commerce, Bureau of the Census. 1978. *1974 census of agriculture. Farms: Number, acreage, value of land and buildings, land use, size of farm, farm debt.* Volume 2, Part 2. Washington, D.C.
31. U.S. Department of Energy. 1979. *The report of the alcohol fuels policy review.* DOE/PE-0012. Washington, D.C.
32. Washington Post. 1980. *Gasohol proves popular here and nationwide.* June 6.
33. Wittwer, S. H. 1979. *Future trends in agricultural technology and management.* In Proceedings, Long-Range Environmental Outlook Workshop. National Academy of Science, Washington, D.C.
34. Zeimetz, Kathryn A. 1979. *Growing energy: Land for biomass farms.* Agricultural Economics Report 425. Economics, Statistics, and Cooperative Service. U.S. Department of Agriculture, Washington, D.C.

5

The Land Planning Urgency: An Ethical Perspective

Jerome L. Kaufman
Professor of Urban and Regional Planning
University of Wisconsin, Madison

Economic and ecological forces assuredly will affect how land resources are used in this country in the next generation. The need for land resource conservation would be much less were it not for the success of the economic system, which has produced such a high standard of living for many Americans, but left in its wake a lot more sprawl and a lot less farmland and natural areas for the public at large. As a countervailing force, the ecological approach is being looked at more as a check on the economic system's incessant drive to "progress," having the potential to pull us back to a more harmonious balance between people and nature, a balance set awry by past economic forces.

In contrast, the influence ethics will have in shaping future land resource use appears much more problematical and uncertain. Despite the occasional land and environmental ethic manifestos, ethical reasons are rarely cited in day-to-day formulation of land resource policies or in land resource decision making. I use the term "ethics" as it commonly applies to those weighty matters of right and wrong, good and evil, duty and obligation (5).

Consider, for example, the reasons environmentalists and land planners give for preserving prime agricultural land, certainly a policy central to any discussion of why a land planning urgency exists. Rarely is the call for such a policy based on grounds that it is right or obligatory to protect such lands. Instead, the reasons given hew to principles of efficiency, economy, or resource protection: Prime agricultural land is the best land for farming because it is generally flat or gently rolling or susceptible to little soil erosion; prime agricultural land is our most energy-efficient land, producing the most food with the least fuel, fertilizer, and labor; preserving prime agricultural land will help control urban sprawl and protect open space and critical resource areas, such as wetlands and marshes; or measures to preserve prime agricultural land will reduce the farmer's tax burden that is rapidly increasing because such lands are assessed at urban speculative value rather than at present use value.

Despite the lack of references to specific ethical principles in ongoing deliberations about land resource issues, it is clear that an ethical perspective could hardly be dismissed as inconsequential to land planning. But that perspective is a difficult one to grasp and articulate. Why? Because ethics is one of those nebulous subjects. Most of us can appreciate ethical principles in the abstract, but when it comes to applying them in specific, concrete situations, more often than not we fail to do so.

What I propose to do here is to shake off some of the cobwebs that shroud the ethical perspective on land resource issues. Specifically, I propose to do three things: Show that ethical considerations, although often camouflaged, are alive and present in the land resources planning and development process; discuss patterns of ethical thinking and ethical dilemmas that underlie that process; and suggest how an ethical perspective might become more prominent and useful in dealing with issues related to future land planning.

I do not intend to argue for an ethical perspective as essential to resolve land resource issues. Rather than to pose as a moralist, my intention is to be descriptive and analytical about ethics.

Two kinds of principles

There are two kinds of ethical principles—ends- and means-oriented principles. Both come into play as far as land resource issues are concerned, but in different ways. In a recent article, "A New Land Use Ethic," Graham Ashworth of Salford University in England developed 10 land ethic prescriptions that embody his personal perspective on American land use ethic issues and imperatives (2). Presented in proper ethical form, as a list of obligations, two of them read:

"You ought to consider land as a resource that may be yours for a time but is also held in trust for the future. Land is not a commodity that any of us can own in the ordinary sense of the word."

"If you are presently trusted with the management of a piece of land, you ought to use it in a manner that benefits the land and does not damage it. Some land uses are abuses that have irreversible consequences, and you ought to avoid such abuses."

These are examples of ends-oriented ethical principles because they imply directions for land policy to follow—view land as a trust, use it in a way that does not damage it, and avoid abusive land uses with irreversible consequences.

Ashworth goes on to contend that land use controls should be developed in the interest of the community and that "you ought to be ready to give time and talents to fight for the land use control." In this instance, the ethical imperative applies to how one should specifically behave—fight for the land use control. This is an example of a means-oriented ethical principle. It is not unlike the standards found in professional codes of ethics, which stipulate how the profession's members should behave in everyday practice.

The distinction between ends- and means-oriented principles is important. Both are needed. Ends without means tend to be impotent, and means without ends tend to be blind. In the context of Ashworth's land ethic prescriptions, it is not enough to say that society should avoid abusive land uses (an end) without also addressing how public officials and others should conduct themselves (the means) in trying to achieve this and other ends.

On the other hand, overemphasizing behavioral norms—be fair, be truthful be loyal to your employer, be objective, etc.—without stipulating the ends to be sought provides insufficient direction to guide personal conduct. Aside from specifying more clearly ends- and means-oriented ethical principles that apply to land resources, a balance between them would be helpful to guide the activity of those involved in the land resources planning and development process.

Right and wrong in land planning

Previously, I noted the absence of references to specific ethical principles in ongoing deliberations about land resource issues. This does not mean that principles of economy, efficiency, and resource protection, or others such as equity, growth, or individual freedom, which are often mentioned in justifying land resource policy decisions, are necessarily void of ethical content. Although I am neither an expert in moral philosophy nor in meta-ethics, I recently have done some reading in these subjects in preparing a course on ethical issues in planning and the public policy professions. So with the excuse of partial knowledge to fall back upon, let me try to make the case that notions of right and wrong, which in part are what ethics deals with, are subsumed, albeit often unconsciously, in the reasoning that underlies a lot of land resource policy and decision making.

If a moral philosopher happened to listen in on a conversation between land resource planners as they ticked off the reasons for an agricultural land preservation policy, he would probably conclude that the planners believe the consequences of implementing such a program would lead to more good than bad things for the public—more open space, more wetlands preserved, more energy efficiencies, and more fairness to farmers as well as less urban sprawl.

On the other hand, he would probably conclude from the discussion that the planners believe that without such a program the public will end up with less of these "goods" and more of the "bads"—more sprawl, less wetlands, less open space, etc. The high-falutin' technical term that best describes the ethical reasoning process used by the planners is teleology. And the moral philosopher would conclude that in this instance the planners are reasoning like teleologists.

A teleologist would say that the basic standard for judging what's ethically right, wrong, or obligatory is the nonmoral value or good that is brought about as a consequence of some action. In this example, more open space, less sprawl, etc., are the nonmoral goods valued by the planners. And since the consequence of acting to preserve prime agricultural land is assumed to produce more of these nonmoral goods than would no action, our land planners (telelogists) therefore reason that such action is right or ethical.

Going further, utilitarians, who are a class of teleologists, might reason that it is right to preserve prime agricultural land because such action would lead to at least as great a balance of good over bad as other available alternatives. This then leads to the familiar utilitarian precept that those actions are right that produce the greatest good for the greatest number. Gifford Pinchot, an esteemed figure in the annals of the conservation movement, clearly spoke as a utilitarian in another context when he announced many years ago that resource conservation should provide the "greatest good for the greatest number for the longest time" (1).

There is yet another form of ethical reasoning that applies to the land resource policy area. It goes by the name of deontology. In contrast to teleologists, deontologists assert that considerations other than an act's consequence of producing nonmoral goods are what makes the act right or obligatory. In effect, deontologists contend that the act itself is what is right or wrong, regardless of its consequences.

Examples of deontological thinking are numerous. The Golden Rule to "do unto others as you would have others do unto you" or Immanual Kant's categorical imperative to "act only on that maxim which you can at the same time will to be a universal law" are well-known examples drawn from religious and moral philosophy. When Aldo Leopold asserted that actions disrupting the biotic community are wrong, he too was speaking as a deontologist (6). For that matter, so is Graham Ashworth, when he says, "You ought to use land in a manner that benefits the land and does not damage it" (2).

While to my knowledge no one has yet asserted that the act of preserving prime agricultural land is ethical in itself, deontological principles form the cornerstone of land and environmental ethic statements. To the extent these principles are drawn upon—indirectly or even subconsciously—in shaping land resource policy, the influence of deontological thinking can be seen.

My feeling, however, is that the teleological approach is more often used than the deontological when an ethical perspective enters into a discourse on land resource issues. I say this because most policy officials characteristically consider the costs and benefits of proposals, even in rudimentary fashion, before recommending or taking any action. And more often than not, this entails some sort of weighting of the nonmoral goods and bads likely to result from the contemplated action. The list of specific "do's and don'ts" in land ethic statements, which reflects the deontological approach, might occasionally enlighten a discussion on a land policy issue, but the principles embodied in these statements in themselves are rarely the grounds upon which land resource policy decisions are forged.

The question of values

I have attempted to sort out some of the ways an ethical perspective can enter the land resources planning process by highlighting distinctions between ends- and means-oriented ethical principles and between the teleological and deontological modes of ethical thought. But what makes the ethical perspective considerably more difficult to apply to land resource issues than either the economic or ecological perspectives is the multiplicity of values built into that perspective. Unlike the economic or ecological perspectives—each of which basically springs from a unified, coherent set of values—the ethical perspective on land covers a much wider range of values, some of which work at cross purposes. One of the knottiest problems in using an ethical perspective, therefore, stems from the conflicts among competing "goods" built into the perspective. As one well-known ethics scholar contends, "most moral problems arise in situations where there is a conflict of duties, where one ethical principle pulls one way and another pulls the other way" (3).

This dilemma is illustrated well in a recently published book, in which the author lays out some conflicting values that often butt up against each other in the real world, compounding the difficulty of making ethical choices affecting environmental issues (4):

1. Economic fuel needs (coal, oil, etc.) versus environmental concerns.

2. The psychological need to grow (inducing a quest for economic growth, jobs, and material products) versus the need to conserve resources.

3. Passive acceptance of nature (based on the Judeo-Christian belief that nature is there to serve man) versus preserving and improving nature (based on an ecological belief).

4. The philosophy of individual freedom versus the philosophy of collective restraint and collective decision making.

5. Faith in human abilities (for example, technology has the answer) versus caution about human error (for example, the problem of nuclear safety).

6. Human rights and needs versus plant and animal welfare.

The author's categorization of these value conflicts is helpful because it clarifies our understanding of the complex ethical milieu in which environmentalists and to some extent land resource planners must operate. One could add other value conflicts to his list that are particularly applicable to the land resources area, for example, environmental protection versus equity and social justice for the have-nots; the growth ethic (producing more job and goods) versus the ecological ethic (favoring a steady state economy and use of more appropriate technology).

The point is that numerous ethical imperatives compete for attention in the real world, which makes it more difficult to sort out right from wrong in a practical sense. Consider the difficulty facing those who would like to achieve the commendable but numerous ethical imperatives embodied in one of Ashworth's land ethic prescriptions (2):

"You ought to ensure that the land use controls developed in your area prevent irreversible damage, avoid waste, protect your natural and cultural heritage, stimulate visual order, regulate and control the unsightly, and safeguard individual liberties (such as mobility and a choice in housing and schooling, so long as those liberties do not impede the liberties of others)."

A tall order indeed!

Education a critical need

Given the difficulty of coming up with a clear, internally consistent ethical perspective on land resource issues, what then might be done to make that perspective a more potent and useful instrument for shaping future land resource policy? I see education of those who will shape future policy as a critical need. By this I mean educating the environmentalists, planners, developers, farmers, and public officials to think more carefully, systematically, and analytically about ethics.

Here we can turn for assistance to the work of those currently rethinking how to teach applied ethics or "moral inquiry directed to making actual choices in moral conflicts" that deal with concrete human problems (5). Interest in applied ethics has increased steadily in the past decade. This interest rises out of symptoms of a moral vacuum in our society, a sense of moral drift and of ethical uncertainty. The field turns on exceedingly difficult ethical dilemmas that are also present in the sphere of land resources planning—tensions between freedom and justice, individual autonomy and government regulation, efficiency and equity, and the rights of individuals and the rights of society.

Drawing upon the summary report (5) of the recently completed nine-volume study by The Hastings Center on how applied ethics is taught in various professional schools, I would suggest a four-pronged educational agenda.

First, we must sort out more clearly the ethical issues and numerous ethical dilemmas involved in working in the land resources area, dilemmas arising out of conflicts among competing ethical principles as well as out of the clash between ends-and means-oriented ethical principles.

Second, we must elicit a greater sense of moral obligation and personal responsibility about what is done to the land resource in our system. We especially need to raise the level of moral anxiety of the public at large about what is being done with our land. As a starting point, those who work as custodians of the public's interest in land should seriously discuss and grapple with the ethical principles embodied in land and environmental ethic statements. If the land custodians pay only lip service to these principles, little progress will be made in educating the general public.

Third, we must develop, hone, and then use the skills of ethical analysis to arrive at ethical judgments. Attention to the following is especially needed:

(a) Carefully examining the multiple concepts of growth, equity, ecology, fairness, justice, individual rights, and others that underlie ethical issues in the land resource area.

(b) Tracing the implications of these concepts, an effort requiring both reason and imagination.

(c) Asking if consequences of ethical choice and action are the only pertinent criteria in judging their validity—characteristic of a teleological approach.

(d) As a corollary, asking if there are some ethical principles so central and critical to resolving land planning issues that the principles must be embraced regardless of the consequences.

And fourth, we must tolerate disagreements and be prepared to accept the inevitable ambiguities in attempting to examine ethical problems. At the same time, no less an attempt should be made to locate and clarify the sources of disagreement to resolve ambiguity as much as possible and to see if ways can be found to overcome differences in ethical views.

What I am proposing is essentially a vigorous, concerted effort at moral education of those in the business of shaping and affecting land resource policy and decisions. This is a formidable task, but in my judgement a necessary one if the ethical perspective is really to become a significant factor in coping with the land planning urgency our society faces.

REFERENCES

1. Applegate, Rick. 1978. *Consider the future—systematically.* Journal of Soil and Water Conservation 33(2): 54-55.
2. Barnes, Chaplin B. 1980. *A new land use ethic.* Journal of Soil and Water Conservation 35(2): 61-62.
3. Frankena, William K. 1973. *Ethics.* Prentice-Hall, Englewood Cliffs, New Jersey. 125 pp.
4. Fritsch, Albert J. 1980. *Environmental ethics.* Anchor Press, Garden City, New York. 309 pp.
5. Hastings Center Institute of Society, Ethics, and the Life Sciences. 1980. *The teaching of ethics in higher education.* Hastings-on-Hudson, New York. 103 pp.
6. Leopold, Aldo. 1966. *A Sand County almanac.* Ballantine Books, New York, New York. 295 pp.

6

The Environmental Imperative of Land Use Planning

Gunnar C. Isberg
Gunnar Isberg and Associates
Northfield, Minnesota

Some recent land use trends in the United States and elsewhere have brought into sharp focus the reality of mankind's dependence upon land and water for food and fiber, recreation, and general well-being. One of these trends is the continuous loss of topsoil. It is estimated that as much as 2 billion tons of sediment are deposited into our streams each year, 1.5 billion tons of which reaches the oceans. The amount of topsoil in some of our most productive areas in the Midwest has declined alarmingly; certain areas now retain less than 6 inches of topsoil. This occurs even though many soil erosion programs and projects have been adopted since the dust bowl days of the 1930s, including, for example, the growing of shelterbelts, contour and minimum tillage farming, and the construction of sediment traps in urban development projects. In fact, there is significant evidence that some of these soil erosion control projects are being abandoned for short-term gains. In the Plains, for instance, shelterbelts are being destroyed to make room for center-pivot irrigation systems, which is likely to have adverse effects on soil erosion.

Another major trend is the loss of some of our most agriculturally productive land to urbanization, which is estimated to consume about 1 million acres of prime agricultural land in the United States annually. Although a few small subdivisions or a few homes in an agricultural area may directly cost only a few acres of agricultural land, indirect effects may occur, such as rises in property taxes from increased demand for services or demands for restrictions on agricultural operations by nonfarm property owners due to dust and odor from normal agricultural operations. Losses of prime agricultural land can also have a significant effect on energy use in that farmers tend to place more marginal land into production. This means greater use of energy in terms of fertilizers, pesticides, and other production inputs.

The United States has been uniquely blessed with abundant resources, including prime agricultural land. As long as these resources remained plentiful, the continued depletion of topsoil or prime agricultural land caused little concern, except perhaps during the dramatic dust bowl. Recent land use trends, though, have raised serious questions. If these trends persist, our choices may narrow. Put another way, perhaps at no time in modern history have we been faced with choices that could have such a profound effect on the future. This requires us to closely examine the traditional ways we have looked at land.

Concepts of land and water

Under a free enterprise system, such as practiced in the United States, land has been viewed historically as an economic commodity. Land use decisions have been made generally on the basis of economic return. The phrase "highest and best use," used in such contexts as land use planning and real estate transactions, refers specifically to the use of the land bringing the highest economic return, whether it be commercial, residential, or agricultural use. Planning and zoning efforts attempt to modify the market system's impact on land use; however, planning is still a relatively recent concept that developed primarily to minimize land use conflicts. Many rural areas often lack planning and zoning programs. In essence, most land use decisions continue to be largely determined by the open market.

Another concept is to view land as a natural resource that needs protection for the good of society as a whole. This value may or may not have a direct relationship to the economic market. For example, a wetland may have little or no value for development purposes and therefore a low market price, yet it may be extremely valuable as part of a local stormwater drainage system or as a wildlife habitat. Those who view land as a vital and unique public resource usually believe that land ought to be held in trust for future generations and that stringent controls need to be placed on the use of the land. This is basically the environmental imperative of protecting land from abuse. Some believe that prime agricultural land in the United States ought to be viewed as a vital natural resource in light of our nation's economic dependence upon agriculture as well as the fact that the United States may indeed become, if it has not already, the "breadbasket" of the world.

Society's dilemma is to face the difficult, if not impossible, task of protecting lands of unique natural resources in the open market. The reason?

The development value of land is usually much higher than its agricultural or natural resource value. Developers can easily outbid farm expansion buyers or governmental units for these lands. Therefore, much prime agricultural land continues to convert to urban development.

Until and unless the value of land for agricultural purposes or open-space purposes reaches that of its development value, the open market system will not protect these lands for future generations. Likewise, unless economic incentives or other regulations are created to encourage or require soil erosion practices, soil erosion will remain a major problem. Furthermore, because of the politically conservative philosophy so prevalent in rural areas of the United States, it will be difficult for society to institute the necessary incentives and controls for regulating land use and management.

Persuasion, economic incentives, or land use controls?

If society determines that prime agricultural land and other environmentally sensitive areas are of critical enough value to warrant protection for posterity, the issue arises as to what programs are required.

Here again, we face the dilemma that most authority over land use controls in the United States rests largely with local governments. Nor is this likely to change in the near future. Local governments are likely to guard their control and resist any proposed shift of this authority to other levels of government. Yet programs to control soil erosion effectively on prime agricultural areas often demand a regional approach and perspective.

Another basic problem is the degree of control necessary to protect this land. Here again, programs can range from tactics of persuasion to strict land use controls, and again, the tendency under a free enterprise system has been to rely exclusively on persuasion or educational programs. For example, soil erosion has been dealt with largely through educational programs. The basic problem with this approach is that its effectiveness depends upon the good will and cooperation of individual landowners. Because of the limitations of this approach, some states and local communities have begun to enact laws that rely more on land use controls.

The type of specific approach to control land use that is most appropriate depends upon the particular jurisdiction. From past experience we know that mere slogans or exhortations from federal or state governments will not be effective in protecting environmentally sensitive areas. We need programs that are relatively simple to implement and inexpensive. Society must be willing to go beyond mere persuasion and rely more on economic incentives. Mandatory land use controls may be necessary in some areas where the problems are critical.

Intergovernmental relations

One other issue pertaining to protection of environmentally sensitive areas concerns the roles of different levels of government. As discussed, authority over land use controls is likely to remain with local governments in the future. Therefore, because of their need to develop effective programs to protect environmentally sensitive areas, local units of government will require technical and economic assistance. They also need standards that are easily adaptable in local land use programs. State and federal governments must develop more effective programs to provide this technical and monetary assistance as well as the standards themselves. This will require a thorough examination of existing programs to consider changes in those programs presently containing inconsistencies.

Transforming current programs

Certain land use trends in the United States suggest that we are reaching a period in history in which choices related to land use may have a profound effect upon future generations. Making these decisions may necessitate that we alter our view of environmentally sensitive lands from one of a simple economic perspective to one that recognizes the intrinsic value of these lands to society, which is to be held in trust for existing and future generations. To protect these lands, we must be willing to move from educational programs to programs with economic incentives and stricter land use controls. This requires effective and consistent programs in which governmental programs at the federal, state, and local levels reinforce one another. In this way we begin to move forward to protect our vital natural resources for succeeding generations.

7

The Land Planning Urgency: A Roundtable Discussion

Jefferson E. Carroll
Coordinator, Environmental Education Programs
Forest Service, Washington, D.C.

A roundtable discussion on the economic, ethical, and ecological perspectives of land use planning generated divergent responses to the questions involved. Participants were asked to rank six discussion questions by order of importance and then recommend the two or more deemed to be of highest priority. Following are responses to the three top-ranked questions.

Should the United States use its agricultural base to improve or maintain the balance of trade with other countries if such trade in the long term degrades the productivity of the nation's land and water base?

The general consensus: "No!" Most participants felt that exporting agricultural products also means, in effect, exporting the land and water necessary to sustain our own production. In an emergency, where national survival might depend upon the ability to produce and export, overdrawing of our resource base might be justified, but it should not be tolerated on a regular basis. On the other hand, most registrants felt that current export levels should be maintained because land used for agriculture would probably then not be lost to nonproductive uses and remain available to meet our own future needs.

Should the U.S. encourage a structure of agriculture that results in fewer but more productive farms?

The response of the majority: "No," but for a variety of reasons. Most participants saw this as a phasing-out of farm family life and the loss of its contributions to American society. Many were concerned about large, absentee, corporate ownerships and their affect on the American farm family, the lack of personal commitment to the land by salaried employees, and possible adverse affects on rural communities. There was approval of large family corporate operations, but the majority disapproved of absentee corporate or government-owned operations of any size.

Other concerns expressed were economic, with an almost even split between those who contended that either large or small farm operations are the more efficient in the long run. Other economic concerns revolved around the disparity of taxes between large corporate ownerships and small individual or family ownerships. In short, the consensus of the group was that bigger is not always better, but it can be in the right context.

What limits or incentives should our society use to motivate landowners to use and care for land without degrading its productivity or polluting water and air?

There was a consistent disclaiming of the desire for regulation, yet participants saw regulation as inevitable. Throughout the responses to all questions ran the acceptance of regulation or, as one group stated, legal incentives that might be most effective when generated and applied at the local level and that would decrease in acceptance in a direct response to the rise through the bureaucratic system of the regulation's point of origin.

Positive incentives to motivate landowners to conserve and to care for the land would also be best applied at the local level where everyone, including elected officials, has a vested interest. Monetary incentives could include tax benefits or rebates or even the purchase of long-term agricultural easements by the county or state. At the federal level, there should be a comprehensive tax incentive program for land remaining in agricultural use or open space.

The key to acceptance of these programs and the conservation ethic that they represent would be found in education, which is itself an incentive. Conservation professionals should be involved as individuals within the politics of their communities. Conservation education should be continued in both the urban and rural sectors, with emphasis on such nontraditional audiences as real estate agents, builders and developers, and construction workers reached through unions and trade schools, as well as the more traditional inclusion of conservation education in the schools and through environmental learning centers and the media.

Perhaps the most positive aspects of the roundtable were the sharing of opinions and concerns by conservationists, agriculturalists, and members of the general public from all over the United States and the realization among participants that although problems may be similar there is a great deal of difference in the way these problems are viewed by those who are affected.

III. The Water Management Crunch

8

The Water Management Crunch: An Economic Perspective

B. Delworth Gardner

Director, Giannini Foundation of Agricultural Economics
University of California, Berkeley
and Professor of Agricultural Economics
University of California, Davis

Water is used in virtually every human activity, especially every economic function concerned with the production, transport, and consumption of commodities. All of us therefore have some stake in policies that help assure the availability of water in sufficient quantity and quality for every desired use. It is in the arid West, however, where irrigation greatly enhances land productivity in agriculture, that concerns about water are most evident. It is there where competition for scarce water from alternative uses has greatly augmented water's value and where quite unique institutions have emerged to govern water development and allocation.

To understand adequately the water management crunch, some historical perspective is helpful. Unfortunately, I am not a historian, but an economist. From my perspective there are problems that might be termed a "crunch." Water is indeed the factor constraining increases in output most in the American West, particularly agricultural output. At the same time, water is misallocated, and the resource is wasted in its capture and distribution. It is as if water is not regarded as an economic good at all, and this is the root cause of the management crunch.

I take as my point of departure the allegation that water is somehow different from other resources and requires quite different mechanisms for its capture and allocation. Most societies treat water as a social resource. That is, the "management tools related to land resources are predominantly in the hands of the land's private owners and users, whereas those related to water resources are predominantly held by the public in spite of the strongly held preferences for private ownership and management of resources" (6).

Our own society is no exception. By statutory enactment in every western state, ownership of water resides in the people (public) or the state. Users of water must obtain rights to put it to some beneficial use. Why is this so? Why has the body politic chosen to treat water differently than land?

Kelso (6) argued, "Land as a resource unit is more clearly definable, more constant, more certain in content and location; water is transient in flows that are variable both in nature and when created by man. Even stored quantities of water are more variable in quantity and quality in nature and as the result of the actions of man than is land."

One of the things Kelso is saying is that land stays put (except for mining and soil erosion), whereas water moves around before, during, and after use, creating positive and/or negative impacts on others. Economists call these impacts externalities. It is this fugitive character of water that perhaps has made society reluctant to endorse private ownership and control. On the other hand, the failure to permit private ownership of water has created uncertainties that have led to serious inefficiencies in development and allocation of water.

Water combines with other resources to produce wealth and utility for human beings. Most people prefer using water in ways that will maximize the income and wealth that constitute the economic well-being of members of society. Economists call this economic efficiency. Efficiency deals only with the total amount of income and wealth produced. The distribution of this total among individuals is the so-called equity issue. It also is of interest to economists. In fact, water policy is and has been a favorite instrument of politicians to bring about redistributions of income and wealh. As a result, special-interest groups have been formed to bring pressure on politicians to make sure the groups' interests are protected and enhanced. This penchant for using water to redistribute income and wealth is one of the greatest sources of inefficiency in water development and allocation; it is thus one of the great contributors to the management crunch.

Efficiency in water development and allocation

Let me begin here by being explicit about the requirements to achieve efficiency in water development and allocation. I use the term "water development" to refer to the situation where scarce land, labor, and capital resources are used to augment the effective supply of water. Water exists in nature but must be harnessed and transported to be available when and where needed. Generally, development occurs on a project-by-project basis.

Economic efficiency imposes two requirements. First, the present value of benefits yielded by a project must exceed the present value of costs. It is assumed here that all costs and benefits can be valued monetarily and that costs are "opportunity costs," that is, the value of the services yielded by the resources in their best alternative uses. The logic of this requirement is compelling; wealth cannot be maximized if resources are used in water development that have higher yields elsewhere in the economy. In the traditional benefit-cost analysis, this requirement is satisfied if the benefit-cost ratio for a specific project exceeds unity or, in other words, if the present value of net benefits (present value of benefits minus present value of costs) exceeds zero.

The second requirement is that project scale be established (both with respect to project size and the durability of the capital stock incorporated in the project), where the present value of benefits at the margin exactly equals the present value of resource costs at the margin. Society's wealth cannot be maximized if a project expands in size beyond the point where additional benefits are equal to additional opportunity costs, or project life is extended beyond the point where the present value of benefits captured thereby are less than the present value of the resource costs expended to get those benefits.

A critical and much-disputed question, even among economists, is the interest rate that should be used in calculating present values of costs and benefits. Space constraints will not permit an adequate treatment of this issue (4). Suffice to say, interest rates generated in the private capital markets, such as the prime rate, are the best indicators of the opportunity cost of capital and the rate of time preference of savers, and these rates should be used to discount benefits and costs of public projects.[1]

Of course, if water projects are not subsidized, the water users, the beneficiaries of the project, must be willing to pay the full development and distribution costs in the form of water tolls. If they are unwilling to do so, there is at least a *prima facie* case that building the project is not an efficient use of resources.

Let's now turn to efficiency in water allocation as contrasted with development efficiency. After water is developed, the fixed development costs are irrelevant to optimal allocation. Real resources have been sunk into project development and thus are no longer relevant marginal costs. If water were only a flow resource (it could not be stored for future use), the allocation problem would be simplified because it would be necessary only to allocate it optimally among prospective users in the current period. Because it can be stored and is stored, however, the allocation decision must consider use by prospective future users as well as by present ones. As a result, there are both spatial and temporal dimensions to the allocation problems.

In general, allocative efficiency is achieved when it is impossible to move a unit of water to another user or another time period where (when) it would be worth more than the costs of moving it (5). Costs include full "oppor-

---

[1]The discount rate issue is especially difficult if there is inflation in the economy. If expected benefits and costs are corrected for price inflation and thus displayed in real terms, the rate of discount should also be a real rate. The real rate can be calculated by subtracting the expected average rate of inflation from the expected average nominal or market rate of interest.

tunity costs,'' which, in addition to conveyance costs, include the value of the water foregone in its previous use and the present value of any future use foregone if the water can be stored. Let's try to clarify these allocation rules with an example.

Suppose water user A values the last unit of surface water at $10 per acre-foot and he has no option of storing it for future use. Also, suppose user B values water at $16 per acre-foot at the margin and the conveyance costs of moving water from A to B is $5 per acre-foot. The conveyance costs include evaporation and seepage losses, valued at A's marginal value. The opportunity costs at the margin of moving an acre-foot from A to B are $15, while B's value is $16. Allocative efficiency would require that water be moved from A to B. Because of the well-known economic law of variable proportions, as water moves from A to B, the marginal value of water to A rises while that of B falls. Thus, allocative efficiency is fully achieved when that quantity of water moves from A to B so that the marginal value of water to B is equal to the opportunity costs of the exchange (A's marginal value plus the conveyance costs).

If either A or B has the option of storing water, the future value of water discounted to the present needs to be considered. If A can store and B cannot and if A has a present value of $12 for some future use and no storage costs, then allocative efficiency would require that A exercise that option and store the water. A's storage option has a value of $12 compared to $10 in current use. Moreover, the opportunity cost of moving water to B is now $12 (A's best use), plus the conveyance cost of $5, which exceeds B's value of $16.

To summarize, allocative efficiency is obtained when the discounted marginal net values of water are equal among all users for all time periods.

One of the practical difficulties in dealing with the temporal allocation is that future net values cannot be known in the present with any degree of certainty; they can only be estimated. Some probability exists that these estimates will be in error when the future becomes the present. Moreover, estimates that are made far into the future are more risky than those made closer to the present. If water users are risk averse, they will attach a lower value to a risky dollar earned in the future than they would to one less risky. The upshot is that risky future net values should be discounted at higher interest rates in making present value comparisons than those less risky.

Now that efficiency has been defined, let's look at some of the evidence to see whether or not it is being achieved and if not, why.

Impediments to the achievement of economic efficiency

Development. Many studies have shown that much water development and allocation are economically inefficient. Much of the development occurring in the late 19th and 20th centuries was privately financed, and it can be safely assumed that it was efficient. Many private mutual irrigation companies still exist that have supplied water to the same lands for over 100 years, a most unlikely outcome if the water development had not been economic. Still, much of the more recent water development has been initiated and even constructed by ambitious federal and state governmental agencies, and here the evidence is much more negative.

It is true that all acceptable federal projects must pass some strict benefit-cost test, one in which the projected benefit-cost ratio exceeds unity or that all costs be covered by user charges. Many studies of water projects, however, have revealed that *ex post* project performance has fallen short of *ex ante* expectations, particularly if benefits and costs are calculated correctly. In practice, *ex ante* benefits are systematically overstated while costs are understated. The most blatant examples are (a) double counting of benefits, such as counting both increases in crop production and increases in land values, where much of the latter is due to the former, (b) counting secondary benefits due to the project's existence, when similar secondary benefits would be generated by the resources in their alternative employment, and (c) using discount rates far below the true opportunity costs of capital.

Many of the reclamation projects under consideration by the Congress are generating separable full costs of irrigation water in the range of $125 to $200 per acre-foot and even higher. Few farmers find it economic to purchase contracts for water at such high prices. In order to generate political support, the government finds ways of subsidizing agricultural water use. Usually these subsidies take the form of (a) calculating the per acre ability-to-pay of farmers by subtracting the nonwater costs of growing crops from crop revenues and then requiring other project beneficiaries, such as power users, to provide the difference between the ability-to-pay and the separable costs of irrigation; (b) deferring any interest and principal payments until project completion, which may involve long periods of time; (c) subsidizing costly additions to projects by allowing (requiring) the distribution agency to charge the average cost for the expensive new water and the cheaper old water; and (d) transferring some of the project costs to landowners by placing a tax on land quite unrelated to water use. Obviously, points three and four are incompatible with the efficient pricing rule.

Another significant impediment to efficient water development is the policy of many state governments to make financial resources available to local entities, public and private, that cannot borrow elsewhere. Often the reason loans are not available elsewhere is that the economic feasibility of the project is doubtful. Such projects may effectively redistribute income and wealth, but they are not efficient in creating new wealth.

It is not surprising that water development is inefficient. Strong political forces are the reason. Senators, congressmen, and state legislators get political mileage out of providing their constituents with a larger share of public largesse, especially when strongly encouraged by well-organized special-interest beneficiaries who stand to gain much if the project is built. The primary loser group, general taxpayers, is much less likely to be well organized, principally because the group is so large and difficult to organize. In addition, the individual losses are much less than the individual gains captured by project beneficiaries. Add to this the governmental agencies at both federal and state levels promoting water development that find it in their best interest to grow and command a larger share of the budget and you have a water lobby that is almost irresistible.

Still, there are powerful countervailing special interests opposing development, primarily environmentalists, who want the water resources left in an undeveloped state, where they might have access to them at little or no cost. The prevailing opinion in the West is that environmentalist forces are very much in the ascendancy in Washington. Witness President Carter's "hit list" of water projects scheduled for completion but for which no funds have been authorized. The battle between developers and anti-development forces is likely to be long and bloody; much will depend upon who occupies the White House and whether or not he or she is a westerner.

Allocation. It is also widely acknowledged that water is spatially and temporally misallocated. We recently completed work in California that looked at conjunctive use of surface and groundwater, both spatially and temporally, using a linear-quadratic, optimal control model (7).

Yolo County, located in the southwest corner of the Sacramento Valley, provides an example of one area in which conjunctive use of groundwater and surface water has evolved without any particular centralized planning. Several water agencies deliver water to various agricultural and urban users. The aquifer was partitioned into six basins for modelling purposes by hydrologists at the University of California at Davis. This partitioning permitted the model to allocate water spatially among the six basins and took account of the very different pumping lifts from the aquifer in the six basins. Subsurface inflows and outflows among the six basins had to be estimated by the hydrologic model. The economic portion of the model estimated shadow prices (marginal values) of the water in current uses in each area as well as the per acre-foot value of the water stock in the aquifer.

The range of marginal values is large—from $2.44 per acre foot in an area near the Sacramento River, where water is quite plentiful and the pumping lift is less than 20 feet, to $61.13 in another area scarcely 25 miles away, where water is pumped from more than 100 feet. This disparity in shadow prices suggests that large efficiency gains could be captured by water transfers from areas of low net values to areas of high net vaues. Regrettably, there are institutional impediments to such economic transfers.

The first impediment may be in the law itself. Most eastern and southern states and California adopted the riparian water right doctrine from English common law. A riparian right entitles water use on land adjacent to a water source. In California, the amount of water entitlement is limited only by applying rules of reasonable and beneficial use. No filing requirement for a permit or right is imposed. By its very nature, therefore, riparian water could not be moved to nonriparian land, regardless of the economic incentive to do so.

Second, in many states using the doctrine of prior appropriation, the water right is held by the irrigation company or by some form of water district. Permission to transfer water must have majority or even sometimes unanimous approval by the voting members. This may be difficult because return flows from water use often are a significant supply source for other users in the company or district.

Third, most states have state agencies that must give approval for transfers—a state engineer; a state water resources control board, as in California; the courts, as in Colorado. As a rule, those state agencies that consider water transfers can usually be appealed to by those negatively affected by a proposed transfer and the transfer can be easily blocked. Because no suitable mechanism exists to compensate losers outside of litigation in the courts, the agencies tend to be reluctant to permit efficient transfers and thereby maintain the *status quo* so as to avoid injury to third parties. Much of this third-party problem could be avoided if transfers of water were limited to the consumptive use of the transferring party. The quantity of return flow, which is the concern of third parties affected, would thus remain in the water source, and third parties would be minimally affected. This policy would also give water users an incentive to improve irrigation (water use) efficiency since they could transfer a larger quantity.

Suppose that a water right permits a diversion of six acre-feet per acre and that irrigation efficiency is 50 percent. The consumptive use is three acre-feet per acre, and return flow is something less than three acre-feet, depending upon a host of factors that affect return flow. If transfer were restricted to consumptive use, three acre-feet could be transferred, and the remaining three acre-feet would be left in the water source to cover other water rights affected by the transfer.

Now suppose irrigation efficiency were 75 percent. A diversion of six acre-feet would permit a consumptive use of 4.5 acre-feet, which could be transferred under the consumptive use rule. Of course, only 1.5 acre-feet now is available to supply return flow rights. So, obviously the consumptive use transfer rule would provide incentive for improving irrigation efficiency but could leave return-flow right holders worse off.

Of course, no voluntary transfers of water will occur unless there is an incentive for both parties (9). Given the current policy of requiring administrative approval for transfers, current appropriators may fear that they will lose their rights if they propose a transfer and it is denied. The administrative agency may argue that the transfer would not be proposed if the water were really needed by the current right holder. If so, they would completely miss the point of different users having different values for water at the margin. What is required is a water market where an appropriator with water to sell can negotiate with a buyer at a price advantageous to both. So long as the exchange is voluntary, it is axiomatic that both parties to the exchange will be better off then they were.

Groundwater use presents a special set of efficiency problems unless use rights have been created that are similar to surface rights. California is one state, among others, that does not have statutory or administrative control over groundwater pumping. As a result, users overlying an aquifer regard water as a common property pool. Since an individual pumper cannot command exclusive rights to the future use of the groundwater stock, he must regard future use as beyond his control. He can be expected to pump in the present so long as the net marginal value in use is greater than the marginal pumping cost. Each pumper using the common pool aquifer can be expected to act similarly. In calculating their individual marginal costs they do not include the costs their pumping imposes on other users of the aquifer in the form of lowering the water table and increasing pumping lifts. The inevitable result is that the pool will be exploited at a faster rate than is socially optimal, which means that all users end up pumping from a greater depth than is economically efficient from a basin point of view. Overinvestment in size of wells, pumps, and other equipment will also occur as each pumper attempts to capture the groundwater before the stock is depleted by other pumpers (2).

As indicated in the section on efficiency, temporal efficiency exists when the marginal present values of water use in all future years equal the marginal value in the current year. In other words, the marginal value of water held in storage will equal the value in current use. If aquifers have been used too rapidly, from the standpoint of all users together, stocks for future use will have higher values than water in current use, and pumping from the stock should be postponed—used at a slower rate.

In the Yolo County study, we estimated these stock values in the aquifers of the six regions with the optimal control model. They ranged from $12.23 per acre-foot to over $1,000 per acre-foot. They are higher than current shadow prices, suggesting that common pool usage is indeed a problem. There are great disparities of value among regions suggesting spatial and temporal misallocation. The conclusion is that use must be controlled if efficiency is to be achieved. Our study also shows that a pump tax is a more efficient way to limit pumping to the optimal level than are per acre pumping quotas, the method used in most states that have groundwater controls.

The Yolo County study is significant because it shows severe misallocation of both surface water and groundwater over space as well as over time for a single use and in a very small geographic area where conveyance costs in transfer would not be high. Almost certainly the disparities in value would be much larger if various uses were considered and larger intrastate and interstate areas were compared. The conclusion is that almost surely the least costly way of increasing effective supplies of water in wealth-producing activities is to find equitable ways of transferring water to higher valued uses and areas. Some will interpret this conclusion as being against agriculture. I do not regard it as such. Except for large-scale energy development in some parts of the West, nonagricultural demands for water can likely be met by transfers that are not large. And given the fact that demand for irrigation water also is relatively inelastic, small shifts in water use will change marginal values significantly. Besides, if farmers had the option of selling their water in a water market at prices greater than its value to them, they would most certainly use it more efficiently and perhaps would shift to crops that use less water. Only rarely, I believe, would we see large areas moving entirely out of agricultural production.

Miscellaneous management issues

No discussion of water management issues in the West would be complete without some reference to water quality and to water allocation for redistributing income.

Many knowledgeable water experts believe that water quality problems resulting from irrigation are the most intractable of all water problems. Warren Hall (3) put the issue eloquently: "Salt problems are particularly insidious. They do not come charging at you with trumpets blowing and battle flags flying, a sight to set stirring the heart of activitists in any century. Rather, they slip in almost unnoticed. They invariably seem to promise to step aside and behave themselves in return for small additional concessions. Then one day, as witnessed by many dead civilizations, they assert their supreme command of the situation. Time is of no concern, for they are supremely confident of their ultimate victory. History is on their side, as are the laws of physics, and chemistry, and biology. They have quietly destroyed, without fuss or fanfare, more civilizations than all of the mighty armies of the world."

Hall's statement has a quality of inevitability about it, that irrigated agriculture is doomed in the long run. My own reading of the evidence is not so pessimistic. There is even some question about whether or not man's actions have much of an impact on salt loading in most of our rivers, since so much of it is caused by natural runoff beyond man's control. What we can say with some degree of certainty is that salt build-up in groundwater aquifers and in surface water sources due to the application of water to the land is a classic externality problem similar to the common-pool problem discussed earlier. Irrigation leaches salts from the soil, and water transports them to locations where the salt build-up becomes a problem for later water users. Under present institutional arrangements there are no financial incentives for irrigators to undertake investments that may reduce the salt loading. If our research could tell us the salt loading that occurs under various water application technologies, then perhaps farmers could be taxed in such a way that these external costs could be internalized, thus providing an incentive for farmers to reduce the damage from an aggregate point of view.

I return finally to one of the most difficult of all water management problems—the income distribution issue. Going back in time at least to the Reclamation Act of 1902, federal funds have been used to build water projects that would induce economic development in the arid sections of the country that require irrigated agriculture. The rationale for restricting acreage to 160 acres per individual owner receiving project water was that irrigation would be subsidized and it would be equitable to spread the subsidy widely among many family-sized farms. For all of its moral appeal in support of freeholding family farms, such a policy was bound to be incompatible with economic efficiency.

In terms of development efficiency, irrigators have not been required to pay the full costs of irrigation development (*10*), resulting in premature and overextended water development. Of course, federal water subsidies have not been restricted to western irrigators. The Rivers and Harbors Act of 1884 and the Flood Control Act of 1936 do not require the project beneficiaries to participate at all in sharing project costs (*1*). The Water Quality Act of 1965 and the Federal Water Pollution Control Act Amendments of 1972 also place most of the financial burden for quality improvement on the federal government. "Federal cost-sharing policy today is a complex web of approximately 185 separate rules that have been developed over the years by congressional acts and administrative decisions" (*1*). It is scarcely any wonder that western irrigators cry "foul" when it is suggested that they pay the full cost for water when so many others pay next to nothing at all.[2] New programs for rehabilitating urban water supply systems are costly and involve huge federal subsidies. From an economic efficiency point of view, these subsidies should be stopped. All classes of water users should be required to pay the full cost of water development. If the federal government, or for that matter state and local governments, must redistribute income and wealth, then it should be done in the most efficient way possible. It is doubtful that new subsidized water development is an efficient redistribution mechanism.

Prescriptions for wise use of limited water

In conclusion, yes, there is a water management crunch. But as a society we are not powerless to do anything about it. Four prescriptions would greatly improve the economic productivity of our scarce water resources:

1. Pay more attention to economic efficiency criteria in developing and allocating water and stop using water policy to redistribute income.

2. Price new water at the relevant marginal cost and reform water institutions to permit them to use this rule.

3. Create firm property rights in water similar to those in land and allow a water market to allocate it among uses and users.

4. When external effects are significant, such as in pumping groundwater from common pool aquifers and in the most severe water quality cases, use depletion and effluent taxes as corrective devices.

---

[2]On 5,000 federal water projects and programs, agricultural water projects repaid 19 percent of real project costs, municipal and industrial projects repaid 64 percent, harbor projects 16 percent, waterways 6 percent, other navigational programs 7 percent, and hydroelectric projects 64 percent (*8*).

REFERENCES

1. Eisel, Leo M., and Richard M. Wheeler. 1979. *Financing water resources development*. In *Western Water Resources, Coming Problems and the Policy Alternatives*. Westview Press, Boulder, Colorado.

2. Gardner, B. Delworth. 1979. *Economic issues in groundwater management.* In Proceedings, Twelfth Biennial Conference on Groundwater. Report No. 45. Water Resources Center, University of California, Davis.
3. Hall, Warren A. 1974. *Statement: Salty solutions to salty problems.* In *Salinity in Water Resources.* Merriman Publishing Company, Boulder, Colorado. p. 166.
4. Harberger, Arnold C. 1968. *On measuring the social opportunity cost of public funds, water resources and economic development of the West.* In *The Discount Rate in Public Investment Evaluation.* Western Agricultural Economic Research Council, Denver, Colorado. pp. 1-24.
5. Helweg, Otto J., and B. Delworth Gardner. 1979. *Groundwater management problems in California.* In *California Water Planning and Policy, Selected Issues.* Water Resources Center, University of California, Davis. pp. 46-56.
6. Kelso, M. M. 1979. *Commentary.* In *Western Water Resources, Coming Problems and the Policy Alternatives.* Westview Press, Boulder, Colorado.
7. Noel, Jay E., B. Delworth Gardner, and Charles V. Moore. 1980. *Optimal regional conjunctive water management.* American Journal of Agricultural Economics 62(3): 489-498.
8. North, Ronald M., and Walter P. Neely. 1977. *A model for achieving consistency for cost-sharing in water resource programs.* Water Resources Bulletin 13(5).
9. Phelps, Charles E., Nancy Y. Moore, and Morlie H. Graubard. 1978. *Efficient use of water in California: Water rights, water districts, and water transfers.* R-2386-CSA/RF. Rand Corporation, Santa Monica, California.
10. Water and Power Resources Service, U.S. Department of the Interior. 1980. *Acreage limitation.* Interim report. Washington, D.C.

9

The Water Management Crunch: An Ethical Perspective

George E. Radosevich
Associate Professor of Water Law and Economics
Department of Economics
Colorado State University, Fort Collins

> If we do not change our direction,
> we are likely to end up where we are headed.
> Chinese Proverb

What is ethics? Volumes of books are written on the subject, religions are based upon ethical principles, and just about every profession sets standards of ethics for its members. But, so as not to miss the forest for the trees, let's identify the commonly applied definition and set our scope of consideration. Ethics can be defined either in a social or professional context and when it comes to water should be seen both ways. In general, let's say ethics are the principles of human duty, moral standards that lead us to decide what is right and wrong. In an Oriental society, at least in China, an ethical perspective would not be too difficult to describe because the social emphasis is upon the duty to use water so as to not cause harm to another user. Western society, and in the western United States specifically, however, emphasizes a right to use water, which focuses upon the concept of self. In this way, ethics becomes much more personal and often resolved in such terms as "standards of the community," "majority rule," or "first come, first serve."

Already our topic is complex, but we may further ask, what is the scope of ethics in the use of water resources? An ethical perspective must include (a) the private water user versus the public concern, (b) present user versus future user, (c) the local, state, regional, national, and international levels of interest over use and control, and (d) the individual and governmental responsibilities associated with each of these considerations.

To put it another way, standing on my father's land in Wyoming, looking over a meadow flooded through the authority of an 1893 water right, is a much different perspective than that of a water planner in the state engineer's office, a member of an environmentalist organization, an eastern congressman, or the chairman of an oil shale company set to develop in northwestern Colorado.

Evolution of ethical standards

Looking at the water management situation in the West from a legal point of view as opposed to technical, economic, or social perspectives, I propose that what one finds is the evolution of intended ethical standards for water allocation, use, and control, at least at the time of enactment of the laws and adoptions of regulations. In early U.S. history, water, like air and open space, was considered a common or free good. Initially, unrestricted use was enabled by the minimal demands on existing supplies. At the same time, in the eastern United States natural precipitation negated the need for major surface diversions. Eastern states recognized the common law concept of riparian rights.

The situation in the West, however, differed because of the lower annual rainfall and the need to supplement natural precipitation with diversions from streams, lakes, or man-made reservoirs. Initially, there was enough water to meet the needs of all the settlers. But as use increased, and as simultaneous uses depleted water flow at particular times of the year, conflicts began to develop along the river systems. Miners, farmers, and other users battled each other until finally people began to recognize the need to develop some order and consistency regarding the use and management of this resource. In social terms, people were willing to give up a little so that all could have more; in economic terms, people were willing to internalize the cost of the externalities created through the use of this common resource. In legal terms, the pen proved to be mightier than the gun or shovel. What emerged was a desire to develop a set of rules and standards using the most socially acceptable tools to govern the management of a valuable resource.

This was an attempt to establish principles of conduct, even duty, in water resource utilization by bringing a public resource into allocations under a property rights system. Some of what resulted was borrowed from the many countries represented by the immigrants to the area. The rest evolved from the natural conditions, types of uses, and the creative capability of the users.

A federated system of water law evolved in keeping with our constitutional philosophy of separate state and federal powers. The federal government holds title to public lands in all western states, and many of those lands are withdrawn from entry or reserved for specific purposes, such as Indian reservations, parks, national forests and monuments, and oil shale reserves. On these lands, the federal government has mandated that sufficient water also be reserved from allocation under state laws to carry out the reservation's purposes. This federal water law is popularly called the Federal Reservation Doctrine. Under the law the federal government also exercises certain control, such as interstate commerce, navigation, and other proprietary interests, over water. Within the last decade it has preempted control over water quality.

Each state was entitled to adopt its own system of water law over waters rising within its jurisdiction. These laws were not to conflict with federal laws. As local customs developed and states were formed, each state adopted its own particular system of water law. Consequently, significant variations for quantity control of surface water and groundwater exist among the states. State water quality control laws are more uniform, however, and follow the pattern set by federal legislation.

State water quantity laws evolved simply and directly. They are a consequence of geoclimatic conditions, supply sources, and need. They also reflect the varying levels of technology that existed at the time pressure on the resource was exerted.

Surface water law. Surface waters developed into two basic philosophies. In the humid eastern half of the country and along the West Coast, the riparian doctrine was adopted. The more arid western half of the country was faced with diversions and return flows and costs involved in constructing new water delivery and application systems. The doctrine of prior appropriation emerged as the basic western water law. As a compromise, because some states have both humid and arid conditions and varying demands placed upon the resource, a mixed riparian/prior appropriaton system was adopted.

Although many variations of the appropriation doctrine exist among various western states, a number of key principles establish commonality, if not relative uniformity:

1. There was to be a diversion from a natural stream or body of water. This has been relaxed in most western states during the last decade to allow in-stream use for recreation and fish and wildlife protection.

2. Water was to apply to a beneficial use. Initially, this was defined in constitutions and/or statutes to be domestic, municipal, stock watering, irrigation, and certain industrial and power uses. Some state laws, such as Wyoming's, reflect the economic influences of one sector over another, as in the way railroad uses were preferred to agricultural uses. In most western states, however, the rural representation ensured agriculture a high position, as a beneficial use also referred to the nature of use.

3. When a diversion and application of water to beneficial use was com-

pleted, a water right was created. This right entitled the holder to continued use as long as the use was beneficial.

4. Every water right acquired a priority date such that priority of right and not equality of right was the basis for distributing water, hence the cliche' "first in time, first in right."

The doctrine of prior appropriaton is based upon the allocation of water under the concept of a property-right interest in water. Simply put, this doctrine creates the right of private use of a public resource under certain conditions and for uses that have been declared to have a public interest. The right does not automatically exist by virtue of the presence of water upon, flowing through, or under land. In all western states, waters are declared to be the property of the public, people, or state, regardless of whether the state or the public (people) own the water. The state is trustee for the proper allocation and distribution of water and the administration and implementation of state water laws.

The right so acquired has two key legal characteristics. First, the right itself is a real property right. It is an exclusive right that, like other property interests, can be defined, is valuable, and can be sold, transferred, mortgaged, or bequeathed. In Colorado the Supreme Court very early in the state's history announced a rule that can be found in the laws of other appropriation doctrine states. The famous *Coffin* v. *Lefthand Ditch Co.* was decided in 1882 and held:

"Water in the various streams thus acquires a value unknown in moister climates. Instead of being a mere incident in the soil, it rises when appropriate to the dignity of a distinct usufructory estate or right of property.... The right to property in this country by priority of appropriation thereto, we think it is and has always been the duty of the national and state governments to protect."

The second characteristic is that it is a usufructory right and a right to use the water when available and in priority, when it can be put to beneficial use. There is no absolute ownership in the corpus of the water prior to diversion. It is a public resource. However, once diverted into a delivery system it becomes the diverter's personal property until it returns back to the stream or escapes his control.

The water right under the appropriation doctrine consists of several elements that give value, dependability, and security to the holder. The water right exists in a definite source of supply; has a definite point of diversion; is for a fixed and stated quantity; is for a specific type and place of use, which together implies the annual time of use; and assures the holder of at least an implied protection to the maintenance of water quality necessary to carry out the purposes for which the water was appropriated.

Several systems were developed by the states to allocate water and provide evidence of water rights. The predominant approach now is the permit system. An application is filed with the appropriate state agency, which then takes the procedural steps of evaluating and determining its disposition, based upon availability of unappropriated water and nonimpairment of existing rights. If approved, a permit is issued that may contain conditions of use. If denied, the applicant is entitled to judicial review of the administrative decision. The finalized water right may be called a license, certificate, or decree.

The cornerstone of water allocation under western law is that beneficial use is the basis and measure of the right to use water. This is often the extent of definition found in state water laws. The concept has two aspects. In order to use water, it must be taken for a beneficial purpose. The other aspect is that the use of water itself must be beneficial and carried out in a beneficial manner.

Another aspect of the water right often overlooked by those not familiar with the doctrine is that it must be exercised. Otherwise it can be lost, totally or partially, through nonuse or misuse. The tool for losing the right is through abandonment or statutory forfeiture. In addition, the right may be condemned for domestic uses by municipalities or lost through adverse possession by another user. So, in order to protect the right, the holder is compelled to divert his full entitlement, often without regard to possible adverse consequences to other users of junior priority or downstream location.

Groundwater law.   Groundwater legislation occurred much later in the growth of the western states due in part to the lack of knowledge of subsurface supplies and in part to adequate surface supplies. The basic principles of use and control often follow the surface doctrines, but again, each state adopted and modified the law to fit its particular needs.

Generally, western states apply one of four doctrines: absolute ownership, reasonable use, prior appropriation, or correlative rights. The doctrine of absolute ownership had its origin in the United Kingdom. Simply stated, the doctrine holds that a landowner can withdraw any water from beneath his land as long as no liability to his neighbors results from such action. In the West, only Texas has retained this rule.

The reasonable use rule states that because the rights of adjacent landowners are similar and their enjoyment in the use of groundwater is dependent upon the action of the overlying landowners, each landowner is restricted to a reasonable exercise of his own water rights and reasonable use of water on his own property in view of the similar rights of others. Nebraska applies the reasonable use doctrine, but also allows out-of-basin diversions for municipal use if no damage is done to overlying landowners in the area where the water is extracted. Considerable attention is now directed to the rapid increase in Nebraska's groundwater use and the problems this may cause to the interstate aquifers common to the High Plains states.

The doctrine of correlative rights in groundwater originated in California and is a further refinement of the reasonable use concept. The doctrine holds that among landowners with lands overlying an underground water supply each landowner can make a reasonable use of that supply as long as the source is sufficient. But when the supply becomes insufficient because of draught or draw-down, each landowner is entitled to water in proportion to the relative percentage of his land overlying the underground waters.

Most of the western states found little reason to adopt a different system of law for surface and groundwaters. Consequently, the theory of the prior appropriation doctrine was applied to both surface and groundwaters. This does not imply, however, that surface water law was to be simultaneously extended to groundwater. In fact, several states initially enacted laws to control groundwater as late as the mid-1950s and 1960s. Kansas applied the absolute ownership doctrine until 1944, then adopted the prior appropriation doctrine. South Dakota and North Dakota have no detailed groundwater laws, but merely apply the surface water principles to groundwater use.

The doctrine of prior appropriation provides that groundwater is subject to appropriation for beneficial use providing the intended user complies with statutory requirements, such as well spacing requirements and pumping rates. The administrative official judges applications on the basis of whether unappropriated groundwater exists and what adverse effects might occur as a result of approval.

In most states, the law allows the state water official to classify the area as a critical or designated groundwater basin upon a determination that a particular groundwater basin or particular aquifer needs close management due to rapid depletion. When this occurs, the users are placed under administrative control for the protection of the aquifer and vested rights.

To fully appreciate the western attitude toward water law, one must accept that without water, the arid West would have a limited productive capability, at least agriculturally. One must also recall that the federal government promoted agriculture as the future of the West. Through a multitude of federal policies, laws, and programs, settlers were assured that their water use would be protected. Private and governmental investments were based upon the security of a continued right to divert water under various state laws. As such, agriculture has become the major use of diverted water in the West, accounting for 90 percent of water consumption. Within this agricultural economy one finds meadows flood irrigated for cattle raising and fields producing high cash-value and forage crops with the use of water pumped or diverted from streams and reservoirs.

Also, during the last half of the past decade, other user groups have increasingly made demands for the limited water supplies. New industries and projected energy projects are seeking water allocations, expanding populations are placing great demands for domestic water, and the public interest in recreational and aesthetic are competing against consumptive users.

Until the mid-1960s, the efforts of federal and state governments and local water user groups was oriented primarily to water development. Then, beginning with a gradual awareness of over-allocation conditions and water quality problems from return flows, we witnessed a shift toward water management. This awareness helped shape the environmental consciousness of the 1970s when users and governments attempted to stress water management over development.

Key issues and problems for water management

Is the water management situation such that we may rightly call it a "crunch"? Yes, quite rightly so. The Council on Environmental Quality (CEQ) stated in its 1979 annual report on environmental quality (2) that "two of the Nation's most valuable resource—fresh water and agriculturally productive soil—are in need of better conservation and management." The report noted that the Water Resources Council projects a decline in total fresh water withdrawal between now and the year 2000 and also sees a concurrent, significant increase in consumption. As a result, the Water Resources Council predicts problems of (a) inadequate surface water supplies, (b) overdraft of groundwater, (c) pollution of surface and groundwaters, (d) flooding, and (e) erosion and sedimentation. A 1979 Government Accounting Office report (5) said "the greatest potential as well as greatest need for better water management and conservation is in the irrigated areas of the West."

A number of more specific issues or problems in the West need to be addressed in the near future (4). One major issue that transcends all concerns is the allocation and reallocation of water for new and increased uses. There exists a finite resource and an infinite demand. Energy development, municipal and industrial growth, public recreation protection and preservation of aquatic and wildlife and their habitat, stabilizing agricultural needs, and water quality control are the major competitors.

Other key issues or problems are development of groundwater, conjunctive use of ground and surface water, water quality control, interstate and international water considerations, federal reserved rights doctrine claims, institutional problem-solving inadequacies, and a tendency toward increased and more complex and costly litigation.

To resolve the many water problems, CEQ has called for a comprehensive approach to management of ground and surface water and related land resources (2). But how, and at what cost? And what are the ethical considerations involved?

An ethical perspective

We know the direction we are headed, but the question is whether this is where we want to go. Decisions and processes considered ethical in the past may not be ethical today or in the future. We are confronted with a dynamic condition and are subject to the changing pressures as we require more advanced technologies and efforts to improve our quality of life. In our property rights and materialistic society, we have allowed the free market and compensation principle to balance the right and wrong of major changing interests. For minor and public adverse effects, the majority rule principle often resolves ethical, economic, and ecological concerns.

Of the list of key issues and problems above, I said the major issue is allocation and reallocation of water for new and increased uses. From an ethical perspective, this has to be our most complex issue because of its impact upon existing water users whose stability, security, and dependability of livelihoods and investments have been based upon rules of the appropriaation doctrine. Is it right or can it be considered our duty to allocate and reallocate water to other users because the rate of return is greater? The law provides sale and transfer mechanisms for water rights, but should the government also provide policy directions for protecting areas of highly productive land that are being converted at a rapid pace to subdivisions? How much water should be reserved for future generations by holding title in the name of the government? Or should we even have a system of private property rights to a resource as fundamental as water?

Out-of-basin transfers have been a solution to many water supply problems in areas of limited source and high demand, but what protection should be afforded the basin? In California just recently, phase two of the state water project was passed by the legislature, diverting excess waters of the north to the growing and arid area of southern California (3). Was it morally right to take water from those who now or will live in the north and transfer it at great costs to those who live in the south? A more basic issue is this: Should man alter the environment to live or should he adapt to the resource base that exists? California and four other states have "area" or "basin of origin" statutes designed to protect an area's future development, but their effectiveness is questionable.

Every state water agency official or board charged with allocation of water has been faced with these tough questions of the impact of their decisions. Some state laws provide criteria, such as the duty of water concept or list factors, to consider factors such as rainfall patterns, soil conditions, and crops grown. As between directly competing applicants for the same water supply, a list of preferences is often provided, with domestic/municipal uses taking top priority. The job of allocating water to competing applicants is no easy task. The impartial decision maker invariably enrages farmers, cities, miners, oilmen, and public interest groups.

Some 15 years ago, an Italian water lawyer, Dante Caponera, wrote an article, "Think Land—Why Not Build It on Water?" The paper described the use of water as a tool for land use development—spatially and temporally. We have seen the reclamation of land in the arid West used as a tool for population location early in our history, but the issue is more complex now. Should arid and semiarid areas be developed and/or continually maintained? Take, for example, the Eden Reclamation Project in Wyoming, where the growing season is 85 to 90 days and only low cash value crops are grown by a few people diverting from 3 to 4 acre feet of water per acre to their land. Some argue that California could make much better use of this water without causing the saline return flows that the Soil Conservation Service (SCS) maintains are occurring from the Eden Project. Yet to those living in Wyoming, the area is home, and they expect the government to recognize their rights to remain there.

Decisions affecting groundwater have strong ethical connotations. Most state laws allow for the designation of critical control areas to protect groundwater reserves from being mined. Other states, like Texas, and to a lesser extent Nebraska, allow almost unrestricted pumping—a "use-now-and-consequences-later" theory. In a recent interview (*1*), the New Mexico state engineer stated: "If unrestricted pumping were allowed, we could have a hell of a boom for maybe ten years. Then everyone would go broke. Our water is public water, and this isn't in the public interest. We shouldn't cut our own throats because the Texans are slitting theirs."

Is one approach more ethical than the other?

Another issue concerns the government granting of low cost loans and other forms of subsidies for crop production where groundwater mining occurs. Broader yet is the issue of whether SCS and state cost-sharing programs that increase agricultural water use efficiency should be continued. Or should farmers be required to improve their efficiency or go out of business, allowing transfer of water to a more efficient use?

Concerning the water quality control issue, is it ethically defensible that the federal government imposes controls over state allocation of water through the use of Section 402 and 404 permits of the 1972 Federal Water Pollution Control Act? Federal and state governments have waged a continual battle over control of water resources. The federal version always pays lip service to states rights and responsibilities over quantity control, but at the same time tries to insure a more superior position in the major decision-making process of large-scale water allocation. The present battle over a national water policy is the latest example of federal encroachment, but more subtle is the use of the water quality control argument to influence quantity control. A court recently ruled that the federal government was interfering with state water rights by refusing to issue a permit for a reservoir on the South Platte in Colorado. What interests should prevail in these types of cases: local, state, or national?

Indian and other reserved rights claims is another area where moral issues are significant. Should the courts take away water rights from existing users who made investments of time, capital, and other resources in good faith? Who should be compensated and by whom?

There are no easy answers, and certainly, as can be seen from just the few examples discussed, ethical standards should not be applied as the sole determinant in these water issues and problems. Ethical considerations must invariably play a role in the decision, along with technological alternatives, economic justifications, and ecological impacts.

Frankly, if we don't like our current direction, I have faith in our system to make contemporary judgements, and the fewer restrictions imposed upon the creativity of persons to argue one way or another, the more likely we will be able to change.

REFERENCES

1. Blundell, William B. 1980. *Hot spot: In New Mexico, water is valuable resource—and so is water boss.* Wall Street Journal (May 1).
2. Council on Environmental Quality. 1979. *Environmental quality: 10th annual report of the Council on Environmental Quality.* Washington, D.C.
3. Hill, Gladwin. 1980. *Major water plan approved on coast.* The New York Times (July 13).
4. Radosevich, George E. 1979. *Better use of water management tools.* In *Western Water Resources: Coming Problems and Policy Alternatives.* Westview Press, Boulder, Colorado. pp. 253-289.
5. U.S. Comptroller General. 1979. *Water resources and the nation's water supply: Issues and concerns.* CED 79-69, Washington, D.C.

10

The Water Management Crunch: An Ecological Perspective

John Cairns, Jr.

*University Center for Environmental Studies and Biology
Department, Virginia Polytechnic Institute and State
University, Blacksburg, and the University of Michigan
Biological Station, Pellston*

My discussion bypasses the first two phases of the environmental problem-solving development—social awareness and documentation.

Focus is on the need to develop a predictive capability to estimate the consequences of a particular course of action and select the best alternative from an array of possibilities. Also, I will illustrate some management capabilities necessary for successful environmental quality control.

Predictive capability in action

The Toxic Substances Control Act (TSCA), the Environmental Protection Act, and other such federal legislation require the development of a predictive capability. TSCA requires determination of the hazard to human health and the environment in the extraction, transportation, manufacture, use, and disposal of both new and old chemicals used for a new purpose. The act requires environmental impact statements for the construction of new power plants, pipelines, and a variety of other activities. Unfortunately, impact statements have generally been a list of species without any attempt to make a probablistic determination based on scientific evidence. TSCA has yet to be implemented partly due to a lack of predictive capability. This shortcoming is striking in the 65 criterion documents on toxic chemicals prepared by the U.S. Environmental Protection Agency (EPA) as a consequence of the consent decree resulting from a suit brought against the EPA administrator by the Friends of the Environment, the Natural Resources Defense Council, and other environmental groups. The criterion documents suffered from a number of deficiencies:

1. The information was not gathered in the systematic, orderly way required for a scientifically justifiable estimate of risk.

2. A large variety of methods, species, and time limits was used, making analysis of conflicting results quite difficult.

3. In some criterion documents, no information was given about "environmental partitioning," "transformation" processes, and other phenomena important to hazard evaluation. Rarely was information about the environmental fate of the chemical linked in any substantive way to the selection of organisms at risk, the length of exposure, the probability of toxicity from secondary transformation products, and the like. In short, not only was the biological information fragmented but essential chemical/physical information was improperly coupled to biological information.

4. Statistical analyses were almost totally lacking.

5. Most of the information used to estimate the "no adverse biological effects concentration" was based on single-species tests. This approach has several weaknesses: (a) Species used were usually those easily cultured in the laboratory. Often they did not inhabit the areas in which the chemical substance was likely to intrude. (b) Virtually no system-level tests were conducted (i.e., energy transfer, nutrient cycling, predator prey interactions, and the like). (c) Tests were usually at a constant concentration with all environmental variables held constant. In the "real world," both the environmental variables and the potential contaminant are likely to vary rather widely, although probably not in concert. (d) There was no description of the types of environmental measurements necessary to check the accuracy of the predations made—in short, no form of error control that would enable one to adjust the predictions based on experience.

I and my associates (1) provided a rationale for the systematic acquisition of evidence to make a hazard estimate. We also (2) provided a series of protocols from industrialized countries that illustrate a variety of ways to estimate hazard from chemical substances. This approach could be readily modified to estimate hazard from other activities, such as clear-cutting forests and building dams. Although the methods require further development, many of the procedures provide practical means of estimating hazard. Even methods known to be effective for more than 30 years (e.g., short-term toxicity tests) are grossly underused. More extensive use of proven methods would provide a basis for more sound management and policy decisions.

Verifying predictions based on single-species tests

A tremendous gap exists between the single-species laboratory toxicity test and other types of bioassays (in which the variables are reasonably well controlled and the stress being administered is reasonably constant) and field studies involving a complex array of species and cause-effect pathways in natural systems (in which the variables are essentially out of control and generally fluctuate frequently and violently). The weaknesses of the single-species toxicity test in predicting system-level effects is being examined in detail by the Committee to Review Methods for Ecotoxicology of the National Research Council. Although the report of the committee is still incomplete, it is sufficiently far along to indicate clearly a serious deficiency in bridging the gap between these two markedly different types of assessments (i.e., single-species versus system-level).

Microcosms provide a means of verifying predictions based on single-species tests before exposing natural systems to the stressor being tested. A microcosm or mesocosm is not a tiny ecosystem, but rather a fragment of an ecosystem particularly suited to examine a particular relationship or function. As a consequence, it is important to decide which parameters are useful in evaluating particular effects of pollution. Without this information, the development of different types of microcosms is not likely to ensure fulfillment of this particular need. Hazard to an aquatic ecosystem from a particular course of action, such as the use of a new chemical, can be estimated crudely with single-species laboratory tests. However, confirmation of the accuracy of the estimates should be made in laboratory microcosms rather than in the "real world." Additionally, in selecting the most desirable from among a variety of courses of action, estimating the ecological consequences of the various alternatives would be markedly enhanced if microcosms and mesocosms could be developed for predictive purposes.

The present state-of-the-art in the construction, use, and interpretation of results from microcosms has been the subject of an Oak Ridge workshop. Preliminary information indicates a promising beginning in this area, but the present array of methods is inadequate. The field is not developing rapidly enough to keep pace with needs in estimating the hazard to aquatic ecosystems by development of new chemicals and other potentially degrading effects. Therefore, it would be prudent to develop this field more rapidly and to a certain extent guide it so that certain types of needs are met.

Rehabilitation of damaged ecosystems

Despite some notable success stories (e.g., Lake Washington) of rehabilitation of damaged ecosystems in the United States, no national plan exists for (a) systematically identifying ecosystems where rehabilitation is desirable, (b) establishing priorities for attention, (c) determining the degree of rehabilitation that provides amenities attractive to the public, (d) estimating the degree of ecological improvement that results from implementing improvements in waste discharges and nonpoint-source discharges into the system and, (e) neither a professionally endorsed set of parameters enabling us to track the improvements as they occur nor a monitoring system ensuring quality control measures to protect the rehabilitated state where improvements have been made. A schematic depicting several policy options for management of damaged ecosystems is given in figure 1. In this diagram, restoration takes the ecosystem back in a rather direct route toward its initial state. Presumably, undesirable features of the initial state are accepted as part of the overall package. Enhancing or improving the current state of an ecosystem without reference to its initial state might lead an ecosystem further from its initial state. This can occur perhaps by adding man-made features and suppressing undesirable natural features. Rehabilitation may be defined as a pragmatic mix of nondegradation, enhancement, and restoration. To the extent that damaged ecosystem recovery can be fostered, we can expect restoration of some desirable features to be a cost-effective tactic within such a mix. Further degradation is always an option, but one that society seems to have rejected in recent years.

The remarkable rehabilitation of the Thames and Clyde Rivers in England provides compelling evidence that present methodologies and waste treatment technologies, however imperfect conceptually, can produce remarkable results in a relatively few years. Furthermore, these projects were not financially ruinous to the industries using the water and can, at least in the case of the Thames, simultaneously turn an ecological eyesore into a multi-use recreational facility. Perhaps the best confirmation of the success of the Thames program was in its ability to solve the problem of meeting a variety of demands that may conflict partially with each other (e.g., sailing and fishing).

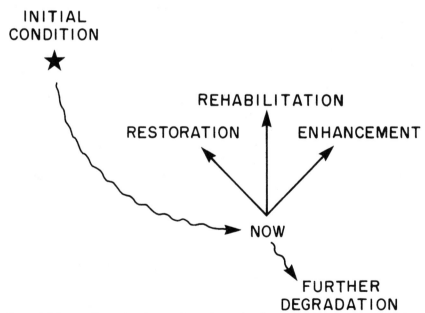

Figure 1. Diagram illustrating the meanings of several policy options for management of damaged ecosystems (3).

In an era when energy costs are skyrocketing, recreation close to one's residence will become increasingly common. Consequently, it seems wise to rehabilitate aquatic ecosystems near large population concentrations.

From an academic standpoint, some urgent needs are obvious:

1. We must determine more precisely the degree of ecological improvement resulting from a specific reduction in point and nonpoint pollutional loading.

2. We must improve the estimation of recovery time once particular pollutional stresses are removed.

3. We must develop means of communicating various ecological options in terms of rehabilitation.

4. We must markedly improve quality control monitoring during the rehabilitation and/or recovery period as well as for the maintenance of desirable quality.

Although the rehabilitation of damaged ecosystems has not had a high priority in EPA in past years, it is one of the items selected for serious consideration in the research and priority recommendation prepared by a group of outside consultants for EPA.[1]

Drainage basin management

Few drainage basin management groups exist in this country. More management groups could lessen some of the following problems:

1. Long-term records of water quality and changes in the organisms that inhabit the system are rarely available. Consequently, determining how much change is normal and distinguishing natural cyclic changes from degradation are difficult.

2. Studies on the Hubbard Brook and Coweeta experimental watersheds have established that the terrestrial system surrounding a drainage basin is a regulator of water quality as well as the primary source of energy. Unfortunately, large-scale events influencing water quality, such as building developments and destruction of woodlands, are rarely studied in a systematic way, and even when they are, careful documentation enabling one to develop correlations with changes in water quality are usually absent.

3. The absence of an organization interested in the entire system almost ensures that system-level questions regarding a particular course of action will not be asked. Thus, water management problems are dealt with in fragments, and rarely is more than superficial attention given to the whole.

4. Remedial quality control measures that might be taken immediately if a monitoring system run by a management group were in place are frequently postponed until a major perturbation occurs.

5. No overall strategy for restoring damaged aquatic ecosystems is available. Even on the few occasions when a plan outline is developed, no

---

[1]The report was coordinated by Pennsylvania State University consultants. (Cooperative Agreement for the Evaluation of Current Environmental Research and Establishment of Priorities, Pennsylvania State University and EPA, April 1979.)

systematic implementation occurs because of this lack of regional authority.

The Ohio River Valley Water Sanitation Commission (ORSANCO) is an interstate agency representing Illinois, Indiana, Kentucky, New York, Ohio, Pennsylvania, Virginia, and West Virginia to assess water quality in the Ohio River and some of its tributaries. ORSANCO's monthly report includes regular water quality analyses of the dissolved oxygen concentration, temperature, pH, conductivity, and flow. The report also includes a comparison with the desired values. Biological data are rarely included, and the data base lacks a frequent assessment of levels of toxicants or other materials in the river that might impair biological integrity. Nevertheless, even these limited data enable one to make some modest predictions about the condition of the aquatic biota. Unfortunately, very few river basin commissions in the United States do as much as ORSANCO, even though it generates relatively limited information, particularly biological information; has little or no police power; and has management plans that pay relatively little attention to the aquatic biota. Even in such important but relatively straightforward matters as water allocation, the Potomac River situation (see reports of the Water Supply Review Committee, National Research Council) provides clear evidence of the difficulties when regional management is not in place.

In contrast, the management of the Thames by the Thames Water Authority has superb allocation and maintenance of water quality. This has been accompanied by a very marked improvement in the condition of the aquatic biota as well as recreation amenities, such as sailing and swimming. For example, few permanent fish resided in the Tidal Thames since the early 1950s, but the situation has been improved so that there are now more than 90 species to be found there. The restoration of the salmon run is a real possibility despite the fact that this is one of the most heavily used rivers in the world, running through one of the largest human concentrations on the globe. The Clyde River has had a comparable, though less well-publicized, recovery.

This clearly illustrates that present technologies and methods are adequate for not only management of river water quality (including preservation of aquatic biota) but for rehabilitation of the river in a cost-effective manner without severe dislocations to municipalities and industries. However, a river basin management group is needed to implement the plans.

A call for appropriate parameters

A number of specific problems require attention: acid rain, degradation of estuaries, hazardous chemicals, effects of particulate matter, accumulation of pesticides and other persistent chemicals, and preservation of rapidly disappearing wetlands. The overriding problem, however, is that the effects cannot be effectively and efficiently studied because aquatic ecologists have not addressed a number of fundamental scientific questions that will ensure adequate studies. Presently there is no substantive professional endorsement, at least in the formal sense common to many other professions, of appropriate parameters required in measuring such effects. Professionals in aquatic ecology have not collectively selected and endorsed parameters that will effectively measure system-level effects of, for instance, acid rain on aquatic ecosystems. Although many methods have been placed in the literature purporting to test such effects, little or no unanimity exists regarding which is acceptable for a particular purpose. Even when parameters are commonly measured, professionals in the field have not felt compelled to go through a formal process of selecting parameters for each purpose. As a consequence, a hodgepodge of parameters combine with an equally confusing array of methods. Mounting a massive program to examine crucial effects, such as those in degradation of estuaries, is difficult when the professional community responsible for doing this is in disarray regarding the most important parameters to be measured. Even when a parameter such as diversity enjoys a temporary success, it is often overworked and inappropriately used. The medical profession has selected certain parameters to be used in determining the health of a human, and while these methods have weaknesses and limitations, they are nevertheless widely and effectively used. Thus, comparative studies on the same problem can be made by a wide array of professionals in different locations with assurance that comparisons will be valid. No such compromise on the selection of parameters for routine use has yet been evident in aquatic ecology.

Selection of standard methods, those methods endorsed by competent professionals in the field in a formal and well-established way, has progressed further than the selection of parameters. Groups producing such methods in aquatic ecology include the American Society for Testing and Materials, the American Public Health Association, the American Water Works Association, and the Water Pollution Control Federation.

In short, the water management crunch is caused by our failure to systematically address the problems. Although new technology and scientific information is helpful, the main problems are organizational, political, and social.

REFERENCES

1. Cairns, J., Jr., K. L. Dickson, and A. W. Maki, editors. 1978. *Estimating the hazard of chemical substances to aquatic life.* STP 657. American Society for Testing and Materials, Philadelphia, Pennsylvania. 278 pp.
2. Dickson, K. L., A. W. Maki, and J. Cairns, Jr., editors. 1979. *Analyzing the hazard evaluation process.* American Fisheries Society, Washington, D.C. 159 pp.
3. Magnuson, J. J., H. A. Regier, W. J. Christie, and W. C. Songogni. 1980. *To rehabilitate and restore Great Lakes ecosystems.* In J. Cairns, Jr. [editor] The Recovery Process in Damaged Ecosystems. Ann Arbor Science Publishers, Ann Arbor, Michigan.

11

The Water Management Crunch: A Roundtable Discussion

Wilber E. Ringler

Assistant Director, Cooperative Extension Service
Kansas State University, Manhattan

Following the presentations by Professors Gardner, Radosevich, and Cairns, registrants attending the session gave their views on several questions dealing with the water management crunch. For example, should water be viewed differently than other commodities that are allocated through the market place?

Participants said yes and cited these reasons: (1) Water is a basic human need; it has many competing uses; and there are no substitutes; (2) water is regionally distinctive, that is, a shortage exists in the arid western regions while adequate or excessive amounts are available in the humid eastern areas; and (3) there is an urgent public need to protect quantity as well as quality of water from pollutants and inefficient uses.

Since many decisions about water resource development are made in the political-economic arena, participants were asked to list ways to include ethics and ecology in the decision-making process. Roundtable reports listed two strategies for getting more ecological input: (1) By electing more ecologically minded public officials, and (2) by developing better predictive capabilities as to consequences of certain actions on ecological matters. For ethics, they said, get more public education, people participation, benefit-cost tests, and discussions of questions dealing with water distribution as well as allocation.

On questions regarding the most important water quality problems, registrants had little difficulty in listing serious ones but were unable to set priorities because of local and regional differences. However, high on the lists were toxic (chemical) wastes and sediment caused by soil erosion. Other problems frequently mentioned were dissolved oxygen, saltwater intrusion, nutrients, salt loading by irrigation, bacteriological contamination, acid rain, thermal pollution, and mine wastes.

Water availability was identified as the most important natural resource constraint confronting North America at SCSA's 34th annual meeting. Participants were asked to list what governments should do to overcome this constraint. The kinds of action suggested were (1) create educational programs that emphasize the dilemma, possible solutions, and consequences; (2) improve identification of existing resources currently available to help solve water problems; (3) develop plans for water availability and distribution; and (4) enforce water-use efficiency technology.

Should water development paid for from public funds be used in population location planning? Participants felt it should be and could be by controlling water distribution and sewage systems that are financed by tax money. This calls for comprehensive regional planning and approval of public expenditures (federal grants and cost sharing) only in support of the regional plans.

In regard to cost of implementation of nonpoint-source water pollution practices on privately owned land, the registrants wanted federal and state governments to continue to share the cost of long-term, permanent practices. The ratio suggested for sharing costs was 75 percent for government and 25 percent for the landowner.

IV. The Energy Squeeze on Land and Water Management

12

The Energy Squeeze and Agricultural Growth

Ralph C. d'Arge
Distinguished Professor of Economics
University of Wyoming, Laramie

Few public policy issues are as pressing as the impact of higher energy costs on the productivity of American agriculture. For some years, there has been expressed concern by leading agriculturalists that the almost explosive growth in yields since about 1940 would taper off in the 1980s. This conjecture was due primarily to the concept of diminishing returns to agricultural research and to quantities of inputs, such as nitrogen fertilier, that could be successfully used per acre of land. But this expected leveling off of yields is not generally observable yet (Figure 1).

Of more dramatic immediate and long-term consequence is the substantial increase in energy costs to agriculture. This is because agriculture is one of the most capital- and energy-intensive sectors of the American economy, more than $220,000 per farm worker in 1978. About 10 to 12 percent of this total was in machinery and vehicles.

In modern agricultural systems, I suggest that capital in general, and machinery and equipment in particular, are complementary with energy. That is, as one increases, so must the other. More machinery and less labor generally implies more energy; particularly more fossil fuel energy must be expended. The agricultural sector thus is one of the most vulnerable to energy supply shortages and to rapidly rising costs.

Farm wage in relation to input costs

Economists like to look at indexes or ratios, and I am no exception (Table 1). Why? Because indexes or ratios often express more clearly what is efficient or not. Benefit-cost analysis is simply a comparison of the value of outputs from an action to the value of inputs. If the ratio of benefits to costs is less than one, it does not pay to make the investment or institute the program. Likewise, when the ratio of two inputs, such as labor and machinery, changes, this implies that, if possible, it is better to change input use rates. For example, if energy is cheap (pre-1973) relative to hired labor, then energy should be used whenever possible in farm operations and labor use reduced. During the past decade or so, however, the ratio of farm wage rates to energy and interest costs has changed dramatically, even in a period of fairly high growth rates in farm wages (Table 2).

To economists, this substantial adjustment in input-cost ratios suggests that, in the long run, a greater proportion of farm tasks as well as input into each task will be accomplished more cheaply by use of more labor and less machinery, energy, and credit. The use of credit, however, may sub-

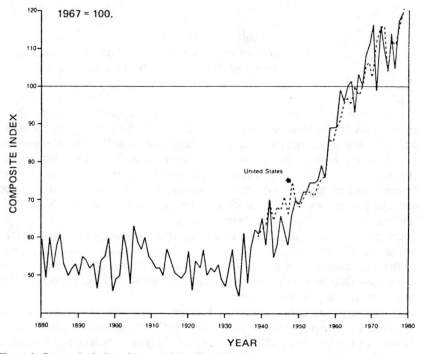

Figure 1. Composite index of crop yields, 1880-1978 (*4*).

Table 1. Selected agricultural statistics (*1*).

Statistic	1967	1979
Farm labor wage rate index	100	265
Index of interest paid by farmers	100	501
Energy cost index	100	276
Agricultural productivity index	100	121*
Index of cost per gallon of diesel fuel	100	378
Index of cost per gallon of gasoline		
(bulk delivery of regular)	100	267

*Preliminary.

Table 2. Farm wage/interest and farm wage/energy cost ratios (*1*).

Ratio	1967	1979
Farm wage/interest	1	.53
Farm wage/diesel fuel cost	1	.70

stantially increase if interest rates move to lower levels in response to lower general inflation rates in the next few months or years.

What appears unlikely is that the ratio of farm wages to energy costs will not be increasingly reduced in the future, thus making farm labor a relatively cheaper input. What will this mean to individual farm or ranch operations? Here are a few examples:

1. Irrigation water will be monitored more carefully to optimize water use. Thus, greater water conservation might be expected.

2. Ditch irrigation systems will become relatively more productive in contrast to pivot or side-roll systems with pump. This leads potentially to less water conservation and more soil erosion.

3. Horsepower and, by implication, energy input will be much more closely matched with the tasks needed to be accomplished; for example, manure spreaders will not be pulled behind 100-brake-horsepower tractors. This implies, everything else the same, a reduction in optimal farm equipment size.

4. Less weed control and fertilizer use with potential reductions in yield. This involves comparison of costs versus reductions in yield and thus value.

5. Introduction at the farm level of limited production of biofuels, such as methane and alcohol, to augment existing fuel supplies.

6. Readjustment in location of farm sales and needed transportation to markets for products and location of input purchases.

Of course, the list is almost endless but implies the following:

1. More labor use.

2. Less fuel consumption.

3. Greater monitoring of fuel-using systems.

4. Attempts to substitute less energy-intensive machinery or systems for more efficient ones.

These and other substitutions among inputs will occur until fairly comparable productivities per dollar of cost are achieved (Table 3). For example, if a dollar spent on diesel fuel is only two-thirds as productive as a dollar spent on labor, then the dollar should obviously be spent on labor.

The farm labor supply

Given the implied need for greater farm labor, how will this labor be supplied? While agricultural wage rates have, in percentage terms, increased more rapidly than most other sectors, they started so low that the absolute differential in dollars is spreading. This spread implies that there is a greater incentive for hired labor to seek employment elsewhere. For example, in Wyoming farm wages are almost $3.50 per hour, but strip-mining wages for comparable skills, for example, heavy equipment operators, are $20-plus per hour (Table 4). Thus, there appears to be no substantial supply response for hired labor unless accompanied by a rapid upward adjustment in hired farm wage rates. And given the mix of tasks of most farm workers, this does not seem likely.

In the past decade there has been a slight tendency toward more hired labor in relation to total farm employment (Table 5). While farm employment will continue to rise, it is doubtful that the hired labor component will

Table 3. Agricultural productivity comparisons, 1967-1979 (1 and preliminary estimates).

Comparison	1967	1979
Agricultural productivity per dollar of farm wage	1.00	.46
Agricultural productivity per dollar of diesel fuel	1.00	.32
Agricultural productivity per dollar of gasoline	1.00	.45

Table 4. Agricultural and nonagricultural hourly wages, 1967-1979, dollars per hour (1, 2, 3).

Industry	1967	1979
Agricultural	1.28	3.38
Manufacturing	2.83	6.65
Construction	4.11	9.08
Mining	3.19	8.42

Table 5. Farm employment by hire or family (1).

Employment	1967	1978
Hired workers (total employment)	0.26	0.32
Family workers (total employment)	0.74	0.68

Table 6. Cost of selected farm equipment, in current dollars (*I*, and personal estimates).

Equipment	1967	1979*
Wheel tractor (50-59 horsepower)	5,440	8,460
Grain drill	900	3,575
Power sprayers	342	1,397
Combines (large capacity)	9,840	56,650
Pitchfork (four-tine)	5.67	13.64

*Estimated from 1978 by assuming a 10 percent inflation factor.

rise. Rather, slack will be taken up by a greater population of farm children remaining on the farm/ranch, cashing in on their higher relative worth due to higher costs of energy inputs.

Impacts of costly energy-using equipment

Finally, a comment or two about the cost of energy-using equipment is in order. Prices of farm equipment have risen so rapidly and become so specialized in the past decade that only through cooperative arrangements can most farm operations sustain themselves these days (Table 6). Short-term credits of many farms exceed several hundred thousand dollars. But cooperative arrangements are costly to corporate farming operations as contrasted to everyday swapping among individual farmers. The cost of transactions is higher because of formal costing and lease arrangements. Thus, as machinery and energy become even more costly, corporate operations will be placed in a position of less competitive advantage and higher hired-labor costs.

Professor Howard Conklin of Cornell University often has remarked that the most resilient farmer is the one with no debt, a small operation, where almost everything can be repaired or done by the operator. I do not believe the small-is-beautiful theme will become dominant in American agriculture, but the long-term energy squeeze will provide strong incentives for a family-based, energy-efficient agricultural system.

Major conclusions

1. Agricultural productivity is increasing but probably will increase at a decreasing rate. Farm income, farm wages, and return on capital will thus increase, but at a slower rate (Figure 2).

2. Farm wage rates have increased substantially during the past decade. But they have increased at a slower rate than primary energy costs or interest rates. The impact of this relative change is to make farm labor relatively more efficient than energy.

3. The opportunities for farm labor to shift to nonfarm jobs will continue to increase, particularly as the demand for coal and other resources increases. Wage differentials between farm and nonfarm employment suggest strong incentives to shift. Thus, there will be increasing scarcity of hired farm workers.

4. Energy prices will continue to increase at least at the rate of interest, net of inflation. Therefore, manual labor will become relatively less costly than capital- and energy-intensive agricultural operations. Either agricultural wages will have to increase substantially or hired labor will be replaced by family labor. Given potential trends in productivity, a substantial wage increase is unlikely. Thus, family labor will substitute for hired labor. The farm unit in terms of size, scale, and intensity will adjust toward an average of family capability.

5. Rapidly increasing energy prices, particularly for diesel fuel and gasoline, will, in the long run, provide incentives toward conservation of fuels. The most efficient farm unit to practice fuel conservation is the family, through variable work-hour patterns; operating small-scale, alternative energy systems (wind, solar, biogas); increasing the fuel efficiency of machinery; and lengthening the life of equipment. Generally, hired labor has few incentives to conserve fuel and other forms of energy. Family-farm units

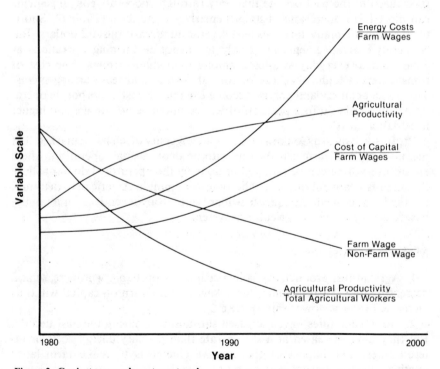

Figure 2. Conjectures on long-term trends.

will, therefore, tend toward being more fuel efficient.

6. Soil conservation practices will become important as a substitute for other productive inputs with high direct or indirect (nitrogen fertilizers) energy costs. Many soil conservation practices involve small decisions on taking care of drainage and irrigation runoff. Again, there are fewer incentives for hired labor or management to practice soil conservation as compared to the family unit concerned with long-term productivity and investment.

7. Large-scale corporate farming has been profitable in the past when interest rates were low in relation to worker productivity on large-equipment systems. However, with higher interest rates (long-term), such investment in equipment will not pay. It will become more efficient to share the use of large-equipment systems, inclusive of tractors, planters, self-propelled combines, and specialized equipment, such as backhows. Corporations tend to have high costs for nonmarket exchanges, such as sharing equipment. They will thus become less competitive as an organizational unit for farming.

8. Given the above conclusions, if valid, one should expect to see a readjustment in American agriculture toward smaller family-operated farm units that are more labor intensive and energy efficient.

REFERENCES

1. U.S. Department of Agriculture. 1979. *Agricultural statistics.* Washington, D.C.
2. U.S. Department of Commerce. 1968. *Monthly labor review.* Washington, D.C.
3. U.S. Department of Commerce. 1980. *Monthly labor review.* Washington, D.C.
4. Witwer, S. H. 1980. *Future trends in agricultural technology and management.* In *Long Range Environmental Outlook.* National Academy of Sciences, Washington, D.C.

13

The Energy Squeeze on Land and Water Management: An Ethical Perspective

Hester McNulty
Past Natural Resources Coordinator
League of Women Voters of the United States
Boulder, Colorado

Beginning in 1973 with the Arab oil embargo, the spectre of massive development of coal reserves and a synthetic fuels industry has been hanging on the horizon. With the recent enactment of the synthetic fuels legislation, the spectre is on the verge of becoming reality, and the implications for uses of water and land have been addressed only superficially.

As E. F. Schumacher emphasized in *Small is Beautiful*, "Among the material resources, the greatest, unquestionably, is the land. Study how a society uses its land, and you can come to pretty reliable conclusions as to what its future will be." And in the High Plains and Rocky Mountains, where most of the nation's energy resources are located, water and land uses are inextricably intertwined.

Agriculture versus energy

For more than 100 years, public policy decisions have stressed the agricultural use of land in the western states. Homestead and reclamation legislation implemented this policy of an agricultural economy. In the Colorado River Basin, for example, 3.5 million acres are irrigated. These acres feed the equivalent of 17 million people. One county in Colorado, Weld, has the third highest total agricultural sales of all counties in the United States.

Public policy now stresses energy development as being in the national interest with little acknowledgement that potential adverse impacts on agricultural lands should be a factor in the decision-making process. An example is a recent analysis by the Department of Energy of which counties in the United States would have the capability of supporting a synthetic fuels industry. Colorado's productive Weld County was on the final list.

Public policy tends to go from one extreme to another. In the rush to develop the West, marginal as well as prime agricultural land was developed and marginal as well as extremely productive irrigation projects were constructed. Now, in the rush to develop energy, there is the same lack of discrimination—a single-purpose ethic.

It would seem with the current national loss of cropland at an estimated 3 million acres a year, energy policy decisions would incorporate mechanisms for the preservation of important agricultural lands and, if irrigated, the water to make them productive. But this is not the case. Coal mining has disrupted aquifers upon which farmers and ranchers in Montana rely; federal coal leasing policy has not incorporated agricultural land productivity as a decision-making element; and energy companies buy up water rights without regard to whether the dried-up land was marginal or prime.

It would also be logical to assume that an energy policy targeted at the resources of the Northern Great Plains and Rocky Mountains would consider the carrying capacity of the land and water resources not only as it exists in the short term but over the long term. What might be the impacts on water and land uses if energy policy is not sensitive to the reality of climatic swings from wet periods to dry periods, especially on these lands west of the 97th meridian that are subject to extended drought?

A policy sensitivity to climatic variation

Tree ring research has shown that there is no definite pattern by which drought years can be predicted, but this research has established that there will be dry years and that these dry periods can last for 20 or more years. A 75-year record of weather in the High Plains states shows that in drought periods there is not only a lack of summer rainfall but also extremely high summer temperatures. This correlation was a factor in the severity of impacts of the "Dust Bowl" drought.

The High Plains and Rocky Mountain states are semiarid. Much of these regions receive only 10 to 14 inches of precipitation a year in nondrought years. Plans for energy development include coal gasification plants, coal-fired generating plants, coal slurry pipelines, uranium mining, oil shale development, strip mining of lignite and coal, and crop production for alcohol fuels. All of these are water and land intensive.

In the context of a long-term drought, there are implications that policy-makers have to come to terms with. First, and perhaps the most obvious, is the failure of strip mine reclamation. Successful reclamation requires at least 10 inches of precipitation a year, and many existing strip mines are borderline now as to whether reclamation can be accomplished. In a drought, strip-mined areas could receive less than 10 inches of moisture and remain without vegetation for many years. The potential for dust bowl conditions would be accelerated.

Second, Missouri River Basin water shortages could create conflicts between energy and food crop production. Out-of-basin diversions would increase the potential shortage and conflicts. Yet, Exxon has proposed an 8-million-barrel-a-day oil shale industry in western Colorado by the year 2010 when available water supplies will support a 400,000-barrel-a-day industry. Exxon, however, is proposing a diversion of "excess" Missouri River Basin water to the oil shale region—at an estimated cost of $5 billion. But this represents less than 1 percent of Exxon's total capital requirements—economics rather than ethics will dictate the feasibility of a water transfer.

Third, a crunch would develop between energy and agricultural uses in the Colorado River Basin that has limited water supplies even in normal years. In a 10- to 20-year drought, how would available water be allocated? Remember, the average flow of the Colorado River at Lee's Ferry of 13.5 million acre-feet is only an average. In 1934 the flow was 5.6 million acre-feet.

Fourth, some energy development processes, such as in situ coal gasification and uranium solution mining, can both contaminate and destroy the integrity of aquifers. Unusable groundwater supplies would further decrease water sources available in a drought for people, livestock, and crops.

Fifth, the Solar Energy Research Institute recently issued a report concluding that the agricultural sector in the United States is sufficiently flexible to absorb large production requirements for fuels and chemicals to be produced jointly with food (2). If there were a long-term drought throughout the Plains states, would this conclusion remain valid? Would a large investment in a gasohol plant give it preference over food crops? An energy or bread conflict could become a reality. In addition, some marginal land is already being used for gasohol crop production. If economic pressures accelerate the use of marginal land for energy feedstocks, the stage is set for another dust bowl under drought conditions.

Sixth, both government and private interests have given serious thought to intensive cultivation to nonfood fuel crops—plant, shrub, or tree farms—in the High Plains, where the only source of water is the already depleted Ogallala aquifer. There is the additional question as to whether these crops would survive in a period of extended drought.

Lessons from the past

An interesting historical analogy is the Timber Culture Act of 1873, which gave a section of public land in the Plains to anyone who would "plant, protect and keep in healthy growing condition for ten years forty acres of timber." The program failed but Congress really believed that by enacting legislation they could make trees grow.

It is interesting to note that there was a national purpose in this legislation—the trees were expected to moderate the climate and lead to a more equal distribution of rainfall throughout the plains. An 1868 General Land Office report, which influenced Congress to pass the Timber Culture Act, stressed "the readiness of nature to second the operations of man in respect to climate and other agencies affecting the productiveness of the soil" (3).

The Chaco civilization flourished in the Four Corners area, then disappeared. Even a sophisticated agricultural base and extensive trade network could not withstand a long-term drought. In Nebraska, along the Republican and Platte Rivers, settlements begun in the 14th century lasted for over 200 years. But the houses and agricultural lands were abandoned in the 1500s when Nebraska tree rings record a great drought that lasted from 1539 to 1564. In more recent times settlers, encouraged by a period of high rainfall, rushed to settle the High Plains. A 12-year drought, beginning in 1884, led to crop failure, great suffering, and widespread emigration.

Should not an ethical energy policy take note of the lessons of the past? Is it ethical to use average water availability as a base for energy development capability in a part of the country where averages tend to be only a statistic? Would it not be more responsible to stage energy development within the limitations of climatic reality and maintain important agriculture while developing energy at a slower pace?

The 1873 Congress thought it could legislate trees and moderate climate. More than a century later, Congress has legislated massive synthetic fuels development, no doubt encouraged by a report to Congress entitled *Water Supply Should Not be an Obstacle to Meeting Energy Goals (1)*.

A member of Congress didn't even have to read the report; on the front cover was the following paragraph:

"This report disputes the common impression that the energy industries thirst for water will create severe shortages throughout the water-short, energy-rich West. Recent evidence indicates that these predictions are unfounded or outdated and that adequate water is available for energy development through at least the year 2000."

Conflicts between energy development and agricultural land

An immediate though secondary impact is that of energy development on land and water resources. Increased population goes hand-in-hand with energy development activities, such as off-shore drilling, mining, or energy facility construction. Agricultural land becomes subdivisions, mobile home parks, or shopping centers. Because farmers and ranchers cannot compete with wages paid by energy companies, a shortage of farm workers develops. A farmer must reduce the acreage cultivated or in some cases give up farming and go to work for the energy company.

One of the most dramatic examples of secondary impact is along the 150-mile-long Front Range in Colorado. Denver has become the energy capital, and energy development is fueling growth along the Front Range at such a pace that preservation of agriculture is uncertain, even in Weld County.

In Colorado, as in most western states, land use planning and implementation have been viewed as somehow violating the frontier ethic, so there is no system in place to protect important agricultural land. Nor is there any mechanism to protect agricultural water. In fact, just the opposite is the case. Water is a very marketable commodity.

In all western states "water flows toward money," but this is probably more true in Colorado because its water laws have undergone little modification since they were enacted over a century ago. Today a farmer's water rights can make him a millionaire. As growth erupts along the Front Range, farmers sell water to cities and subdivisions.

This conflict is most evident with Colorado-Big Thompson water, which was brought from the western slope of the Rocky Mountains, through the continental divide, in the early 1950s at a cost of $159 million. At that time 90 percent of the 200,000 acre-feet of storage was used for agriculture, mostly on prime agricultural land in the Front Range counties north of Denver. That percentage today is 70 percent, and it will decrease as the pressure to sell mounts. The price in recent years has jumped from $40 to $2,867 an acre-foot, with a predicted rise to $20,000 an acre-foot by 1984.

As a result, productive farmland is removed from agriculture although it may be miles from the urban development to which the water was sold. Energy companies can also buy water rights and dry up important agricultural land. Should it be a right for uses of water and land to be determined by the highest bidder?

The United States has, as yet, no real national commitment to the preservation of prime and important agricultural land. Public policy decisions, such as the location of highways and water and sewer lines, have accelerated the conversion of vast amounts of productive farmland. Energy policy has not yet recognized the importance of agricultural land over the long-term, and accelerated energy development has the potential to reduce significantly the land available for food crop production.

An ethical perspective

This nation, first of all, needs to develop a land use ethic acknowledging that potential adverse impacts on important farmland should be a factor in the decision-making process. Then, a system must be developed to preserve those lands that respect public as well as private interests.

Also needed is a conservation ethic for both energy and water use. A real commitment to energy conservation can reduce the pressure for quick-fix solutions at the expense of the energy-rich regions, while water conservation can make limited water supplies serve more purposes.

Then, a new water ethic is needed in the West so that water will be available for a balance of uses and will not always "flow towards money." Re-use and exchanges of water can also be developed that will alleviate the crunch between agricultural and other water uses.

Finally, the nation needs a carrying capacity ethic. Energy policy decisions must reflect an awareness that energy resources are located in a semiarid part of the United States subject to periodic drought. These lands are fragile, and the winds can blow the lands away.

REFERENCES

1. Comptroller General, General Accounting Office. 1980. *Water supply should not be an obstacle to meeting energy development goals.* CED-80-30. Washington, D.C.
2. Hentzmark, D., D. Ray, and G. Parvin. 1980. *The agricultural sector impacts of making alcohol from grain.* Solar Energy Research Institute, Golden, Colorado.
3. U.S. Commission of the General Land Office. 1868. *Report.* Washington, D.C.

14

The Energy Squeeze on Land and Water Management: An Ecological Perspective

Herman E. Koenig
Director, Center for Environmental Quality
Office of Vice-president for Research and Graduate Studies
Michigan State University, East Lansing

The rising real cost, uncertainty of supply, and changing technical characteristics of available U.S. energy resources in the 1980s will motivate many changes in the physical, ecological, and social structure of agriculture and related sectors of the economy. But these changes are likely to be essentially diametric to those of the last century or more. The critical issue in agricultural policy is to assist market processes in making timely and productive adaptations toward the future. The critical questions both from the policy and the operators' perspectives are these: What specific structural adaptations are likely to become economic in the foreseeable future and when?

If we are to avoid premature obsolescence of capital stock and many other economic and social costs, these questions must be answered with at least a decade of lead time, considering the context of a rapidly changing and highly uncertain economic environment. Both private and public decisions pertaining to these questions must be supported by an expanded capability in the design and management of agroecosystems.

A recent history of energy and the structure of agriculture

The nature of structural changes in agriculture, the time scale for change, and the economic forces motivating them have their origins in the technical principles and economic costs involved in making energy in our environment useful to human societies.

A number of important trends in the structure of U.S. agriculture and its intersectorial relationship to human settlements and other sectors of the economy can be related to the changing costs, forms, and sources of energy, especially the fluid fossil fuels. Energy production and consumption in the United States by fuel types from 1920 to 1977 is shown in figure 1. The dominance of natural oil and gas as the universal fuel for industrial and agricultural growth for the past half century is clearly evident from these data.

The cost of energy relative to labor, land, and other economic factors (the real cost) has been and will continue to be the dominant factor in shaping agriculture and its intersectorial relationship to the durable goods industries, urban settlements, and other sectors of the economy. One practical measure of the real cost of energy is the ratio of the consumer cost in dollars per unit of energy to the average industrial wage rate in dollars per hour. Data from *U.S. Statistical Abstracts* show that this ratio, which represents the average hours of labor required to deliver a unit of energy to final consumption, declined by more than 5 percent per year from 1950 to 1973 (Figure 2).

Although reliable data are not readily available, we can infer that the hours of labor involved in acquiring a unit of energy undoubtedly declined yearly from at least the early part of this century when inexpensive oil and natural gas became the dominant fuels for industrialization. Now for the first time in perhaps a century, the energy/wage ratio is increasing. From 1973 through 1977, the real cost increased at a rate of 4.8 percent per year for electricity and 14.7 percent for natural gas. Similar changes are true for all petroleum-based fuels.

In production agriculture, cheap fluid fossil fuels for transportation, tillage, grain drying, synthetic fertilizers, and pesticides fostered large-scale regional specialization and increased scale of operation. On many accounts, these structural changes have resulted in the opening of important nutrient cycles and otherwise disrupted long-term balances between man-made and natural ecosystems, and they have increased the susceptibility and sensitivity of production systems to insects and disease. The highly specialized, large-scale cash crop farming operations now characteristic of the north central region of the United States, for example, would certainly not be economically feasible without cheap and reliable supplies of fossil fuels to provide low-cost pest control, transportation of grains to centralized animal feeding operations, and the requisite high levels of synthetic nitrogen and grain drying.

Energy supplies, real costs, and technical characteristics

Projections of future gross energy supplies by major fuel types through the year 2000 are also shown in figure 1 in relationship to several scenarios of growth in energy consumption. These projections were developed inde-

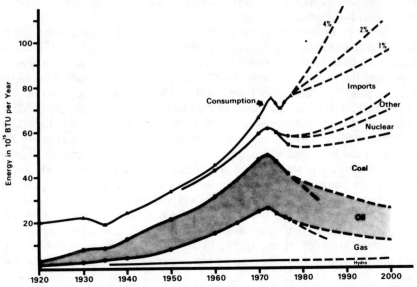

Figure 1. Fossil fuel consumption in the United States, by fuel types, from 1920 to 1977 and projections of possible supplies to the year 2000 (*1, 2*).

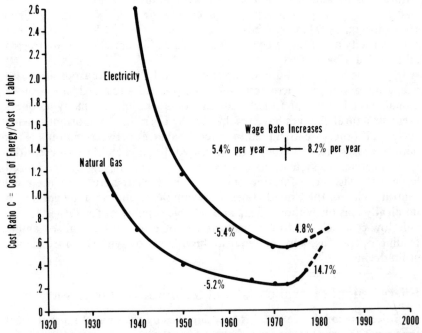

Figure 2. Real cost of energy in the United States as measured by the consumer cost in dollars per unit of energy to average industrial wage rates in dollars per hour.

pendently (*1, 2*) and represent levels that, from technical and engineering perspectives, potentially could be produced without regard for cost. Sources labeled "other" include various forms of solar-based energy resources (solar-thermal, wind, biomass, etc.), geothermal, and nonconventional oil and gas (shale, geopressurized brine, etc.).

The nearest substitute in quality and quantity to the fluid fossil fuels is coal. Under the best of conditions, conversion of this resource to refined fluid fuels can probably only take place with efficiencies of 55 to 65 percent. The capital costs of the conversion technologies are very high also, and water resources to support the processes is a serious limiting factor. Under present economic conditions, synthetic fuels derived from coal will cost two to four times as much as natural fluid fuels. Furthermore, the environmental effects are serious and hard to manage.

Nuclear energy cannot serve as a portable fuel to drive mobile vehicles required in the present transportation systems, agriculture, and many other sectors of the economy, except indirectly through hydrogen or some other synthetic fuel.

Biomass is a near substitute for the solid fossil fuels, except that it has not been concentrated in time and space by natural geophysical processes. Compared with coal, it is dilute and geographically dispersed.

Solar-thermal energy is also diffuse and dilute. In addition, it is intermittent. Solar-thermal energy is also difficult to store in large quantities and is virtually nontransportable as heat. It must be developed primarily as a decentralized source in very close proximity to the end use, or it must be converted to electrical form.

Hydro and wind power are primarily work forms of energy, which in the pre-fossil fuel era were used directly at the point of collection to drive grist mills, water pumps, weaving looms, and the like.

It is the dispersed or dilute and intermittent nature of most of the various solar forms of energy rather than their absolute quantities that limit their economic use (*4*). As fossil fuels are depleted, biomass that was accumulated, stored, and processed by nature over an extremely long time must be processed by man on vastly shorter regeneration cycles, using manmade materials, devices, and energy. From this perspective alone, there appears to be little hope that we can ever produce synthetic fluid fuels from biomass sources on a continual basis in quantities and at costs comparable to the natural fluid fuels.

Much of the divergence in assessments of the longevity of natural petroleum and gas as well as the potential development rates, costs, and availability of alternatives to the fluid fossil fuels centers on the distinction that must be made between gross energy production and the accessible or net energy that can be derived from geological reserves or from renewable alternatives.

The net energy available for end use from alternative sources can be quantified in terms of the energy gain (*3*). Gain is defined as the ratio of the gross energy delivered by an energy deployment system over its useful lifetime to the energy invested in building, operating, and maintaining a facility. A comparison of the range of energy gains attainable from alternative energy systems is shown in figure 3, along with the net energy ultimately available for end use from these sources, expressed as a fraction of the gross.

A theoretical cost coefficient, C, defined as the ratio of the dollar cost of energy to the pecuniary cost of conversion (all non-energy costs including labor), is shown in figure 4 as a function of the energy gains of conversion systems. This coefficient is in effect another measure of the real cost of producing energy that reflects the physics of energy production. It shows that as the gain of our aggregate resources declines the real costs of energy will continue to increase.

During the era of fluid fossil fuels, when the gain of our energy resources was well above 10, net energy returns, time delays, and other factors of energy balance were not of major concern in economic planning. But as the economy becomes increasingly dependent upon renewable resources this parameter becomes increasingly significant. Labor and pecuniary costs (nonenergy costs of agricultural and other economic systems) typically decline as the scale of operation increases. On the other hand, the energy cost (energy

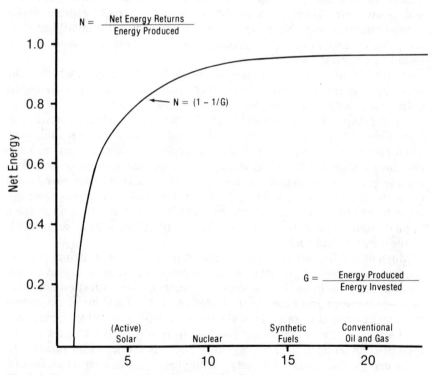

Figure 3. Net energy as a function of energy gain, G.

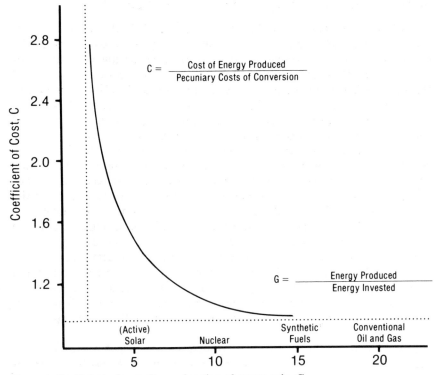

Figure 4. Coefficient of cost, C, as a function of energy gain, G.

per unit of output) for harvesting and collecting dilute resources typically increases with scale because of the increased area over which the feed stock must be gathered. For high-gain systems ($G > 10$) these latter costs are relatively insignificant compared with the economies of scale to labor and other nonenergy factors. However, for low-gain systems ($G < 10$), the reverse is true. For such systems (Figure 4), small increases in gain are made possible through technological innovation, substitution of labor for mechanization, small-scale operation, or integration with other economic processes. The lower the gain, the greater this significance of such structural changes. The energy gain of ethanol, for example, produced from agricultural grains (corn) in the context of present agricultural production systems and most proposed distillation technologies is in the vicinity of 1. The relative economics of this fuel will not improve much, if at all, with rising costs of conventional fuels unless changes are made in the structure of the agricultural/alcohol system to improve the overall energy gain. But small improvements so achieved will have large impacts on net energy returns and real cost.

Agricultural and regional economic development

Statistics show that during the 30 years prior to 1973 the real cost of virtually all agricultural commodities, as measured by the ratio of market price of the commodity to average industrial wage rate, declined by factors of two to four. These reductions in real costs of production were achieved through specialization and progressive increases in scale of individual farming enterprises. Most of the reductions occurred at the expense of increased transportation and food processing requirements, open material and energy "loops," and increased ecological instabilities in the farming system.

In the present era of rising real energy costs, sustained reductions in the real cost of basic agricultural commodities may not be possible under any conditions. The hope is to retard the rate of increase in the real cost of food, energy, and other consumer products, and to reduce the sensitivity of the food production system and the economy to disruptions in external energy supplies. In the long term these results can be achieved through the selective integration of unit operations and regional diversifications rather than continued differentation, expanding scale, and regional specialization. Such systems will capitalize on shorter transportation lines, closed material and energy loops, more stable ecological structures that reduce chemical pesticides, and shorter, less energy-intensive food processing and distribution systems. These adaptations are essentially diametric to those of the past half century or more.

In the north central region of the United States, for example, grain drying, synthetic nitrogen, and pesticides account for the largest fossil fuel inputs to agricultural production. As the cost of energy relative to labor continues to increase, regional integration of cropping systems with livestock will eventually be economically motivated as a means for reducing simultaneously all three of these energy inputs. The basic hypothesis is that these adaptations can and probably will take place without a significant loss in overall edible food produced per acre of land in the United States. And they will be more stable ecologically.

This hypothesis is based on potential increases in the resource efficiencies and ecological stability of combining animal feed and human food chains from photosynthesis to human consumption, not merely the resource efficiencies of the individual operation within these combined chains. More than 90 percent of the corn and soybeans produced by U.S. agriculture, for example, is used in the animal feed chain. The important economic and agricultural questions are not just yields per acre of corn and soybeans, but the pounds of beef, pounds of pork, or the pounds of milk that can be produced per acre of land, per unit of energy, and per man-hour of labor.

An interesting and important unanswered question remains: To what extent has the availability of cheap fossil fuels actually increased the overall

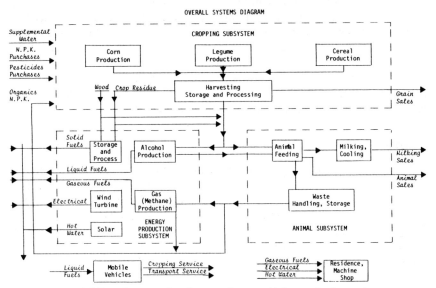

Figure 5. **Material-flow diagram of an integrated energy/dairy production system.**

yield of U.S. agriculture in human food per acre and to what extent has it simply provided the means for specialization?

The rising real cost of energy and the increased dependence of the overall economy on biologically derived resources will also bring certain critical integrations between energy and food production—integration of liquid and gaseous fuel production from crop residues, grain, animal waste, and other forms of biomass. If ethanol production from corn, for example, is properly scaled and integrated with cropping systems and animal feeding as illustrated in figure 5, it is possible to reduce significantly transportation requirements, eliminate grain drying, and close critical nutrient cycles at the farm or regional levels. The yield of land resources in food, industrial feed stocks, and energy and the economic cost of production through integrated agroecosystems designed and engineered to regional ecological and economic conditions remains critical to the future.

Human settlements then will become increasingly dependent upon the integrated use of agricultural land, forests, and other ecological and physical resources. As this happens, such energy forms as wind, hydro, wood, solar-thermal will serve as supplements or partial replacements for nonrenewable materials and energy resources. Cities and towns will have important "feedback" effects on the structure of agriculture in terms of employment opportunities and land use. The basic hypothesis is that rising energy costs and shifts to renewable resources will eventually curtail urban sprawl and redirect urban growth toward multinucleated cities of limited size. This requires an increase in the housing intensity and economic diversity of land use around existing shopping malls and community centers so as to support both public transportation and district heating and reduce the need to travel. Areas between centers that are currently dominated by 5 to 80 acre plots will remain low density, preserving the option for high intensity garden farming, biomass fuel production, and future recreation. Such land use patterns also provide a framework for implementing smaller-scale, less energy-intensive human waste recycling systems, all of which will surely impact on the long-term future structure of agriculture.

Transitional issues

Rising real costs of energy and uncertain supplies of natural fluid fuel as direct inputs to agriculture, continued biological adaptation of pests to man-made chemicals, and indirect impacts of changing urban form will eventually give economic impetus to structural adaptations in agriculture along the lines indicated in the previous section. From a policy point of view the critical issue is to assist market processes in promoting timely adaptations.

Economic issues: The future as a moving target

Economically viable agricultural production and food systems of the future are moving targets. The critical questions both from the policy maker's and operator's perspective are these: What specific structural adaptations are likely to become economic in the foreseeable future and when? If we are to avoid premature obsolescence of capital stocks and other economic losses and social costs, we must anticipate real costs and the changing forms of energy resources. Also, we must incorporate these changes in private and public development plans with at least a decade of lead time. We must support both public and private decisions pertaining to the economics of transition by greatly expanding our capabilities for designing regionally integrated food/energy systems, such as that illustrated in figure 5. This design capability must provide quantitative procedures for assessing the technical (economic and physical) performance of alternative regional food/energy systems in the context of a rapidly changing and uncertain economic environment. Because the agricultural, economic, and resource environment is likely to be much more uncertain and volatile than it has been in recent history, economically viable systems must be robust enough to survive a wide range of economic scenarios.

Ecological issues: Achieving more stable strategies

Adaptations in agriculture already outlined provide a new context for integrated pest management—a context in which the structure of regional food/energy systems becomes a major component of the pest control strategy. Preliminary studies and other empirical evidence suggest that through proven crop rotations, interplantings, and regional diversification of plant species and insect habitats the use of chemical controls can be greatly reduced or eliminated entirely in certain instances without economically significant damage. Such control strategies are perhaps appropriately referred to as "ecological control" strategies because they are based on the design of balanced or nearly balanced species communities.

The central hypothesis is that combined ecological/chemical control strategies in principle can be more stable than chemically based strategies and that economic forces will over time give rise to regional agroecosystems that are increasingly susceptible to such controls.

Management issues: Shaping a robust system

During the pre-1973 era of declining real cost of energy, the expanding base of scientific information was dealt with through specialization in research, education, and the farming enterprise. Microcomputers can play a significant role in assisting the operator, the researcher, and the student in understanding and dealing scientifically with the added complexity of integrated systems. However, management of the more integrated agroecosystems of the future may be a limiting factor in the practical applications of computers unless an overall system can be designed to be ecologically and economically robust, without a significant loss of resource efficiency.

Declarations of regional independence

It is difficult to anticipate the social feasibilities and consequences of previously indicated adaptations in agriculture and human settlements. In general, it can only be said that in the long term increases in the cost of energy relative to labor will lead to more labor-intensive agricultural systems and human settlements that are more effectively organized to use dispersed food and energy resources. These structural adaptations are key factors in mitigating inflation, reducing detrimental environmental impacts, and maintaining a high quality of life. Increased regional economic diversity and the increased use of local renewable resources provide the foundations for increased local autonomy in government.

New courses and questions

Limitations on future energy supplies and costs are determined not simply by the combined quantities of energy present in our environment or by the gross production capacity of an energy industry, but by the fraction of gross production that can be made available for end use at any given point in time—the net energy gain. Crucial to planning for the future is the fact that the combined energy gain from resources will continue to decline and that the real cost of energy resources will increase as the nation and the world move from natural fluid fuels to alternatives.

These basic and apparently irreversible changes in the technical characteristics of our energy resources provide a new context for the world food
question in general and U.S. agriculture in particular. It mandates new directions in the evolution of agriculture and its relationship with the rest of
the economy. Continued reductions in the real costs of U.S. agricultural
commodities may not be possible under any conditions. Reductions in the
rate of increase of real costs are, however, apparently to be found in selective integration of unit operations and regional diversifications rather than
in continued differentiation of operations and regional specialization. Food
yields remain an open question.

There are many economic, ecological, management, and social/cultural
problems involved in identifying and carrying out timely transitions toward
selective integrations and regional diversification in agriculture in response
to rising real costs and changing forms of energy. Therefore, we must carefully reassess present policy in virtually all phases of agriculture, research,
and development.

REFERENCES

1. Duane, J. W. 1977. *World and national oil and gas demand and supply.* Aware Magazine
   (October).
2. Hayes, E. T. 1979. *Energy resources available to the United States, 1985 to 2000.* Science
   203(4377): 233-239.
3. Michigan Transportation Research Program, Highway Safety Research Institute. 1979.
   Coping with energy limitations in transportation: Proposal for Michigan. University of
   Michigan, Ann Arbor.
4. Pollard, W. G. 1976. *Long range prospects for solar derived fuels.* American Scientist
   64(4).

15

The Energy Squeeze on Land and Water Management: A Roundtable Discussion

Lee B. Shields
Assistant Director, Information and Public Affairs
Soil Conservation Service, Washington, D.C.

Registrants participated in a roundtable discussion on "The Energy Squeeze on Land and Water Management" following the presentations by Professor D'Arge, Ms. McNulty, and Dr. Koenig.

Consensus was difficult to reach in answering the eight questions posed, mainly because participants were from several different regions of North America, the issues involved are extremely complex, and discussion time was short. The thoughts articulated by registrants were these:

1. What possibilities exist for resolving conflicts between the use of water for development of energy resources and use of water for irrigated agriculture?

Concentrate coal mining where there is little potential for irrigaton (but don't process coal in areas of low water supply; reclamation requires water, too). Use integrated solutions, such as building slurry lines from humid regions, to carry coal from and water to the arid West. Use the heat from power plants to run greenhouses, which can reduce the need for irrigation.

2. What effects would reduced water for agriculture in the West have on agriculture in other regions of the country?

Other marginal land may be brought into production in the East and South, particularly wet soils. Intensified agricultural production in nonirrigated areas could accelerate soil erosion. There would be effects on the West, too. Marginal land will be brought into production in areas that have sufficient irrigation water.

Where groundwater is not available, much of the West may go back to dryland farming, since land values are too high to go to grassland farming (some land presently in major grain production would support only 10 cows per quarter section).

3. *What factors are important in choosing between national priorities and regional, state, provincial, or local preferences?*

Public involvement and not vested interests should determine agency decisions, but how are we to be sure the public is really involved? We need more local input into energy development and other policies and more attention to social, economic, and environmental impacts of mining. We need better communication among all levels of government and better communications by government and industry. Nations do exist; therefore, we do need to be concerned about national, continental, even global problems, such as acid rain. We cannot rely only on local and state or provincial initiatives, yet we need not sacrifice one for the other.

4. *Can decisions regarding priorities be made by existing institutions?*

Yes, if they cooperate more closely than they have (by force, if necessary); if citizen groups are substantially more active; and if federal agencies, such as the Environmental Protection Agency, Department of Energy, and U.S. Department of Agriculture, develop an integrated approach to some kind of national land use planning (by some acceptable name).

5. *What should be the shape and structure of any new institution needed to help make such decisions?*

We do not need or want any new super agency. It could not work.

6. *How can important agricultural lands be protected or preserved from unnecessary impacts of energy development or energy-related activities?*

Prime agricultural lands must be reclaimed to an "equal or better" condition after mining. Practical reclamation laws must be developed and enforced. Also, different methods of transportation must be considered and a method selected that is the most energy efficient and environmentally acceptable. Land use regulations must be adopted for our best farmland, or we must make widespread use of Canada's point system for setting high-priority areas for protection and firm local ordinances to support it. Steps must be taken to resolve saltwater pollution of streams and groundwater in oil-producing areas.

7. How can we go about giving ethics a seat at the table where political-economic decisions about resources are made?

We must let people make the decisions (although we have had a problem of credibility of some of the inputs, and much greater attendance is needed at public meetings). Maximum use should be made of citizen groups. There is need for follow through on a holistic approach in discussions and decisions that weigh social, economic, and environmental trade-offs and examine more alternatives and more externalities. We must weigh off-site effects of energy development in the future. We must take the emotion out of decision making and use the best available documented facts and sound technical advice. Producers should be given a voice in USDA decisions as well as processors. An objective system of zoning should be adopted. Environmental education should be provided at the elementary, secondary, and university levels as well as for adults (especially legislators).

8. How can we go about giving ecology a seat at the decision table?

The same suggestions offered in response to question 7 were given here. Also: Remember that legislators are not totally unethical. If we understand ecological principles and ideas, why don't some of us run for legislative office ourselves and directly influence the process? We must make sure that public program regulations reflect ecological principles and provide for full public participation.

Finally, a good starting point for giving ecology and ethics a seat at the decision tables would be to double the membership of the Soil Conservation Society of America to aid the blending of ideas and perspectives.

V. Assessing the Future

16

Global 2000:
Imperatives for the Future

Gerald O. Barney
Director, Global 2000 Study
Council on Environmental Quality
and U.S. Department of State, Washington, D.C.

If present trends continue, the world in 2000 will be more crowded, more polluted, less stable ecologically, and more vulnerable to disruption than the world we live in now. Serious stresses involving population, resources, and environment are clearly visible ahead. Despite greater material output, the world's people will be poorer in many ways than they are today.

For hundreds of millions of the desperately poor, the outlook for food and other necessities of life will be no better. For many it will be worse. Barring revolutionary advances in technology, life for most people on earth will be more precarious in 2000 than it is now—unless the nations of the world act decisively to alter current trends.

This, in essence, is the picture emerging from the U.S. government's projections of probable changes in world population, resources, and environment by the end of the century, as presented in the Global 2000 Study. The study does not predict what will occur. Rather, it depicts conditions that are likely to develop if there are no changes in public policies, institutions, or rates of technological advance, and if there are no wars or other major disruptions. A keener awareness of the nature of the current trends, however, may induce changes that will alter these trends and the projected outcome.

Principal findings

Rapid growth in world population will hardly have altered by 2000. The world's population will grow from 4 billion in 1975 to 6.35 billion in 2000, an increase of more than 50 percent. The rate of growth will slow only marginally, from 1.8 percent a year to 1.7 percent. In terms of sheer numbers, population will be growing faster in 2000 than it is today, with 100 million people added each year compared with 75 million in 1975. Ninety percent of this growth will occur in the poorest countries.

While the economies of the less developed countries (LDCs) are expected to grow at faster rates than those of the industrialized nations, the gross national product per capita in most LDCs remains low. The average gross national product per capita is projected to rise substantially in some LDCs (especially in Latin America), but in the great populous nations of South Asia it remains below $200 a year (in 1975 dollars). The large existing gap between the rich and poor nations widens.

World food production is projected to increase 90 percent over the 30 years from 1970 to 2000. This translates into a global per capita increase of less than 15 percent over the same period. The bulk of that increase goes to countries that already have relatively high per capita food consumption. Meanwhile, per capita consumption in South Asia, the Middle East, and the LDCs of Africa will scarcely improve or will actually decline below present inadequate levels. At the same time, real prices for food are expected to double.

Arable land will increase only 4 percent by 2000, so that most of the increased output of food will have to come from higher yields. Most of the elements that now contribute to higher yields—fertilizer, pesticides, power for irrigation, and fuel for machinery—depend heavily on oil and gas.

During the 1990s world oil production will approach geological estimates of maximum production capacity, even with rapidly increasing petroleum prices. The study projects that the richer industrialized nations will be able to command enough oil and other commercial energy supplies to meet rising demands through 1990. With the expected price increases, many less developed countries will have increasing difficulties meeting energy needs. For the one-quarter of humankind that depends primarily on wood for fuel, the outlook is bleak. Needs for fuelwood will exceed available supplies by about 25 percent before the turn of the century.

While the world's finite fuel resources—coal, oil, gas, oil shale, tar sands, and uranium—are theoretically sufficient for centuries, they are not evenly distributed; they pose difficult economic and environmental problems; and they vary greatly in their amenability to exploitation and use.

Nonfuel mineral resources generally appear sufficient to meet projected demands through 2000, but further discoveries and investments will be needed to maintain reserves. In addition, production costs will increase with energy prices and may make some nonfuel mineral resources uneconomic. The quarter of the world's population that inhabits industrial countries will continue to absorb three-fourths of the world's mineral production.

Regional water shortages will become more severe. In the 1970-2000 period population growth alone will cause requirements for water to double in nearly half the world. Still greater increases would be needed to improve standards of living. In many LDCs, water supplies will become increasingly erratic by 2000 as a result of extensive deforestation. Development of new water supplies will become more costly virtually everywhere.

Significant losses of world forests will continue over the next 20 years as demand for forest products and fuelwood increases. Growing stocks of commercial-size timber are projected to decline 50 percent per capita. The world's forests are now disappearing at the rate of 18 to 20 million hectares a year (an area half the size of California), with most of the loss occurring in the humid tropical forests of Africa, Asia, and South America. The projections indicate that by 2000 some 40 percent of the remaining forest cover in LDCs will be gone.

Serious deterioration of agricultural soils will occur worldwide, due to erosion, loss of organic matter, desertification, salinization, alkalinization, and waterlogging. Already, an area of cropland and grassland approximately the size of Maine is becoming barren wasteland each year, and the spread of desert-like conditions is likely to accelerate.

Atmospheric concentrations of carbon dioxide and ozone-depleting chemicals are expected to increase at rates that could alter the world's climate and upper atmosphere significantly by 2050. Acid rain from increased combustion of fossil fuels (especially coal) threatens damage to lakes, soils, and crops. Radioactive and other hazardous materials present health and safety problems in increasing numbers of countries.

Extinctions of plant and animal species will increase dramatically. Hundreds of thousands of species—perhaps as many as 20 percent of all species on earth—will be irretrievably lost as their habitats vanish, especially in tropical forests.

The future depicted by the U.S. Government projections, briefly outlined above, may actually understate the impending problems. The methods available for carrying out the study led to certain gaps and inconsistencies that tend to impart an optimistc bias. For example, most of the individual projections for the various sectors studied—food, minerals, energy, and so on—assume that sufficient capital, energy, water, and land will be available in each of these sectors to meet their needs, regardless of the competing needs of the other sectors. More consistent, better integrated projections would produce a still more emphatic picture of intensifying stresses, as the world enters the twenty-first century.

Conclusions

At present and projected growth rates, the world's population would reach 10 billion by 2030 and would approach 30 billion by the end of the twenty-first century. These levels correspond closely to estimates by the U.S. National Academy of Sciences of the maximum carrying capacity of the entire earth. Already the populations in sub-Saharan Africa and in the Himalayan hills of Asia have exceeded the carrying capacity of the immediate area, triggering an erosion of the land's capacity to support life. The resulting poverty and ill health have further complicated efforts to reduce fertility. Unless this circle of interlinked problems is broken soon, population growth in such areas will unfortunately be slowed for reasons other than declining birth rates. Hunger and disease will claim more babies and young children and more of those surviving will be mentally and physically handicapped by childhood malnutrition.

Indeed, the problems of preserving the carrying capacity of the earth and sustaining the possibility of a decent life for the human beings that inhabit it are enormous and close upon us. Yet there is reason for hope. It must be emphasized that the Global 2000 Study's projections are based on the assumption that national policies regarding population stabilization, resource conservation, and environmental protection will remain essentially unchanged through the end of the century. But in fact, policies are beginning to change. In some areas forests are being replanted after cutting. Some nations are taking steps to reduce soil losses and desertification. Interest in energy conservation is growing, and large sums are being invested in exploring alternatives to petroleum dependence. The need for family planning is slowly becoming better understood. Water supplies are being improved and waste treatment systems built. High-yield seeds are widely available and seed banks are being expanded. Some wildlands with their genetic resources are being protected. Natural predators and selective pesticides are being substituted for persistent and destructive pesticides.

Encouraging as these developments are, they are far from adequate to meet the global challenges projected in this study. Vigorous, determined, new initiatives are needed if worsening poverty and human suffering, environmental degradation, and international tension and conflicts are to be prevented. There are no quick fixes. The only solutions to the problems of populaton, resources, and environment are complex and long-term. These problems are inextricably linked to some of the most perplexing and persistent problems in the world—poverty, injustice, and social conflict. New and imaginative ideas, and a willingness to act on them, are essential.

The needed changes go far beyond the capability and responsibility of this or any other single nation. An era of unprecedented cooperation and commitment is essential. Yet there are opportunities—and a strong rationale—for the United States to provide leadership among nations. A high priority for this nation must be a thorough assessment of its foreign and domestic policies relating to population, resources, and environment. The United States, possessing the world's largest economy, can expect its policies to have a significant influence on global trends. An equally important priority for the United States is to cooperate generously and justly with other nations, particularly in the areas of trade, investment, and assistance, in seeking solutions to the many problems that extend beyond our national boundaries. There are many unfulfilled opportunities to cooperate with other nations in efforts to relieve poverty and hunger, stabilize population, and enhance economic and environmental productivity. Further cooperation among nations is also needed to strengthen international mechanisms for protecting and using the "global commons"—the oceans and atmosphere.

To meet the challenges described in this study, the United States must improve its ability to identify emerging problems and asssess alternative responses. In using and evaluating the government's present capability for long-term global analysis, the study found serious inconsistencies in the methods and assumptions employed by the various agencies in making their projections. The study itself made a start toward resolving these inadequacies. It represents the government's first attempt to produce an interrelated set of population, resource, and environmental projections, and it has brought forth the most consistent set of global projections yet achieved by U.S. agencies. Nevertheless, the projections will contain serious gaps and contradictions that must be corrected if the government's analytic capability is to be improved. It must be acknowledged that at present the federal agencies are not always capable of providing projections of the quality needed for long-term policy decisions.

While limited resources may be a contributing factor in some instances, the primary problem is lack of coordination. The U.S. government needs a mechanism for continuous review of the assumptions and methods the federal agencies use in their projection models and for assurance that the agencies' models are sound, consistent, and well documented. The improved analyses that could result would provide not only a clearer sense of emerging problems and opportunities, but also a better means for evaluating alternative responses, and a better basis for decisions of worldwide significance that the president, the Congress, and the federal government as a whole must make.

With its limitations and rough approximations, the Global 2000 Study may be seen as no more than a reconnaissance of the future; nonetheless its conclusions are reinforced by similar findings of other recent global studies that were examined in the course of the Global 2000 Study. All these studies are in general agreement on the nature of the problems and on the threats they pose to the future welfare of humankind. The available evidence leaves no doubt that the world—including this nation—faces enormous, urgent, and complex problems in the decades immediately ahead. Prompt and vigorous changes in public policy around the world are needed to avoid or minimize these problems before they become unmanageable. Long lead times are required for effective action. If decisions are delayed until the problems become worse, options for effective action will be severely reduced.

17

Resources Conservation Act: New Window on the Future

Norman A. Berg
Chief, Soil Conservation Service
U.S. Department of Agriculture, Washington, D.C.

The Global 2000 report confirms other sobering reports prepared in the past few years—reports that indicate that the growing world population will create increasing pressures on our natural resources. The available evidence leaves no doubt that the world, including the United States, faces enormous, urgent, and complex problems in the decades immediately ahead. The world needs prompt and vigorous changes in public policy to avoid or minimize these problems before they become unmanageable. We require long lead times for effective action. If decisions are delayed until the problems become worse, options for effective action will be severely reduced.

As its title indicates, the Global 2000 report is a worldwide forecast. But worldwide problems are resolved on a far smaller scale. They are ultimately solved by actions of people in their own area of control. Most of these actions are taken by individuals in their own backyard. It is the summary of individual actions that solves nationwide or even worldwide problems.

Concern for the future is being voiced elsewhere. In his recent speech in Toronto at the first Global Conference on the Future, Edward Schreyer, governor general of Canada, named three major preoccupations of the future: food and agriculture, pollution of the biosphere, and resource and energy conservation.

In spite of these gloomy forecasts of the future, I believe humanity will survive. But survival requires our action now; it will not come automatically. Obviously, as those in agriculture know all too well, we cannot manage all the elements that will affect the future. Lest we forget, Mount St. Helens forcefully reminds us of this. To a large extent, however, we create our future. The future will be what we make it.

Humankind has two basic goals for the future: survival and growth. For survival, we need to know the answers to questions such as: Why? How long? How will people organize themselves for continued survival? For growth, we need to know the answers to the "how" questions; we need technology. The Soil and Water Resources Conservation Act (RCA) will help answer some of these questions, and thus it is a new window on the future.

RCA and public response to the process

The U.S. Department of Agriculture's interagency RCA Coordinating Committee published four documents in early January 1980. These draft documents included two appraisals, a program report and environmental impact statement, and a summary. These documents contain (a) recognition that currently within USDA there are 34 different programs relating to soil and water conservation, (b) facts about the status and condition of the nation's land and water resources, (c) assumptions about the future to the year 2030, (d) analyses of seven important natural resource areas, (e) proposed objectives, (f) proposed activities that support each objective and the estimated costs of these activities, and (g) seven alternative strategies for carrying out these objectives.

Wide discussion of these documents was encouraged, and the public was invited to comment between January 28 and March 28, 1980. The U.S. Department of Agriculture (USDA) held more than 9,000 local and 18 regional public meetings and set up a Response Analysis Center in Athens, Georgia, to handle the 64,872 responses bearing the signatures of 118,213 interested persons. These responses contained 1,513,556 separate, identifiable comments about the RCA draft document and related issues. Responses came from every state in the nation and the Caribbean area.

Analysis of these responses showed that (a) almost three-fourths were from individuals; (b) responses from the South and Midwest were proportionately greater than the nonmetropolitan populations of those regions; (c) nearly half of the individuals did not identify themselves by occupation or affiliation; (d) nearly one-fourth of the responses were from those who identified themselves as farmers or ranchers; (e) one-fourth were from respondents who identified themselves as employees of federal, state, or local government; (f) well over half were structured response forms; (g) many different structured response forms were used; (h) about half of all comments addressed the alternative strategies for conserving soil and water resources; (i) more than one-third of all comments addressed the conservation objectives; and (j) the remaining comments addressed present programs, conservation activities, RCA assumptions and projections, USDA agencies, soil and water resources, and miscellaneous topics.

An evaluation team was formed in Washington to prepare a report on the comments. Respondents told us many things. Those commenting on soil, water, and related resources (a) valued highly the nation's soil, water, and related resources; (b) were concerned about the capacity of the nation's resources to meet future needs; and (c) were troubled by the definition of wetlands.

Respondents commenting on the conservation objectives (a) viewed the proposed objectives as important issues in developing a national conservation program and supported all RCA objectives, (b) supported the objectives to reduce soil erosion and retain prime farmland more than all other objectives, (c) supported energy conservation, and (d) expressed the least support for the objective to reduce loss of wetlands and the objectives associated with irrigation water use.

Those commenting on the activities to reach the objectives (a) said, by a 3 to 2 margin, that activities for achieving conservation objectives were adequate rather than inadequate; (b) most frequently said that erosion control measures, structural flood control measures, conservation tillage, and drainage were effective conservation measures; (c) supported incentives and farm management for solving soil and water resource problems, and advocated a conservationist philosophy, research and education, and technical assistance as solutions to those problems; (d) favored a public-private partnership for solving water resource problems; and (e) acknowledged farmers' commitments to a conservation ethic.

Persons commenting on USDA agencies and their conservation programs (a) generally believed that the programs were effective but said that the agencies could do an even better job if they had more funding, if they could provide more technical assistance, and if they were more efficient; (b) said that education and research—but not regulation—are appropriate areas for governmental involvement in conservation activities; and (c) wanted red tape and regulations reduced.

Those commenting on related agricultural issues (a) favored a strong export policy and related this to energy needs, (b) endorsed the traditional American concept of small family farms, and (c) supported preservation of farmland for agricultural use.

The most popular alternative strategy—redirecting present conservation programs—and the least popular alternative—regulation combined with a strong conservation assistance program—appeared to be two extremes in a range of alternatives, but actually they were not. The two extremes were not even proposed as alternative strategies because it did not seem to the RCA Coordinating Committee that either extreme would be feasible.

At one extreme we could envision a situation in which the federal government assumed full financial responsibility for protecting the nation's natural resources, while farmers, ranchers, and foresters continued to have broad discretion over how they use their land. At the other end of the spectrum is a situation in which laws are passed providing severe penalties for those who do not manage natural resources with society's best interest in mind. As a practical matter, our choices were, and are, within these two extremes.

Respondents commenting on the alternative strategies (a) most favored redirecting present conservation programs and conservation performance bonuses; (b) least favored the regulatory emphasis and cross compliance; and (c) generally said that they would support a national conservation program that is well funded, voluntary, and responsive to local conditions and needs.

Respondents commenting on the RCA process (a) endorsed the RCA public participation effort; (b) said that the review period was too short, that too few copies of the documents were available, and that the documents should have had more exposure; (c) expressed some doubts about the accuracy of the data in the RCA draft documents; and (d) questioned data collection methods.

The thousands of concerned citizens who took the time to respond to the RCA effort were most interested in programs for erosion control, prime farmland retention, conservation tillage, and drainage. They showed the least interest in programs for wetland retention and data collection.

Respondents generally agreed with the appraisal of our country's natural resources. They said that erosion reduction should be the primary objective of USDA and that increased emphasis should be placed on water quality and energy conservation as well.

Respondents wanted more technical assistance for on-the-ground implementation, more funding, less regulation, and less red tape. They also recommended better communication and coordination among USDA's conservation agencies. What these comments boil down to is support for a voluntary, locally controlled, subsidized program. Whether or not this is the program that emerges remains to be seen. But decision makers are taking the public's comments into consideration in developing the program.

The final USDA program recommendation was to go forward to the president and the Congress later in 1980. Before that happened, though, the public had an opportunity to comment again, this time on the recommended program. Another 60-day review period began early in the fall of 1980.

Maintaining the land base

As for predicting the final outcome, one thing I can foretell with certainty is that the program will not please everybody. This is certain, because everyone does not view public and private rights regarding conservation the same. Some insist that the rights of the public should prevail in determining land use, but others proclaim the sanctity of private land rights. There is a delicate balance between the public interest and private rights. We have no intention of making major changes in this balance—even if we could.

We want to maintain our base for producing food and fiber and still preserve as much of our individual initiative and economic freedom as possible. RCA decision makers are fully aware of the fact that the American people will not practice conservation because they are forced to do so, but because they want to do so.

Maintaining our land base means reducing soil erosion that exceeds the maximum level of erosion, determined with the use of the universal soil loss equation, to be tolerable on a given area. This objective will be the keystone of the new program. After nearly a half century of trying to control it, soil erosion is still our country's number one conservation problem, one that affects our ability to feed ourselves and our global neighbors. And it is a problem that impacts on the environment, including water quality and fish and wildlife habitat. Thus, controlling soil erosion affects all three of the future preoccupations identified by Governor General Schreyer: food and agriculture, pollution of the biosphere, and resource/energy conservation.

Soil erosion decreases productivity if it occurs faster than the topsoil can be replenished by natural processes. And this is the usual case because it takes as much as 200 years to rebuild 1 inch of topsoil. The average loss that can be tolerated on cropland, pasture, and forest land is 5 tons per acre per year. Rangeland is more fragile and can tolerate an average of only 2 tons per acre per year. The national average for sheet and rill erosion in this country is a loss of about 5 tons per acre per year, although it varies from region to region. In some places, the loss is three or four times that much. This type of erosion is more serious in the Midwest and South, our most important cropland areas.

The RCA staff groups made projections of how maximum crop yields in the year 2030 would be affected by the assumed continuation of present erosion losses. They concluded that the greatest declines in productivity—up to 46 percent—would be in land capability classes IV and V, those lands generally less suited to cultivation. This does not sound ominous—the greatest losses in yields would be on those soils that are the least productive and the least desirable for growing crops. But population pressures and demand for food could cause cultivation of more of these lands, and if that happens, erosion will increase. Then, overall reduction in yields could be substantial. For example, a 3 percent decline in today's production of wheat would equal 60 million bushels, worth $240 million at recent prices. Such a decline, extended to all crops, would be a serious blow for the U.S agricultural economy.

In addition to sheet and rill erosion, we also have a serious problem with wind erosion, especially in the 10 Great Plains States. Wind moves billions of tons of soil each year, particularly during drought. Erosion from streambanks, gullies, and roadbanks also is serious, accounting for at least a billion tons of soil moved each year.

An increasingly serious problem in some areas is soil compaction, which restricts root penetration and lowers crop yields. One study indicated that such losses amounted to more than $1 billion in 1971. The same loss in current dollars would triple that figure by the year 2030.

Fighting erosion and sedimentation on cropland, of course, would be but one objective of the national conservation program. We are also concerned about reducing erosion on forest land and on rangeland. The latter can tolerate even less soil loss than cropland. At the same time that we reduce erosion, we want to help land users to increase productivity of range and forest. One avenue of help will come from implementation of the Renewable Resources Extension Act of 1978 (RREA), administered by USDA's Science and Education Administration (SEA), through the Cooperative Extension Service.

Today, about 71 percent of the commercial forest land and 64 percent of the rangeland in the contiguous United States are privately owned. According to SEA, these private forests and rangelands provide the greatest single opportunity to increase the supply of renewable natural resources. Under RREA, Extension will provide better management information to owners, managers, processors, and users of such lands. These efforts will complement federal and state programs of technical and financial assistance for conservation.

Other threats to agricultural productivity include possible energy shortages, soil and water salinity, and reduced agricultural research. For instance, irrigation increases soil and water salinity, making some soil unsuitable for growing crops. Some 25 to 35 percent of the irrigated lands in the West have salinity problems.

In the past, the United States has been able to increase yields per acre despite physical and natural constraints, thanks to government research. Unfortunately, research funding has been declining in real dollars. As a result, there will be a lag before we can expect to see new technological changes introduced that could offset rising energy prices.

U.S. agricultural productivity is expected to increase about 1 percent annually in the years ahead, compared with the 2 percent annual growth rate that we experienced over the past three decades.

Besides its effects on agricultural productivity, soil erosion and the resulting sedimentation pollute streams, lakes, and reservoirs. As much as 2 billion tons of sediment are deposited every year in the nation's stream systems; half a billion tons reach the oceans. That makes sediment the greatest single water pollutant by volume.

The program that finally emerges from the RCA process should not be limited to only one concern—the land and its ability to produce. It should encompass all natural resources. The public demands it. In the area of water quality, for example, 85 percent of the people who responded to the RCA draft documents agreed with the objective to reduce sediment; 76 percent agreed with the objective to minimize nutrient pollution. As a result, the new national program should take into consideration the traditional factors of agricultural production and also respond to nonmarket factors of value to society, such as maintaining fish and wildlife habitat, preserving wetlands, and retaining prime and other important farmland for agricultural purposes. When considered separately, these nonmarket factors may not seem important enough to compensate for the public's cost of providing them. Yet, collectively, their value to society becomes obvious. And their cost may actually be offset because they help reduce production costs by controlling soil erosion.

Who will pay for what?

The whole question of costs, and who's going to pay for what, should be addressed in the recommended RCA program. The total cost, both public and private, of meeting all of the proposed objectives is at least double what is now being spent. Where will the additional funds come from? What proportion of cost should be borne by the landowners, by society, by the federal government? Many respondents to the RCA strategies asked for cost-sharing, saying that the federal government should pay 51 to 100 percent of the cost of conservation practices. The new national program should propose workable answers to these questions. It should encourage farmers and ranchers to apply to the land those conservation measures that will benefit themselves in the short run. And the program should reimburse them, in part or in full, for measures they cannot otherwise afford.

Finally, in my view of the future through the RCA window, the program should entail an expanded and more viable role for state and local governments. It should be a program that is more in tune with the needs and desires of the American people.

Citizens of the United States are keenly interested in wise resource stewardship, as we found out clearly through public meetings, written comments, and the nationwide public opinion survey on soil and water resources conducted for USDA. Some of the survey findings: (a) Americans are knowledgeable about conservation and are aware of conservation issues, (b) half of all Americans consider the misuse of soil and water resources a very serious problem, (c) half of all Americans also consider the loss of good farmland to be a very serious problem, (d) two out of three Americans see conservation as a shared public and private responsibility, (e) by 7 to 1, Americans feel that federal action to protect farmland from erosion is a proper role for the federal government, and (f) 8 out of 10 Americans feel that the federal government should grant money to farmers and other landowners so that they can protect the soil and water.

The program that develops from this first RCA cycle will be carefully monitored for effectiveness. Some of the questions we will have to ask ourselves as we prepare for the 1985 RCA process include:

How well is the program working?

How serious are natural resource problems?

How do these problems impact on crop yields?

We also will have to consider other factors.

I recently served as the co-chairman for a joint U.S.-Canadian water quality study. Called PLUARG (Pollution from Land Use Activities Reference Group), the six-year study examined conditions in the Great Lakes

Basin that relate to water quality, including the impacts of sedimentation.

In July 1978, the Reference Group made recommendations to the International Joint Commission, which had requested the study. A few of the recommendations included: (a) improve and expand erosion and sediment control programs to reduce the movement of fine-grained sediment from land surfaces; (b) reduce phosphorus loads to achieve target loads in the individual lakes and to prevent future degradation; (c) reduce inputs of toxic substances—for certain toxics, a target load of zero will be necessary; (d) retain the best farmlands for agricultural purposes; and (e) preserve wetlands.

Based on the PLUARG study and public meetings held throughout the Great Lakes Basin, the Commission made its final recommendations to the U.S. and Canadian governments. The Great Lakes study showed that the effects of soil erosion are far-reaching. Soil erosion is a problem that impacts on people and their environment. Soil erosion control deserves to be the cornerstone concern of the new national conservation program. America has the ability to produce abundantly for our domestic needs as well as supply a portion of the world's needs for food and fiber. This capability cannot be expanded to meet infinite demands, however; nor can it even be maintained if we continue to allow the present rate of loss of our resources base. At present, there is no national policy for the United States that places value on the soil resource or on conserving the soil resource.

There are some programs and regulations of agencies that conflict with, offset, or duplicate each other that reduce the effectiveness of the national soil conservation program. We need to answer the question: "What are the costs of not applying or properly maintaining soil conservation practices or systems on various kinds of land?"

It should be stressed that the true legacy one generation leaves for the next is the capacity to produce. Humankind's goal is not simply to survive, to preserve our natural resources, but is also to grow. Our obligation to future generations is to progress. Through the RCA, Forest and Rangeland Renewable Resources Act, and RREA, these questions and considerations should be worked into new and improved programs for protecting and using America's soil and water resources—to enable us to meet the ever-increasing demands on these resources for the next 10, 20, and 50 years.

18

Forests of the Future

R. Max Peterson
Chief, Forest Service
U.S. Department of Agriculture
Washington, D.C.

What will the forests of the future look like? What needs will they be called upon to meet? And whom will they serve?

As a nation, we are answering these questions right now. We can choose the future that we want. And right now we are planning for that future.

The Forest and Rangeland Renewable Resources Planning Act (RPA) became law in 1974. In January 1976 the president sent the first assessment of all the nation's forest and rangeland resources and the first long-term recommended program of Forest Service activities to Congress. The president sent the 1980 updates to Congress on June 20 with his statement of policy. The program will be updated again in 1985 and the assessment in 1990.

A planning triumverate

RPA is only one of the U.S. Department of Agriculture's triumverate of planning efforts. There are also the Soil and Water Resources Conservation Act (RCA) and the Renewable Resources Extension Act (RREA). Together, these laws give the secretary of agriculture authority for planning land management programs that affect virtually all of the United States, except for urban areas. This is enormously important because we are talking about the future of renewable resources.

Like most planning processes, these did not develop ideally. For one thing, the timing was not synchronized; one grew out of the other. RPA became law in 1974, and two sets of documents have already been sent to Congress. The Soil Conservation Service is still working on the RCA program, and the Science and Education Administration has sent a tentative plan for RREA to Congress.

USDA is working to pull these three efforts together. The three lead agencies and others have cooperated closely. We already have developed working relationships and are ready to unite our efforts so that each benefits and strengthens the others. In 1985 all three programs will be updated at the same time. This will produce better coordinated plans.

Forests of the future

Now, what will the forests of the future look like, and what demands are likely to be made on them? The 1980 assessment gives us some good clues. It provides four kinds of information: (a) the existing resource situation or base, (b) supply trends, (c) demand trends, and (d) opportunities to improve the outlook.

The assessment is based on assumptions involving low, medium, and high levels. For instance, with the medium projection, U.S. population would increase about 81 million by the year 2030, Gross National Product would roughly quadruple, and each person's disposable income would more than double.

The assessment looked at forest and rangeland ownership and location and at the nation's water supply.

Then, it focused on projected demands. For example, outdoor recreation demands are projected to rise anywhere from 50 to 250 percent. Hunting and fishing show large increases also, as much as 250 percent for saltwater fishing. Water use is expected to increase, with irrigation remaining the major use. A 40 percent increase in range grazing is projected.

Timber demands show large increases also. Sawtimber consumption would almost double; roundwood consumption would more than double. Softwood demand should reach 15.5 billion cubic feet in 2030, with supply at 13 billion cubic feet, given base-level prices. The equilibrium price would be reached at about 14 billion cubic feet. Meanwhile, new housing production is expected to rise and then fall to about 2 million new houses per year in 2030.

Regionally, softwood timber demands and supplies show that the South will have the greatest supply increases. Hardwood sawtimber demands and supplies should increase much more than softwood proportionately. And imports are projected to continue to be much larger than exports.

In 1976 timber growth exceeded removals in the East, and removals exceeded growth in the West. But the potential growth in some areas is twice what it is at present.

In addition to biological opportunities, many economic opportunities exist. Regionally, the greatest opportunities are in the South. Most of these are on the nonindustrial private lands.

In summary, the assessment tells us once again that the nation is faced with rapidly increasing demands for renewable resource products and slower increases in supplies—demands are expected to far exceed supplies.

This outlook also has some important economic, social, and environmental impacts: intensifying competition for the available supplies of renewable resource products, higher costs to consumers for forest renewable resource products, rising environmental costs resulting from use of substitute materials, accelerated rate of use of nonrenewable resources, fewer and less satisfying outdoor recreational experiences, and a general deterioration in the quality of life for many people.

But this gloomy scenario is not necessarily inevitable for the future. This country also has a huge forest, rangeland, and water base. These land and water resources have the capacity to produce much larger quantities of forest and rangeland products, enough to meet most projected demands for these products.

The 1980 program

The 1980 program, as submitted to Congress by the Carter Administration, provides a range of options during this time of tight federal budgets. It is described in terms of high and low bounds. Funding for the national forest system will rise over the long term. State and private forestry funding is anticipated to rise in the near term in response to assessment findings about needing increased production from the private sector. Research funding also shows increases, especially under the high bound, but even the low bound is proportionally greater than for other areas.

In terms of individual output from the national forest system, recreation output would decrease, then rise again. Wilderness output reflects the second Roadless Area Review and Evaluation decisions. Funding would rise rapidly.

Wildlife and fish output and funding rise, then level off. Timber output rises more gradually and funding would follow accordingly. Range output would rise slightly over the long term. The emphasis would be on improving range condition. Range funding would be fairly constant.

Water and mineral resource outputs and funding could vary dramatically, depending upon the options chosen.

Examples of funding for state and private forestry programs include cooperative assistance to nonindustrial private owners, assistance to those owners for forest management plans for their land, reforestaton of nonindustrial private lands, and improved utilization of wood.

Compared with 1980, research initiatives under the recommended program would increase. (On December 12, 1980, in Public Law 96-514, 94 stat. 2957, as provided for by the Resources Planning Act of 1974, Congress amended the president's Statement of Policy for implementing the recommended program. The amendment generally endorsed the high bound of the recommended program.)

RPA and land management planning

The Forest Service administers 190 million acres of national forests and grasslands. Regional plans for the system and individual plans for each national forest must likewise tie to the RPA program. So must plans for research and for state and private forestry.

By law, all plans must respond to the RPA program. The 1980 recommended program set the scope and focus of regional plans. The alternatives in regional plans represent different ways to meet regional RPA targets, for example, different mixes of outputs from individual national forests.

In theory, regional plans reconcile the national RPA program with forest or state capabilities. But forest plans must consider a wider range of alternatives to reflect the forest's total capabilities. These "capability alternatives" will then feed back into the next RPA data base. This ascertains how each forest can help meet RPA goals and how it can contribute to setting new goals for the next go-round.

RPA's value to forests of the future

When the late Senator Hubert Humphrey proposed RPA, he had several ideas in mind. First, he was concerned that previous approaches to legislate and plan for one resource at a time, such as timber or recreation, were overlapping on the same land base, so he wanted an assessment of the total forest and rangeland resource. Second, he wanted long-term planning direction for these lands. And third, he wanted the assessment and program to be a funding vehicle and a progress chart for Congress. RPA has the potential to accomplish these goals. From 1977 to 1980, Congress increased Forest Service funding substantially and reordered the agency's priorities. This was during a period of budget cuts for many other agencies.

RPA and the future

If RPA looks at the future of the nation's forests, what about the future of RPA itself? The Forest Service is looking critically at the 1980 assessment and program. Both must be improved where possible. The Forest Service also wants to cooperate closely with its two sister agencies in the 1985 update. Most of all, the agency wants to keep RPA a living, dynamic process.

RPA was meant to change with the nation's needs, to respond to new national priorities. The last several years have shown that it can do just that. It is possible to plan for the long-term future and yet respond to contemporary necessities. This is the true role of any long-range planning. With RPA, the nation's forests of the future are not just a far-distant vision, but a constantly evolving reality, changing as people and the nation change.

19

America's Agricultural Lands: Today and Tomorrow

Robert Gray
Executive director, National Agricultural Lands Study
Washington, D.C.

The National Agricultural Lands Study (NALS) began in June 1979 with a memorandum signed by the secretary of agriculture and the chairman of the Council on Environmental Quality (CEQ) agreeing to co-chair the study, which now involves 12 federal agencies. The work is to be completed January 1, 1981, with a report to the president.

The study's purpose is to measure the causes and extent of farmland conversion nationally and to make whatever legislative or administrative recommendations, if any, are necessary to mitigate some of the impacts of agricultural land conversion.

In the fall of 1979 NALS held 17 public meetings on this issue around the country. About 2,000 people attended and gave us their impression of land problems in their particular communities. In addition, our research staff has worked on a series of technical papers dealing with farmland conversion.

What I would like to address here is what we have seen as a result of our work so far. First, it is clear that concern at the national level grows from the fact that in the last few years our food exports have increased dramatically. Only a decade ago we were exporting as much as one in six acres of our grain crop. Now the figure is about one in three acres, and some of the projections that the Soil and Water Conservation Resources Act (RCA) process has used in other studies show that it is conceivable by the turn of the century that our exports might be as high as 50 percent under certain conditions. So we have tremendous pressures on our land. Our balance of trade, of course, hinges strongly on our continued ability to produce food for export markets. The other area of concern at the national level is what effects federal programs and other federal involvement in such activities as construction of highways, sewage treatment facilities, and housing have on agricultural land.

A data base for NALS

One of the biggest hurdles in starting NALS was to form a data base for use throughout the U.S. Department of Agriculture and the many other participating federal agencies. We used the 1975 Conservation Needs Inventory, the Potential Cropland Study started in 1975, and the National Resource Inventory completed in 1977. We analyzed this information and are using it as a basis for looking at the agricultural land conversion rate that has occurred and for determining the actual cropland phase in the so-called reserve bank.

Why this method? It was pretty obvious to us that this information was clearly the best available. It had been accumulated by an on-the-ground look at land-use changes that had occurred in a decade and probably came as close as any current information in determining what had happened during the late 1960s and through the 1970s. Of course, what was shown was an increase in the conversion rate during the period from 1967 to 1977 of close to three billion acres a year—rural land being converted to other uses—and at least 700,000 acres coming from croplands—some of the better cropland when you consider the reserve figure. Probably close to a million acres of our prime and better cropland are being converted or at least taken out of production for other uses. Whether or not these figures are accurate is something people are going to argue about for a long time, and there is still some disagreement about these figures among U.S. Department of Agriculture agencies. Basically, however, it seems to us that, while the Natural Resource Inventory and other data can be improved in the years ahead to capture more completely land-use changes, the information does form a good basis to begin to look at where we are today.

The important thing now, of course, is to look ahead. NALS is focusing on a 20-year horizon—to the year 2000. We are attempting to foresee what changes are going to take place during the next 20 years and what impact these changes are going to have on agricultural land.

Some elements of the agricultural land issue

During the 1970s, of course, there was a tremendous migration back to rural areas, some of it fed by the improvement of the highway system and some of it probably generated by the fact that land was cheaper in rural areas, the lifestyle better, and the local regulations fewer. Developers found it easier to purchase land and have people move everything from mobile homes to pre-fab homes or custom-built homes onto agricultural lands. We have discovered in rural areas a tremendous increase in the number of septic tanks, siting for homes, individually drilled wells, and fairly large lots. The difference between the figures picked up in the Conservation Needs Inventory and the Natural Resource Inventory showed the acceleration of this trend.

One of the more interesting figures to emerge recently is the amount of acreage in developments less than 10 acres. About 4.5 million acres of land fall into this category. The category is not included in the overall conversion rate because there is no comparable data from the previous decade with which to compare it. But as we look at these changes and examine population trends, the question is what is going to happen in the next 20 years. Household formation after 1990 will probably diminish as the baby boom generation peaks in the 1980s and levels off somewhat. The real question is whether or not people will continue moving to rural areas. If pressure on agricultural land continues to mount during the next two decades as a result of increased household formation in rural areas, this problem will continue to be one of our most difficult.

Another part of this issue relates directly to federal policies and programs. The Environmental Protection Agency (EPA) has less funding available for infrastructure in rural communities. Budget projections show that funds will probably be leveling off or decreasing. This obviously means that there will be less funding available to build such infrastructure as sewage treatment facilities that is needed for rural communities. The effect will be to prevent some of spread of growth.

I have talked with many state and local officials about what changes are going to occur in rural areas in the next 10 to 20 years. Many of them see the current trend continuing because it will still be cheaper for a person to buy a few acres of land in a rural area and build a home than to move into an urban area. This is the basic decision that an individual has to make. The biggest investment that most of us make in our lifetime is our home. Whether or not energy costs escalate is not as much a major factor as what the cost of that home will be and where the home can be located.

Federal policies will have to play a key role in this situation through the Farmers Home Administration, which has tremendous effects on rural areas in funding everything from water lines to sewer lines to houses; through EPA's program; and through the Department of Housing and Urban Development programs and policies enticing people back to urban areas.

The state role in agricultural land protection

I think it is clear that the states must play a key role in considering land-use policy and the effect it is going to have on their agricultural land base.

We have evaluated many state and local programs being used to protect agricultural land. In the study follow-up we will issue a separate reference guide that will evaluate all state and local programs, including programs like Wisconsin's, which uses a variety of tax credits, incentives, zoning, and local planning, and Oregon's, which is more comprehensive. We will consider a variety of other approaches, including purchase of development rights, transfer of development rights, and zoning, which is being practiced now by nearly 250 counties across the country.

If states are going to take a larger part in land-use planning, what kind of help can they get from the federal government? Illinois, for example, has put together a program that gives its agriculture department the opportunity to review state and federal projects that might affect agricultural land. This is one of the first steps a state can take in responding to projects that are going to have an impact on the agricultural land base.

One of the major findings of our study has been the "depermanent" syndrome. Possibly the most serious effect of this first development in rural areas is not necessarily the amount of actual land that it takes out of production but the sort of exaggerated expectations that it creates among farmers concerning the perceived value of their land. Furthermore, complications arise from conflict between farmers and rural residents, such as accessibility to fields and highway use, and many environmental concerns, such as water quality.

These are some of the more significant concerns, and we are going to have to try to deal with them at the federal level, providing states and local governments with a variety of educational information, technical assistance, and other services. We also need to plan at the local level. Many local governments simply are not geared to deal with some of the changes occurring in their areas.

Many people ask whether or not this is a national issue. Of course, it is a national issue. Through its projects, the federal government is constantly involved in making changes in local resource decisions. Of course, the federal government has to be concerned about the available land base because in the long run the local situation has regional impacts, which in turn add up to national impacts. I think that the true test of whether or not our study is successful is whether some of the ideas that we come up with for handling this particular problem can be implemented over the next four or five years in a relatively successful manner.

20

The Agricultural Research System: A New Evaluation

Omer J. Kelley
Contractor, Food and Renewable Resources Program
Office of Technology Assessment
U.S. Congress, Washington, D.C.[1]

Agricultural research is defined broadly to include basic and applied research that directly or indirectly influences the quantity or quality of the food supply. Thus, our definition includes research on both land and aquatic food production as well as research on processing, distribution, marketing, and nutrition. I will not deal with extension and education, even though both of these activities are essential to reap the benefits of research.

Research provides new knowledge and technologies to enhance and sometimes multiply the value of resources. It is a fundamental requirement for the advancement of modern society. The U.S. food and agricultural industry has benefited tremendously from research and is based on an ever-increasing use of new technologies—technologies that have made American agriculture the most efficient agricultural production system in the world (based on manpower inputs per unit of output). The effectiveness of these technologies and the development of new technologies, however, seems to be decreasing at a time when the research problem base is expanding and some problems are intensifying. Further, financial support and professional man-years devoted to many research areas are declining. These and other

---

[1]The ideas expressed in this paper are those of the author and do not necessarily represent the views of the Office of Technology Assessment.

150

problems prompt concern in assessing the future of agricultural research.

I am assisting the Office of Technology Assessment (OTA) of the U.S. Congress in assessing U.S. food and agricultural research. The assessment was requested by the Senate Committee on Appropriations and the Senate Committee on Agriculture, Nutrition, and Forestry. The House Agriculture Subcommittee on Department Investigations, Oversight, and Research has endorsed the request. This assessment is broader than my discussion here; however, many of the issues are closely related. The objectives of the OTA assessment are to: (a) examine the scientific base for establishing national, regional, and local research problems; (b) identify the role of federal, state, and private research institutions in the development of technologies for solutions of national, regional, and state or local problems; (c) evaluate methods by which federal, state, and private research organizations can cooperate in identifying priority research areas and the role of each actor in solving top-priority problems; (d) update evaluations of the adequacy of present research efforts in relation to research priorities for basic, applied, and developmental research; and (e) evaluate public policy options for the Congress that will maximize our research potential.

The agricultural research establishment in the United States

An examination of agricultural research requires an understanding of the institutional structure for agricultural research in the United States. U.S. agricultural research is conducted by both the public and private sectors. In the past, responsibility for publicly supported agricultural research was shared largely by state agricultural experiment stations and the U.S. Department of Agriculture (USDA), and in the private sector by numerous food and agricultural industries or organizations. These organizations have been primarily responsible for the tremendous advances in U.S. agricultural technologies.

The land grant colleges were established by an act of Congress in 1862 (8). As late as 1887 only five colleges had established experiment stations. During the early history of the development of the state agricultural experiment stations, there was concern about the relationship between research stations and the land grant colleges. There was an even greater concern about the acquisition of federal funding through USDA for support of state experiment stations, free from excessive domination by the federal commissioner of agriculture. The Hatch Act of 1887 successfully resolved this issue and provided for a high degree of autonomy for individual states in designing and conducting research.

Additional legislation providing support for state agricultural experiment stations clearly recognizes the stations as distinct entities in the land grant colleges as follows:

1. The Hatch Act of 1887 establishes agricultural experiment stations in connection with the colleges established in several states under provisions of the Morrill Act of 1862 and supplementary acts.

2. The Adams Act of 1906 provides for and regulates an increased annual appropriation for agricultural experiment stations.

3. The Purcell Act of 1925 authorizes the more complete endowment of agricultural experiment stations.

4. The Bankhead-Jones Act of 1935 provides for research into basic laws and principles relating to agriculture. The act also provides for the future development of cooperative agricultural extension work and more complete endowment and support of land grant colleges.

5. The amendment of the Bankhead-Jones Act and the Agricultural Marketing Act of 1946 provides for further research into basic laws and principles relating to agriculture. It also improves and facilitates the marketing and distribution of agricultural products.

6. The Agricultural Act of 1955 consolidates the Hatch Act of 1887 and supplementary laws relating to the appropriaton of federal funds for the support of agricultural experiment stations.

In earlier years, state agricultural experiment stations were concerned almost totally with state and local research problems. However, as they grew, their research broadened to include regional, national, and international activities.

One of the earliest, systematic federal efforts to improve U.S. agriculture dated back to 1819 when the Department of Treasury directed U.S. consulates to collect seeds, plants, and information on crops and soils in their assigned countries (2).

USDA, established May 15, 1862, was given broad authorization "to acquire...useful information on subjects concerned with agriculture in the most general and comprehensive sense of the word" (8). USDA has developed a wide range of research laboratories, stations, and functions that include not only national, regional, and international activities but at times local concerns as well. Some field locations are practically local demonstration farms.

The role of USDA in the national research system has been highly flexible; so has the role of the states. The lack of a hard-and-fast distinction between federal and state responsibilities is well expressed in a statement by a special commission (8) appointed in 1906. It determined that "the organization and policy that in the opinion of the commission should prevail in the expenditure of public money provided for scientific experimentation and research in the interests of agriculture, to the end that such funds shall be applied in the most economical, efficient, and worthy manner in the production of results of permanent value."

The recommendation continued: "There should be a clearer definition of the relative fields of work of the United States Department of Agricuture and the (state) experiment stations. The dominance of the stations within their respective fields should be preserved and their growth fostered, as agencies for the investigation of local questions and of the more individual scientific problems. The federal agency, on the other hand, should cultivate the almost limitless field offered by questions having national or interstate relations, and by those broad scientific problems requiring heavy expenditures, elaborate equipment, long continued study, and the correlation of the results of many investigators, which efforts are usually beyond the means of an individual station. On many questions the harmonious cooperation of the two agencies is essential to the highest efficiency of effort.

"Any research agency charged with a single main line of investigation should be organized so that it may employ within itself all necessary processes in any branch of science. The cooperation of any or all of the departments of an experiment station on a single problem, when necessary, should be a fundamental requirement."

This broad base for application of federal and state resources to research on national, regional, or local problems, together with the recognition of the need for interdisciplinary approaches, as stated in 1906, has been an important factor in U.S. agricultural research for more than half a century.

But it has also led some, including Congress, to question the degree of planning and coordination of existing research, especially at the top levels of administration. There appears to be considerable duplication of effort and competition for funds. The question of research priorities continues to be a subject of disagreement—basic versus applied, commodity versus discipline, marketing versus production, and so on—and Congress and other interested groups have grown increasingly concerned.

Previous studies and reports

Research problems have prompted numerous studies and reports—the Pound Report (6), the World Food and Nutrition Study (5), NAC-BRR (5), and Agricultural and Food Issues and Priorities-USDA (11). The latter study reviewed most of the approximately 50 previous reports and studies dealing with the subject of state, regional, and national research programs and a strategy for their implementation, coordination, and management. Thirty-two of the studies and reports addressed the adequacy of funding of agricultural research and called for its strengthening. In addition, the General Accounting Office released a report in 1977 that focused on how the Agricultural Research Service could improve its research through better internal management (2). One result of these studies was an attempt to coordinate research between USDA and state agricultural experiment stations (SAES) and provide a means to categorize all such research in the Cooperative Research Information System (CRIS). Nevertheless, little attempt if any has occurred to define local, regional, and national problems scientifically. Nor has there been an effort to identify the role of participants in the solution of such problems.

Public Law 95-113 gave clear-cut responsibility to USDA, working with SAES and others, to improve on and identify constraints to these problems. The law clearly spells out the role of USDA and other institutions in the coordination and planning of agricultural research, extension, and teaching. The following are excerpts from this law:

• Responsibilities of the secretary and Department of Agriculture

"Sec. 1405. The Department of Agriculture is designated as the lead agency of the federal government for agricultural research (except with respect to the biomedical aspects of human nutrition concerned with diagnosis or treatment of disease), extension, and teaching in the food and agricultural sciences....

"The Secretary shall coordinate all agricultural research, extension, and teaching activity conducted or financed by the Department of Agriculture and, to the maximum extent practicable, by other agencies of the executive branch of the United States Government."

• Joint Council on Food and Agricultural Sciences

"Sec. 1407. (a) The Secretary shall establish within the Department of Agriculture a committee to be known as the Joint Council on Food and Agricultural Sciences which shall have a term of five years.

"The primary responsibility of the Joint Council shall be to foster coordination of the agricultural research, extension, and teaching activities of the Federal Government, the States, colleges and universities, and other public and private institutions and persons involved in the food and agricultural sciences."

• National Agricultural Research and Extension Users Advisory Board

"Sec. 1408. (a) The Secretary shall establish within the Department of Agriculture a board to be known as the National Agricultural Research and Extension Users Advisory Board which shall have a term of five years.

"The Advisory Board shall have general responsibility for preparng independent advisory opinions on the food and agricultural sciences."

The Joint Council and the Users Advisory Board are operational. A committee on research priorities also has been established.

The Joint Council established an Interim Research Planning Committee having four regional planning councils. This is basically the same research committee structure that existed under the Agricultural Research Policy Advisory Committee. The primary objectives of the Interim Research Planning Committee are to determine local, regional, and national priorities (developing them from local to regional to national) and to provide for cooperation and coordination among the various actors. This structure appears to be effective in obtaining a consensus for priority ratings and in providing a coordinating mechanism. *There is no evidence to date, however, that the Joint Council is identifying state, regional, and national problems, or focusing on which organization should do what.*

Creation of the Science and Education Administration (SEA) (*9*) within USDA was also a response to Title XIV, which emphasized that agricultural research, extension, and teaching are distinct missions of USDA.

Evaluating the private sector

Private industry conducts much food and agricultural research and development that is important to U.S. agriculture (*10*). Private industry in the

U.S. agricultural sector is made up of a large number of individual firms of varying size and diverse interests. Many are too small to be able to conduct their own research and rely on publicly supported research. A lesser number are of sufficient size to have their own research programs. Those that have their own research programs tend to view their role in research and development (R&D) primarily from a business investment standpoint. They conduct research in areas of interest to the company and in areas that may give it proprietary advantages.

Much of the research conducted by agribusiness has general use and is of great value to the public, but agribusiness cannot be depended upon to conduct a wide array of research in any given area. It seems likely that industry might underinvest in research if the public sector were conducting similar research. The public sector, as well as the industrial firms themselves, have difficulty foreseeing what research will be important to agribusiness. Therefore, the public sector must maintain a research effort commensurate with public interest. Even though agribusiness finances research at SAES and other public agencies, the amount and purposes of funds used for in-house research of a proprietary nature usually are unavailable. Thus, it is even more difficult, if not impossible, to evaluate research and technologies developed in this part of industry's activities. Nevertheless, we can evaluate developed technologies and their role in U.S. agriculture, since industry usually tends to finance development at a higher level than basic research.

Industry has been complaining recently that regulatory programs are forcing them to spend more of their research budgets on defensive research just to stay in business and that frequently only a fracton of their research budget can be allocated to investigating new processes and products.

Assessing the future

Thus far we have identified the three main actors in U.S. agricultural research and their past roles. Many factors must be considered in looking ahead at future agricultural research:

General expansion of research areas and a tightening of the national budget for agricultural research. During the last 40 years, federal research and development has included an everwidening array of research. Military, space, health, environment, and energy represent some of the larger areas. In relation to other R&D, support for food and agricultural research and development has declined continually. In its first annual report to the president, the National Agricultural Research and Extension Users Advisory Board indicated that USDA's R&D budget had declined as a percentage of the total R&D budget from 39 percent in 1940 to 2 percent in 1980 (Table 1).[2] The administration's 1980 fiscal year R&D outlays in the current budget

---

[2]Office of Technology Assessment. Project Statement, "U.S. Food and Agricultural Research" assessment, February 8, 1980.

of USDA declined by 2.6 percent from fiscal year 1979, while the average R&D outlay of all federal agencies rose by 7.6 percent during the same period. This certainly indicates a change in emphasis: Agriculture just does not have the priority it once had.

However, funds for food and agricultural research have increased by nearly one-third since 1966, when considered in terms of constant dollars (Table 2). All three performing sectors—USDA, SAES, and industry—have contributed to the increase, but there are marked differences among them. The increase in constant dollars in SAES has been 40 percent (nonfederal support) compared to 32 percent in USDA and 26 percent in industry.

Even though funds have increased in terms of constant dollars, the cost of conducting research has increased even more. Research now requires more sophisticated and costly equipment and support staff than it did 10 years ago. For example, new research horizons, such as genetic engineering and systems approaches to agriculture, are much more costly than past traditional research. Also, in additon to the traditional research areas, such as production efficiency, resource conservation, and crops and livestock, there are many new areas of concern that require research, such as energy, organic farming, environmental concerns, community services, living standards of rural people, and consumer health and well-being. Many research areas thus are receiving less funding today than before because the total research funds are being applied to additional research areas that require considerable support.

Scientific man-years may be even more important than dollars. As stated earlier, constant dollar funds have increased about 30 percent since 1966. The total number of scientists has increased overall by only 10 percent. In USDA the number of scientists actually decreased since 1966. These data, if indicative of things to come, show that U.S. agricultural research faces serious problems both in funding and in staff scientists.

Sylvan Wittwer (13) recently compared U.S. and Soviet Union agricultural research. He pointed out that in the mid-1970s, one-third of the world's agricultural research was conducted in the United States. This is no longer true. In 1968 the Soviets edged out the United States in percentage of gross national product (GNP) committed to total R&D. Today they are spending 3.4 percent of their GNP on R&D. The United States commits 2.2 percent.

Table 1. Federal and USDA R&D budget.

Fiscal Year	Total Federal R&D Budget Amount ($ million)	USDA Percentage of Total R&D Budget
1940	74	39
1950	1,083	5
1960	7,744	2
1970	15,736	2
1980	31,165	2

Table 2. Expenditures for food and agricultural research by performers.*

Year	SAES	USDA	Industry	Total
		million	$	
1966	$230	$132	$321	$ 684
1967	280	139	346	766
1968	270	132	381	784
1969	292	137	403	834
1970	314	150	444	909
1971	336	162	450	949
1972	356	211	448	1,015
1973	384	220	497	1,102
1974	423	228	574	1,226
1975	482	248	612	1,343
1976	517	280	695	1,492
1977	594	322	750	1,666
		1966 constant dollars = 100		
1966	100	100	100	100
1967	118	103	105	109
1968	109	93	110	106
1969	112	92	111	108
1970	115	96	116	112
1971	117	98	112	111
1972	118	122	107	114
1973	121	121	112	117
1974	122	114	118	119
1975	126	114	115	118
1976	129	122	124	125
1977	140	132	126	132

*OTA Project Statement, "U.S. Food and Agricultural Research" assessment, February 8, 1980.

In agricultural research the difference is even greater. The Soviets have more than 60,000 agricultural scientists and 150,000 supporting personnel. In the United States there are about 12,000 agricultural scientists supported by public funds (USDA and SAES) and another 12,000 to 13,000 supported by private industry, making a total of some 25,000.

What is the appropriate level of federal support for agricultural research? This includes funds, scientists, and other resources. This question is not peculiar to agricultural research—it is the same question being asked in other areas of research. Nor is it easy to answer. It can be related to size of the industry, level of support per scientist, or to a number of different parameters.

In any event, research is nearly always associated with problem solving. There must be problems to solve for research to be relevant, and these must be easily reviewed and identified as part of the budget-justifying process. In the health field, everyone knows someone who has a heart problem, cancer, or any of a number of other health problems. It is easy to perceive these problems and judge them to be important. Quite the opposite is true in agriculture. Few people perceive that we have problems in agriculture. U.S. agriculture provides an ample surplus of nutritious food at low cost for all Americans and has enough left over to help feed much of the world. Why do we need agricultural research? Those of us interested in agricultural research have a real challenge in articulating the problems and the role of research in providing the scientific and technological advances necessary for the future well-being of agriculture in its broadest concept. If this is done effectively to both laymen and legislatures, it will be much easier to obtain adequate support for agricultural research.

A perception that the national research effort is not organized and managed well. Previously, I identified the three early actors and their roles in U.S. agricultural research. The number of actors has been steadily increasing. Today they include: USDA, which has three research agencies—Agricultural Research (AR), Cooperative Research (CR), and Economics, Statistics, and Cooperatives Service (ESCS) (this paper deals with food issues; hence, Forest Service research is not included); at least nine additional federal agencies [Department of Defense (DOD), Department of Energy (DOE), Department of Health and Human Services (DHHS), Department of Interior (DOI), Department of State (DOS, including the Agency for International Development, AID), Environmental Protection Agency (EPA), National Oceanic and Atmospheric Administration (NOAA), National Science Foundation (NSF), Tennessee Valley Authority (TVA)]; 56 state agricultural experiment stations, 61 schools of forestry, 16 land grant colleges of 1890, Tuskegee Institute, non-land-grant universities, colleges of veterinary medicine, and numerous private food and agricultural industries and foundations.

Yet there is no formal understanding of who does what. Mechanisms have been set up for coordination among federal agencies and between USDA and SAES, and to a lesser degree with other research organizations. However, coordination is one thing; research planning and administration is another. The question has been raised: Is there a rationale, scientific or otherwise, for determining which organization should do what? This includes private industry. There are those who believe that improved administration and management among federal, state, and private sectors could produce more efficient use of research funds. Others maintain that too much administration and management is detrimental to efficient research. This is an area of great concern to many people, especially the researchers and the Congress. Publicly supported agricultural researchers must develop a management system upon which they can agree and that identifies who does or should do what and/or their relationship to each other. If agricultural research is to receive the support it deserves and must have for the well-being of not only the U.S. agricultural industry but also consumers, we must articulate these research problems and work to produce sound solutions for them.

Some perceive problems not only with how the research organizations do or do not work together but with the lack of management within the organizations. Consider some questions with respect to SEA/AR and the SAES.

ARS within USDA was reorganized in 1972. This reorganization set up what appears to be four autonomous regions for the present SEA/AR. These regions were divided into two or three state areas, each with an area director who some believe is also autonomous. Successful management requires many things—essential among them being the control of funds and the authority to advance and locate staff and provide facilities and other resources. The responsibilities of AR are usually associated with regional, national, and some international activities, yet there is the perception that no technical staff within AR has these types of responsibilities along with any control of the resources. It seems that the area directors may be simply conducting research on the basis for two or three states versus the experiment station directors conducting research on a one-state basis, and thus it appears that AR may have lost its ability to plan and carry out regional and national research programs.

At one time the staff of SAES was nearly all full-time research workers, and most, if not all, of their resources came through the experiment station directors. Over the years most of SAES's staff has become involved in instruction and/or extension. They now have two or three "bosses." Some observers feel that the ability of an experiment station director and other state research administrators to plan and carry out a research program has been severely eroded. The easy availability to staff of public and private grant or contract funds adds to the staff independence, sometimes further distancing researchers from problems of the state.

Whether or not these perceptions are true, they deserve consideration. If they are true, are they beneficial or detrimental to the overall research objectives? These and other questions need to be answered as interest in agricultural research intensifies, and this interest includes not only supporters of research but also detractors.

Problems not only exist with how the various researchers work together but with methods of funding, particularly at the federal level. The Hatch Act funds have been allotted to SAES by formula and are referred to as formula funding. This is the only federal research program funded by this process. Some concede that there may have been a need for formula funding in the early days of agricultural research, but question it today. If there is a need, what is the rationale for this need? What is the role of competitive grant funding?

Some contend that research quality is higher under competitive grant funding than formula funding. What are the facts? One thing is certain: Money is harder to get at the federal level and probably will become even more difficult with time. There are many who believe, and this includes members of Congress and the Office of Management and Budget (OMB), that the administration and management of U.S. agricultural research can be improved. Some say research cannot be managed and be effective. However, certain facets of research—allocating funds to priority problems, insuring that such funds are used properly, insuring that scientists have adequate facilities and funds, insuring that the appropriate mix of scientific disciplines are available, and insuring that the products are of high quality—are subject to some degree of management. Once the problem and area of investigation have been identified, however, the scientists' freedom must be safeguarded to attack the problems as they see fit. This assumes some duplication of effort (which is considered necessary for efficient research) because different scientists will attack the problem in different ways.

The private sector conducts about one-half of all U.S. R&D. Individual firms usually consider investment in research as any other investment—namely, from the profit motive. The present administration and recent past administrations have attempted to shift some of the R&D effort (especially post-harvest technology) from the public to the private sector. They rationalized that the private sector was conducting this type of research already and the public sector should not be duplicating their effort. Generally, each time the administration proposed a decrease, Congress has restored most of the funds. The shift in R&D to the private sector has been attempted with no overall plan for the role of each actor—SEA/AR, SAES, and private industry. There was no evaluation of what might happen to U.S. R&D efforts if the private sector were to change its share of R&D. However, some believe that as long as federal funds are available for certain types of research, private sources will not be. Similarly, if federal sources were discontinued, private funding would become available. The ramifications of this funding change have not been explored. The principle concern, it seems, is determining what research needs are best addressed by whom. As indicated earlier, to date no scientific basis has been used to determine national, regional, or local research problems; the role of the various actors—federal agencies, SAES, and private industry—is not well defined. And there is a question of whether present methods are satisfactory in bringing expertise and interest of federal, state, and industrial organizations together on the identification and conduct of priority research.

Research priorities. As funds become tighter and agricultural problems grow, the problem of identifying research priorities becomes more important. There are several levels or magnitudes requiring priority determination, and there are a number of actors involved in setting priorities. One level concerns policy. This level decides how much funding is available for total U.S. research and how much is assigned specifically to agriculture. Certainly each agency conducting research, OMB, the Office of Science and Technology Policy (OSTP), the Congress, and the president, are involved at the policy level. Within the agricultural arena, these same officials have some input into where and how much money is appropriate. USDA develops a budget that by the nature of its breakdown identifies areas of priorities. These are nearly always changed in review by OMB (including OSTP) and actions by the Congress.

How much of this process represents improvement of the agricultural research effort? Some changes and specifications may be so specific as to affect given field locations. After funds are approved for given lines of work—regional activities, local stations, SAES, etc.—in each region, state, or location, additional priorities must be made. What is the role of USDA, research agencies, experiment station directors, scientists, producers, processors, labor, consumers, and regulatory agencies in setting priorities? Certainly at the project level the scientist has the comparative advantage. But all of these other interested groups are becoming more involved. The lawsuit involving the *California Agrarian Action Project* v. *the University of California* is a good example. There are mechanisms for involving most of these interested groups in one way or another. Are they sufficient? The future will probably see greater effort to involve the more interested groups in more meaningful ways.

In the OTA assessment three papers pertaining to priorities are being prepared. One deals with how we say priorities are determined, the second with how priorities are actually determined (and in some cases there are considerable differences), and the third with how priorities should be determined. This paper will include a review of the latest applicable scientific methodology.

There are crops and other areas of research that some believe are not now receiving sufficient research attention under our present methods of setting priorities. These include both new food and industrial crops. The NSF (7) has studied this subject and in two volumes gives reasons why research efforts should be stepped up on some 20 crops.

Consider guayule, a good example of one of these crops. It appears to have considerable economic and strategic potential. In 1942 the U.S. government initiated the Emergency Rubber Project, a massive effort that eventually involved more than 1,000 scientists and technicians and 9,000 support staff to develop guayule rubber. By 1945 some 32,000 acres of guayule had been planted in Texas, Arizona, and California. Fifteen tons of guayule rubber could be processed daily at facilities in California (3).

The end of World War II brought a severe setback to guayule rubber. Natural rubber was available again, and rapid developments in the synthetic rubber industry seemed to make guayule obsolete. Thousands of acres of guayule were dramatically burned off to make way for orange groves, and by 1953 all federal and most private research on guayule had ended.

To the surprise of many forecasters, the synthetics never completely replaced natural rubber, although they did come to claim about 70 percent of the world market. Natural rubber continued to be preferred in applications that demanded high elasticity, resilience, tackiness, and low heat buildup. Natural rubber is an indispensable component of tires for buses, trucks, and airplanes where frictional heat buildup is a major cause of failure, and is used in most of the recently introduced, increasingly popular radial auto tires.

Suddenly, however, the U.S. supply of rubber again seemed to be extremely uncertain. The formation of OPEC led to dramatically increasing costs and decreasingly dependable supplies of petroleum feedstocks for synthetic rubber.

The demand for natural rubber continues to increase at a steady rate and will likely outstrip supply by the late 1980s—a situation that could be further complicated by cartel-type arrangements among rubber-producing countries. Hence many concerned persons and institutions are again turning to guayule as a major source of rubber.

But in view of the difficulty of obtaining increased funds for agricultural research and its low priority in USDA, it is unlikely that guayule will ever receive the attention it needs through the agricultural budget. If DOD decided that guayule rubber were critical, sufficient research funds might be made applicable to develop guayule into a stable commercial crop. To accomplish this will require a sizeable research effort on a continuing basis, but an investment that is small compared to the value of a domestic source of natural rubber. Guayule and a number of other potentially important crops to the United States are not now receiving adequate priority. Some means need to be found to correct this situation.

Beneficiaries of agricultural research. The question of who are the beneficiaries of agricultural research is being asked more frequently, particularly in relation to who should pay for agricultural research. It has generally been assumed that the public is the ultimate beneficiary. Undoubtedly, the public or consumer benefits greatly from agricultural research, but are there groups that benefit more than others? Farm size has increased drastically over the past 50 years. Most farmers have the capacity to store one or more years' crops to wait for improved markets. This gives them the opportunity to have an increasing share of the new benefits of research. But as more of U.S. crops are marketed overseas, the benefits of this portion of production go increasingly to the farmer and the middleman handling the sale and transportation of these commodities. However, some of the benefits still go to the public in the forms of increased foreign exchange and balance of payments. Processors and retailers share not only from research directed to their part of the industry but also from increased efficiency and improved quality of farm production.

Farm labor has benefited in terms of increased wages and less drudgery, but has been harmed in the loss of jobs caused by increased use of chemicals and equipment. Other beneficiaries include the research worker and research institutions. With the sale of more farm products overseas, the foreign consumer is becoming a larger beneficiary. The future will see a better understanding of these benefits, and it is likely that this information will play a role in future research policy and funding.

Productivity of agricultural research. Many investigators have studied productivity of agricultural research. Evenson and others (1) recently summarized a number of these investigations. Although various aspects of economic returns were studied, only the annual rate of return will be considered here. They broke the period from 1868 to 1971 into three periods based on availability and detail of data. All agricultural research during the period from 1868 to 1926 had an annual rate of return of 65 percent. During the period from 1927 to 1950, the researchers broke agricultural research into technology-oriented and science-oriented research, which they defined as follows: technology-oriented—research where new technology was the prime objective (includes plant breeding, agronomy, animal production, farm management)—and science-oriented—research answering scientific questions relating to production of new technology (genetics, biology, zoology, etc.). During this period, technology-oriented research had an annual rate of return of 95 percent and science-oriented research 110 percent. During the period from 1948 to 1971, another segment was broken out—namely, farm management and agriculture extension. During this period, technology-oriented research had an annual rate of return of 130 percent for the South, 93 percent for the North, and 95 percent for the West. The researchers attributed the high value in the South to a lower level of research there prior to this time period. Science-oriented research had an overall annual rate of return of 45 percent, and the annual rate of return from farm management and agricultural extension was 110 percent.

All of these are phenomenal rates of return. They indicate a gross underinvestment in agricultural research. The authors related this underinvestment primarily to two cases. They state that the consumers are the primary beneficiaries of research, but that the individual consumer receives such a small share of the benefits that he does not recognize it. As a result, consumers support collective actions only when food prices rise rapidly. They further state that much of the political legislative history of farm support since the mid-1920s can be viewed as a effort to slow the transfer of gains to the consumer.

The annual rate of returns referred to here does not include some social and environmental gains and losses. In the future, all benefits and costs—to all members of society—will be important in considering agricultural research productivity. Both those who gain and those who lose will need to do a better job of communicating their interests to the legislatures, Congress, and concerned institutions.

The role of the United States in international agricultural research. In order to keep pace with population growth and rising food demand, developing countries must increase their food production by at least 4 percent per year over the next quarter century—a rate significantly higher than historical performance. Most of the increases will have to come from increased yields on land now under cultivation. This will require strengthening national research systems in developing countries and developing new and better technologies for various climates and soils of the respective developing countries. The U.S. agricultural research community has the capability and the responsibility to assist with these tasks. Even though the U.S. capability for agricultural research in temperate agriculture is among the best in the world, it is obvious to most who have worked in the tropics and subtropics that we, like so many others, still have much to learn. Public Law 89-808, Section 406, authorizes USDA to conduct research in tropical and subtropical agriculture. An amount not to exceed $33 million for any given year was authorized for activities described in this section. The administration has requested only a small amount of money over the years, and this year the budget contained slightly over $2 million for this purpose. This is not enough for a meaningful program.

AID has the main responsibility for assisting less-developed countries to improve their economic development and well-being. This includes agriculture. A primary contribution to a country's lack of development is a lack of technology and its use in maximizing their resources. This is true for agriculture as well as other sectors of the economy. AID has had a great deal of difficulty in finding ways to bring to the less-developed countries the capability in U.S. agricultural research and technology on agricultural problems. Public Law 94-161, Title XII, authorized a closer linkage with the land grant colleges and others in this effort as well as a Board for International Food and Agriculture Development (BIFAD). It appears to many that little progress has been made in getting U.S. technical expertise into country program planning and execution. The charges are still made that AID is without a technical capability, that AID has no recognized scientists or people with technical capability at the decision-making level in Washington or as mission directors in the field. Yet agriculture is the major industry in most developing countries, and until progress is made in agriculture it is unlikely that general economic development will improve.

Many believe that if the U.S. agricultural scientific community is to play its full role in international agricultural development, there will have to be an upgrading of the importance of international agriculture in both AID and USDA—in AID from the standpoint of internal management and in USDA from the standpoint of resource allocation.

Much progress, however, has been made in certain areas of international agricultural research, especially the international agricultural research centers and their outreach programs. AID is a foremost supporter of these centers, and frequently AID and other bilateral programs support the outreach activities. The Green Revolution of the late 1960s and early 1970s was an outgrowth of these activities, as have been other recent increases in food production in a number of developing countries.

Summary

U.S. agriculture has benefited tremendously from research, and continued agricultural productivity is dependent upon an ever-increasing use of new technologies. Recently the agricultural research base has widened. Agricultural problems have grown more complex, and requirements to meet research of regulatory agencies have increased. At the same time there has been a decreasing emphasis on agricultural research in relation to other research areas and a continuing loss of positions for inhouse research at the federal level.

The number of actors in agricultural research has grown considerably over the years. There seems to be no agreed-upon criteria, scientific or otherwise, for determining the role of the various actors. While productivity of agricultural research remains high, this has not been translated into effective demand for increased research. The role of the various sectors of society that are affected by agricultural research, in setting research priorities and as beneficiaries, is poorly articulated. And the effectiveness of the U.S. scientific community in international agricultural research has been limited severely by a lack of technical competence at the decision-making levels in AID and a lack of interest or high priority in USDA.

The future will see a greater interest in these problems by all affected groups, and much more attention and responsiveness will be necessary at the administrative levels of the various actors in agricultural research if U.S. agricultural research is to prosper and carry out its function and responsibilities effectively.

The U.S. system of agricultural research, while seemingly complex, has a simple structure. Essentially, it is a composite of national, regional, and local programs with varying degrees of cooperation and participation from USDA, states, and private resources. The system has served U.S. agriculture well, and criticisms are not leveled at destroying the system, but at preserving it. For any cooperative system to work well, the cooperators must know and understand their respective roles. And each must be strong.

REFERENCES

1. Evenson, Robert E., Paul F. Waggoner, and Vernon W. Ruttan. 1979. *Economic benefits from research: An example from agriculture.* Science 205: 1,101-1,107.
2. General Accounting Office. 1977. *Management of agricultural research: Need and opportunities for improvement.* Washington. D.C.
3. Lawless, Edward W., and Ralph R. Wilkinson. 1980. *Guayule—rubber crop of the future.* Midwest Research Institute, Kansas City, Missouri.
4. Moseman, Albert H. 1970. *Building agricultural research systems in the development nations.* Agriculture Development Council, Washington, D.C.
5. National Academy of Sciences, Board on Agriculture and Renewable Resources. 1975. *The world food and nutrition study.* Washington, D.C.
6. National Academy of Sciences, Committee on Research Advisory to the U.S. Department of Agriculture. 1975. *The Pound report.* Washington, D.C.
7. National Science Foundation. 1975. *Feasibility of introducing food crops better adapted to environmental stress.* Volumes 1, 3. Washington, D.C.
8. U.S. Department of Agriculture. 1962. *A history of research policy and procedure.* Miscellaneous Publication 904. Cooperative State Experiment Station Service, Washington, D.C.
9. U.S. Department of Agriculture. 1980. *USDA's Science and Education Administration. What it is—what it does.* Washington, D.C.
10. U.S. Department of Agriculture, Agricultural Research Institute. 1977. *Survey of U.S. agricultural research by private industry.* Washington, D.C.
11. U.S. Department of Agriculture and National Association of State Universities and Land Grant Colleges. 1978. *Agriculture and food research issues and priorities—a review and assessment.* Washington, D.C.
12. Wittwer, Sylvan. 1980. *U.S. and Soviet agricultural research agendas.* Science 208(4,441).

21

Making Choices for the Future: The Critical Role of the Conservation Professional

Robert Theobald

President, Participation Publishers, Wickenburg, Arizona

How many of you read science fiction? How many of you don't read science fiction? How many of you don't know if you read science fiction? That question used to get a titter a couple of years ago, but the response is moving rapidly toward a belly laugh because people are very nervous about the news these days. It is not at all clear whether what we are reading is real or whether it is science fiction.

One reason is because there is an enormous split now between the public and the private dialogue. We say things to each other in private that we are not prepared to say in public, for what seem to be good and sufficient reasons to us. But I am going to suggest to you that they are not good and sufficient reasons. It is time for us to level with each other in places where we can be heard and quoted.

How many of you believe in extrasensory perception (ESP)? How many of you don't believe in ESP? How many of you don't know?

How many of you believe that our educational system is preparing people for the world in which they are going to live? (Response: less than 1 percent.) A 1 percent response is usually very high in any audience.

How many of you believe that we are going to be able to maintain full employment by any reasonable definition? (Response: less than 1 percent.) This group is even less optimistic than many. It is therefore time that we come to grips with new issues.

I want to suggest to you that the failure of this year's election process is because people know a change has to happen and that none of the candidates are speaking to that reality. John Anderson, and I hope that I am not treading on anybody's toes, is what I call a vacuum candidate, called into existence by the frustration about candidates of both major parties. People are ready for change and are aware that the election process is not dealing with that issue.

Some credentials

What gives me a right to be at this podium? First, I have worked for the Office of Technology Assessment on two studies in the last three years, one on residential energy consumption and another dealing with biomass. The biomass study says, as many of you have seen in the press, that we can produce a significant proportion of America's energy from biomass, about 20 percent if good management decisions are made.

That leads me to my second experience, which was with the U.S. Department of Agriculture (USDA). I was invited to a meeting on renewable natural resources as one of the keynote speakers and was rude enough to entitle my speech, "Why effective management is today impossible." I was rude enough to tell those present why the conference would not work as it was set up, and I was further rude enough during the conference to say that it was not working. USDA is the only organization to whom I have given that treatment and not been chucked out by my neck. Instead they gave me a contract.

That says something interesting about USDA. While I would like to believe that most administrators are in the business of accepting criticism, it is not normally my experience. Administrators tend to be defensive about criticism. To find the level of openness in USDA that said "OK, you've raised questions that we ought to deal with" was to me exciting and surprising. The report that came out of my USDA experience I believe is one of the most remarkable educational tools available, not only within the U.S. government but within the overall educational movement in terms of what is going to happen to us in the future.

The third experience I bring is that of a small town person—a small town person from the West. Following a recent comment, I should state that I too feel the West does not get a fair share. I also feel that if the East does not realize that the West is not getting its fair share and that the West is becoming extremely powerful, we are going to see strong dangers of regionalism in the worst possible sense. My views on this subject were picked up recently in one of the Arizona papers. It was quite startling to me how many people now agree with what I said about the costs of growth. If America expects the West to provide its energy, it is going to have to come up with fairer methods of dealing with the secondary consequences of development.

If America is going to stop losing an enormous amount of agricultural land, it is going to have to strengthen its small towns and counties in ways far beyond current thinking. The movement into rural areas started in the mid-1970s and was not understood until the late 1970s. I worked with a reporter as late as this year in describing that trend in the *Wall Street Journal*. It is still not perceived as a major national trend, and its potential for disruption, particularly in the Sun Belt where you have migration from north to south and from urban to rural, is quite extraordinary.

I am a small town person in one other sense. That is, I watch us struggling in our communities with bureaucracies. I hear a lot of agencies saying, "We would like to help you." I go to those agencies (and obviously with the reputation I have I have a lot more leverage than the average small-town guy), and I say, "What do you mean and how real is your offer to help us?" I find the mesh between what we want and what these agencies will give is bad at best and disastrous at worst. What I usually hear is this, "Yes, we have a program, and if you can fit into our program, we would love to help you, but don't expect us to fit into your needs." If we mean our rhetoric about helping people resolve their own problems, if we mean our rhetoric about farmers and ranchers working out of their perceived self-interest, we are going to have to make much bigger changes in the way we run our systems than is under consideration at this time.

I am extremely impressed that the Resources Conservation Act effort tried a citizen participation process, but when I hear that they tried to process 1.5 million comments, I know that nothing "real" happened. The only place citizen participation can work is in a local area where there is an opportunity to truly affect local dynamics. That is what has to begin to happen, and this implies a fundamentally different institution than we now have. I use institution in the classic anthropological sense. If you remember your sociology, bureaucracies are set up to manage stable systems. The whole point about today's world is that our systems are not stable, and bureaucracies therefore are not good forms for managing them.

Bringing about change

I want to give one other quiz. How many of you found the picture presented in Gerald Barney's discussion of the Global 2000 Report to be credible and reflecting your view of the future? How many of you did not? How many of you are not sure? You need to be sure, not because he is necessarily right, but because if he is we face a quite different situation than we have ever faced in the past.

I believe Mr. Barney is right. I believe he is right in his comment that the problems are understated. And I believe above all that the study's time frame is much too optimistic; the crunch is now, not in the year 2000. If we are to affect those dilemmas and directions, it will be on the basis of changes and policies over the next five years. That does not mean everything has to happen in the next five years, but it does mean we must start to shift our policies in the next five years.

Now you can say to me, look at the political picture. Fundamental change clearly is not possible. The whole point I am making, though, is that it clearly is possible. People are ready for change. The failure is not in people, the failure is in the political process that refuses to listen to people and their readiness. If you don't believe that, go out and talk to the people in your hometown. I can give you lots of evidence, but you must find it for yourself if you are to believe it.

I am not saying we know all of the things we need to do. Yes, a lot of people will say, "Isn't it possible to go back to the good old days?" It is not a totally bright picture I am painting, but I am saying that people know that the status quo model is not working. And I also know that people will buy into a model that suggests we can create a more human and humane society, that they do believe we can cope with what I call the driving forces, the fact that the world is changing, must change, but that we can act to create a more human and humane society.

The coming communications era

Let me state my central argument briefly. A large proportion of the population is now aware that we are in the middle of a transition from the industrial era to the communications era. This shift is causing changes in attitudes and values as profound as those that took place as we moved from the agricultural era to the industrial era. But these alterations are taking place far more rapidly and, indeed, are concentrated in the 1980s.

I want to give some evidence of these contentions, if I may. I visited Dallas recently to work with Eastfield Community College. We decided to discuss our concerns about rapid change. We went to four groups—the Jaycees, the YWCA, a church, and the college itself. I first presented the fact that change was coming, why it was coming, that the relationship between rich and poor countries was changing, that migration factors were moving us, that telecommunications were moving us....

By the way, one of the remarkable things we have not mentioned this morning is the fact that the world will be changed radically by telecommunications in the next decade. One more quiz: How many of you feel you have any sense of the telecommunications and the microelectronic revolution that is taking place? Your response (about 15 percent) is encouraging. It is the best response I have ever seen and it fits with what I am hearing in USDA, the Forest Service, and the Science and Education Administration, all of which have been pushing this revolution. Most audiences have no sense of how changes in communication will profoundly alter the world. Home computers are now down to $400. They will cost less than $100 by the end of the decade, which means they will be much cheaper than color television. Office computers will cost less than $1,000. How are people going to compete?

It follows that the recession through which we are moving is not an "economic" recession but a "structural" recession. What do I mean? We said we must use less energy. Less energy means fewer cars, which in turn means less mileage, right? What happens? If you are going to produce fewer cars, somebody is going to get in trouble. Well, who got into trouble? Chrysler! We then said, "No, we are not going to allow that to happen." So instead we put the whole auto industry into a bind, and the car manufacturers managed to lose $1.5 billion in one quarter. We have done great harm by refusing to accept that there is structural change going on and that there must be structural change.

We can also look at home building. We can do a lot more with a lot less space. I suspect that we will all have to use less space than we have become used to. Go back a hundred years and think what sort of space a family "needed" and think what we have grown used to, then wonder whether we can really maintain our present standards. Can we have the level of household formation that we are talking about that assumes cheap housing, or are we going to see the re-creation of the extended family? Mobility created the nuclear family. It is pretty clear to me that mobility is going to decline. It is too expensive. People are ready for change.

To return to Dallas. We got through the discussion of change, which normally bogs people down. We went on to ask what we might do about this? All of the groups involved decided to bring in people to meetings to take the discussion further. You know the defense mechanisms we all have to prevent action. We have all sorts of skills. One of the best ones is "Well, we haven't quite discussed this far enough to come up with an action model."

The fact that four groups were willing to forego this defensive pattern is to me extraordinary. It suggests that we have a small window of time. It is small because the chances of moving into an authoritarian society here and in the rest of the world, together with the chances of moving into protectionist systems here and in the rest of the world, are very high. The chances of trouble between north and south, in other words the rich and the poor countries where the dialogue has broken down, is very high. And the chances of major trouble between East and West as Russia comes to a time where her oil supplies begin to be a limit to growth is very high.

One of the most terrifying developments of the last few years has been the re-creation of the possibility of nuclear war. I thought one of the things we had achieved in the 1970s was to recognize that there were no victors in nuclear war. I thought we had also come to understand that there is no scenario one can write about a limited nuclear exchange that makes sense. People write scenarios about limited nuclear exchanges assuming that war is a rational process. Some of you went through a war, and you know it is not rational. The idea that a country that has just had a nuclear bomb dropped on it is going to sit down and talk about how it should react is not very probable.

We must start thinking about new ways of resolving disputes. In the end, the Global 2000 report comes down to a matter of how we create new national discussion and transnational discussion. There are no channels presently available for the sort of discussion that we ought to be having because you cannot solve questions by violence anymore, either internally or externally. Violence is too dangerous; we are going to have to learn to cooperate. We traditionally define peace as the absence of war. That is not enough. Peace is the ability to maintain a functioning world without war, which is a very different statement.

What "you" can do

Now some things you can do. You—because change is not going to come out of Washington. If it is going to come from anywhere, it is going to come out of our small towns and our cities and our states.

First, the report I wrote for USDA, "Challenges in Renewable Natural Resources," enables you, and any audience you choose to work with, to look at the new issues, discuss them, and decide whether you want to move on them. The report begins with today's driving forces. These are written in terms of a report to the president suggesting that the president should hold some sort of national meeting to enable people to understand those driving forces. It ends up with material on natural resource issues. In between are some scenarios for the year 2000 and a statement on the social issues and how they can be managed. Social issues were stated in terms of television programs we could produce to enable people to look at such issues as employment, health, housing, etc.

The report is designed for people to use in the field. It is a report supported by USDA, which gave me remarkable freedom to write it. It has the support of the secretary. The problem is distributing it, because we are not used to doing this sort of thing through these channels. If we are going to face fundamental issues, you are going to have to ask Washington, "Why haven't we heard more about this? We are willing to support it; we want to see it happen."

The report is also available on a computer system. We have created, again with USDA support, what we call a computer educational system, a programmed educational system. (The distinction here is between programmed training and programmed education. Training says you have a fixed body of knowledge, and we will take that body of knowledge and run you through it until you get it right: Two plus two equals four! If you do not understand that, we will take you through a new group of loops until you do understand that two plus two equals four. Our system presents a body of knowledge that you must interact with and improve.)

My report argues that we have to choose among alternative futures. A biomass future is radically different from other futures, not only in patterns of land use but in the attitudes and values of society. The problem is that the important issues of this moment are not quantifiable. We must talk about value shifts. We have a wasteful culture. It was the way to make the industrial system function. If we now need a nonwasteful culture, we require profound value shifts.

Here is a second suggestion: rural development councils. Let me suggest to you that those states that have not yet created rural development councils could create them in a way that would not be top-down models but bottom-up models. Are you willing to truly give power to people? Use a videotape recorder to start discussions in small communities. Ask people in small communities, on the basis of a meeting with its total power structure—everything from 4-H to the city council to the churches to the schools—what their priorities are and ask them to elect delegates to a governor's conference. I wonder how many states would be prepared to allow the agenda to be set that way, rather than through the agriculture department?

My challenge to you, therefore, is to deal with these issues in your state. Change your priorities by recognizing that the key issue is not conservation, although heaven knows this is important, but that conservation is impossible without changes in values. While you are saving one farm by getting somebody to till it properly, you are losing another dozen because somebody has put a subdivision in. It is much easier to have narrow vision; I know that. A lot of mornings I wake up wishing I could go back to having narrow vision, but that kind of attitude will not help deal with the issues we all care about.

A third suggestion would be to support the leadership in USDA by making it clear that the field is willing to move. Remember, USDA is under political pressure. All bureaucracies, all institutions in Washington, are under political pressure. One of your jobs is to use your political representatives to make it clear that the issues of attitudes and values are important and must be handled. The issues discussed in the Global 2000 Report must be handled, but handled in a way that is truly democratic.

Finally, we need to make up our minds about whether we are indeed going to struggle to be the country the founding fathers envisioned. If the founding fathers were here today, they would be horrified. This is not the society they thought about. It does not have the values they believed in, and it certainly does not have the political system they thought about. A part of the problem is that we have grown so much. Our forefathers thought in terms of a population of 12 million to 15 million people existing in the eastern part of the country. Now, we are 225 million people spread across the whole continent. The time has come to go back and ask how the dreams of the founding fathers can be realized under the actual conditions of today.

Choosing between better or worse

What I want to leave with you is my conviction and that of many futurists, business people, and decison makers that during the 1980s society, both at the national and world levels, will either have to start to improve significantly or it will get significantly worse. There are going to be drastic breaks in trend during this decade. As the Chinese put it, this will lead to crises, and in these crises there are two possibilities—one danger and one opportunity. At the moment we are heading straight for danger because we are not willing to cope with these issues.

To return to an old lesson: We must admit, first, that the emperor has no clothes on; second, that he is about to catch double pneumonia; third, that the antibiotics we got for him do not work because he has had it too many times before; and fourth, that it is our job, not somebody else's, to find him some clothes to put on and convince him he is not wearing any.

The key issue we face is this: Can we learn to cooperate? When we interact with people, are we going to be afraid that their prime motivation is to "take us," or are we going to believe that we can work with, learn with, and cooperate with other people? If we cannot take that first step, we have no hope. If we can, perhaps we will create the sort of world we all want.

VI. Resource Conservation Technology for the Future

22

CREAMS: A System for Evaluating Best Management Practices

W. G. Knisel

*Hydraulic Engineer, Southwest Rangeland Watershed
Research Center, Science and Education Administration—
Agricultural Research, Tucson, Arizona*

and

G. R. Foster

*Hydraulic Engineer, Science and Education
Administration—Agricultural Research
West Lafayette, Indiana*

Mathematical models to assess nonpoint-source pollution and evaluate the effects of management practices are needed to respond adequately to the water quality legislation of the past 10 years. Action agencies must assess nonpoint-source pollution from agricultural areas, identify problem areas, and develop conservation practices to reduce or minimize sediment and chemical losses from fields where potential problems exist. Monitoring every field or farm to measure pollutant movement is impossible, and landowners need to know benefits before they apply conservation practices. Only through the use of models can pollutant movement be assessed and conservation practices most effectively planned.

In 1978 the U.S. Department of Agriculture's Science and Education Administration—Agricultural Research began a national project to develop relatively simple, computer-efficient mathematical models for evaluating nonpoint-source pollution. A model that does not require calibration was planned because little data suitable for calibrating a model were available. Initial efforts concentrated on a field scale because that is where conservation management systems are applied. A field was defined as an area with a relatively homogeneous soil under a single management practice and small enough so that rainfall variability was minimal. Requirements for the model were that it be simple and yet represent a complex system, be physically based and not require calibration, be a continuous simulation model, and have the potential to estimate runoff, erosion, and transport of chemicals in solution and attached to the sediment. The result of this project was CREAMS, a field-scale model capable of assessing these conditions and meeting these requirements (*14*).

Our purpose here is to present the concepts, to describe briefly each component of the model, and to describe an application of CREAMS (Chemicals, Runoff, and Erosion from Agricultural Management Systems). A complete description of the model and instructions for its use have been published by the U.S. Department of Agriculture (*14*).

Model development

Simple mathematical expressions have been used for years as models in hydrology, erosion, and sedimentation. The universal soil loss equation (USLE) is a simple mathematical model that relates average annual soil loss (A) to an average annual rainfall erosivity factor (R), a soil erodibility factor (K), a slope length and steepness factor (LS), a cover-management factor (C), and a supporting practice factor (P) in the form $A = RKLSCP$ (*17*). The USLE is a much-used and powerful model for estimating long-term erosion. Values for its factors are readily available, and calculations are quick and easy. Values for the C and P factors can be changed to represent different management and cover conditions, and model calculations can be repeated to estimate the influence of a change in management.

With present-day needs for evaluating runoff, percolation, erosion/sediment transport, and associated dissolved and sediment-adsorbed chemical losses from farms, one simple relationship is insufficient. Also, long-term averages can be meaningless, as in the case of a toxic pesticide that may only be a problem for a few days after application. Interactions between the various components of the transport system prevent the use of single, straightforward calculations. However, the physical processes can be represented by a logical series of mathematical expressions that can be solved repetitively and easily with high-speed computers. First, the modeler identifies the important physical processes that must be represented to provide the accuracy and detail of information needed from the model. Formulation of the model expresses the modeler's concepts of the physical system and ideas of the order of processes. Computer efficiency is also important, especially when a model is to be used many times to evaluate a system as complex as that in nonpoint-source pollution. If a model is to show effects of management practices, the necessary equations and parameters that reflect the practices must be incorporated into the model.

Models are developed for specific purposes. Their application outside these specific conditions can result in erroneous answers. For example, use of a model for estimating streamflow from large basins would likely give misleading estimates of runoff from a five-acre area. Average infiltration might be satisfactory for the basin scale, but for the field scale temporal and spatial variations in infiltration might be important. Sediment yield estimates for large basins often require careful description of channel processes, whereas accurate descriptions of erosion by raindrop impact on overland flow areas may be most important for estimating sediment yield from fields.

Review of models

Passage of the Federal Water Pollution Control Act Amendments, Public Law 92-500, in 1972 resulted in the need for mathematical models to evaluate pollution from diffuse agricultural areas. These needs resulted in a proliferation of model development. Although hydrology and erosion models were available, there were few models for chemical transport. Models for evaluating nonpoint-source pollution were assembled, oftentimes by "piggy-backing" erosion and chemical components onto hydrology models for both field-size and basin-size areas.

Crawford and Donigian (3) developed the pesticide runoff transport (PRT) model to estimate runoff, erosion, and pesticide losses from field-size areas. The hydrologic component of the PRT model is the Stanford watershed model (4); the erosion component was developed by Negev (11). The Stanford watershed model was among the first computer simulation models developed for basin-size areas.

Donigian and Crawford (5) incorporated a plant nutrient component with the basic PRT model to develop the agricultural runoff model (ARM). The hydrology, erosion, and pesticide components are the same as the PRT model. ARM is also for field-size areas. Both the PRT and ARM models require data for calibration.

Frere and associates (7) developed an agricultural chemical transport model (ACTMO) to estimate runoff, sediment yield, and plant nutrients from field- and basin-size areas. The hydrologic component is the USDA Hydrograph Lab model (9), which is based on an infiltration concept. The erosion component is based on the rill and inter-rill erosion concepts and USLE modifications developed by Foster and colleagues (6). The ACTMO model does not require calibration.

Bruce and associates (2) developed an event model—WASCH—to estimate runoff, erosion, and pesticide losses from field-size areas for single runoff-producing storms. The model requires calibration to a specific site.

Beasley and colleagues (1) developed the ANSWERS mode to estimate runoff, erosion, and sediment transport from basin-size areas. The model does not have a chemical component. It is used to identify sources of erosion and areas of deposition within a basin.

The ARM, WASCH, and ANSWERS models are expensive to operate and cannot be used economically for long-term simulation. Long-term simulation and risk analysis are desirable for examining probabilities of exceeding toxic pesticide concentrations.

Models that require calibration to evaluate parameter values are generally calibrated for a specific site and practice. If relationships for the physical processes are not carefully formulated, parameter values can be seriously distorted. Calibration of a model with data for a specific site and management practice can give erroneous results when the model is applied to a different site or management practice without recalibration. Minimizing the need for calibration is desirable. A model is most useful when values for its parameters are readily available as functions of easily measured features of the evaluated site and practice. Both modelers and model users should be aware of problems associated with calibration, availability of parameter values, parameter distortion by inadequate watershed representation, inaccurate results from poorly formulated equations, and excessive use of computer time. We sought to minimize these problems with CREAMS.

CREAMS model structure

CREAMS consists of three major components: hydrology, erosion/sedimentation, and chemistry. The hydrology component estimates runoff volume and peak rate, infiltration, evapotranspiraton, soil water content, and percolation on a daily basis. If detailed precipitation data are available, the model calculates infiltration at histogram breakpoints. The erosion component estimates erosion and sediment yield, including particle distribution at the edge of the field on a daily basis. The chemistry component includes elements for plant nutrients and pesticides. Stormloads and average concen-

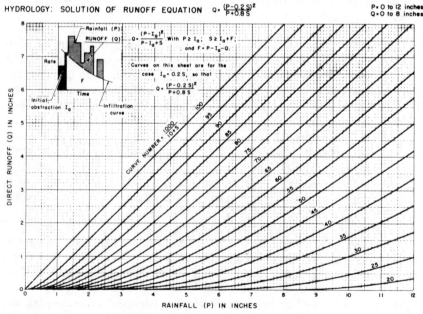

Figure 1. Soil Conservation Service curve number method of storm runoff estimation (*15*).

trations of adsorbed chemicals and dissolved chemicals in the runoff, sediment, and percolate fractions are estimated.

The hydrologic component. The hydrologic component consists of two options, depending upon availability of rainfall data. One option estimates storm runoff when only daily rainfall data are available. If hourly or breakpoint (time-intensity) rainfall data are available, a second option estimates storm runoff by an infiltration-based method.

Option 1: Williams and LaSeur (*16*) adapted the Soil Conservation Service (SCS) curve number method (*15*) for simulation of daily runoff. The method relates direct runoff to daily rainfall as a function of curve number (Figure 1). Curve number is a function of soil type, cover, management practice, and antecedent rainfall. The relationship of runoff, Q, to rainfall, P, is

$$Q = \frac{(P - 0.2S)^2}{P + 0.8S} \tag{1}$$

where S is a retention parameter related to soil moisture and curve number. An equation for water balance is used to estimate soil moisture from:

$$SM_t = SM + P - Q - ET - O \tag{2}$$

where SM is initial soil moisture, SM_t is soil moisture at day t, P is precipitation, Q is runoff, ET is evapotranspiration, and O is percolation below the root zone.

The percolate component uses a storage routing technique to estimate flow through the root zone. The root zone is divided into seven layers. The first layer is 1/36 of the root zone depth, the second layer 5/36 of the total depth, and the remaining layers, all equal in thickness, are 1/6 of the root zone depth. The top layer is approximately equal to the chemically active surface layer and the layer where inter-rill erosion occurs. Percolation from a layer occurs when soil moisture exceeds field capacity. Amount of percolation depends on saturated hydraulic conductivity.

The peak rate of runoff, q_p, (required in the erosion model) is estimated by the empirical relationship

$$q_p = 200 \ D^{0.7} \ C^{0.159} \ Q^{(0.917D^{0.0166})} L^{-0.187} \tag{3}$$

where D is drainage area, C is mainstem channel slope, Q is daily runoff volume, and L is the watershed length-width ratio (*14*). Although equation 3 was developed and tested for basin-size areas, testing of CREAMS has shown it to be applicable to field-size areas as well.

Option 2: The infiltration model is based on the Green and Ampt equation (*8, 13*). The concept defined in figure 2 assumes some soil water initially in a surface infiltration-control layer. When rainfall begins, the soil water content in the control layer approaches saturation and surface ponding occurs at a time, t_p (Figure 2). The amount of rain that has infiltrated by the time of ponding, designated F_p in figure 2, is analogous to initial abstraction in the SCS curve number model (option 1), but is also a function of rainfall intensity. After the time of ponding, water is assumed to move downward as a sharply defined wetting front with a characteristic capillary tension as the principle driving force. The infiltration curve of figure 2 is approximated to give the infiltrated depth, ΔF, in a time interval, Δt, as

$$\Delta F = [4A(GD + F) + (F - A)^2]^{1/2} + A - F, \qquad [4]$$

where $A = K_{si} t_i / 2$, $D = \Theta_s - \Theta_i$, Θ_s is water content at saturation, Θ_i is initial water content, G is the effective capillary tension of the soil, and K_s is the effective saturated conductivity. The average infiltration rate $\bar{f}_i$ for the ith interval is

$$\bar{f}_i = \frac{\Delta F_i}{\Delta t_i} \qquad [5]$$

and runoff/rainfall excess, q_i, during the interval is rainfall rate for the interval minus the infiltration rate, $r_i - \bar{f}_i$. Total runoff is the sum of all q_i for the storm. The infiltration-based model has three parameters: G, D, and K_s.

Percolation is estimated as in option 1, except that a single layer below the infiltration control layer represents the root zone. Percolation is calculated using average profile soil water content above field capacity and the saturated hydraulic conductivity, K_s. Peak rate of runoff is estimated by attenuating the rainfall excess using the kinematic wave model with parameter values to account for nonuniform steepness and roughness along the slope (*18*).

The evapotranspiration (ET) element of the hydrologic component is the

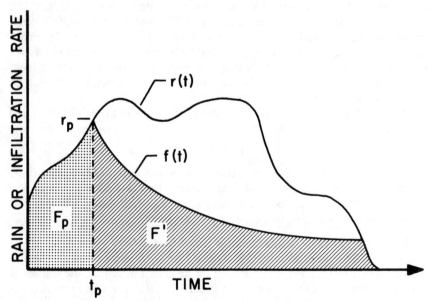

Figure 2. Schematic representation of runoff model using infiltration approach (*13*).

same for both options. The ET model, developed by Ritchie (*12*), calculates soil and plant evaporation separately. Evaporation, based on heat flux, is a function of daily net solar radiation and mean daily temperature, which are interpolated from a Fourier series fitted to mean monthly radiation and temperature (*10*). Soil evaporation is calculated in two stages. In the first, soil evaporation is limited only by available energy and is equal to potential soil evaporation. In the second, evaporation depends upon transmission of water through the soil profile to the surface and time since stage two began. Plant evaporation is computed as a function of soil evaporation and leaf area index. If soil water is limiting, plant evaporation is reduced by a fraction of the available soil water. Evapotranspiration, which is the sum of plant and soil evaporation, cannot exceed potential soil evaporation.

The erosion component. The erosion component considers the basic processes of soil detachment, transport, and deposition. The concepts of the model are that sediment load is controlled by the lesser of transport capacity or the amount of sediment available for transport. If sediment load is less than transport capacity, detachment by flow may occur, whereas deposition occurs if sediment load exceeds transport capacity. Raindrop impact is assumed to detach particles regardless of whether or not sediment is being detached or deposited by flow. The model represents a field comprehensively by considering overland flow over complex slope shapes, concentrated channel flow, and small impoundments or ponds (Figure 3). The model estimates the distribution of sediment particles transported as primary particles—sand, silt, and clay—and large and small aggregates that are conglomerates of primary particles. Sediment sorting during deposition and consequent enrichment of the sediment in fine particles is calculated.

Detachment is described by a modification of the USLE for a single storm event (*6*). Rate of inter-rill detachment, D_{IR}, in the overland flow element is expressed as

$$D_{IR} = 0.210 \, EI \, (S_{of} + 0.014) \, KCP \, (q_p/Q) \qquad [6]$$

where EI is the product of a storm's energy and maximum 30-minute intensity, S_{of} is the slope of the land surface, q_p is peak runoff rate, Q is runoff volume, K is a soil erodibility factor, C is a cover-management factor, and P is a contouring factor. Rate of detachment, D_R, by rill erosion is expressed as

$$D_R = 37983 \, nq_p^{4/3}(x/72.6)^{n-1} \, (S_{of})^2 \, KCP \qquad [7]$$

where x is the distance downslope and n is a slope-length exponent. The factors K, C, and P are from the USLE. Inter-rill erosion is primarily a function of raindrop impact on areas in between the rills; it is not a function of runoff as the term q_p/Q suggests in equation 6. This term converts total erosion for the storm to an average rate. Rill erosion is a function of runoff rate. Sediment transport capacity for overland flow is estimated by the Yalin transport equation (*19*), modified for nonuniform sediment having a mixture of sizes and densities.

The concentrated flow or channel element of the erosion model assumes that the peak runoff rate is the characteristic discharge for the channel. Calculation of detachment or deposition and transport of sediment are based on this discharge. Discharge is assumed to be steady but spatially varied, increasing downstream from lateral inflow. Friction slope of the flow is estimated from regression equations fitted to solutions of the spatially varied flow equations so that drawdown or backwater from a control at the channel outlet can be considered.

Detachment can occur when sediment load is less than transport capacity of the flow and shear stress of the flow is greater than the critical shear

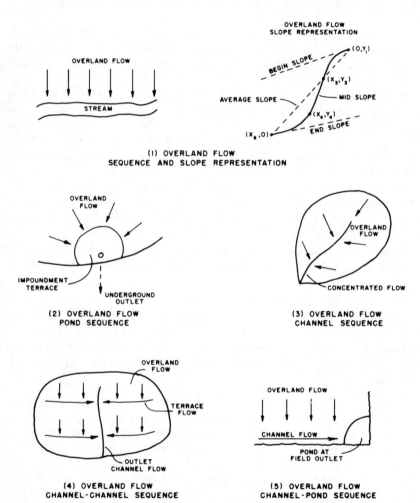

Figure 3. Schematic representation of typical field systems in the field-scale erosion/sediment yield model.

stress for the soil in the channel. Both bare and grassed waterways, combinations of bare and grassed channels, and variable slope along the channel can be considered.

Water is often impounded in fields, either as normal ponding from a restriction at a fence line, a road culvert, a natural pothole, or in an impoundment-type terrace. These restrictions reduce flow velocity, causing coarse-grained primary particles and aggregates to be deposited. Deposition depends upon whether fall velocity of the particles causes the sediment to reach the impoundment bottom before flow carries them from the impoundment. The fraction of particles passing through the impoundment, FP, of a given particle class, i, is given by the exponential relation

$$FP_i = A_i e^{B_i d_i} \tag{8}$$

where d_i is the equivalent sand-grain diameter and A_i and B_i are coefficients that depend upon impoundment geometry, inflow volume, infiltration through the impoundment boundary, and discharge rate from the impoundment.

In addition to calculating the sediment transport fraction for each of five particle classes, the model computes a sediment enrichment ratio based on specific surface area of the sediment and organic matter and the specific surface area for the residual soil. As sediment is deposited, organic matter, clay, and silt are the principle particles transported. This results in high enrichment ratios. Enrichment ratios are important in transport of chemicals associated with sediment.

Chemistry component—plant nutrients. The basic concepts of the nutrient component are that nitrogen and phosphorus attached to soil particles are lost with sediment yield; soluble nitrogen and phosphorus are lost with surface runoff; and soil nitrate is lost by leaching from percolation, by denitrification, or by extraction by plants.

The nutrient component assumes that an arbitrary surface layer 1/2 inch deep is effective in chemical transfer to sediment and runoff. All broadcast fertilizer is added to the active surface layer, whereas only a fraction is added by fertilizer incorporated in the soil; the rest is added to the root zone. Nitrate in the rainfall contributes to the soluble nitrogen in the surface layer.

Soluble nitrogen and phosphorus are assumed to be thoroughly mixed with the soil water in the active surface layer. This includes soluble forms from the soil, surface-applied fertilizers, and plant residues. The imperfect extraction of these soluble nutrients by overland flow and infiltration is expressed by an empirical extraction coefficient. The amounts of nitrogen and phosphorus lost with sediment are functions of sediment yield, enrichment ratio, and the chemical concentration of the sediment phase.

When infiltrated rainfall saturates the active surface layer, soluble nitrogen moves into the root zone. Incorporated fertilizer, mineralization of organic matter, and soluble nitrogen in rainfall percolated through the active surface layer increase the nitrate content in the root zone. Uniform mixing of nitrate in soil water in the root zone is assumed. Mineralization is calculated by a first-order rate equation from the amount of potential mineralizable nitrogen, soil water content, and temperature. Optimum rates of mineralization occur at a soil temperature of 35 °C. Soil temperature is estimated from air temperature in the hydrologic component.

Nitrate is lost from the root zone by plant uptake, leaching, and denitrification. Plant uptake of nitrogen under ideal conditions is described by a normal probability curve. The potential uptake is reduced to an actual value by a ratio of actual plant evaporation to potential plant evaporation. A second option for estimating nitrogen uptake is based on plant growth and the plant's nitrogen content.

The amount of nitrate leached is a function of the amount of water percolated out of the root zone, estimated by the hydrologic component and the concentration of nitrate in the soil water. Denitrification occurs when the soil water content exceeds field capacity. The rate constant for denitrification is calculated from the soil's organic carbon content; it is adjusted by a twofold reduction for each 10-degree decline in temperature from 35 °C.

The plant nutrient component thus estimates nitrogen and phosphorus losses in sediment, soluble nitrogen and phosphorus in the runoff, and changes in the soil's nitrate content due to mineralization, uptake by the crop, leaching by percolation through the root zone, and denitrification in the root zone for each storm. Nitrogen and phosphorus concentrations in runoff and sediment are computed. Individual storm losses are accumulated for annual summaries that are used to compute average concentrations.

Pesticides. The pesticide component estimates concentration of pesticides in runoff (water and sediment) and total mass carried from the field for each storm during the period of interest. The model accommodates up to 10 pesticides simultaneously in a simulation period. Foliar-applied pesticides are considered separately from soil-applied pesticides because degradation of pesticides is more rapid on foliage than in soil. The model considers multiple applications of the same chemical, such as insecticides. Figure 4 is a flow chart of the pesticide component.

As in the plant nutrient component, an active surface layer about 1/2 inch deep is assumed. Movement of pesticides from the surface is a function of runoff, infiltration, and pesticide mobility parameters. Pesticide in runoff is partitioned between the solution phase and the sediment phase by the following relationships:

$$(C_w Q) + (C_s M) = a C_p \qquad [9]$$

and

$$C_s = K_d C_w \qquad [10]$$

where C_w is pesticide concentration in runoff water, Q is volume of water per unit volume of surface active layer, C_s is pesticide concentration in sedi-

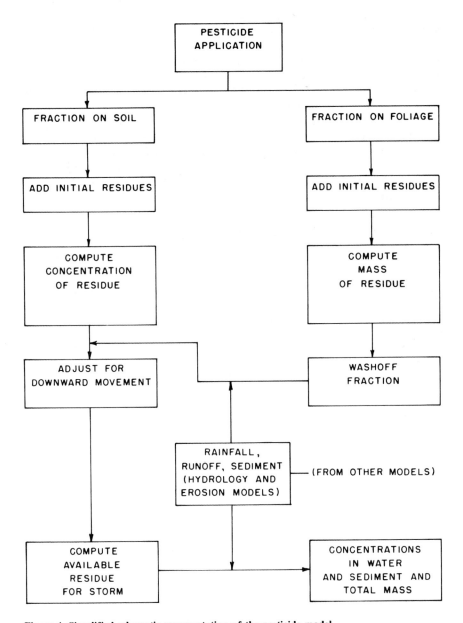

Figure 4. Simplified schematic representation of the pesticide model.

ment, M is mass of soil per unit volume of active surface layer, a is the extraction ratio of the concentration of pesticide extracted by runoff to the concentration of pesticide residue in the soil, C_p is the concentration of pesticide residue in the soil, and K_d is the coefficient for partitioning the pesticide between sediment and water phases. The concentration, C_w, of the pesticide in solution in runoff from the field is less than the soluble concentration in the surface layer because of inefficient extraction by runoff. The pesticide concentration, C_s, is that in the soil material of the surface layer. Selective deposition, as expressed by enrichment ratio, enriches this concentration in the sediment leaving the fields. The amount of pesticide attached to the sediment leaving the field is the product of the concentration C_s, sediment yield, and enrichment ratio.

Pesticide washed off foliage by rain increases the residual pesticide concentration in the soil. The amount calculated as available for washoff is updated between storms by a foliar degradation process. Pesticide residue in the surface layer is reduced by imperfect extractions by overland flow and infiltrated rainwater and by degradation described by an exponential function with a half-life parameter.

Application of CREAMS

A major use of CREAMS is evaluation of alternate management practices for control or minimization of runoff of sediment and chemicals. Several alternate practices might be proposed for a given site. Each could be

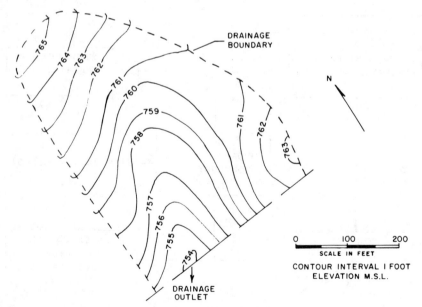

Figure 5. Topographic map for the Georgia Piedmont field.

Table 1. Hydrologic analysis of several farming practices for the example Georgia watershed. Values are from CREAMS simulations.

Management Practice	Rainfall* (in)	Runoff (in)	Percolation (in)	Evapotranspiration (in)	Product† $Q (q_p)$ Total	Product† $Q (q_p)$ Average/Event
1	116	14.4	24.3	78.4	38.7	0.74
2	116	14.4	24.3	78.4	38.7	0.74
3	116	8.9	29.2	78.8	22.1	0.61
4	116	8.9	29.2	78.8	19.7	0.55
5	116	14.5	24.4	78.4	38.7	0.74

*Total for the period May 1973-October 1975.
†Product of runoff volume, Q, and runoff peak rate, q_p (in²/hr).

evaluated with CREAMS, and a farmer could select a practice from those judged satisfactory.

Example area and practices. A 3.2-acre area from the Georgia Piedmont physiographic area illustrates the application of CREAMS. Figure 5 shows the topography of the field. The fenceline restricts surface drainage, which results in temporary ponding of runoff. The soil is a Cecil sandy loam, 24 inches deep to the B2 horizon.

Five management practices were analyzed for continuous corn:

Practice 1. Conventional tillage—moldboard plow in the spring, disk twice, plant, and cultivate twice. Rows run across the drainage, more or less on the contour in the upper end of the field and generally up-and-down slope at the lower end. Runoff is restricted at the fenceline.

Practice 2. Same as practice 1, except with a grassed waterway in the concentrated-flow area.

Practice 3. Chisel plow is used instead of moldboard and no cultivation; grassed waterway is used in the concentrated-flow area.

Practice 4. Conventional tillage, same as practice 1; channel-type terraces with 0.2 percent grade; tillage on contour; grassed terrace outlet channel.

Practice 5. Same as practice 1 with a tile outlet impoundment at the fenceline.

The plant nutrient component was run twice, once with practice 1 for a single application of 125 pounds per acre nitrogen and 25 pounds per acre phosphorus at planting time and again with a split application of nitrogen—25 pounds per acre incorporated at planting time and 100 pounds per acre topdressed 30 days after planting. A soluble pesticide, atrazine, and one adsorbed type, paraquat, were assumed to be surface-applied at planting time at the rate of 3.0 pounds per acre and 1.83 pounds per acre, respectively, for each management practice. Paraquat used in this application is considered only as an indicator for transport of any strongly soil-adsorbed chemical that is applied annually or is present as a residue from previous applications.

Results from hydrologic component. The daily rainfall hydrologic option was used to generate hydrologic values required by the erosion and chemistry components. Table 1 shows the results. Hydrologically, the only changes were in management practices 3 and 4 as compared with practice 1. Reduced curve numbers resulted in less computed runoff for these two practices. The roughness and the surface cover of corn residue in the chisel plow system accounted for its reduction in runoff. In practice 4, terraces and contouring reduced runoff volume and attenuated the peak rate of runoff because of a longer total flow path (increased effective length:width ratio). The parameters were not chosen to reflect a hydrologic influence of the grassed waterway or impoundment at the fenceline.

The effect of terraces and contouring on runoff was equal to that of chiseling and associated crop residue. Runoff volume and thus percolation and evapotranspiration did not change between practices 3 and 4. Runoff, percolation, and evapotranspiration were the same for practices 1, 2, and 5. However, runoff from these practices was 1.6 times that from practices 3 and 4.

The last column of table 1 gives the sum of the product of volume of runoff and peak runoff rate for the period of record, which is an index of the potential power of runoff for sediment transport. The index provides a relative comparison of the management practices. Since runoff volumes and peak rates did not change among practices 1, 2, and 5, the index value did not change. The peaks associated with lower volumes for practice 3 resulted in a much lower value, and the peak attenuation caused by the terraces in practice 4 further reduced the index even though volumes were the same for practices 3 and 4. The empirical relationship for peak rate (equation 3) does not reflect an increased hydraulic roughness for grassed waterways, as in practice 2, or the effect of impoundments, as in practice 5.

Results from erosion/sediment yield component. To apply the erosion component, an overland flow element and a concentrated flow element were used to represent the watershed for practices 1, 2, and 3. An impoundment element was added for practice 5. Practice 4 was represented by an overland flow element and a series of two channel elements. Parameter val-

Table 2. Erosion/sediment yield analysis of several farming practices for the example Georgia watershed. Values are from CREAMS simulations.

Management Practice	Sediment Yield* (t/a)	Enrichment Ratio (ER) Based on Specific Surface Area	Product (SY•ER) (t/a)
1	9.47	2.1	19.89
2	4.80	2.7	12.96
3	1.79	2.3	4.12
4	1.72	2.9	4.99
5	0.96	4.3	4.13

*Total for the period May 1973-October 1975.

Table 3. Summaries of total plant nutrient components for five management practices for the Georgia Piedmont, 1973-1975. Values are from CREAMS simulations.

	Management Practice					
	1A*	1B	2	3	4	5
Nitrogen (lb/a)						
Inputs						
Fertilizer	375.0	375.0	375.0	375.0	375.0	375.0
Rainfall	21.1	21.1	21.1	21.1	21.1	21.1
Mineralization	65.0	65.0	65.0	65.3	65.3	65.9
Outputs						
Runoff	3.3	3.0	3.3	1.9	1.9	3.3
Sediment	33.7	33.7	19.7	8.2	7.8	4.8
Plant uptake	287.6	196.4	287.6	285.6	285.6	287.6
Leaching	51.9	94.9	51.9	61.2	61.2	51.9
Denitrification	95.8	182.7	95.8	91.6	91.6	95.8
Phosphorus (lb/a)						
Inputs						
Fertilizer	75.0		75.0	75.0	75.0	75.0
Outputs						
Runoff	1.2		1.2	.7	.7	1.2
Sediment	12.8		7.4	3.0	2.9	1.8

*Practices 1A, 2, 3, 4, and 5 had 25 pounds per acre of nitrogen fertilizer incorporated at planting and a topdressing of 100 pounds per acre about 30 days after corn emergence. Practice 1B had 125 pounds per acre incorporated at planting time.

ues for 10 overland flow paths around the watershed were averaged for a representative overland flow path. The fenceline at the watershed outlet was assumed to restrict flow, causing backwater.

Simulation results indicate the factors affecting erosion and sediment yield at this site (Table 2). Deposition occurred with practice 1 because the enrichment ratio, ER, of 2.1 was greater than 1.0. If the model computes no deposition, this ratio is 1.0. Deposition was on the toe of the concave overland flow slope, but most was in backwater immediately above the fenceline. The model predicted that the natural waterway upstream from the backwater would erode.

A grassed waterway, practice 2, eliminated erosion by concentrated flow in the previously unprotected waterway and caused deposition of some sediment eroded on the overland flow area. The increase in enrichment ratio from 2.1 to 2.7 resulted from increased deposition. Fines were not reduced in the same proportion as sediment yield (SY) because the enrichment ratio increased. The product of sediment yield and enrichment ratio, a relative measure of both sediment yield and specific surface area, indicates the carrying capacity for chemicals attached to the sediment.

Deposition in and at the edges of the grassed waterway would cause maintenance problems and should be reduced by reducing erosion on the overland flow area. Chisel plowing, practice 3, provided that reduction, which would also help maintain soil productivity.

Instead of conservation tillage, the farmer may prefer conventional tillage with conventional terraces, practice 4, and a grassed outlet channel. Sediment yield was reduced 82 percent, but the enrichment ratio increased because of considerable deposition in the terrace channels and in the grassed outlet channel. Another possibility was an impoundment terrace, practice 5, which further reduced sediment yield, but greatly increased the enrichment ratio. The resulting product of sediment yield and enrichment ratio was as high as that for practice 3, in which sediment yield was 1.8 times that of practice 5.

As expected, enrichment ratio increased as sediment yield decreased, but in a scattered fashion. Furthermore, the relationship may be quite different for other sites.

Results from nutrient component. Table 3 summarizes the results from the plant nutrient component for the 30-month period. Two runs were made for management practice 1 to demonstrate the effects of possible fertilizer treatments. Fertilizer application was the same for management practices 1A, 2, 3, 4, and 5, where 25 pounds per acre of nitrogen was incorporated at planting time and 100 pounds per acre of nitrogen was topdressed about 30 days after corn emergence. In practice 1B, 125 pounds per acre of nitrogen was incorporated at planting time.

The results for practices 1A, 2, 3, 4, and 5 reflect differences caused by changes in runoff and sediment yield for the different practices. Practices 3 and 4 resulted in less runoff and more percolation than did practices 1A, 3, and 5. Thus, nitrogen and phosphorus in runoff was less for practices 3 and 4, but more nitrate was leached out of the root zone, and more denitrification occurred. Plant uptake of nitrogen changed little because there was little change in evapotranspiration. These changes in nitrogen uptake reflect slightly different crop yields due to differences in water and nitrogen availability.

A split application versus a single application of nitrogen can be evaluated by comparing results for practices 1A and 1B. Part of the difference in nitrogen loss was due to storm rainfall/runoff/sediment loss events relative

Table 4. Summary of total pesticide losses for five management practices on the example Georgia watershed, 1973 to 1975. Values are from CREAMS simulations.

	Pesticide					
	Atrazine			Paraquat		
Management Practice	Total Applied (lb/a)	Total Loss (lb/a)	Percent of Application	Total Applied (lb/a)	Total Loss (lb/a)	Percent of Application
1	9.0	0.049	0.55	5.5	0.237	4.32
2	9.0	0.048	0.54	5.5	0.135	2.46
3	9.0	0.020	0.22	5.5	0.035	0.65
4	9.0	0.020	0.22	5.5	0.056	1.03
5	9.0	0.048	0.53	5.5	0.048	0.88

to time of application and part was due to all of the nitrogen being incorporated into the soil for practice 1B. Nitrogen uptake was less for the single application than for the split application for the same evapotranspiration because leaching and denitrification depleted the high soil nitrate following the single application. This illustrates the influence of storm sequence. If rainfall had been more frequent but less in total amount, the results might have been entirely different. Nitrate leaching among the five practices reflected the change in percolation. Surface losses of nitrogen and phosphorus largely reflected runoff and sediment losses.

Results from pesticide component. Table 4 summarizes pesticide losses for the five management practices during the simulation period. Atrazine and paraquat represent a dissolved and a sediment-attached pesticide, respectively, and the losses show the effects of the management practices on runoff and erosion. Atrazine is transported mainly in water, and the reduced runoff from chisel plowing and terracing (Practices 3 and 4, Table 1) reduced losses by about 60 percent. The slight changes in loss from practices 1 to 2 to 4 reflect the small amount of atrazine transported by sediment. Since paraquat is transported mainly in sediment, losses are generally closely associated with sediment yield. The exception is for practice 5, where the impoundment resulted in the lowest sediment yield (Table 2). Deposition of coarse particles in the impoundment resulted in the highest enrichment ratio and sediment having the highest fraction of fines. The fine sediment is the main carrier of pesticides attached to sediment. Enrichment of fines resulted in more paraquat loss from practice 5, the impoundment system, than from practice 3, the chisel plow system, where sediment yield was greater.

Utility of results. The relative results of applying the CREAMS model may change for the same practices in other land resource areas or other fields in the same land resource area. Application of the model is site specific, and the examples represent a specific topographic and climatic situation. However, these results demonstrate the utility of CREAMS as a tool to evaluate alternative management practices and the complex interactions among the components for the several practices. The results show that a specific management system may not minimize all pollutants (sediment, plant nutrients, and pesticides). Factors other than minimizing pollutants must be considered in selecting a management practice, such as farm machinery requirements and the farmer's economic constraints.

REFERENCES

1. Beasley, D. B., E. J. Monke, and L. F. Huggins. 1977. *ANSWERS: A model for watershed planning.* Agricultural Experiment Station Journal Paper No. 7038. Purdue University, West Lafayette, Indiana. 34 pp.
2. Bruce, R. R., L. A. Harper, R. A. Leonard, W. M. Snyder, and A. W. Thomas. 1975. *A model for runoff of pesticides from small upland watersheds.* Journal of Environmental Quality 4(4): 541-548.
3. Crawford, N. H., and A. S. Donigian, Jr. 1973. *Pesticide transport and runoff model for agricultural lands.* EPA-660/274-013. Office of Research and Development, U.S. Environmental Protection Agency, Washington, D.C. 211 pp.

4. Crawford, N. H., and R. K. Linsley. 1962. *The synthesis of continuous streamflow hydrographs on a digital computer.* Technical Report No. 12. Department of Civil Engineering, Stanford University, Stanford, California.
5. Donigian, A. S., Jr., and N. H. Crawford. 1976. *Modeling pesticides and nutrients on agricultural lands.* EPA-600/2-76-043. Office of Research and Development, U.S. Environmental Protection Agency, Washington, D.C. 317 pp.
6. Foster, G. R., D. L. Meyer, and C. A. Onstad. 1977. *A runoff erosivity factor and variable slope length exponents for soil loss estimates.* Transactions, American Society of Agricultural Engineers 20(4): 683-687.
7. Frere, M. H., C. A. Onstad, and H. N. Holtan. 1975. *ACTMO, an agricultural chemical transport model.* ARS-H-3. Agricultural Research Service, U.S. Department of Agriculture, Washington, D.C. 54 pp.
8. Green, W. A., and G. A. Ampt. 1911. *Studies on soil physics, I. The flow of air and water through soils.* Journal of Agricultural Science 4: 1-24.
9. Holtan, H. N., and N. C. Lopez. 1971. *USDAHL-70 model of watershed hydrology.* Technical Bulletin 1435. U.S. Department of Agriculture, Washington, D.C. 84 pp.
10. Kothandaraman, V., and R. L. Evans. 1972. *Use of air-water relationships for predicting water temperature.* Report of Investigations No. 69. Illinois State Water Survey, Urbana. 14 pp.
11. Negev, M. A. 1967. *Sediment model on a digital computer.* Technical Report No. 76. Department of Civil Engineering, Stanford University, Stanford, California. 109 pp.
12. Ritchie, J. T. 1972. *A model for predicting evaporation from a row crop with incomplete cover.* Water Resources Research 8(5): 1,204-1,213.
13. Smith, R. E., and J. Y. Parlange. 1978. *A parameter-efficient hydrologic infiltration model.* Water Resources Research 14(3): 533-538.
14. U.S. Department of Agriculture, Science and Education Administration. 1980. *CREAMS—A field-scale model for chemicals, runoff, and erosion from agricultural management systems.* Conservation Research Report No. 26. Washington, D.C. 643 pp.
15. U.S. Department of Agriculture, Soil Conservation Service. 1972. *National engineering handbook.* Section 4, Hydrology. Washington, D.C. 548 pp.
16. Williams, J. R., and W. V. LaSeur. 1976. *Water yield model using SCS curve numbers.* Journal of the Hydraulics Division, American Society of Civil Engineers 102(HY9): 1,241-1,253.
17. Wischmeier, W. H., and D. D. Smith. 1978. *Predicting rainfall erosion losses—a guide to conservation planning.* Agriculture Handook No. 537. U.S. Department of Agriculture, Washington, D.C. 58 pp.
18. Wu, Y. H. 1978. *Effects of roughness and its spatial variability on runoff hydrographs.* Report No. CED 77-78 YHW7. Civil Engineering Department, Colorado State University, Fort Collins. 174 pp.
19. Yalin, Y. S. 1963. *An expression for bedload transportation.* Journal of the Hydraulics Division, American Society of Civil Engineers 89(HY3): 221-250.

23

Use of Manures: Fertilizer, Feed, or Fuel?

R. K. White

Extension Agricultural Engineer
Ohio State University, Columbus

Livestock manure can be a valuable resource when it is used to fertilize crops, fed to livestock, or used for fuel production. In many cases, manure is not effectively used, is wasted, or may cause pollution when improperly handled.

Resource recovery from animal manure offers an economic incentive for use of management practices that will protect environmental quality. Historically, manure has been used for fertilizing crops. This method of disposal is still the major use of manure. Alternative economic returns can be obtained by using manure products for feed and fuel. Benefits can thus accrue to environmental quality as well as agricultural productivity and energy production.

The quantity of manure available for economic recovery is always less than that produced. Manure from livestock on range or pasture is not recoverable in one sense, although it is recycled. Other losses occur due to the manure handling system and methods of disposal. A loss that is of much concern is the volatilization of nitrogen (ammonia) in a manure handling system. Van Dyne and Gilbertson (7) estimated the amount of manure and its nutrients that can be economically recovered. Table 1 gives the estimated manure production and nutrient contents in the United States for 1974 and the amount that is economically recoverable. Less than 50 percent of the manure, on a dry weight basis, is economically recoverable. Only 34 percent of the nitrogen (N) and about 50 percent of the phosphorus (P) and potassium (K) are recoverable.

Use of manure as fertilizer

When the manure is recoverable and spread on cropland or pasture, the amount of N, P, and K available to the plants can be predicted. These data are available in *Manure Production and Characteristics for Manure Nutrient Quantities* (*1*), the *Midwest Plan Service Handbook* (*6*) or the *Ohio Livestock Waste Management Guide* (*10*).

There are two principal objectives to meet in applying animal wastes on land: maximum use of the manure nutrients by crops and minimizing the water pollution hazard. To meet these objectives, several factors should be taken into account in developing a manure application plan. These include:

1. *Characteristics of manure.* The amount of plant-available nutrients in the manure, especially N.

2. *Number of animals and land available for application.* This will determine the amount of manure produced and the frequency and rate of manure applicaton.

3. *Type of crops and rotation.* The rate, time, and method of application will depend upon the types of crops grown and crop rotations used.

4. *Topography of application area.* Slope of the land and position relative to farm ponds, drainage ditches, and streams will determine the potential nutrient loss and pollution hazard.

5. *Time of year.* Crop cover, form of precipitation, winter application on snow, or frozen ground will affect nutrient loss and potential water pollution.

The factor that limits the annual amount of manure that should be applied to cropland is the amount of N. All manure contains appreciable

Table 1. Livestock manure production in the United States in 1974 (1,000 tons per year).

Species	Manure and Nutrients Produced by Livestock				Manure and Nutrients Economically Recoverable			
	Manure (dry wt)	N	P	K	Manure (dry wt)	N	P	K
Beef cattle (range)	52,057	1,267	370	807	1,897	41	17	38
Feeder cattle	10,428	399	117	254	16,000	263	92	132
Dairy cattle	25,210	814	137	652	20,358	498	119	617
Hogs	13,360	1,086	252	391	5,538	284	142	236
Sheep	3,796	147	37	150	1,700	48	18	75
Laying hens	3,374	158	68	68	3,259	92	68	68
Turkeys	1,251	76	21	24	983	36	13	21
Broilers	2,086	136	37	44	2,434	122	37	44
Total	111,562	4,083	1,039	2,390	52,169	1,384	506	1,231

Table 2. Percent nutrient losses under various management systems.

	Loss of Nutrient		
Management System	N* (%)	P (%)	K (%)
Solid handling			
1. Bedded building, regularly surface spread	40	-	-
2. Manure pack, surface spread	50	-	-
3. Confined housing, daily scraped and surface spread	40	-	-
4. Open paved lot, scrape, 6-month storage, surface spread	60	30	25
5. Poultry pit under cages, surface spread	50	-	-
Liquid handling			
6. Pit, earthen basin or above ground storage, surface spread	40	-	-
7. Anaerobic lagoon, surface spread	80	50	40
8. Aerobic (aerated) lagoon, surface spread	40	30	25

*It is ammonia N that is lost. Injection or immediate soil incorporation will decrease loss, saving from 20 to 25 percent of the N.

Table 3. The nutrients available from four different livestock facilities for growing 160 bushels per acre continuous corn.

Species (No. Livestock)	N*		P		K	
	Amounts (lbs/yr)	Acres Needed†	Amounts (lbs/yr)	Acres Supplied‡	Amounts (lbs/yr)	Acres Supplied‡
Dairy						
(100 cows at 1,400 lbs)	10,500	21	3,700	140	13,800	370
Beef						
(200 head at 750 lbs)	9,300	19	6,000	227	13,200	353
Swine						
(1,000 pigs at 135 lbs)	11,000	22	7,300	277	14,600	390
Poultry						
(20,000 layers at 4 lbs)	10,500	39	8,200	311	9,000	240

*A 50-percent loss of N is assumed due to handling, storage, and surface spreading.
†The minimum number of acres needed to avoid pollution of water based on a yield of 160 bushels/acre of continuous corn with 40 percent of the N available in the year spread for dairy, beef, and swine and 75 percent for poultry.
‡The acres that the manure will provide the crop needs of P or K for 160 bushels/acre of corn on regularly fertilized soils.

amounts of N, and levels greater than the N requirements of the crop may lead to N entering surface waters or leaching into groundwater where it may cause pollution. In designing the manure application rate, the N losses due to storage, handling, and spreading must be considered (Table 2) (10).

Under Ohio conditions, about one-third of the N in animal manure, except poultry, is available to crops in the year in which it is applied; the remaining two-thirds, residual organic N, becomes part of the soil organic matter. It is mineralized or becomes available at the rate of about five percent a year. In the case of poultry waste, about 75 percent of the N is available the first year; the remainder also mineralizes at about five percent annually. To determine how much N will be available to crops from manure applications, the grower must take into account the mineralized N that will become available from previous manure applications.

Manure is also a good source of P and K, with most of the P and K in manure available to the crop in the year it is applied, except as noted in table 2.

Table 3 presents a comparison of four livestock facilities in terms of supplying the fertilizer nutrient for a yield goal of 160 bushels per acre of continuous corn. The livestock numbers give about the same amount of manure N each year after allowing for a 50 percent loss. Dairy beef and swine manure are similar in N availability, but the poultry manure will have twice as much available. If manure is applied regularly to the same ground over many years, the mineralization of organic N in the soil will contribute a significant amount of N to the crop. It is noted that the P supplied by the manure will fertilize 7 to 12 times as many acres as will the N. Similarly, dairy, beef, and swine manure will provide K for 18 times the acres supplied by the N and poultry for 6 times the acres. Therefore, it may be better to use more acreage, approaching the acreage requirement based on P or K, and apply additional chemical N as needed.

Manure is best applied when it can be injected or incorporated as soon as possible. This means prior to plowing or tillage. Manure can be spread without incorporation in the fall or spring on ground with sod cover or crop stubble to retard runoff. When necessary to spread on frozen, sloping, snow-covered ground, spread on the least sloping ground with good vegetative cover away from streams and drainageways. This will assure maximum conservation of nutrients for crop production and minimize the pollution potential.

Use of manure as feed

Processed manure as a feedstuff is a valuable resource that contains energy, crude protein, and P. Consumption of manure by animals or birds is not new. Coprophagy is common in many species. The first widespread use of manure for feeding domestic livestock was the production of swine in finishing cattle lots in the Midwest in the early 1900s. Interest in feeding processed manures has intensified of late, particularly during periods of high feed cost when the price of meat and livestock products were low. The current information of feeding animal manures is summarized in a recent report prepared by a Council for Agricultural Science and Technology (CAST) task force (2).

Animal manures are most efficiently used by ruminants, such as sheep or cattle. Ruminants are able to digest fiber and use nonprotein N. Poultry wastes have the highest nutritional values. Broiler litter has an energy value similar to that of hay, and the N, P, and calcium contents are higher than that of hay. Caged layer manure is almost as high in nutritional value as broiler litter. Cattle manure is relatively low in energy and protein but is being successfully used in waste supplemented rations or as a ration for animals in low production. The feeding of swine manure has only recently been done on a commercial scale.

The Food and Drug Administration summarized the present status of feeding animal manures and raised several concerns regarding the safety of animals fed manure and the safety of the animal products for human food (4). The safety concerns about feeding manures are the potential for harmful residues of pesticides, drugs, minerals (metals), toxins, and the hazard of disease transmission. The CAST report (2) indicated there is no research to indicate that feeding manure to animals presents hazards to human health. The only documented evidence of a harmful effect on animal health of feeding manure is copper toxicity, which occurred in ewes fed broiler litter high in copper as a result of putting copper sulfate in the broiler feed.

Because manures may contain large numbers of pathogenic organisms, treatment of manure prior to feeding is a standard practice. Processes that can effectively destroy or significantly reduce certain pathogens in manure to be fed include ensiling, dehydration, composting, aerobic treatment of slurries, chemical treatment, or single-cell protein production. Because of the high moisture content of manure, frequent collection and processing are desirable to minimize the loss of energy and protein as well as to maintain palatability. Materials-handling problems arise in attempting to collect, transfer, blend, and store manure. Solid-liquid separation is being used

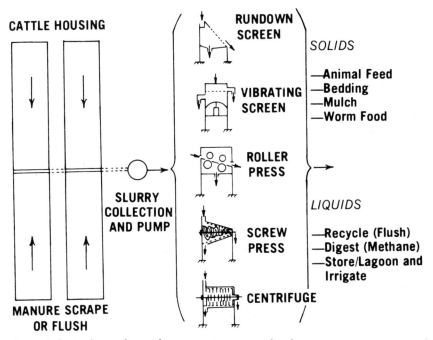

Figure 1. Separation equipment in a manure management system.

when applicable, for example, with liquid swine manure (*9, 10*). Solid-liquid separation equipment used includes screens, presses, and centrifuges. Figure 1 shows separation equipment in a manure system.

The development of organic acids and the anerobic conditions contribute to the success of ensiling manures. Broiler litter can be ensiled directly. Mixing crop material, such as corn stover, hay, bermuda grass, etc., with poultry or fattening beef manure is being done. A mixture of 40 percent manure and roughage with a resulting moisture content of 50 to 70 percent will ensile, and the final product will compare favorably with corn or sorghum silages. Coliform bacteria are usually eliminated in less than 10 days.

The drying of poultry (layer) manure has been done and the dried material fed back to poultry on a 10 to 20 percent basis or mixed with feed for ruminants. Poultry manure is the only manure that lends itself to dehydration because the moisture content is 75 percent. This compares with a moisture content of 87 to 92 percent for cattle and swine manures unless the facility is in an arid climate.

Feeding of swine manure after aerobic treatment is being done. The aerated, mixed liquor can be provided to the pigs as the source of water; the treated manure is thus consumed. Aerated swine manure can also have the solids separated out; it is then usually fed to gestating sows. There are commercial systems marketed to separate the solids and feed them (*9*).

Composting, chemical treatment, or single-cell protein production have not found acceptance or been developed at an economical level for treating manures to be fed.

In 1978 the American Association of Feed Control Officials published model regulations for processed manure to be sold commercially as a feed ingredient. These regulations do not apply to on-farm recycling. They specify quality control criteria and general prohibitions on extraneous materials, pathogens, parasites, and chemical residues. According to the FDA report (*4*), six states have adopted regulations for feeding animal manures (Alabama, California, Colorado, Mississippi, Virginia, and Washington).

On the basis of 1976 and 1977 costs of feedstuffs, the value of processed animal manure for replacing soybean meal in ruminant rations containing corn, corn silage, and soybean meal as the principal ingredients ranges from $125 to $280 per ton of dry matter (*2*). Cost of processing, storage, and transportation are not included so the net return to a farmer could be significantly less, or even be a cost.

One other point is noteworthy. For every ton of manure processed and fed, there is one less ton as a potential environmental pollutant.

Use of manure as fuel

Energy recovered from manures was identified as a priority research item at a national conference on Research Needs Assessment-Livestock Manure Management in the United States, held in 1978 (*8*). Two methods of energy recovery from manure are being researched: thermo-chemical processes and anerobic digestion.

Most thermo-chemical processes are at the laboratory or pilot-plant stage. These processes involve controlling pyrolysis or converting the products of pyrolysis so that liquid or gases for fuel are obtained. Also, catalysts can be used to convert the fuel to an end-use product, such as ammonia or methanol. These processes are directed toward applications with waste production capacities ranging from 100 to 1,000 tons per day. Most investment/cost evaluations indicate that the current thermo-chemical designs will not have the necessary economy-of-scale for single on-farm applications.

Anaerobic digesters to produce methane (biogas) using manure have been working in India and South Africa for many years. Recent research on generating methane from manure has centered in the United States because large concentrations of cattle in confinement offer a unique opportunity for economic production of methane. As an example, 4.5 million tons per year of cattle feedlot manure could be converted into nearly 10 billion cubic feet of methane (natural gas) worth about $20 million a year. In addition, digester residue valued at $40 million a year could be used as a feedstuff. The liquid effluent from the digester would contain as much as $30 million worth of plant nutrients. There are no appreciable losses of N, P, or K in the digestion process. Another benefit of anaerobic digestion is the reduction in offensive odors when digester residue is applied to land.

A methane production system should incorporate the following components:

1. Manure handling—collection and transport.

2. Material preparation—mixing and pumping.

3. Digester—with internal agitation and capability to heat.

4. Gas clean-up—removal of carbon dioxide, moisture, and other contaminants.

5. Gas handling—storage, on-site use, or marketing.

6. Byproduct recovery—land application for fertilizer use and/or solids recovery for feed.

The anaerobic digester has two optimum operating temperatures: 95 °F (mesophilic) and 135 °F (thermophilic). Thermophilic digesters provide peak methane yield and can be one-half to one-third the size of mesophilic digesters. However, they suffer higher heat losses and are reportedly more subject to bacterial upset. Mixing is normal in high-rate digesters, which renews bacterial contact with the substrates and releases gases. Because mixing requires energy, a mixing frequency of 15 minutes per hour or less is used. A "plugflow" digester with no mixing for dairy and beef feedlot manure has been developed at Cornell University (5). Anaerobic digesters should be loaded "continuously," at least once per day.

For methane production to be practical, the lowest cost digester that will reliably produce biogas at an acceptable level is a necessity. Rigid-wall, above-ground digesters, complete with slurry pumps, mixing equipment, and gas-handling systems, typically cost between $5 and $20 per cubic foot. A plugflow digester in a trench with membrane liners and insulated cover costs $3 to $7 per cubic foot.

Jewell and associates (5) reported methane production for a 40-cow and a 100-cow dairy operation and a 1,000-head beef feedlot. They estimated actual costs for use of the methane produced in a plugflow digester at $20, $9.80, and $2.80 per million Btu's for the 40- and 100-cow dairies and the 1,000-head beef feedlot, respectively. The combined benefits of the energy, nutrient conservation, and odor control would offset costs on the dairies and potentially produce an income on the beef feedlot. Farms with more than 100 dairy cows can begin to consider digestion as an income-producing operation.

An economic study of swine anaerobic digesters by Fischer and colleagues (3) included an internal combustion engine-electric generator system that supplied electrical and thermal energy marketing 3,200 hogs per year. They reported that the system was profitable with a $64,000 investment ($15 per cubic foot for digester and $11,000 for engine-generator) at an electric price at $0.08 per kilowatt hour and the price of supplemental propane at $1.10 per gallon. If electricity costs $0.06 per kilowatt hour, then an investment cost of $42,000 is profitable. This would require about $10 per cubic foot for digester costs.

The technologies of digester design and operation are being developed to the point where it is becoming economical for facilities with over 100 dairy cows, 1,000 to 1,500 head of beef, or 2,500 hogs to generate methane. The major obstacles to implementaton of this technology is use of the methane. If it is to be used for heating, less is available when it is needed during the winter because of heating the digester; during the summer, when more gas is available, less is needed. Methane, a very light gas, cannot be liquified economically. The methane should be used with very little gas storage provided. The advent of the engine/electric generator using methane may be the answer to this problem. Also, the exhaust heat from the engine can be used for heating water, etc. The use of the digester residue as a feedstuff or as a soil fertilizer is essential for the technology of methane production to be economical.

REFERENCES

1. American Society of Agricultural Engineers. 1980. *Manure production and characteristics* ASAE D384, Agricultural Engineers Yearbook. St. Joseph, Michigan.
2. Council for Agricultural Science and Technology. 1978. *Feeding animal waste.* Report No. 75. Ames, Iowa. 48 pp.
3. Fischer, J. R., N. F. Meador, D. D. Osburn, and C. D. Fulhage. 1979. *Economics of a swine anaerobic digester.* ASAE Paper No. 79-4580. American Society of Agricultural Engineers, St. Joseph, Michigan. 14 pp.
4. Food and Drug Administration. 1975. *Recycled animal wastes.* Federal Register 42(248): 64,662-64,675.
5. Jewell, W. J., H. R. Davis, W. W. Gunkel, D. J. Lathwell, J. H. Martin, Jr., T. R. McCarty, G. R Morris, D. R. Price, and D. W. Williams. 1976. *Bioconversion of agricultural wastes for pollution control and energy conservation.* TID-27164. National Technical Information Service, U.S. Department of Commerce, Washington, D.C. 321 pp.
6. Midwest Plan Service. 1975. *Livestock waste facilities handbook.* Iowa State University, Ames. pp. 4-5.

7. Van Dyne, D. L., and C. B. Gilbertson. 1978. *Estimating U.S. livestock and poultry manure and nutrient production.* ESCS-12. U.S. Department of Agriculture, Washington, D.C. 145 pp.
8. White, R. K. 1978. *Research needs assessment-livestock manure management in the United States.* EPA-600/2-79-179. U.S. Environmental Protection Agency, Washington, D.C. 52 pp.
9. White, R. K. 1980. *The role of liquid-solid separation in today's livestock waste management systems.* Journal of Animal Science 50(2): 356-359.
10. White, R. K., editor. 1980. *Ohio livestock waste management guide.* Bulletin 604. Ohio Cooperative Extension Service, Ohio State University, Columbus. 32 pp.

24

Organic Farming: Opportunities and Obstacles

Garth Youngberg

Organic Farming Coordinator, Program Planning Staff
Science and Education Administration
U.S. Department of Agriculture, Beltsville, Maryland

Only four years ago, a leading spokesman for the organic farming movement in the United States proclaimed, "It will be at least a generation before the USDA recognizes us." At the time, there seemed little reason to dispute the proclamation's accuracy. The view was shared widely in the organic community (*12*). Yet just last month, Secretary of Agriculture Bob Bergland, in his "Foreword" to USDA's *Report and Recommendations on Organic Farming*, wrote:

"Many large-scale producers as well as small farmers and gardeners are showing interest in alternative farming systems. Some of these producers have developed unique systems for soil and crop management, organic recycling, energy conservation, and pest control.

"We need to gain a better understanding of these organic farming systems—the extent to which they are practiced in the United States, why they are being used, the technology behind them, and the economic and ecological impacts from their use. We must also identify the kinds of research and education programs that relate to organic farming.

"As we strive to develop relevant and productive programs for all of agriculture, we look forward to increasing communication between organic farmers and the U.S. Department of Agriculture."

Moreover, in the "Preface" to that same USDA report, the director of the Science and Education Administration, Anson R. Bertrand, explained at least in part why USDA is interested in organic farming:

"One of the major challenges to agriculture in this decade will be to develop farming systems that can produce the necessary quantity and quality of food and fiber without adversely affecting our soil resources and the environment. This study was conducted to learn more about the potential contribution of organic farming as a system for the production of food and fiber."

What accounts for USDA's relatively new and accelerating interest in organic farming? To what extent is it the result of changing structural variables that impact upon American agriculture? Is it partly the result of the so-called new agenda in food and agriculture and the changing character of food and agricultural politics? What aspects of the new agenda relate to organic farming?[1] What potential opportunities does organic farming offer for the future of food and fiber production in the United States and throughout the world? In particular, what are the potential benefits of organic farming for environmental quality, especially soil and water conservation? What are the primary obstacles to the wider adoption of this mode of agricultural production?

A socio-political context

Before exploring the character of organic farming practices and their potential impact upon U.S. and world agriculture, it is important to note that questions about the future role of organic farming are no longer the sole concern of organic true believers; nor are they questions of strictly academic interest. Clearly, the basic tenets and potential benefits of organic farming address a number of growing social problems and concerns.

Organic agriculture is rooted in a set of highly integrated ideological propositions. As these tenets and their direct application to a host of interrelated social concerns become more widely known, organic beliefs, such as the following, will likely assume increasing importance: nature is capital; soil is the source of life; feed the soil, not the plant; diversify production systems; personal independence; and anti-materialism.

Throughout preparation of the USDA report on organic farming, for example, it became apparent "that there is increasing concern about the adverse effects of our U.S. agricultural production system, particularly in regard to the intensive and continuous production of cash grains and the ex-

---

[1]The so-called new agenda refers generally to a broad and relatively new set of concerns within the area of food and agriculture policy, such as environmental protection, less energy intensive modes of agricultural production, soil and water conservation, farm worker safety, protection of prime farmland, preservation of the family farm, and food quality and safety. A host of consumer, nutrition, and environmental groups have worked to place these issues on the agricultural agenda. Economist Don Paarlberg provides an excellent overview of the new agenda, its actors and concerns, in two recent publications (7, 8).

tensive and sometimes excessive use of agricultural chemicals." The most frequently expressed concerns were:

1. Sharply increasing costs and uncertain availability of energy and chemical fertilizer and our heavy reliance on these inputs.

2. Steady decline in soil productivity and tilth from excessive soil erosion and loss of soil organic matter.

3. Degradation of the environment from erosion and sedimentation and from pollution of natural waters by agricultural chemicals.

4. Hazards to human and animal health and to food safety from heavy use of pesticides.

5. Demise of the family farm and localized marketing systems.

The relationship between these concerns, organic ideology, and the politics of the new agenda in food and agriculture are clear and unmistakable. Although some new agenda issues transcend organic philosophy (organic ideology does not, for example, directly address such issues as food stamps and school lunches, important items on the new agenda), this philosophy certainly does relate to such central concerns of the new agenda as environmental protection, soil and water conservation, the protection of prime farmland, reduced reliance on petrochemical-based farm inputs, the quality of food, and the basic structure of American agriculture. For example, according to Robert Rodale (4), one of the leading contemporary spokesmen of the organic farming movement:

"Organic farmers and gardeners not only wish to avoid the use of many pesticides that can cause damage to wildlife, and create toxic effects in a variety of ways, but they also are very much concerned about the prevention of erosion, the adding of humus and other organic matter to soil to improve fertility, the preservation of small family farms, localized marketing of food, energy conservation, and proper nutrition. It is a rare organic grower who does not share those concerns, or pursue those activities."

The overlap between these basic organic tenets and the policy objectives of the new agenda coalition could provide the basis for a broad-based political structure in support of organic agriculture. In the past, there has been no over-arching, umbrella organization representing the interests of organic farmers. A number of individuals and groups have expressed concern over the absence of a single political voice for organic agriculture. In fact, during the latter months of 1979 and continuing into 1980, several Washington-based environmental, resource conservation, small-farm, and consumer groups held a series of meetings in Washington, D.C., for the purpose of discussing the feasibility and advisability of forming a coalition that would seek to advance organic concepts before governmental officials in both the legislative and executive branches. Although little concrete organizational progress has been made to date, the mere presence of such an effort suggests the growing visibility of organic ideology and its potential linkage to broader political coalitions. Should this effort succeed, new-agenda advocates would have added an important political force as well as a possible integrating ideology to their otherwise disjointed causes. In any case, it seems clear that the socio-political context of organic agriculture has changed markedly in recent years.

What is organic agriculture?

According to the USDA report on organic farming, "there is no universally accepted definition of organic agriculture." Continuing, the report asserts:

"Organic farmers use various combinations of technological and cultural practices because of certain underlying values and beliefs. The organic agricultural spectrum ranges from so-called pure organic farming on one extreme to more liberal interpretations of organic philosophy on the other. At this latter end of the spectrum, organic agriculture begins to merge with so-called conventional agriculture. At this point, the two systems share many common agricultural practices and organic and conventional farmers express a number of common concerns."

Several points about the character of organic farming, particularly the spectrum of organic systems and practices, warrant brief elaboration:

1. Organic farmers, regardless of their individual location on the organic spectrum, have not regressed to agriculture as it was practiced in the 1930s and 1940s. As a matter of fact, "today's organic farmers use modern farm machinery, recommended crop varieties, certified seed, sound livestock management, recommended soil and water conservation practices, and innovative methods of organic waste and residue management."

2. Some organic farmers reject totally the use of any synthetically compounded fertilizers, pesticides, growth regulators, and livestock feed additives. Others, while still calling themselves organic farmers, will, as a last resort, allow the restricted use of some or all of these resources.

3. A legume-based rotation with green manure or cover crops is an integral part of most organic farming systems. Ordinarily, legume crops comprise 30 to 50 percent of cultivated acreage with the overall crop rotation following patterns similar to those used 30 to 40 years ago.

4. Most organic farmers avoid use of the moldboard plow, favoring chisel or disk-type implements for primary tillage. Shallow tillage, which mixes the soil but does not invert it, is also common among organic farmers.

5. Organic farmers are strongly committed to soil and water conservation. Heavy use is made of terraces, stripcropping, grassed waterways, and contour farming. Most organic farmers included in the USDA case studies appeared to be highly successful in controlling erosion.

6. Organic farming is not necessarily limited by scale. The USDA case studies included farms ranging up to 1,500 acres.

7. Organic farmers obtain nitrogen (N) primarily from legumes, animal manure, crop residues, and "to a limited extent from organic and inorganic fertilizers applied as a supplement for high N use crops.... Rock phoshate and greensand (unprocessed glauconite) are acceptable sources of phosphorus (P) and potassium (K), respectively...."

8. Weed control on organic farms is, for the most part, achieved by "crop rotations, tillage, mowing, and to a lesser extent by selective use of herbicides and hand weeding. Preventive methods were emphasized."

9. Organic farmers attempt to control insects in field crops "by selective rotations and natural insect predators."

10. Well-established organic farming systems appear to generate per-acre crop yields that are comparable to nearby chemical intensive farms.

11. Most organic farmers market their produce as conventionally grown.

12. Although accurate data are unavailable, organic farmers probably constitute less than one percent of the total U.S. farming population. Within the organic population, however, the USDA study revealed that organic farmers are distributed throughout all major production regions of the United States, highly experienced, well-educated, excellent farm managers, and own either all or most of their land.

Given the diversity of organic farming, it seems quite clear that the future of this mode of agriculture depends largely on how organic farming is defined. For example, an utterly purist definition, excluding use of synthetically compounded fertilizers, pesticides, growth regulators, and livestock feed additives, would probably tend to limit organic farming to relatively small farm operations. On the other hand, if organic farming is defined so to allow for limited use of such production inputs, then organic farming operations would not necessarily appear to be limited by scale. While there is disagreement over what constitutes a bonafide organic farm, the assumptions, propositions, and conclusions found here are based upon the following definition, developed by the USDA Organic Farming Study Team:

"Organic farming is a production system which avoids or largely excludes the use of synthetically compounded fertilizers, pesticides, growth regulators, and livestock feed additives. To the maximum extent feasible, organic farming systems rely upon crop rotations, crop residues, animal manures, legumes, green manures, off-farm organic wastes, mechanical cultivation, mineral-bearing rocks, and aspects of biological pest control to maintain soil productivity and tilth, to supply plant nutrients, and to control insects, weeds, and other pests."

Opportunities for soil conservation

Organic farming practices can reduce soil erosion significantly and, to a lesser extent, help to conserve water. The following analysis of organic farming as a potential tool for enhanced soil and water conservation is paraphrased from the USDA report.

Effective erosion control methods practiced by organic farmers include the use of grass, legume, and small grain crops that reduce the percentage of row crops in the rotation; use of cover crops; green manure crops; and tillage methods that conserve surface residues. Organic agriculture also emphasizes application of manure and other organic materials to maintain or increase soil organic matter, which, in turn, increases water infiltration and storage, decreases nutrient and pesticide runoff, and reduces soil erosion.

The effect of soil and crop management practices on soil erosion by water can be evaluated with the cover and management factor, or C factor, in the universal soil loss equation (*11*). The C factor, which ranges in value from about 0.001 for well-managed woodland to 1.0 for continuous fallow, is directly proportional to soil loss on a given site and reflects only differences in soil and crop management.

Crop rotations. Many organic farmers maintain from 25 to 40 percent of their cropland acreage in sod crops, such as grass and legumes, whereas the chemical-intensive (conventional) farmer often grows mostly row crops, such as corn and soybeans, with little or no grass or legume crops in the rotation. The chemical-intensive farmer also uses conventional planting and tillage practices.

With conventional tillage, as the percentage of row crops in rotation decreases, the potential for soil loss decreases markedly. Where sod crops comprise 25 to 40 percent of the rotation, average annual soil loss is one-third to one-eighth of that occurring with conventional tillage and continuous row cropping.

Cover crops used by organic farmers may also reduce soil erosion by as much as 50 percent when they follow crops that leave only small amounts of residue after harvest, such as potatoes, most vegetables, and silage corn.

Tillage. Many organic farmers in the USDA case studies had already shifted from the moldboard plow to the chisel plow and disk-type implements, which provide even greater erosion control than conventional methods. Studies in the Midwest show that when chisel and disk implements are used in primary tillage operations, soil loss is reduced by 20 to 75 percent from that occurring under conventional tillage. The favorable results from chisel and disk implements are due mainly to effective placement of residues at or near the soil surface. This type of tillage, which is not unique to organic farming, is becoming well accepted in wide areas of the Corn Belt and parts of the Pacific Northwest.

One of the most effective erosion control methods that could be adopted in chemical-intensive systems is conservation tillage, which includes minimum tillage and no-till methods. Conservation tillage systems generally are not a viable option for organic agriculture because they require pesticides for weed and insect control. With no-till planting, soil erosion losses from a corn-soybean sequence are one-third to three times greater than with sod crops in the rotation. No-till continuous corn has a C factor comparable to that of meadow rotations with conventional tillage. Conservation tillage systems, though not yet extensively used in the United States, are gaining popularity among some farmers.

Organic matter. Increases in soil organic matter that are associated with organic farming practices can also reduce erosion significantly. Differences in the content of soil organic matter from manure applications and crop rotations may range from a fraction to several percentage points. For example, at Rothamsted, England, soil cropped with barley and treated continuously since 1852 with N, P, and K fertilizers had an organic matter content of 1.90 percent, while soil treated continuously with manure had an organic matter content of 4.85 percent (3). This research also showed that grass and legumes in the rotation tend to maintain soil organic matter at higher levels (0.5 percent or more) than continuous arable cropping.

The effect of increased soil organic matter content on soil erosion is quantified by the soil erodibility factor, K, in the universal soil loss equation (11). The change in the K factor, which results from a change in organic matter, can be estimated for many soils from a soil erodibility nomograph (11). This nomograph shows that an increase in organic matter content of 1 percent on some soils, for example, changing the organic matter content from 3 to 4 percent, will reduce the K factor by 10 percent. This would, in turn, reduce the potential for soil erosion by this percentage. This does not take into account changes in the structure index or permeability class, which might also be improved by increasing the organic matter content.

Use of supporting practices. USDA's case studies showed that organic farmers make good use of erosion control support practices, such as terraces, contour stripcropping, contour farming, and grassed waterways. However, the studies did not assess whether organic farmers used these practices to a greater extent than their conventional neighbors.

Opportunities for water conservation

Many practices frequently employed by organic farmers increase water infiltration and storage, but these practices do not necessarily conserve water for subsequent crops. Moreover, these practices do not conserve water as effectively as some practices used in conventional farming.

Tillage. The organic farmers' choice of the chisel plow or offset disk over the moldboard plow, which is used frequently by conventional farmers, knowingly improves water conservation. Also, long-term use of the organic farmers' method of shallow tillage, which incorporates residues near the surface, may temporarily increase water infiltration compared with moldboard plowing (5). On the other hand, conservation tillage practices, which include forms of minimum tillage or no-till, are even more effective for water conservation. These systems as yet are not viable options for organic farming because pesticides are required to control weeds and insects in residues. Additional pre-plant or post-plant tillage as a substitute for pesticides would decrease the effectiveness of conservation tillage systems.

Cropping practice. Sod crops produce some residual benefits, such as increasing water infiltration for a year or so after the sod is plowed out. This effect declines rapidly thereafter, however. Apart from this, sod, especially deep-rooted alfalfa, and cover crops often used in the organic rotation consume large amounts of water. This may contribute to a water deficit for the subsequent crop in areas of lower rainfall.

Organic matter effects. The infiltration capacity of fallow soils increases as soil organic matter content increases (*10*). However, experiments show that short-term changes in soil organic matter due to soil management are difficult to measure unless extremely large amounts of organic material are added (*6*).

Obstacles to organic farming

Despite the relative advantages and opportunities afforded by organic farming technology and management practices for soil and water conservation, a number of factors exist that may severely limit their adoption on a significantly broader scale. The following potential limitations and barriers delineated in the USDA report would not necessarily impact upon all organic farmers. Some organic farmers could be relatively free of most or all of these constraints. Many organic farmers do not consider these factors to be serious barriers to successful and profitable organic farming.

Limiting phosphorus and potassium. Farming systems that have negative P and K budgets and soils with a low P- and K-supplying capacity generally will not sustain crop production over the long term at high yield levels without the use of organic and/or inorganic sources of these nutrients. On most soils, high levels of crop production cannot be sustained indefinitely under negative P and K budgets.

Organic sources of plant nutrients are limited. America's highly productive agriculture requires large amounts of N, P, and K fertilizers; and large-scale substitution of these fertilizers with organic sources would be limited by both cost and availability (*9*). Extensive use of symbiotic N-fixation would require large-scale changes in land use.

Restrictions on symbiotic N-fixation as a source of N. Organic farming systems, which rely heavily on use of leguminous meadows to provide N through symbiotic N-fixation, are often less satisfactory than those systems where N is supplied from inorganic sources and may be unsatisfactory under conditions of lower rainfall. In such cases, the yield of the first crop following the leguminous meadow is often reduced because of the severe depletion of subsoil water by deep-rooted legumes.

Low-solubility nutrient sources. Low-solubility sources of P and K, which are most commonly used in organic farming, are often of limited value as nutrient sources for high-yield levels of many common crops.

Demand for organic food. The current demand for organically grown food is somewhat limited, but indications are that it may increase. At present, relatively few organic farmers can depend upon receiving a premium price for organic products. A large percentage of organically grown produce is now marketed through conventional channels.

Lack of organized marketing. Organic farmers have no concentrated marketing effort. There is little information on kinds of organic products available, the location and source of these products, and their price. There is some confusion as to what can be defined as "organically produced" food. There is also a lack of well-developed alternative marketing strategies available to organic farmers. In addition, lack of certification programs for organic food and poor understanding of certification standards by consumers are often barriers to the marketing of organically grown products.

Increased transportation costs. The geographical dispersion of organic producers and the low volume of organic products increases the cost of transportation and marketing.

Reduced production. While individual farmers may find it economically feasible to adopt organic farming, a full-scale shift to organic practices probably would reduce total farm output. Thus, macroeconomic factors may be a barrier to significant expansion of organic farming, at least in the short term.

Low income crops in rotational systems. Because of the need for crop rotations, organic farming results in greater diversification than conventional farming. Consequently, organic farmers may have to substitute low-income crops for high-income crops. This results in lower income for organic farmers compared to conventional farmers whose standard practice is production of high-value crops.

Economic loss during transition from conventional to organic farming. The shift from conventional or organic farming requires a three- to five-year transition. During this period, weeds and insects can be serious problems. Significantly lower crop yields may result.

Greater risks from weeds and insects. Organic farmers may be subject to greater crop losses from weeds and insects. Controlling weeds and insects is a major problem for some organic farmers, especially those producing fruit and vegetable crops.

Increased cost of labor. The availability and cost of labor, especially hand labor, may limit the success and profitability of organic farming.

The need to maximize economic return. Organic farming is sometimes limited because of economic returns. In the short run, high input costs, especially for land, and low farm prices put continuous pressure on farmers to use practices and methods that provide the greatest return on investment.

Lack of credit and financing. Many organic farmers, or would-be organic farmers, report difficulties in convincing loan officers that organic farming can be a viable economic operation.

Lack of communication and understanding. According to USDA's case studies, lack of communication and understanding between organic farmers and the agricultural research and extension communities has hindered the transfer and application of research and educational information. The negative attitudes of many conventional farmers and of the agricultural establishment toward organic farming have sometimes limited the acceptance of this method of farming.

Attitudinal barriers and inadequate knowledge about the benefits of organic farming. Many agricultural scientists, extension workers, and farmers strongly believe that organic farming is impractical or not feasible. To some extent, these views are the result of misperceptions and misunderstandings about the contemporary character of organic farming. Similarly, agricultural policy makers are not fully aware of the environmental, conservation, and energy-related benefits of organic farming. Educational programs could help overcome these attitudinal and institutional barriers.

Ambiguity of organic farming concepts. The ambiguity of certain basic concepts of organic farming prevents their use as a firm basis for decision making. For example, the concept of feeding the soil rather than the plant is unclear, difficult to interpret in physically meaningful terms, and difficult for scientists to relate to soil physical and chemical characteristics. This barrier can be overcome by mutual education and understanding.

Lack of information on organic farming. Little research and published information are available to help organic farmers resolve the problems they encounter in the development and implementation of organic production methods.

Farm ownership patterns. Organic farmers tend to own a large portion of the land they farm. Thus, they are in a unique position to experiment, to conserve, and to take less than optimum yields if necessary. Absentee landlords and local landlords as well may not be so willing to allow their tenants to practice organic farming.

Lack of adaptable crop varieties. Organic farmers generally grow recommended crop varieties. However, these varieties are most often selected for their response to a high soil fertility regime and may not respond well when grown in organic systems. Thus, the lack of adaptable crop varieties may limit successful organic farming.

Future prospects for organic farming

The future role and scope of organic farming in U.S. and world agriculture is uncertain. Despite such potential advantages as reduced pesticide and nutrient pollution, reduced soil erosion, enhanced food safety and quality, energy and water conservation, improved soil tilth and productivity, lower farm production input costs, improved farm worker safety, and long-term food production sustainability, a number of obstacles may severely limit the wider adoption of organic farming. Given this complex mix of advantages and barriers, what factors may impact most heavily upon the future expansion of organic farming?

1. Cost and availability of energy.
2. Demand for organically grown food.
3. Public support for research and education programs in organic agriculture.
4. Cost and availability of chemical fertilizers, pesticides, and other conventional farm production inputs.
5. Public concern over the adverse affects of conventional agricultural practices on environmental quality.
6. Soil productivity.
7. Public policy and farm structure.

For example, rapidly rising energy costs, accompanied by increased public concern over the character and direction of agricultural production and its possible adverse effects, could provide the basis for a serious reevaluation of organic farming's role in U.S. and world agriculture. Should these events trigger a serious research and education effort in organic farming, as well as certain policy changes designed to foster organic farming, for example, policy incentives to decentralize animal production, it is conceivable that this mode of agriculture could play a far larger role in the future.

The headline of a recent *Science* article (*2*) dealing with the USDA report on organic farming declared, "Organic Agriculture Becomes 'Legitimate'." According to students of public policy, achieving agenda status, that is, getting policy makers to be aware of and take seriously a given policy area, is an essential first step in the overall policy process (*1*).

If, indeed, organic farming has now achieved agenda status, one of the principal obstacles to its wider adoption has already been overcome. Resolution of the remaining obstacles may well constitute one of the most fascinating and important chapters in agricultural history.

REFERENCES

1. Anderson, James, et al. 1978. *Public policy and politics in America.* Duxbury Press, North Scituate, Massachusetts.
2. Carter, Luther. 1980. *Organic farming becomes "legitimate."* Science 109; 254-256.

3. Cooke, G. W. 1977. *The roles of organic manures and organic matter in managing soils for higher crop yields: A review of the experimental evidence.* In Proceedings, International Seminar on Soil Environment and Fertility Management in Intensive Agriculture, Ministry of Agriculture, Agricultural Research Council, London, England
4. Federal Trade Commission. 1976. *Hearing on food advertising, November 17.* 16 CFR Part 437. Washington, D.C. p. 4.
5. Johnson, C. B., and W. C. Moldenhauer. 1979. *Effect of chisel versus moldboard plowing for soil erosion by water.* Soil Science Society America Journal 43: 177-179.
6. Lucas, R. E., and N. L. Vitosh. *Soil organic matter dynamics.* Research Report Number 358. Michigan Agricultural Experiment Station, East Lansing.
7. Paarlberg, Don. 1980. *A new agenda for agriculture.* In Don F. Hadwiger and William P. Brown [editors] *The New Politics of Food.* Lexington Books, Lexington, Massachusetts
8. Paarlberg, Don. 1980. *Farm and Food Policy: Issues of the 1980s.* University of Nebraska Press, Lincoln.
9. U.S. Department of Agriculture, 1978. *Improving soils with organic wastes.* Report to Congress in response to Section 1461 of the Food and Agriculture Act of 1977. Washington, D.C.
10. Wischmeier, W. H. 1966. *Relation of field-plot runoff to management and physical factors.* Soil Science Society America Proceedings 30: 272-277.
11. Wischmeier, W. H., and D. D. Smith. 1979. *Predicting rainfall erosion losses.* Agricultural Handbook 537. U.S. Department of Agriculture, Washington, D.C.
12. Youngberg, Garth. 1978. *Alternative Agriculturists: Ideology, politics, and prospects.* In Don F. Hadwiger and William P. Brown [editors] *The New Politics of Food.* Lexington Books, Lexington, Massachusetts

25

Remote Sensing Applications for Resource Management

Chris J. Johannsen
Visiting Professor, Department of Land, Air and Water Resources, University of California, Davis,
and
Terry W. Barney
Research Associate, Geographic Resources Center University of Missouri, Columbia

Many people familiar with remote sensing do not consider it useful in their work. The technology was oversold in its early stages. People were told they could detect plant diseases and insects, see nutrient deficiencies, determine differences in plant temperatures, and many other claims. Remote sensing is also flashy. Color-infrared images, multicolored classification maps, and similar products make beautiful wall hangings, but managers and administrators look at these displays and question their usefulness.

Most remote sensing specialists are aware that remote sensing, on its own, is not the answer to many resource problems. Resource managers currently use topographic maps, soil surveys, black and white aerial photography, land ownership maps, and similar reference information in their decision making. The renewed look at remote sensing focuses on use of remote sensing products in conjunction with standard reference information.

Remote sensing is currently defined as the science and art of acquiring information about material objects from measurements made at a distance, without coming into physical contact with the objects. Recognizably, this definition covers photography, scanning images, radar, sonar, and similar data-gathering techniques.

An important aspect of the definition is information extraction or data analysis to obtain useful information. Remotely sensed data are measurements of variations in electromagnetic energy that may reveal spectral, spatial, and temporal variations in the scene (20). Resource managers need to think seriously about these variations before planning to acquire or to use a remote sensing product. An agricultural scene, for example, can be identified by the color of light emanating from the scene (spectral variations), by the relatively uniform rectangular areas distinguished by the local crop types (spatial variation), by the manner in which the scene changes over the course of the local growing season (temporal variations), or by a combination of all three factors.

Data bases

There are many techniques available for analyzing remotely sensed data (29, 31, 33). Emphasis here is on combining ancillary data, such as surface observations, soil maps, and weather measurements, with remotely sensed data. Correlation of this information in an orderly format, such as geographically arrayed by computer, is referred to as a data base.

An example of the use of a data base would be the combination of elevation data with Landsat data (15). In mountainous terrain, certain tree species exist within certain elevation ranges. Therefore, digital geographically oriented topographic data can be merged with Landsat data to separate species that appear similar spectrally.

Data bases also permit more feasibility in the use of remote sensing data as well as ancillary data. Weismiller and his colleagues (35) spatially registered Landsat data at a scale of 1:24,000 and overlaid this with digitized township, watershed, and physiographic boundaries. This enabled separation of soil associations by three landscape positions. With this data base, one can also delineate, by categories, the acres of soil and vegetation by slope group and by watersheds. This greatly increases the accuracy of runoff estimates in watershed analysis. With the addition of temporal remote sensing data and additional ancillary data, one could determine land cover by soil type, provide soil interpretations, determine erosion hazard areas, chart land use changes, and carry out a variety of other applications. Some of these data base applications can be obtained without direct use of remote sensing data.

Development of data bases ultimately leads to the need for a geographic information system (34). A geographic information system is a formal process for gathering, storing, analyzing, and disseminating information about natural resources and socioeconomic data. Many resources managers have found that such a system provides a cost-effective procedure for planning, developing, managing, and conserving natural resources.

Remote sensing applications

Scientific and nontechnical literature contains many reports on remote sensing applications that are important to resource managers. These reports discuss techniques for processing, analyzing, and interpreting information in the areas of agriculture, rangelands, forestry, hydrology, geology, cartography, land use, thermography, environmental protection, oceanography, disaster warning, and human and animal health. The results of many experiments have been reported in a series of major symposia for which review reports are available, including the Purdue University Symposia on Machine Processing of Remotely Sensed Data between 1970 and 1980 and the University of Michigan Symposia on Remote Sensing of the Environment between 1964 and 1980 (*11, 27, 28*).

The true users of remote sensing information have been coming forth only during the past four years. The time lag can be attributed to four factors: First, the technology was ahead of many potential users. Second, the time interval between collection and delivery of data was too long to answer many resource questions. Third, there was uncertainty as to the continuity in acquiring satellite data. Fourth, it was difficult to satisfy such a broad range of users who had different spectral, spatial, and temporal needs.

Land resources. Many resource managers require land use data, information, and maps. While land use classification systems have been developed for remote sensing (*3*), their use with photography appears more acceptable than with Landsat images. It is not unusual to see users modify or develop their own land use classification system based upon the time of year that data was collected (temporal), the resolution of the data, the scale of the photograph or image, the geographic location, and other factors.

Many users are able to separate land cover categories using Landsat data from which they can interpret land use. Barney and associates (*5*) were able to separate grain crops, hay and pasture, timber, and urban categories using Landsat images at a scale of 1:250,000 (Figure 1). They used tonal differences and land patterns to help in the separation process, then verified their interpretations with aerial photographs and ground observations.

The utility of such maps (Figure 1) can be assessed from the general but helpful information they convey. To the fertilizer or chemical company looking for dealer and distribution-center locations, the grain crop map shows where crops are located. The proportion of area in grain crops helps reaffirm available U.S. Department of Agriculture figures. Agricultural workers, such as extension specialists, can use the locational information in program planning for more effective educational efforts. A livestock specialist would know the location of cow-calf operations by observing hay and pasture distribution. A wildlife specialist could predict the location of specific animals or fowl based upon the relationship of timber to the other cover categories (*21*).

The maps in figure 1 demonstrate the utility of a data base. They were registered to a common base and digitized along with three generalized slope maps prepared from a U.S. Geological Survey 1:250,000 topographic map and a soil association map of the county (*6*). Interaction of the land cover maps with the slope and soil maps produced data showing the acres of

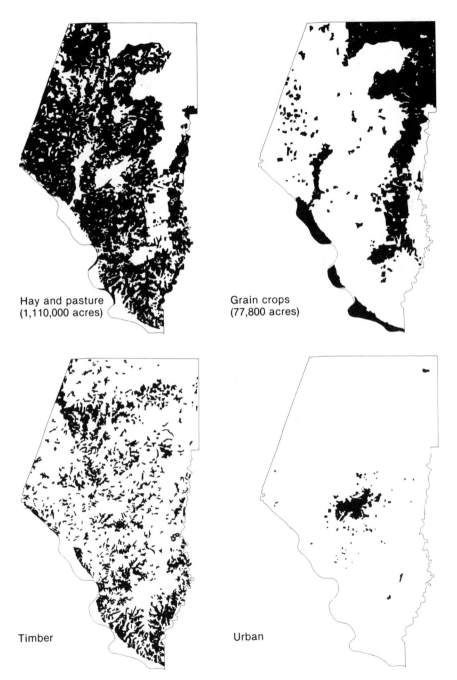

Figure 1. Distribution of land cover types in Boone County, Missouri, as determined by analysis of Landsat data. Acreage figures are crop area data reported by the U.S. Department of Agriculture for the same year.

each cover type by topographic position within each soil association. The intensity of land use on certain soil types becomes more evident to conservationists when viewing the data.

One should not overlook aerial photography, which has been used for years to map land use. Use of different dates of coverages provides the opportunity to show the rate of change of residences, mobile homes, and businesses in rural areas (*17*) and the documentation of land use change occurring before and after a freeway was announced and built in a Los Angeles suburb (*13*). An index of aerial photography for Missouri enables users to see what photography has been flown and is available for their area (*4*).

Soil resources. Use of aerial photography in mapping soils is evident by the use of the photograph as a base map, the delineation of slope units through stereo observation, the use of the photo tones to delineate soil boundaries more accurately, and the publishing of soil maps on aerial photographs to assist the user with orientation.

Landsat images have been used to map soil associations by photo-interpretation techniques (*22, 36*). The following Landsat characteristics are applicable to a state soil survey program: synoptic view, multispectral data collection, ability to collect temporal data, and the near orthographic aspect of the data (*37*). Landsat data can also be merged with ancillary data, such as elevation, and with vegetation patterns in noncultivated areas to increase mapping capabilities.

An important application of remote sensing in soil mapping involves the use of soil color information. Recent work (*8, 25*) shows that the most important factors influencing soil color are mineralogy and chemical constituents, soil moisture, soil structure, particle size, and organic matter content. Johannsen and de Costa (*19*) used spectral reflectance from laboratory and Landsat measurements to predict soil physical and chemical properties. This work illustrates the opportunity to not only make soil boundaries remotely but to predict organic matter, clay and sand content, and iron content. However, these applications are limited. They are subject to surface moisture variabilities as well as seasonal conditions when soils have been tilled. In addition, reflectance data is limited by the fact that conventional soil series are differentiated by both surface and subsurface properties.

Soil erosion in conjunction with nonpoint pollution control has become an increasing concern to resource planners. Remotely sensed data from satellites can provide a continuous flow of information about land cover and land use conditions in a watershed. Color infrared aerial photography is satisfactory for assessing eroded areas in grassland and timber locations but unsatisfactory with Landsat pictures because of the coarse resolution (*24*). Remote sensing techniques also can provide cover data—the C-factor in the universal soil equation—for predicting erosion on cropland (*26*).

Vegetation resources. Those features on the earth's surface that produce the greatest contrast, such as green vegetation, bare soil, and water, are the easiest to separate. Sundanese scientists (7), using Landsat images over southern Sudan, were able to map natural and cultivated vegetation, clayey soil areas, sand dunes, and surface water, which provided valuable resource planning data. The application of providing current resource maps in developing countries is obvious to anyone who has struggled with the problem of obtaining resource information for planning purposes.

Selection of images at particular times of the year increases the chances of separating certain categories of vegetation. An early spring scene over the central Corn Belt is ideal for distinguishing row crops (bare soil), wheat (dark green vegetation), hay and pasture (light green vegetation), and timber (brownish green vegetation). There is likely to be some confusion between wheat and hay or pasture. To separate the wheat, one need only compare the spring scene with a fall scene of the same area, just after wheat seeding. Areas that feature bare soil in the fall and green vegetation in the spring can only be wheat. This is making use of the temporal aspect of Landsat data.

Analysis of a spring scene in Missouri illustrates a variety of uses for the agricultural industry (Figure 2). An accurate estimate of wheat acreage is important to elevator and storage facilities as they plan for harvest and the purchase of grain. Location of bare soil areas can be an important feature for determining the quantity and type of chemicals and fertilizers that dealers should have in inventory. Comparison of a Landsat scene from 1978 with one from 1973 documents the acres of pasture plowed up and seeded to soybeans. This information is important for ordering seed, fertilizer, and chemicals. Combining the Landsat classification (Figure 2) with soil survey maps, one can predict the chemical inventory more accurately as well as arrive at realistic production figures for selected trade areas.

The forecasting of crop yields is a question that is frequently brought to remote sensing technologists. The identification of crop types and measurement of acreage, which can be accomplished by Landsat under specific conditions, is only one step in the process of forecasting crop production. Crop yield must be estimated using a combination of plant phenology information as well as weather data. Some direct estimates of yields in remote sensing have been attempted, however (16). The Large Area Crop Inventory Experiment (LACIE) used crop yield models that required the date of planting or stage of maturity as well as moisture and temperature data. The results with these Landsat data produced cautious optimism for the application of improving crop production forecasting by acreage estimates in developing countries.

Monitoring of range conditions is important to ranchers and land managers. Measurements of existing biomass (32) with weather predictions can assist in planning for grazing schedules. The location of areas to be reseeded; the location of weeds, brush, and other unwanted plant species; the location and extent of surface water, and the areas mowed for hay are other additional forms of information that can be obtained by interpreting remote sensing products (23).

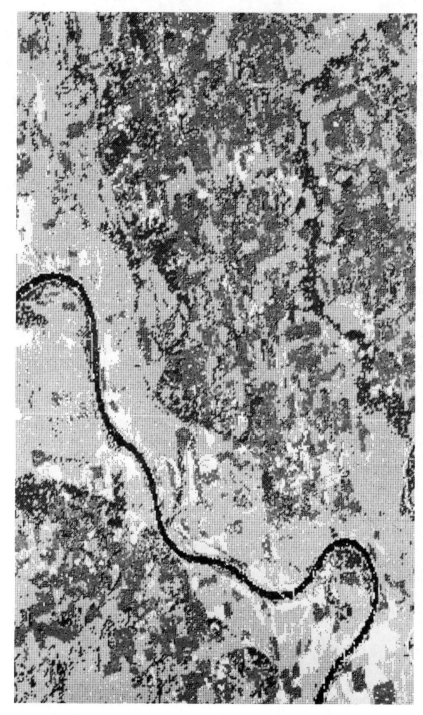

Figure 2. A Landsat classification of a 200-square-mile area in central Missouri showing bare soil, wheat, hay and pasture, timber, and water.

Foresters have used computer-aided analysis of multispectral remotely sensed data to delineate the areal extent and boundaries of recent forest fires (*14*); to map detailed timber categories, such as aspen, ponderosa pine, and douglas fir (*12*); and to detect tree stress (*1*). The accuracies of forest-type mapping can also be increased using data bases and reference materials, including U.S. Geological Survey topographic maps, stand compartment-type maps and related information, aerial photographs, Forest Service land use maps, and ground observations (*10*).

Mineral resources.   One of the earliest uses of aerial photography was in geological exploration. Remote sensing's principal application in mineral resources development is to inventory areas known to contain minerals and to estimate potential yield. New remote sensing technology finds its way rapidly into mineral exploration because of the potential economic returns. Many new remote sensing techniques, procedures for computer analysis, and development of data bases are being funded through petroleum and geological exploration (*29*).

Use of remote sensing in assessing surface mine reclamation efforts has received increased attention with the passage of federal legislation on reclamation. Rogers and colleagues (*30*) employed computer processing of Landsat data to identify reclaimed areas, partially reclaimed areas, water, and water with sedimentation on minelands in a five-county area of eastern Ohio. Landsat data was also used to measure strip-mined acreage in western Maryland (*2*).

Surface-mined areas were successfully located and revegetated zones delineated on Illinois and Missouri mine sites using low-cost Diazo processing and manual interpretation techniques (*38*). Carrel and associates (*9*) used overlays on aerial photography to darken vegetative areas with a pen, then measured the darker areas using a leaf meter to measure the percentage of groundcover.

Computer techniques involving the scanning of color-infrared aerial photography over strip mine lands proved to be a low-cost approach to assessing the degree of revegetation on individual surface mines (*9*). These techniques were used to measure the vegetal cover, bare soil, and water areas on active mines by the Missouri Land Reclamation Staff (*18*). Repetitive coverage of the same areas will provide information on the rate of vegetation establishment, reclamation of abandoned mines, and identification of problem areas that need specific attention and study.

Conclusions

Many applications of remote sensing depend upon resource managers' access to information, the correlation of this information with current ancillary data, the type of analytical equipment available, and the managers' training or that of their staff people in remote sensing. Use, understanding, and acceptance of this new technology takes time, money, and patience.

The need for technology transfer in remote sensing is ever-increasing. Colleges and universities as well as state and federal agencies are attempting to meet this need, and resource managers should not hesitate to seek their assistance. Prototypes of second-generation Landsat systems and operational uses will be further demonstrated for many disciplines during the coming decade. Remote sensing data applied to natural resources, especially when combined with ancillary data, such as soil maps, topographic information, and watershed boundaries, will be of enormous value to resource managers.

REFERENCES

1. Aldrich, R. C., and R. C. Heller. 1969. *The use of multispectral sensing techniques to detect ponderosa pine trees under stress.* Space Science Laboratory Report. University of California, Berkeley. 25 pp.
2. Anderson, A. T., D. T. Schultz, and N. E. Buchman. 1975. *Landsat inventory of surface mined areas using extendible digital techniques.* In Proceedings, NASA Earth Resources Survey Symposium (volume I-A). National Aeronautics and Space Administration, Houston, Texas. pp. 329-345.
3. Anderson, J. R., E. E. Hardy, and J. T. Roach. 1972. *A land use classification system for use with remote-sensor data.* Circular 671. U.S. Geological Survey, Washington, D.C.
4. Barney, T. W., and C. J. Johannsen. 1976. *Index to aerial and space coverage of Missouri.* Extension Division M-102. University of Missouri, Columbia. 114 pp.
5. Barney, T. W., C. J. Johannsen, and D. J. Barr. 1977. *Mapping land use from satellite images—a users guide.* Marshall Space Flight Center, National Aeronautics and Space Administration, Huntsville, Alabama. 45 pp.
6. Barr, D. J., and C. J. Johannsen. 1978. *Application transfer activity in Missouri.* NASA CR-150805. Marshall Space Flight Center, National Aeronautics and Space Administration, Huntsville, Alabama. 41 pp.
7. Bashii, H. S., Y.I.M. Bushara, Y. Y. Mohammed, E.M.A. Hassan, K.A.K. Ibrahim, and A.R.A. Mohammed. 1978. *Remote sensing in the Sudan.* International Development Research Center, Ottawa, Ontario. 36 pp.
8. Beck, R. H., W. W. McFee, B. F. Robinson, and J. B. Peterson. 1976. *Spectral characteristics of soil moisture, organic carbon, and clay content.* Information Note 081176. Laboratory for Applications of Remote Sensing, Purdue University, West Lafayette, Indiana. 82 pp.
9. Carrel, J. E., C. J. Johannsen, T. W. Barney, and W. D. McFarland. 1978. *Remote measurements of vegetative cover in surface mines.* In Proceedings, International Symposium on Remote Sensing of Environment. Environmental Research Institute of Michigan, Ann Arbor. pp. 1,652-1,664.
10. Dodge, A. G., and E. S. Bryant. 1976. *Forest type mapping with satellite data.* Journal of Forestry 74: 526-531.
11. Earth Satellite Corporation and Booz-Allen Applied Research Corporation. 1974. *Earth resources survey benefit-cost study: Economic, environmental, and social costs and benefits of future earth resources survey systems.* Prepared for U.S. Department of Interior-Geological Survey, 12 volumes. Earth Satellite Corporation, Washington, D.C.
12. Fleming, M. D., J. S. Berkebile, and R. M. Hoffer. 1975. *Computer-aided analysis of Landsat-1MSS data: A comparison of the three approaches including a "modified clustering" approach.* In Proceedings, Machine Processing of Remotely Sensed Data Symposium. Laboratory for Applications of Remote Sensing, Purdue University, West Lafayette, Indiana. 8 pp.
13. Goehing, D. R. 1971. *Monitoring the evolving land use patterns on the Los Angeles Metropolitan fringe using remote sensing.* Technical Report T-71-5. Department of Geography, University of California, Riverside. 106 pp.
14. Hitchcook, H. C., and R. M. Hoffer. 1974. *Mapping a recent forest fire with ERTS-1MSS data.* Information Note 032674. Laboratory for Applications of Remote Sensing, Purdue University, West Lafayette, Indiana. 13 pp.
15. Hoffer, R. M. 1975. *Natural resource mapping in mountainous terrain by computer analysis of ERTS-1 satellite data.* Research Bulletin 919. Laboratory for Applications of Remote Sensing, Purdue University, West Lafayette, Indiana. 124 pp.
16. Idso, S. B., R. D. Jackson, and R. J. Reginato. 1977. *Remote sensing of crop yields.* Science 196: 19-25.

17. Johannsen, C. J. 1976. *Agricultural applications of remote sensing.* Statement to special oversight hearings of Committee on Science and Technology, U.S. House of Representatives, Report 51. Washington, D.C. pp. 695-724.
18. Johannsen, C. J., T. W. Barney, J. E. Carrel, A. D. Coble, W. D. McFarland, and D. J. Barr. 1979. *Characterization of vegetation and drainage in strip mined land utilizing remote sensing techniques.* Environmental Protection Agency and U.S. Department of Agriculture, Washington, D.C. 98 pp.
19. Johannsen, C. J., and L. M. deCosta. 1980. *Using soil color/reflectance in predicting soil properties.* In Proceedings, Remote Sensing and Soil Survey Symposia. Laboratory for Applications of Remote Sensing, Purdue University, West Lafayette, Indiana. p. 283.
20. Landgrebe, D. 1976. *Computer-based remote sensing technology—a look to the future.* Remote Sensing of Environment 5: 229-246.
21. LaPerriere, A.J.L., III. 1976. *Use of Landsat imagery for wildlife habitat mapping in northeast and east central Alaska.* Report, National Academy of Science 5-20195. University of Alaska, Fairbanks. 39 pp.
22. Lewis, D. T., P. M. Seever, and J. V. Drew. 1975. *Use of satellite imagery to delineate soil associations in the Sand Hills Region of Nebraska.* Soil Science Society of America Proceedings 39: 330-335.
23. Maxwell, E. L. 1975. *Applications of ERTS to rangeland management* In Proceedings, Remote Sensing of Earth Resources Conference (volume IV). Tennessee Space Institute, University of Tennessee, Tallahoma. pp. 105-136.
24. Michelbacher, V. M. 1978. *Vegetative-soil relationships used to identify soil erosion with remote sensing.* Masters thesis. School of Forestry, Fisheries and Wildlife, University of Missouri, Columbia. 137 pp.
25. Montgomery, O. L., M. F. Baumgardner, and R. A. Weismiller. 1976. *An investigation of the relationship between spectral reflectance and the chemical, physical and genetic characteristics of soils.* Information Note 082776. Laboratory for Applications of Remote Sensing, Purdue University, West Lafayette, Indiana. 147 pp.
26. Morgan, K. M., G. B. Lee, R. W. Kiefer, T. C. Daniel, G. D. Bubenger, and J. T. Murdock. 1978. *Prediction of soil loss on cropland with remote sensing.* Journal of Soil and Water Conservation 33: 291-293.
27. National Research Council, Commission on Natural Resources, Committee on Remote Sensing Programs for Earth Resources Surveys. 1974. *Remote sensing for resource and environmental surveys: A progress review.* National Academy of Science, Washington, D.C.
28. National Research Council, Space Applications Board of the Assembly of Engineering. 1975. *Practical applications of space systems.* National Academy of Sciences, Washington, D.C.
29. Reeves, R. G., editor. 1975. *Manual of remote sensing.* American Society of Photogrametry, Falls Church, Virginia. 2,144 pp.
30. Rogers, R. H., L. E. Reed, and W. A. Pettjohn. 1973. *Automated strip mined and reclamation from ERTS.* In Proceedings, Earth Resources Technology Satellite-1 Symposium (volume II). National Aeronautics and Space Administration, Johnson Space Center, Houston, Texas. pp. 1,519-1,531.
31. Rohde, W. G. 1978. *Digital image analysis techniques required for national resources inventories.* In Proceedings, National Computer Conference. U.S. Department of the Interior, Washington, D.C.
32. Seevers, P. M., J. V. Drew, and N. P. Carlson. 1975. *Estimating vegetative biomass from Landsat-1 imagery for range management.* In Proceedings, NASA Earth Resources Survey Symposium (volume I-A). National Aeronautics and Space Administration, Houston, Texas. pp. 1-8
33. Swain, P. H., and S. M. Davis, editors. 1978. *Remote sensing: The quantitative approach.* McGraw-Hill, New York, New York. 396 pp.
34. Tessar, P. A., and L. M. Caron. 1980. *A legislator's guide to natural resource information systems.* National Conference of State Legislatures, Denver, Colorado. 59 pp.
35. Weismiller, R. A. I. D. Persinger, and O. L. Montgomery. 1977. *Soil inventory from digital analysis of satellite senser and topographic data.* Soil Science Society America Journal 41: 1,166-1,170.
36. Westin, F. C., and V. I. Myers. 1973. *Identification of soil associations in western South Dakota on ERTS-1 imagery.* In Proceedings, Second Symposium on Significant Results Obtained from the Earth Resources Technology Satellite. Goodard Space Flight Center, Greenbelt, Maryland.
37. Westin, F. C., and C. J. Frazee. 1976. *Landsat data, its use in a soil survey program.* Soil Science Society of America Journal 40: 81-89.
38. Whitebay, L., and D. J. Barr. 1977. *Evaluation of Landsat imagery for mined land studies.* In Proceedings, Missouri Academy of Sciences Annual Meeting, Columbia. 8 pp.

26

Effects of Conservation on Wheat Yields

G. Larry Edmonds
Agricultural Economist, Soil Conservation Service
Spokane, Washington
and
Robert H. Dawson
Agricultural Economist, Economics and Statistics
Service, Corvallis, Oregon

Loss of topsoil and its related productive and environmental effects is one of the important natural resource problems in the dryland farming area of Washington.

Resource management systems can be developed to solve these problems, but the effects of these systems on farm income must be determined. To identify the differences in effects among resource management systems, it is necessary to separate the systems into elements. Herein we address the effect on wheat yields of certain components in the resource management systems. The components are farm management, tillage, cropping systems, crop residue, contour farming, stripcropping, and terraces.

The study's data base

The national inventory and monitoring system was used as a base for resource data. The 8 percent Land Inventory and Monitoring (LIM) sample sites in Asotin, Garfield, Columbia, and Walla Walla Counties of southeastern Washington were selected as the study base. There were 1,287 cropland sites in these four counties. A supplemental data sheet was added to the standard LIM inventory form. This sheet enabled the identification of all conservation practices and systems listed in local Soil Conservation Service

(SCS) technical guides. After this inventory was completed, a list of conservation practices was developed for each site.

The LIM data sheets were then used to identify the major soil mapping unit for each site. Information was added on the expected average annual precipitation for each site to the nearest inch (determined by placing a precipitation map overlay on the LIM site map) and the farm operator for each site [from SCS and Agricultural Stabilization and Conservation Service (ASCS) records]. At this point the list included conservation practices, soil, precipitation, and operator data.

The district conservationist and other experienced SCS personnel were asked to estimate residue level for each operator at seeding. There were three categories: over 1,000 pounds of crop residue at seeding, 500 to 1,000 pounds of crop residue at seeding, and less than 500 pounds of residue at seeding.

The district conservationists were then asked to estimate management levels. Indicators included seeding dates, adapted varieties, fertilization, pest management, and timeliness of tillage. The group was divided into above average, average, or below average.

Next, yield data were obtained for each sample point. ASCS offices had records of yields for most farms in the county. These yields were supported by the operators providing ASCS with elevator receipts for a five-year period. The yield records were matched with the farm and LIM site. If the LIM site was not representative of the farm as to soils, precipitation, etc., the data for that site were not used in the analysis. Example: One site was on a shallow soil with rock outcropping, while the majority of the farms had deep loess soils. In these cases, the yield data for that farm were not representative of that site and, therefore, were not used. The data base then included information on conservation practices, soil, precipitation, operator, management, residue, and yields. These data were developed by county, then aggregated, including a connotation for each county. Data were available for 852 sites after nonrepresentative sites and sites without yield information were excluded.

The soil mapping units were then combined into nine soil associations. These associations were (1) Ritzville-Ellisford, which included 174 observations; (2) Walla Walla-Chad-Asotin, 266 observations; (3) Athena-Palouse, 250 observations; (4) Snow-Yakima-Patid, 27 observations; (5) Esquatzel, 12 observations; (6) Adkins-Quincy, 4 observations; (7) Starbuck, 64 observations; (8) Klicker-Tolo-Anatone, 13 observations; and (9) Gwin-Waha-Palouse, 42 observations.

Means, standard error of mean, sample variance, sample standard deviation, and coefficient of variation were computed. The T test was used to identify the upper and lower yields at the confidence level for each of these associations. At the 80 percent confidence level there was no significant difference in yields for associations 1,2,5,6,7,8. These were combined to give us an elevation group with 533 observations. The next-sized sample was the Athena-Palouse with 250 observations, the Gwin-Waha-Palouse with 42 observations, and the Snow-Yakima-Patit with 27 observations.

Data at this point had been collected and arrayed so it could be analyzed by (a) soil mapping unit, (b) soil associations, (c) soil associations with similar yields, (d) residue level, (e) management level, (f) precipitation, (g) county, (h) conservation practice, and (i) combinations.

Work is currently being done to include cropping system, land ownership status, enumerator, and erosion rates.

Results of data analyses

The yield data collected through the evaluation procedure were compared with yield data collected for the soil survey report. The soil survey data matched well with that collected in this study on a site-by-site basis. The Walla Walla and Ritzville soils are adjacent topographically, and the yield data collected from ASCS records indicate that on a farm-by-farm basis the yields are more comparable than might be expected. The upper yielding area of the Walla Walla is closer in yields to the lower yielding area of the Ritzville than to the overall average of the Walla Walla. Table 1 summarizes yields by soil association.

Table 1. Average wheat yields, by soil association, all counties, 95 percent confidence.

Significant Soils Treatment	Observations	Average Yield	Standard Error of Mean	Confidence Level Lower	Confidence Level Upper
Ritzville-Ellisford	174	48.5	0.8	46.9	50.1
Walla Walla-Chard-Asotin	266	47.8	0.7	46.4	49.2
Athena-Palouse	250	58.2	0.7	56.8	59.6
Snow-Yakima-Patia	27	53.7	2.0	49.5	57.9
Esquatzel	12	53.7	2.0	42.9	51.7
Adkins-Quincy	4	-	-	-	-
Starbuck	64	47.2	1.5	44.2	50.2
Klicker-Tolo-Anatone	13	49.3	2.7	43.5	55.1
Gwin-Waha-Palouse	42	41.4	1.9	37.6	45.2

Table 2. Average wheat yields, by residue level, all counties, 95 percent confidence.

All Soils Residue Levels	Percent Operators	Observations	Average Yield	Standard Error of Mean	Confidence Level Lower	Confidence Level Upper
1,000 lbs +	25	210	52.5	0.8	50.9	54.1
500 lbs +	44	378	50.6	0.6	49.4	51.8
500 lbs −	31	264	49.7	0.9	47.9	51.5

Table 3. Average wheat yields, by management level, all counties, 95 percent confidence.

All Soils Management Level	Percent Operators	Observations	Average Yield	Standard Error Of Mean	Confidence Level Lower	Confidence Level Upper
High	24	205	51.8	0.8	50.2	53.4
Average	57	488	52.6	0.6	51.6	53.6
Low	19	159	44.1	0.9	42.3	45.9

Table 4. Average wheat yields, by residue and management, Gwin-Waha-Palouse soils, all counties, 80 percent confidence.

Significant Soils	Treatment	Observations	Average Yield	Standard Error of Mean	Confidence Level Lower	Confidence Level Upper
Gwin-Waha-Palouse		42	41.38	1.88	38.93	43.83
,,	Mgt. A	2	46.00	17.00	-	-
,,	Mgt. B	26	45.69	2.03	43.02	48.36
,,	Mgt. C	14	32.71	2.64	29.15	36.27
,,	Low residue	3	48.33	10.09	29.30	67.36
,,	Medium residue	30	44.40	1.95	41.84	46.96
,,	High residue	9	29.00	2.27	25.83	32.17

Table 5. Average wheat yields, by residue and management, Ritzville-Walla Walla soils, all counties, 80 percent confidence.

Significant Soils	Treatment	Observations	Average Yield	Standard Error of Mean	Confidence Level Lower	Confidence Level Upper
Ritzville-Walla Walla	Population	533	47.92	.49	47.29	48.55
,,	High mgt.	128	48.60	.97	47.35	49.85
,,	Medium mgt.	128	49.27	.66	48.42	50.12
,,	Low mgt.	99	42.89	.99	41.61	44.17
,,	Low residue	156	51.22	.91	50.05	52.39
,,	Medium residue	232	47.17	.64	46.35	47.99
,,	High residue	145	45.57	1.06	44.20	46.94

Table 6. Average wheat yields, by residue and management, Snow-Yakima-Patit soils, all counties, 80 percent confidence.

Significant Soils	Treatment	Observations	Average Yield	Standard Error of Mean	Confidence Level Lower	Confidence Level Upper
Snow-Yakima-Patit	Population	27	53.74	2.04	51.06	56.42
,,	Mgt. A	21	51.24	2.20	48.33	54.16
,,	Mgt. B	3	68.00	4.73	59.08	76.92
,,	Mgt. C	3	57.00	All observations	55.36	58.64
,,	Low residue	22	51.91	2.20	49.00	54.82
,,	Medium residue	3	57.00	-	55.36	58.64
,,	High residue	2	69.00	8.00	44.38	93.62

Table 2 demonstrates the effect of residue at seeding time on yield. Residue had no effect on yield in comparing the high to medium levels of residue and the medium to low levels. However, the difference was significant between the high and low levels of residue when the four-county data were combined.

There proved to be no difference in yields between operators in the high and average management classes. Operators in the low-management class experienced significantly lower yields than operators in the other two.

For the Gwin-Waha-Palouse soil groupings (Table 4), low management resulted in lower yields and 500 to 1,000 pounds of residue increased yields significantly over the overall average. Yields on the Ritzville-Walla Walla soils (Table 5) were affected by management similarly to the Gwin-Waha-Palouse group. However, yields declined significantly as residue declined, which was the opposite of what had been expected.

Management and residue trends reversed on the Snow-Yakima-Patit soil group (Table 6), but there were few observations.

The high-yielding Athena-Palouse soil group showed significantly lower yields for low management and high residue (Table 7).

Obviously, yield response to residue and management varies, depending upon soil characteristics. No broad statement can be made about the effect of residue on yields for the entire evaluation area. However, operators who were poor managers experienced significantly lower yields than the average operators.

Table 7. Average wheat yields, by residue and management, Athena-Palouse soils, all counties, 80 percent confidence.

Significant Soils	Treatment	Observa-tions	Average Yield	Standard Error of Mean	Confidence Level	
					Lower	Upper
Athena-Palouse	Population	250	58.23	.75	57.27	59.19
,,	Mgt. A	54	59.91	1.39	58.10	61.72
,,	Mgt. B	153	60.05	.95	58.83	61.27
,,	Mgt. C	43	49.63	1.67	47.45	51.81
,,	Log residue	29	60.51	2.18	57.65	63.37
,,	Medium residue	113	59.15	1.03	57.82	60.48
,,	High residue	103	56.64	1.22	55.06	58.22

Table 8. Average wheat yields, by residue and management for no conservation treatment, all soils and counties, 80 percent confidence.

Significant Soils	Treatment	Observa-tions	Average Yield	Standard Error of Mean	Confidence Level	
					Lower	Upper
All	None	208	52.53	.82	51.48	53.58
,,	Mgt. A	34	51.00	2.10	49.69	52.31
,,	Mgt. B	139	53.78	1.02	52.47	55.09
,,	Mgt. C	35	49.06	1.70	46.83	51.29
,,	Low residue	61	52.15	1.53	50.17	54.13
,,	Medium residue	74	51.05	1.24	49.44	52.66
,,	High residue	73	54.34	1.51	52.38	56.30

Table 9. Average wheat yields, by residue and management for conservation cropping systems, all soils and counties, 80 percent confidence.

Significant Soils	Treatment	Observa-tions	Average Yield	Standard Error of Mean	Confidence Level	
					Lower	Upper
All	Conservation cropping	20	58.20	2.37	55.06	61.34
,,	Mgt. A	6	66.00	2.25	62.68	69.32
,,	Mgt. B	10	56.80	3.13	52.47	61.13
,,	Mgt. C	4	50.00	6.12	39.98	60.02

Table 10. Average wheat yields, by residue and management for contour farming, all soils and counties, 80 percent confidence.

Significant Soils	Treatment	Observa- tions	Average Yield	Standard Error of Mean	Confidence Level	
					Lower	Upper
All	Contour farming	14	47	3.24	42.63	51.37
"	Mgt. A	2	38	0.0	-	-
"	Mgt. B	12	48.5	3.61	43.58	53.42
"	Mgt. C	0	-	-	-	-
"	High residue	0	-	-	-	-
"	Medium residue	13	47.54	3.45	42.86	52.22
"	Low residue	1	40.00	-	-	-

Table 11. Average wheat yields, by residue and management for crop residue use, all soils and counties, 80 percent confidence.

Significant Soils	Treatment	Observa- tions	Average Yield	Standard Error of Mean	Confidence Level	
					Lower	Upper
All	Crop residue use	392	49.57	.67	48.71	50.43
"	Mgt. A	83	51.29	1.33	49.57	53.01
"	Mgt. B	210	52.79	.90	51.68	53.95
"	Mgt. C	99	41.31	1.06	39.94	42.68
"	High residue	50	52.4	1.86	49.97	54.83
"	Medium residue	195	51.9	.87	50.78	53.02
"	Low residue	147	45.5	1.12	44.06	46.94

Table 12. Average wheat yields, by residue and management for minimum tillage, all soils and counties, 80 percent confidence.

Significant Soils	Treatment	Observa- tions	Average Yield	Standard Error of Mean	Confidence Level	
					Lower	Upper
All	Minimum tillage	15	51.8	3.03	47.74	55.86
"	Mgt. A	4	43.5	5.5	34.49	57.51
"	Mgt. B	8	56.0	3.63	50.86	61.14
"	Mgt. C	3	51.67	8.33	35.96	67.38
"	High residue	0	-	-	-	-
"	Medium residue	14	50.64	3.01	46.58	54.70
"	Low residue	1	68.00	0.	-	-

Management and residue effects were also analyzed by conservation practice (Table 8). There were 208 sites with no conservation practice. A lower percentage of high-level managers had no conservation practice than might be expected when compared with the percentages for all operators (Table 9). The low-management group continued to experience lower yields. High-residue operators had slightly higher yields than the lower residue groups.

A conservation cropping system was applied only to a small portion (2 percent) of the samples. However, it is interesting that the high management group had significantly higher yields than the rest of the population.

Contour farming was also applied to only 2 percent of the population (Table 10). Contour farming was practiced primarily by average managers and average residue operators. Apparently, operators in the upper and lower management groups avoid this practice. Yields with contour farming were lower than the average for all operators.

Forty-six percent of the operators used crop residues during the evaluation year (Table 11). Management level did not affect practice application. However more managers in the low residue group applied this practice than might be expected. Yields were not significantly affected by residue use.

Minimum tillage was also applied on only 2 percent of the sites (Table 12). The average management group experienced significantly higher yields—56.0 bushels compared to an overall average of 52.6 bushels.

Table 13. Average wheat yields, by residue and management for strip cropping, all soils and counties, 80 percent confidence.

Significant Soils	Treatment	Observa- tions	Average Yield	Standard Error of Mean	Confidence Level Lower	Confidence Level Upper
All	Strip cropping	49	54.06	1.69	51.86	56.26
"	Mgt. A	15	55.80	2.29	52.72	58.88
"	Mgt. B	34	53.29	2.22	50.38	56.20
"	Mgt. C	0	-	-	-	-
"	High residue	9	58.56	2.96	54.42	62.70
"	Medium residue	26	50.11	2.35	47.02	53.20
"	Low residue	14	58.5	2.98	54.48	62.52

Table 14. Average wheat yields, by residues and management for terraces, all soils and counties, 80 percent confidence.

Significant Soils	Treatment	Observa- tions	Average Yield	Standard Error of Mean	Confidence Level Lower	Confidence Level Upper
All	Terraces	80	51.68	1.27	50.03	53.33
"	Mgt. A	38	50.42	1.71	48.18	52.66
"	Mgt. B	37	54.27	1.95	51.72	56.82
"	Mgt. C	5	42.0	3.39	36.80	47.20
"	High residue	23	52.87	2.32	49.81	55.93
"	Medium residue	48	52.75	1.67	50.57	54.93
"	Low residue	9	42.89	2.05	40.03	45.75

Table 15. Average wheat yields, by residues and management for the summary, all soils and counties, 80 percent confidence.

Significant Soils	Treatment	Observa- tions	Average Yield	Standard Error of Mean	Confidence Level Lower	Confidence Level Upper
All	None	208	52.53	.82	51.48	53.58
"	Conservation cropping	20	58.20	1.37	55.06	61.34
"	Minimum tillage	15	51.8	3.03	47.74	55.86
"	Crop residue use	392	49.57	.67	48.71	50.43
"	Contour farming	14	47.	3.24	42.63	51.37
"	Strip cropping	49	54.06	1.68	51.86	56.26
"	Terraces	80	51.68	1.27	50.03	53.33

Stripcropping (Table 13) was applied on about 6 percent of the sites. Operators in the low management group did not apply strips. Operators in the high management group experienced slightly higher yields than the operators overall, but these yields were not significantly different from those obtained by operators in the average management group. There was a greater percentage of managers in the medium residue group than expected, and yields were slightly higher for managers in the high and low residue groups.

Terracing was the last practice evaluated. Table 14 summarizes the effect of residue and management on yields for soils protected with terraces. The average yield for average management exceeded the confidence limits for the total population. All other categories were not significantly different from the yields for the total population.

Table 15 compares practices. Yields under conservation cropping were significantly higher than those on no-treatment sites. This indicates that a conservation system has the potential for increasing yields at certain locations. Minimum tillage showed no significant yield difference from the no-treatment sites. Crop residue use resulted in a significant reduction in yields. Part of this reduction was due to the fact that some no-treatment sites were fallowed, while crop residue use only applied to continuous cropping systems. In most cases, wheat following fallow yields more than wheat under continuous cropping. Contour farming reduced yields for some unknown reason. Stripcropping increased yields slightly because of a reduction in wind erosion, a reduction in losses due to voiding by water rills, and increased moisture retention. Operators in the low management group rarely use this practice. Finally, terraces did not significantly increase yields.

Conclusions

Following are the conclusions reached in this study:

1. Components of resource management systems do affect yields.

2. Yields vary significantly, depending upon soil, residue level, and management level.

3. Extreme care must be taken when expanding site-specific data for broader based evaluations.

4. The deductive approach may also be misleading.

5. Poor farm managers are not applying complex resource management systems.

VII. Education for Productive Conservation

27

Harmonization and Reconciliation: E Pluribus Unum

Alexander J. Barton

Program director, Development in Science Education
National Science Foundation, Washington, D.C.[1]

If ever you travel the Blue Ridge Parkway along the crest of the Appalachian Mountain chain through Virginia and North Carolina, don't fail to stop at an overlook called Wildcat Rocks. To find it, you have to park your car near milepost 241 and walk up a forest path that terminates abruptly at a rock ledge overhanging a deep, steep ravine. A panorama of jumbled mountain, creek valley, and forest—a hundred square miles or more—stretches out beneath your gaze.

Of all the views I can recall from 35 years of field work as a professional ecologist in the Appalachians, this is the one that conveys most forcefully the isolation of the early American pioneer. In all this great expanse there is not a sign of human habitation to be seen—until you look almost straight down. There at your feet, 2,000 vertical feet below, a tiny, old log cabin sits alone on the edge of a pathetically small patch of cleared land. Not even a wilderness road reaches this solitary outpost; it was four miles down the hollow by foot or horseback to the wagon road, and then four miles more to the nearest hamlet. The couple who built this remote home so long ago wrested a living for themselves and their 14 children from the forest. Large-

[1]The opinions expressed in this article are those of the author and do not necessarily represent the official views of the National Science Foundation.

ly dependent upon themselves, they feasted briefly at the peak of the harvest or when there was fresh game in the larder, but subsisted pretty meagerly most of the time; they shivered in the cold and sweated in the heat; they grew or made or caught most of what they needed (or did without); if the time was inconvenient, the wife gave birth without outside assistance; when primitive home medicines were insufficient remedies for accident or disease, people died. But because they were a strand of a robust, burgeoning young nation, that wilderness did not conquer them. They mastered it.

If you tear yourself away from Wildcat Rocks and drive just a few miles north, you come to Brinegar Cabin. Its garden still grows a little flax, just as it has for more than a century and a half. Inside the cabin, by far the largest object is the massive old four-poster hand loom. The gracious park attendant weaves mostly cotton rugs on it these days, but that old loom originally was devoted to the weaving of linsey-woolsey—a coarse homespun fabric that unites the durability of linen with the warmth (and the itch) of wool to produce the garments that enabled these hardy pioneers to withstand the cold and wet as they clawed their laborious way westward across the Appalachian Mountain barrier.

I'd like you to think a moment about that loom and the pieces of linsey-woolsey that were woven so painstakingly upon it. Visualize the shuttle traveling back and forth across the warp, combining scarce animal hairs and plant fibers into a cloth more serviceable than either one could produce alone. Focus, if you will, upon the idea of *integrating several individual qualities into a whole that is stronger than the separate parts.*

While you are thinking about the enhanced strength that comes when many diverse assets are combined into one whole, reflect upon the fact that while these hardy pioneers were generalists who could get by pretty much on their own devices, there also was a degree of interdependence among them. Not every home had a loom, for instance, but everyone needed its cloth.

Down the road a few miles, beyond Brinegar, stands the cabin in which Miz Puckett, the local midwife, lived for 74 of her 102 years. She delivered over a thousand babies to families in those hills (most of whom I hope had better success than she had with her offspring, for not one of her own 24 babies survived infancy). Many a time Miz Puckett's services were paid for with a length of linsey-woolsey. And Mr. Mobry who owned the mill further north sometimes was paid in cloth in return for his services in grinding everyone's corn and grain. So was the blacksmith and the preacher.

The primitive society of these parts was itself a great loom upon which the talents and resources of many families were woven, like flax and wool, into a social fabric that combined in one the strengths of its members.

The present situation

What analogy to the current environmental crisis would I have you draw from the experience of these early pioneers? What has linsey-woolsey to do with acid rain? Just this:

1. The environment that sustains all life on earth is under steadily intensifying stress on every side. It cannot long survive an extension of the present trends.

2. The human race has at its disposal a vast array of resources—knowledge, technique, and talent—for amending the destructive aspects of its environmental behavior.

3. These resources are splintered, fragmented—even contentious—as each seeks to win for itself a disproportionate share of the finite support base.

4. Our species has not yet evolved any process for weaving into a unified whole the various useful environmental strands available to it. It is imperative that we do so at once. We are facing in these closing decades of the 20th century not the loss of a crop but of the farm!

Reflect with me upon the area that in recent years has occupied my deepest thoughts—*environmental education* or, as the sectional topic of this book so aptly phrases it, *education for productive conservation.*

Environmental education is like a huge weaving mill loaded with useful materials. Great piles of wool spill over into the cotton; the silk is snarled with the nylon and orlon; the flax has gotten mixed into the sisal and hemp. The whole thing is a mess and, frankly, the world's top managers don't know where to begin in dealing with the problem. So they call upon their technical people for advice as to how the world can sort out its environmental household and begin to make some useful educational cloth.

Among these technical experts, the predominant group are the educators, who insist that the whole environmental education problem can be solved by concentrating upon delivery methods. "Just get the conveyors rolling," they say, "and all the problems will be solved." But unfortunately, the samples of cloth they offer to validate their claims are sad, thin, threadbare specimens that won't keep anybody warm. Useful as the educators' expertise is, *by itself* it is inadequate to meet the nation's needs.

Turning elsewhere for more effective advice, management calls upon its scientists—its researchers and professional problem-solvers. "The educators are wrong," these savants tell us. "Content is all that really matters." The output of the scientists is just the opposite of the educators'. The samples of cloth they present prove to be so densely woven that no ordinary tailor can cut or sew them into useful garments. Indeed, it seems as if the scientific fraternity takes perverse pleasure in creating goods that only their fellow initiates can handle. So by itself, the scientists' output too is unserviceable in meeting society's broader needs.

There is one more place for the world to turn for solutions—to the users' representatives, to the consumers of environmental education. Their response is absolute bedlam. It is virtually impossible for society to sort any signal out of the noise created by the cacophony of their shrill, competing voices. Everytime the marine specialist begins to say something interesting and helpful, the energy protagonist snatches away the microphone. Industrialists and bankers generally are fighting the Sierra Clubbers; the representatives of organized labor, with a cheerful impartiality, take potshots at both. Developers and keep-things-just-like-they-are conservationists both preach that theirs is the only true gospel; that for the public to pay any attention to the other is the sure road to perdition. A control-through-regulation proponent steals the show by bringing out his model dressed in an elegant suit. But when the model turns around, even the friendliest observer cannot fail to note that the designer has left out the seat of the pants! So, there is a serious problem with the advice that comes from the user groups.

Lost in ghettoes of special interest, well-meaning enthusiasts from the various environmental factions miss the very essence of environmental knowledge—its holism. The interrelationships, the feedback mechanisms, the interconnecting linkages, the indivisible integrity of the ecosystem totally escapes their understanding as they loudly recommend overly simple, partial solutions that, if pursued, would defeat their own most cherished goals. By themselves, none of these designers—educators, scientists, or users—seem able to give us any pattern for creating a sound environmental fabric.

Recent studies

All of us have grown tired of hearing Malthusian prophets of doom predict that humankind will choke to death in its own effluent at 10 p.m. on August 6, 2024. I would not have you mistake me as being one of their number. However, no thinking person can ignore a rising tide of evidence that says unmistakably that our present course is leading us toward global disaster. The capacity of the biosphere to sustain life as we know it is infinitely better buffered and more able to sustain insults than is the fragile socioeconomic system that maintains our quality of life. Neither one, however, is infinitely capable of sustaining our current abuses of them.

Ocean sediment corings taken recently from the floor of the Atlantic present startling indications that surficial marine life also died off about the same time the dinosaurs became extinct. One plausible hypothesis is that some extraterrestrial event—a comet or some other enormous physical phenomenon—temporarily created conditions that were lethal to higher life forms on a worldwide scale, so that the then-dominant species, together with many lesser types, were utterly exterminated in a relatively brief period. Whatever the cause of this massive die-off was, my point is this: Because it already *has* happened here; it *can* happen here!

Confirming warnings that were sounded in 1972 by the Club of Rome in its *The Limits to Growth* (8), three new reports issued this year all concur that it might happen again—not as a result of some cosmic cataclysm, but through human improvidence. You will find these reports briefly summarized by Luther Carter in the August 1, 1980, issue of *Science.*

North-South: A Program for Survival (6) is the report of an international commission headed by West Germany's Willy Brandt that warns that society must make major political and economic decisions that will alter the way the earth's resources are spent. The commission's basic recommendation is that the nations of earth stop their massive spending on arms (currently some $450 billion per year) that diverts to military applications resources that otherwise might go to conservation and development.

Many would agree that this is a laudable goal, but one unlikely to be achieved.

The *World Conservation Strategy* (7), which was put forward last March with endorsements from the United Nations, the Organization of American States, and other international bodies, seeks to make conservation and development efforts mutually supportive. The strategy correctly identifies the dual imperative; on one hand, development cannot be sustained if ecological systems are disrupted and renewable resources are abused; on the other hand, human poverty and degradation cannot be relieved without economic growth.

I pass over these earlier reports hurriedly to concentrate upon one that is more recent. The latest and most exhaustive of the three studies, *The Global 2000 Report to the President* (*15*) is a three-volume, 800-page work prepared by a task force involving 13 federal agencies and more than 100 international experts working steadily since 1977. Based upon a mass of real data that has been poured into the group's mathematical "global model," this report describes conditions that probably will pertain in the year 2000. The task force's prognostications do not make for light reading.

Unless major steps are taken, the president was told, the world 20 years from now will be a filthy, unstable planet with billions of poor people scrambling for scarce, high-priced resources:

1. The world population will have risen from 4 billion in 1975 to 6.35 billion people and will be growing by 100 million a year. Most of this growth will be in the poorer, less developed countries where 4 out of 5 persons will live—mostly in urban slums and shantytowns:
   a. Mexico City, already crowded by only 10 million will bulge with 31 million people.
   b. The Orient will be the most overpopulated: Calcutta will have nearly 20 million; more than 15 million each will jam Bombay, Jakarta, and Seoul. In the Middle East, Cairo will have equally as many.
2. The environment will have lost important life-supporting capabilities:
   a. By 2000, 40 percent of those forests that still remained in the less developed countries in 1978 will have been destroyed.
   b. The atmospheric concentration of carbon dioxide will be nearly one-third higher than preindustrial levels.
   c. Acid rain will poison many lakes and rivers, making their waters uninhabitable to fish and other aquatic life.
   d. In little more than two decades, one-fifth or more of the earth's total species of plants and animals will have become extinct, a loss of 500,000 to 2 million species. Rare plants needed to create new blight-and pest-resistant hybrids will have vanished from the earth.
   e. Desertification, including salinization, may have claimed a significant fraction of the world's rangeland and cropland.

    f. Demand for firewood, the world's most widely used fuel, will exceed supply by at least 25 percent.

    g. Even if every spring, well, river, and lake that exists today continues to yield a constant supply of potable water (and you can guess how likely that will be), between 1975 and 2000, per capita water supplies will decline by 35 percent because of greater population alone.

    h. The world's remaining petroleum resources per capita can be expected to decline by at least 50 percent.

    i. The number of malnourished people will rise from an estimated half-billion in the mid-1970s to 1.3 billion by the year 2000.

    j. Starvation will claim increasing numbers of babies born in less developed countries. Many of the survivors will grow up physically and mentally stunted.

3. Prices will be higher:

    a. To meet projected demand, a 100 percent increase in the real price of food will be required.

    b. To keep energy demand in line with anticipated supplies, the real price of energy is assumed to rise more than 150 percent over the period 1975-2000.

4. The world will be more susceptible both to natural disaster and to disruptions from human causes:

    a. Most nations are likely to be more dependent on foreign sources of energy in 2000 than they are today.

    b. Modern mass food production will be vulnerable to disruptions of fossil fuel energy supplies and to weather fluctuations.

    c. As cultivation expands to more marginal areas and as monoculture increases, the risk of massive crop failures will increase.

    d. Larger numbers of people will be less able to cope with higher food prices when production fails. Outbreaks of famine are likely to increase.

    e. The world will be more vulnerable to the disruptive effects of war, while tensions that could lead to war will have multiplied.

As one reels at the impacts of these figures, it is important to note that, strictly speaking, they are not predictions of the future. Rather they are to be understood as projections made from current trends, as conditions likely to exist in the year 2000 *unless* the present course of events is changed by significant shifts in public policies, major advances in technology, or unforeseeable events, such as an outbreak of war or the depressive effects that a lack of food for the urban poor, a lack of jobs, and increasing illness and misery might have in slowing and altering the trends.

Global 2000 contains no recommendations. The commission that produced the report was mandated only to create a workable world model and then employ it to extrapolate data curves—not to make or interpret policy.

Even before the report officially had been delivered to him, however, President Carter acted to initiate the essential next step by creating an Interagency Task Force on Global Resources and Environment. *Science* goes on to report, "The President said that 'the projected deterioration of the global environmental and resource base' was among the world's 'most urgent and complex challenges', and he called on the task force to give high priority attention to the global resource, population, and environmental problems and seek ways to improve the government's capability for analyzing global trends. The task force will in effect develop policy recommendations to go with the report...."

Conclusions

I have little doubt that by now the *Global 2000* "two by four" has arrested your attention, as it did mine. As citizens and as persons responsible in our various jobs for at least some aspects of environmental education, what should we be doing?

Major answers for the United States have been available for several years. Mary Berry, for instance, summarized them nicely in her introduction to *Toward an Action Plan: A Report on the Tbilisi Conference on Environmental Education* (*14*): "We must move toward a coherent national strategy for environmental education that takes full advantage of the strength of our diversity. We must make sure that all essential items are provided for, that unnecessary redundancies do not squander our resources, and that adequate coordination is maintained."

Rather than engaging in an endless cycle of iterations, we need to review already available answers and then to devote our energies to implementing them. A good starting point is the 1977 Declaration of the Tbilisi Intergovernmental Conference on Environmental Education (*16*) that stated: "Education utilizing the findings of science and technology should play a leading role in creating an awareness and a better understanding of environmental problems. It must foster positive patterns of conduct toward the environment and the nations' use of their resources.

"Environmental education should be provided for all ages, at all levels and in both formal and nonformal education. The mass media have a great responsibility to make their immense resources available for this educational mission....

"Environmental education, properly understood, should constitute a comprehensive lifelong education, one responsive to changes in a rapidly changing world. It should prepare the individual for life through an understanding of the major problems of the contemporary world, and the provision of skills and attributes needed to play a productive role toward improving life and protecting the environment, with due regard given to ethical values. By adopting a holistic approach, rooted in a broad interdisciplinary base, it recreates an overall perspective which acknowledges the fact that natural environment and man-made environment are profoundly interdependent. It helps reveal the enduring continuity which links the acts of today to the consequence for tomorrow...."

The National Environmental Education Leadership Conference, convened in Washington in 1978 to examine the 41 recommendations emerging from Tbilisi (*11*), reported a priority listing of those that are especially relevant to the United States. Their finding was that the creation of a National Center for Environmental Education is the goal of greatest urgency.

Walter Jeske, George Pratt, and I have published (*1*) a rationale that supports that conclusion. It is our conviction that such a national center can form a rallying point at which the common elements of our environmental concerns will be emphasized and the differences minimized, where federal, state, and privately controlled environmental bodies can join forces to coordinate and vastly increase the effectiveness of the nation's environmental education efforts. The entire issue of *Trends*, in which the Barton-Jeske-Pratt article appeared, is full of interesting insights into the current environmental education scene in the United States.

Robert Cahn, in the 19th Horace M. Albright Conservation Lecture (*2*), suggested that the conservation challenge of the eighties is one of ethics and values, of will, and of philosophy. Cahn said:

"As we begin the new decade, however, we are confronted by a set of conditions entirely new to this nation, and which will require a reordering of priorities, some changes in our system of values, and a willingness to alter our lifestyles and even some of our very basic philosophies.

"What I see as the conservation challenge of the 80s is to reshape our attitudes and values and our practical approaches in such a way that we can live in an era of scarcity without ruining the life systems on which we depend.

"It was the seemingly endless frontier and boundless resource based that allowed our nation to achieve world leadership in the brief span of two centuries and give full vent to individualism, ingenuity, and freedom of movement and action. Now we are within sight of physical boundaries. We are feeling restrictions closing in on our use of resources. We are beginning to recognize that conservation can no longer be the pet province of an aware minority; it is now an absolute and universal requirement.

"I am not suggesting that the limitations we now face will rob us of the individualism and freedom that are so basic to the American psyche, but that these ideals will have to stretch their bounds to include a wider acceptance of community interest—sometimes at the expense of personal self-interest—and an enlightened sense of our relationship with the planet and its inhabitants that can be called an environmental ethic.

"One of our cherished philosophies that has already been shattered is that 'a man's house is his castle'—that we can use land we own according to our personal dictates. Of course, we have learned to abide by laws that limit how and where we can develop our property, and how and where we can dispose of our refuse—laws enacted out of necessity because it was discerned that the welfare of the entire community superseded the indulgence of oneself or family. And in the world of commerce the time-honored philosophy that 'the business of business is profits' is being somewhat tempered by a growing concern for wider and longer-range considerations which include social and environmental responsibility."

There is heartening evidence that Cahn is not alone in seeing attitudinal changes taking place in America. One needs only to examine the August 18, 1980, issue of *U.S. News and World Report* to see the wide attention currently being directed toward environmental issues. In one article, Jerome Wiesner is reported as arguing that, after affluence, America is "not prepared to go back to a totally different lifestyle." Analyzing the effects of technology on our "open and democratic society," he worries about the nation's "paralysis of decision making," calling for decisions that "provide environmental protection and at the same time permit the evolution of technical processes that are required for industry."

"When the scale of technology was small," Dr. Wiesner goes on to observe, "benefits so exceeded peripheral new problems that people didn't have to be concerned about the problems. Today, we have to measure costs as well as benefits in everything we undertake in the technological realm. And we have to be concerned about the side effects of what we are doing...." This article is a very substantial exercise in environmental education, led by a national luminary and given full exposure in one of the nation's leading news weeklies!

But it is even more fascinating to note that this one issue devotes more than 12 full pages to environmental education matters. In addition to the Wiesner interview, the magazine's editorial coverage treats hurricanes, world population forecasts (in two pages of text and graphs), and endangered species (in two more pages, complete with 10 full-color photos). Equally interesting is the environmental content of the advertising pages! I spotted "Clearing the Nation's Air" (Chemical Manufacturers Association); "Environmental Protection or Environmental Perfection. There's a Big Difference" (U.S. Steel); "New Environmental (weather) Satellite"; "Energy Savings" (Hughes Aircraft); and "Gas Additions to Reserves" (American Gas Association). This sampling leaves no question that environmental issues are commanding great prominence in the national forum and that various interests are competing vigorously for the peoples' favor. Much of the energy now being expended in these ways could be captured and channeled into better and more effective environmental education if we but had the wit and political acumen to do it.

Useful work is being done. John Disinger has edited a fine compendium of *Environmental Education Activities of Federal Agencies* (3) that first was issued in 1978 and just now is being revised. William Stapp, together with his colleagues and students at the University of Michigan, has thought deeply about possible options for the nation's strategy for environmental education and has published on the topic (12). Harold Hungerford, Ben Payton, and Richard Wilke (5) have published an extremely useful paper on goals for curriculum development in environmental education. David Dodson Gray (4) has directed attention to the public anger reaction with which the American citizenry increasingly is meeting the frustrations of a limited-growth society. No recital of current environmental education references is complete until mention is made of the perennially standard outline of environmental education topics, *The Fundamentals of Environmental Education* (*13*).

Clay Schoenfeld is the sparkplug of a promising effort to develop a definitive agenda of research work that is needed to create a firmer theoretical foundation for environmental education. Finally, Norman Miller of Dartmouth College, producer of the anthropology film series, "Faces of Change," contributor to the excellent United Nations Environment Programme Review 1978 (*10*), and author of the *United Nations Environmental Programme* (*9*), is organizing an invitational conference for mid-fall 1980 intended to give fresh impetus to the movement advocating a National Environmental Education Center. The functions both of a national policy center and of a North American regional teaching resource center for environmental education will be reexamined at that time.

This partial checklist of activities persuades me that the nation's environmental education community is spinning some strong threads, but spinning thread is only a preliminary to weaving cloth. Strong cross connections and linkages are what are needed now, unifying structures that will unite the good threads into a durable fabric.

I should like to leave you with just two urgent personal agenda items:

1. All of you, regardless of your background or persuasion, join together in raising a loud call for the new Interagency Task Force on Global Resources and Environment to make extensive use of education as an instrument of environmental preservation. Education's track record as an effective instrument for forming the wills and informing the minds of the people earns it such a place in this national council. Insist through your institutions, organizations, and personal influence that adequate environmental education expertise be added to the task force at once so that the insights of environmental educators may become integral parts of the national policies this task force is to formulate.

2. Charge from here determined to foster stronger bonds between environmental science and environmental education and also to forge the links that should unite responsible development with prudent preservation. How might you do this?

a. Those of you who belong to one or more professional scientific societies, give their education committees no rest until environmental education occupies a prominent place on their standing agenda.

b. Those of you whose affiliations are closer to educational associations, press these bodies to be less parochial in their outlooks, more rigorous in their environmental scholarship, more willing to sink their teeth into really tough urban and natural ecological issues, and to chew hard untill significant gains have been made. Urge them also to join hands with the doers, so that their fine intellectual structures may be built more quickly into practical operational programs.

c. Those of you who are farmers, ranchers, and foresters, plant the environmental ethic with every row of seed you sew. By precept and example, persuade other agriculturists to so conduct their operations that the land they manage retains its productivity until their stewardships end and the farms descend to their children.

d. Try to convince your associates that not all environmentalists are a bunch of woolly headed extremists who put the welfare of butterflies ahead of human needs. Those of you who are members of conservation organizations, work to rid your friends of the notion that all businessmen are mercenary beasts who slaver over every chance to rape the earth of its last remaining resources. Resolve personally to be less suspicious of potential environmentalist allies whose professional, occupational, educational and social backgrounds differ from your own. Take a developer to lunch, share with him or her some mutually broadening explorations into education for productive conservation.

REFERENCES

1. Barton, Alexander J., Walter E. Jeske, and George L. B. Pratt. 1979. *A national center for environmental education.* Trends 16(1): 16-20.
2. Cahn, Robert. 1980. *The conservation challenge of the 80s (The 19th Horace M. Albright Conservation Lecture).* College of Natural Resources, University of California, Berkeley.
3. Disinger, John F., editor. 1978. *Environmental education activities of federal agencies.* Subcommittee on Environmental Education. Federal Interagency Committee on Education, U.S. Department of Health, Education, and Welfare, Washington, D.C., and ERIC/SMEAC, Columbus, Ohio. 167 pp.
4. Gray, David Dodson. 1980. *Goodbye more—hello less.* Joint Strategy and Action Committee. Grapewine 11(6): 1-5.
5. Hungerford, Harold, R. Ben Payton, and Richard Wilke. 1980. *Goals for curriculum development in environmental education.* Journal of Environmental Education 7(3): 42-47.
6. Independent Commission on International Development Issues. 1980. *North-south, a programme for survival.* MIT Press, Cambridge, Massachusetts. 304 pp.
7. International Union for the Conservation of Nature and Natural Resources. 1980. *World conservation strategy.* Gland, Switzerland.
8. Meadows, Donella H., et al. 1974. *The limits to growth; a report for the Club of Rome's project on the predicament of mankind.* New American Library, New York, New York. 207 pp.
9. Miller, Norman N. 1979. *The United Nations Environmental Programme.* American Universities Field Staff Reports. Hanover, New Hampshire. 36 pp.
10. Miller, Norman N. 1980. *Environmental health and human behavior: UNEP's twin challenge,* and *An independent evaluation.* In *Annual Review of the United Nations Environment Programme.* Nairobi, Kenya. pp. 74-83.
11. Stapp, W. B., editor. 1978. *From ought to action in environmental education: A report on the National Leadership Conference on Environmental Education.* ERIC/SMEAC, Columbus, Ohio. 98 pp.
12. Stapp, William B., et al. 1979. *Toward a national strategy for environmental education.* In Arthur B. Sacks and Craig B. Davis [editors] *Current Issues V: The Yearbook of Environmental Education and Environmental Studies.* ERIC/SMEAC, Columbus, Ohio. pp. 92-125.
13. Subcommittee on Environmental Education. 1976. *Fundamentals of environmental education.* U.S. Department of Health, Education and Welfare, Washington, D.C. 30 pp.
14. Subcommittee on Environmental Education, Federal Interagency Committee on Education. 1978. *Toward an action plan: A report on the Tbilisi Conference on Environmental Education (October 14-26, 1977).* U.S. Department of Health, Education and Welfare, Washington, D.C. 33 pp.
15. The Global 2000 Task Force. 1980. *The global 2000 report to the president; entering the twenty-first century.* Council on Environmental Quality and U.S. Department of State, Washington, D.C.
16. United Nations Educational Scientific and Cultural Organization. 1977. *Declaration, working papers of the Intergovernmental Conference on Environmental Education.* New York, New York.

Addendum

To extend the voice of SCSA's annual conference to nationwide audiences in the United States and Canada, Mr. Barton was asked to tape several audio actualities by Robert W. Buis, public information specialist at the Soil Conservation Service Midwest Technical Service Center in Lincoln, Nebraska.

Mr. Buis's questions and the responses they elicited from Mr. Barton summarize the nature, role, and importance of environmental education in late 20th century America. Following is a transcript of the tapes that were distributed continent-wide by radio:

Mr. Barton, we're hearing a lot about environmental education and we would like to know just what it is, and why the Soil Conservation Society of America, for example, is establishing a special division for environmental education?

Environmental education deals with the living world and what makes it work—relationships between various plants and animals and the nonliving factors in the environment—things such as water and soil, sunshine, and air. Old-time nature study concentrated on the whats of nature, for example, what kind of bird is that, or what kind of soil am I plowing? Ecology and environmental science, on the other hand, concentrate on the whys of nature. Why does poison ivy flourish on land that has been disturbed recently? Why do cattails grow in areas that are permanently moist? Why do people who function well when they are surrounded by fresh air and growing green plants begin to make more mistakes and become irritable when their air supply grows stale and warm? The answers to these kinds of questions are the business of environmental education—answers that better enable us to understand ourselves and the world we occupy.

We feel that environmental education uses the findings of science and technology to play a leading role in creating a wide public awareness and a better understanding of environmental problems. It seeks to foster positive patterns of conduct toward the environment, and toward the nation's use of its resources. Environmental education is for people of all ages, at all levels, whether they are in the formal education system or outside of it. (The mass media thus have a great responsibility to make their immense resources available for this educational mission.)

Environmental education should constitute a comprehensive, lifelong process that is responsive to changes in a rapidly changing world. It should prepare the individual for life through an understanding of the major problems of the contemporary world. It should provide the skills and attributes that are needed for people to play a productive role toward improving life and protecting the environment. Proper concern, too, is given to ethical values.

An important strength of environmental education is the way in which it adopts a holistic outlook. Environmental education is rooted in a broad interdisciplinary base; it creates an overall perspective that acknowledges the fact that the natural environment and the man-made environment are profoundly interdependent. Perhaps its most important feature is the vital way in which it helps to reveal the enduring continuity that links the acts of today and the consequences of tomorrow.

With so much concern being shown nationwide for improving the ability of our schoolchildren to perform basic functions like reading and writing, why should schools take time to teach environmental education?

Well, everybody I know always concentrates on what they think is important. To put it the other way, people don't react to what they think is unimportant. The job of education is to enable people to make better and more accurate estimates of what really is important.

Maintaining the ability of the earth to support high-quality human life is terribly important. If we were in a submarine and our experts notified us that our air supply was going bad, we would give high priority attention to that problem—right now! If we were just getting into a spaceship and the man in charge said that he has decided to put twice as many people into the ship as originally planned, to go just as far on the original supply of food and water, I don't know about you, but I wouldn't get on that spaceship.

Why would the submarine or spaceship passengers react so strongly? It is because they realize that their air, food, and water supplies are strictly limited, and that if they run out it might not be possible to replenish them.

One central message being sounded at this conference is this: Whether we want to believe it or not, this spaceship earth has a strictly limited capacity to provide clean air, food, and water to living things. If we poison or exhaust that capacity, it may not be possible to replenish the supplies, or to go on supporting the kind of life that we are willing to accept.

Our kids are going to have to cope effectively with the problems of limited food, water, wood, animal feed, soils—you name it. I think it's terribly important, therefore, that our schools teach people how to deal with these very real dangers. The media ought to play an important role in telling people about them, too.

You can see that I quite disagree with those who want to push our earth's growing environmental problems back into the shadows in the hope that they will go away somehow. I think these problems can be solved, but only if people learn how to work on them. Learning how to work on them is the task of environmental education.

Just how serious is this matter of environmental misuse? Isn't it merely one of those trendy issues that young people get all excited about and then blow up into something a lot bigger than it deserves to be?

Young people certainly are concerned over environmental misuse, but I'm convinced that both they and the older generation have very good reasons to be concerned. This matter of environmental well-being is not just a kooky issue of concern for a few extremists. Nobody thinks that the more than 100 international experts who worked on the Global 2000 Study are a bunch of radical alarmist kids, and neither are the 13 different federal agencies that have just completed this three-year study of what the world might look like in the year 2000 if we don't do anything to correct current trends.

These responsible folks agree that unless major steps are taken, the world 20 years from now will be a filthy, unstable planet with billions of poor people scrambling for scarce, high-priced resources. The world population will have risen from 4 billion in 1975 to 6.35 billion, and will be growing by the rate of 100 million a year. Most of this growth will be in the poorer, less-developed countries, where four out of five people will live by then.

The environment will have lost important life-supporting capabilities. By the year 2000, 40 percent of those forests that still remain in the less-developed countries of the world in 1978 will have been totally destroyed. The atmospheric concentration of carbon dioxide will be nearly one-third higher than in preindustrial levels. Acid rain will poison many lakes and rivers, making their waters uninhabitable to fish and other aquatic life. In little more than two decades, one-fifth or more of the earth's total species of plants and animals will have become extinct, a loss of between one-half million and two million species.

Desertification may have claimed a significant fraction of the world's rangelands and croplands. The demand for firewood (the world's most widely used fuel) will outstrip supply by at least 25 percent. Even if all of our springs and rivers and lakes were to remain pure and drinkable, the per capita water supplies of the earth would decline by 35 percent between 1975 and 2000 because of greater population alone! The world's remaining petroleum resources per capita also can be expected to decline by at least 50 percent.

The number of malnourished will rise from an estimated half billion people in the mid-1970s to 1.3 billion people by the year 2000. Starvation will claim increasing numbers of babies born in less developed countries; many of the survivors will grow up physically and mentally stunted. Modern mass food production will be vulnerable to disruptions of fossil fuel energy supplies and to other fluctuations. Larger numbers of people will be less able to cope with higher food prices when production fails and the world overall will be vulnerable to the disruptive effects of war as the tensions that can lead to war will have multiplied.

Since now is the time to make the decisions and initiate the actions that would insure that this unpleasant future will not befall us, I think that environmental education is an imperative today, and for every one of us, not just concerned kids.

28

What Kind of Environmental Education for the Eighties?

John F. Disinger
Professor, Division of Environmental Education
School of Natural Resources
and Associate Director
ERIC Clearinghouse for Science, Mathematics, and
Environmental Education
Ohio State University, Columbus

It is not only fashionable but appropriate in this tenth anniversary year of Earth Day to reflect on the progress of environmental education during the past decade, assess its current status, and project what the new decade may portend. But this task of projection must be approached with caution. A number of projections from 1970 have already proved wildly inaccurate (*33*).

Nonetheless, the task is an interesting one. If Winston Churchill's admonition—those who do not understand history are doomed to repeat it—is honored, the approach of the computer-armed futurist in analyzing how the past has created the present and how they together propel us into the future (*3*) may be instructive in examining the question: What kind of environmental education for the eighties?

Earth Day, an amalgamation

Of course, it is no more accurate to suggest that environmental education was born on Earth Day 1970 than it is reasonable to define it as education for environmental activism. Pre-1970 predecessors of environmental education have commonly been identified as nature study, conservation education, and outdoor education (*20, 31*). What occurred in 1970 selectively absorbed the content, techniques, and clientele of each, then attempted to refocus the result on survival of the human species.

The procedure commonly used was to reconstitute the philosophies, goals, and objectives of those predecessors, then redefine them, as did the National Environmental Policy Act of 1969 (Public Law 91-190), in terms of "the profound impact of man's activity on the interrelations of all components of the natural environment, particularly the profound influences of population growth, high-density urbanization, industrial expansion, resource exploitation, and new and expanding technological advances and recognizing further the critical importance of restoring and maintaining environmental quality to the overall welfare and development of man."

This clearly called for education directed toward "a systematic, interdisciplinary approach which will insure the integrated use of the natural and social sciences and the environmental design arts in planning and in decision-making which may have an impact on man's environment" (P.L. 91-190), but in so doing also demanded a reorientation of educational procedures, administrative and instructional, within the formal educational establishment. Such reorientation has proved difficult at best to achieve and seems little closer to reality now than in 1970.

The institutional response

Certainly the formal educational establishment at the federal level made the right noises 10 years ago. An Office of Environmental Education was established in the U.S. Office of Education, and a widely circulated statement by the assistant secretary for education in the Department of Health, Education, and Welfare, proclaiming that "environmental education is the education that cannot wait" (*15*), fostered a belief that the weight of the federal educational establishment was firmly committed to nurturing the new thrust. But this anticipated support has not materialized. Particularly lacking have been federal leadership and funding (*24, 25*).

State educational agencies generally have done no better. Two surveys in the 1970s (*4, 19*) reported glaring unevenness in state support, again in terms of leadership and funding. State agencies apparently waited for federal leadership and money. When such support was not forthcoming, most state agencies were not particularly supportive, nor innovative. California and Florida are exceptions.

The higher education community apparently has recognized the importance of environmental education over the past decade. There has been a substantial increase in the number of courses containing one of the terms "ecology/ecological," "environment/environmental," or "energy" in their titles (*28*). Case studies provide additional evidence of this recognition (*28*).

Problems have been encountered in college/university settings, however.

These typically include perceived encroachment by environmental education on the domains of established departments; difficulties encountered by faculty involved in such efforts in demonstrating academic respectability in an ill-defined, nontraditional field; and in the case of environmental education for teacher education, the twin obstacles of limited job opportunities for teachers trained as environmental educators and resistance to making curricular space for new offerings at the expense of established courses and programs.

The curricular space problem is also evident in the nation's K-12 schools, particularly in the departmentalized settings characteristic of secondary education. Is environmental education science or social studies? How can it be both? The school curriculum is already crowded, and other new and in some cases mandated offerings compete for curricular space. Also, teachers are not prepared to deal with environmental education, and schools are beleaguered by other pressures, such as those generated by social welfare programs, the back-to-the-basics phenomenon, and public resistance to higher taxes. A series of surveys (*5, 6, 7, 8, 9*) indicates widespread but spotty K-12 involvement in environmental education. There are a few outstanding efforts, a number of adequate ones, and far more schools than environmental education programs or activities.

Why the lack of progress

There are a number of reasons why progress in environmental education has not been greater.

1. Environmental education has been and remains difficult to define, particularly in operational terms. In addition to the long-time staples—nature study, conservation education, outdoor education—foci associated with environmental education over the past decade have included citizenship education, energy education, experiential education, marine education, population education, urban environmental education, values education, and others.

Turf problems have become multitudinous. A sufficiently broad definition of environmental education proclaims it as the overarching umbrella for all of these (*21, 22*). And while there appears to be general philosophical agreement, many prefer to concentrate their efforts on those segments of environmental concern of greatest interest to them (*14, 16*). Why? There is comfort in operating at a disciplinary rather than a transdisciplinary level (*35*), access to limited funding in specific areas, and the logical belief that smaller problems can be dealt with more efficiently than large ones, thus leading to eventual solution of the larger ones—which some argue is not the case (*11*).

2. One of the strongest and most telling criticisms of environmental education is its lack of academic respectability. Its content represents an uncertain mixture of various disciplines. It contains a strong attitude/value component that can lead to the simplistic preaching and moralizing often asso-

ciated with attempts to tell people what they ought to do and how they ought to do it, without providing a knowledge base as to why (12). This criticism, leveled at environmental education throughout the 1970s, with cause, cannot be resolved until the content component of environmental education becomes the basis upon which learners form their own attitudes, modify their own values, and decide for themselves on their courses of action.

3. Leadership in environmental education is lacking. There are many competent leaders, but most are viewed as leaders in subsets of the field, and they behave in that manner. An orchestration of these leaders has yet to occur—and may not.

4. Financial support from governmental agencies has not been generous. There has been no equivalent to the support of science education in the 1950s and 1960s by the National Science Foundation (NSF) or any other organization. NSF is in the business of science education, but it has yet to decide how to bring environmental education into the fold. As mentioned, the Department of Health, Education, and Welfare, as well as the new Department of Education, have been frugal in their support of environmental education. The U.S. Environmental Protection Agency, a regulatory agency, has its hands full with the business of interpreting, then enforcing complex legislation and regulations. The Department of Energy and its predecessor agencies, while providing significant funding for energy education, have been criticized for "not drawing the line between education and propaganda" (34). The Sea Grant Program of the National Oceanic and Atmospheric Administration has and continues to provide support, but only in the area of marine education.

A position statement (25) by federal agency representatives attending a 1975 conference in Snowmass is worth noting:

"We recognize that the federal government does not view environmental education as an end in itself, but rather serves it as the mission responsibilities of the several agencies dictate. This is likely to mean in the future (as in the present) federal support for environmental education will be modest in amount and uneven in coverage. Environmental education will receive federal support only when it represents the delivery mode of choice, competing against legislation, regulation, delegation to state or local jurisdiction, etc. The federal government will, however, attempt to target its efforts in a manner calculated to achieve significant results."

One can easily take a negative view of progress in environmental education over the past 10 years. The urgency and evangelical fervor of 1970 that were expected by some to revolutionize education have not produced the desired institutionalized change. Matthew J. Brennan, a founding father of environmental education and a stalwart of conservation education before that, recently pointed out that those goals identified in 1970 are no nearer achievement today (2):

"So we have failed to develop a program of environmental education for the same reason that we do not have an energy program, or a land use policy, or an environmental policy—we do not have the will. Conservation is a philosophy that runs counter to our American way of life. We recognized this ten years ago, but along the way we lost sight of it."

Some environmental education successes

Environmental education efforts in the 1970s were not all failures. There were accomplishments. Some of these portend trends that if taken into the 1980s presage accelerated progress and maturation for the field.

1. Numerous environmental education efforts are being conducted in K-12 schools across the nation. Generally, with time and experience, such efforts are becoming more substantive. Many have progressed beyond a shakedown period to achieve levels of permanence and effectiveness. A recent survey (8) produced 402 recommendations for K-12 environmental education efforts from 49 states. The 284 responding efforts indicated progressively greater maturity than those reported in earlier surveys. The era of emotionalism, moralizing, and preaching may not be over, but evidence of scientific rigor, interdisciplinary approaches, reasoned logic, and balanced analyses mounts.

2. The proliferation of environmental courses and programs in colleges and universities also presages a continuing impact upon the higher education establishment. Environmental education's marriage to post-secondary institutions appears to be in no immediate danger of divorce.

3. The environmental movement was originally conceived, or at least advertised, as a grassroots movement. In many situations, such grassroots efforts have actually worked (27, 29). And while these efforts tend to cease when their tasks are completed, new ones continue to emerge. Their leadership, often local, generally appears from colleges and universities, K-12 schools, the Cooperative Extension Service, conservation districts, League of Women Voters, or any number of other federal, state, and local conservation agencies and organizations. Their impacts may not be national in scope, but neither is their purpose. These efforts often are highly effective, sometimes accomplishing more education than a lifetime of courses.

4. More and more coalitions committed to environmental education are exerting influence, and continued growth of their vitality may make them keystones of environmental education in the 1980s. Among the coalitions are the following:

The *Subcommittee on Environmental Education* of the Federal Interagency Committee on Education, a Washington-based group consisting of representatives from 25 federal agencies, coordinates the educational functions of their offices with respect to environmental education. The Subcommittee in 1976 published a series of concepts about the environment (10). Subcommittee members developed the concepts themselves "so that they would share their basic philosophies about education and environment and so that all members could keep the content of environmental education in a holistic perspective" (13). A second major accomplishment was preparation and coordination of U.S. input for the 1977 Tbilisi Intergovernmental Conference on Environmental Education (*32*).

The *Alliance for Environmental Education* (AEE) "joins together 32 nongovernmental organizations with the common goals of interests and programs in environmental/energy education at the regional and national levels, for the purpose of encouraging development, implementation, and coordination of effective environmental education programs among members, as well as exploring cooperative ventures with other groups and segments in the environmental education field. The membership includes groups representing youth organizations, professional educators and other professionals interested in environmental education, civic, conservation/environmental, and industry/labor organizations" (*17*).

The Alliance sponsored or cosponsored the 1975 Snowmass Conference (*24, 25*), the 1976 St. Louis Conference (*1*), and the 1978 Washington, D.C. Leadership Conference (*30*).

The *State Environmental Education Coordinators Association* (SEECA) attempts to provide communication and cooperation among environmental education specialists of the state educational agencies.

The *Western Regional Environmental Education Council* (WREEC) is a unique group in that its membership consists solely of representatives from state educational agencies and state resource management agencies in the 13 western states—one of each from each state (*23*). WREEC worked with AEE in sponsoring the 1975 Snowmass Conference. It also was instrumental in developing several curriculum projects, most notably the American Forest Institute's Project Learning Tree (*18*).

The *Southern Regional Environmental Education Council* (SREEC), a new organization modeled after WREEC, is developing activities similar to those of WREEC in the 13 southeastern states (*36*).

5. Two highly visible offspring of the environmental movement are the *Journal of Environmental Education* (JEE) and the *National Association for Environmental Education* (NAEE). Both are young, neither is strong, but each is developing rapidly into an effective voice for professionals in any field who also are or see themselves as environmental educators. *JEE* has become a recognized scholarly journal. NAEE is in many ways a coalition itself, though its members generally do not seem to see it in that light. Its members, who come from a variety of places, including academic, government, and industry, are in the process of learning what they have in common, how they can work together, and if trying to understand one another is worth the effort. Two or three years ago, the prognosis for NAEE's success, even survival, may have been doubtful; now the organization appears to be viable. At least its factions are open about their differences and communicating about how these differences might be resolved.

Lessons learned

An optimist might conclude that environmental education is maturing, though he would have to be placed in the "wild-eyed" category if he were to suggest that the field has already matured. A pessimist may find sufficient indicators to conclude that environmental education is stagnant, dying, or dead, but unaware of its embalmment, depending on his propensity for varying degrees of pessimism. But each must be aware that over the past 10 years some valuable lessons apparently have been learned:

1. Looking to the federal government for leadership has not been productive, and there is no reason to expect that things will change during the 1980s. Environmental education exists without federal leadership and can continue to do so.

2. Looking to the federal government for massive funding has not been useful, and there is no reason to expect changes during the 1980s. There are and likely will continue to be funds available for specific subareas, such as energy or marine education, or for whatever future crises emerge, but such funds are limited in their uses and cannot be used for environmental education per se. Too much time has been spent chasing federal funding. Too much complaining has been heard about its absence. If similar time and energy had been expended productively, environmental education would be further ahead proportionately. Environmental education can survive without blanket funding from the federal government.

3. The real gains in environmental education have been achieved through the cooperative efforts of individuals and coalitions of concerned agencies and organizations. The support provided to and by these agencies and organizations has been more in the form of technical assistance—help might be more descriptive—than funding. Through the 1980s and beyond, these relationships will be more productive than either outside funding or outside leadership.

4. An element of maturity is appearing. Matthew Brennan expresses regret for his role in replacing the term "conservation education" with "environmental education" because the change apparently clouded recognition of what needed, and needs, to be done (2). Clay Schoenfeld, president of the National Association for Environmental Education, in a recent address (26), proposed that "we dedicate ourselves to a decade of integrated environmental management education, participated in by all segments of society—a sober consideration of the challenges posed by the 1980s, but a reasoning together of ways that will help enhance environmental quality and energy conservation without jeopardizing human needs, and that will help meet human needs without jeopardizing the quality of our environment and our energy requirements."

Brennan's call for a return to conservation education is clearly equivalent to Schoenfeld's plea for integrated environmental management education. They are essentially saying the same thing about the appropriate mission for environmental education. The difference is in the choice of words. Both are right with respect to what the focus must be.

By whatever name, it is time for environmental education to mature. For that to happen, environmental educators must get on about the business of learning and educating people about the delicate balances between and among resource base, resource use and abuse, and human needs—individual as well as societal. Those involved in environmental education, by whatever name, must learn to capitalize on their considerable similarities. To do that they must recognize and honor their differences, but not dwell upon them. This is the task of environmental education for the 1980s.

REFERENCES

1. Aldrich, J. L., A. M. Blackburn, and G. A. Abel. 1977. *A report on the North American Regional Seminar on Environmental Education.* ERIC/SMEAC, Columbus, Ohio. 106 pp.
2. Brennan, M. J. 1979. *Where are we and what time is it?* Journal of Environmental Education 11(1): 45-46.
3. Diebold, J. 1969. *Man and the computer: Technology as an agent of social change.* Praeger Publishers, New York, New York. 156 pp.
4. Disinger, J. F., and M. L. Bowman. 1975. *Environmental education 1975: A state-by-state report.* ERIC/SMEAC, Columbus, Ohio. 319 pp.
5. Disinger, J. F. 1972. *A directory of projects and programs in environmental education for elementary and secondary schools.* ERIC/SMEAC, Columbus, Ohio. 520 pp.
6. Disinger, J. F. 1975. *A directory of projects and programs in environmental education* (third edition). ERIC/SMEAC, Columbus, Ohio 389 pp.
7. Disinger, J. F. 1976. *A directory of projects and programs in environmental education* (fourth edition). ERIC/SMEAC, Columbus, Ohio. 330 pp.
8. Disinger, J. F. 1979. *A directory of projects and programs in environmental education for elementary and secondary schools* (fifth edition). ERIC/SMEAC, Columbus, Ohio. 860 pp.
9. Disinger, J. F., and B. M Lee. 1973. *A directory of projects and programs in environmental education for elementary and secondary schools* (second edition). ERIC/ SMEAC, Columbus, Ohio. 670 pp.
10. Federal Interagency Committee on Education, Subcommittee on Environmental Education. 1976. *Fundamentals of environmental education.* Office of the Assistant Secretary for Education, U.S. Department of Health, Education and Welfare, Washington, D.C. 30 pp.
11. Forrester, J. W. 1971. *World dynamics.* Wright-Allen Press, Cambridge, Mass. 142 pp.
12. Goodlad, J. I., R. von Stoephasius, and M. F. Klein. 1966. *The changing school curriculum.* Fund for Advancement of Education, New York, New York. 122 pp.
13. Jeske, W. E. 1978. *Subcommittee on Environmental Education, Federal Interagency Committee on Education.* In J. F. Disinger [editor] *Environmental Education Activities of Federal Agencies.* ERIC/SMEAC, Columbus, Ohio. pp. 159-163.
14. Lanier, J. A. 1979-80. *Letter to the editor: The dung heap syndrome.* Journal of Environmental Education 11(2): 4-5.
15. Marland, S. P., Jr. 1971. *Environmental education cannot wait.* American Education 7(4): 6-10.
16. McMahon, J. J. 1980. *Letter to the editor: The dung heap syndrome.* Journal of Environmental Education 11(3): 48.
17. McSwain, J. 1978. *The Alliance for Environmental Education.* In J. F. Disinger [editor] *Alliance Affiliate Activities: Non-Governmental Organizations in Environmental Education.* ERIC/SMEAC, Columbus, Ohio. pp. 5-13.
18. McSwain, J. 1977. *Project Learning Tree.* In A. C. Schoenfeld and J. F. Disinger [editors] *Environmental Education in Action-I: Case Studies of Selected Public School and Public Action Programs.* ERIC/ SMEAC, Columbus, Ohio. pp. 231-239.
19. Rocchio, R., and E. Lee. 1974. *On being a master planner...a step by step guide from a nationwide study of environmental education planning.* ERIC/SMEAC, Columbus, Ohio. 155 pp.
20. Roth, C. E. 1978. *Off the merry-go-round and on to the escalator.* In W. B. Stapp [editor] *From Ought to Action in Environmental Education: A Report of the National Leadership Conference on Environmental Education.* ERIC/SMEAC, Columbus, Ohio. pp. 12-22.
21. Schafer, R. J. H. 1979. *The dung heap syndrome and other destructive phenomena detrimental to the progress of environmental education.* Journal of Environmental Education 11(1): 4-5.
22. Schafer, R. J. H. 1980. *Multichotomization-or, how thin can you slice the environmental mozzarella and still come up with a satisfying pizza?* Environmental Education Report 8(2): 6-7.
23. Schafer, R. J. H. 1977. *Western regional environmental education council.* In A. C.

Schoenfeld and J. F. Disinger [editors] *Environmental Education in Action-I: Case Studies of Selected Public School and Public Action Programs.* ERIC/SMEAC, Columbus, Ohio. pp. 274-295.

24. Schafer, R. J. H., and J. F. Disinger, editors. 1975. *Environmenta education perspectives and prospectives: Key findings and major recommendations.* ERIC/SMEAC, Columbus, Ohio. 18 pp.

25. Schafer, R. J. H., and J. F. Disinger, editors. 1975. *Environmental education perspectives and prospectives: Supporting documentation.* ERIC/SMEAC, Columbus, Ohio. 84 pp.

26. Schoenfeld, A. C. 1980. *Earth Day '70, '80, '90.* In A. B. Sacks, C. B. Davis, L. L. Bammel, and L. A. Iozzi [editors] *Current Issues VI: The Yearbook of Environmental Education and Environmental Studies, Selected Papers from the Ninth Annual Conference of the National Association for Environmental Education.* ERIC/SMEAC, Columbus, Ohio.

27. Schoenfeld, A. C., and J. F. Disinger, editors. 1977. *Environmental education in action-I: Case studies of selected public school and public action programs.* ERIC/SMEAC, Columbus, Ohio. 343 pp.

28. Schoenfeld, A. C., and J. F. Disinger, editors. 1978. *Environmental education in action-II: Case studies of environmental studies programs in colleges and universities today.* ERIC/ SMEAC, Columbus, Ohio. 499 pp.

29. Schoenfeld, A. C., and J. F. Disinger, editors. 1978. *Environmental education in action-III: Case studies of public involvement in environmental policy.* ERIC/SMEAC, Columbus, Ohio. 202 pp.

30. Stapp, W. B., editor 1978. *From ought to action in environmental education: A report of the national leadership conference on environmental education.* ERIC/SMEAC, Columbus, Ohio. 98 pp.

31. Swan, M. D. 1975. *Forerunners of environmental education.* In N. McInnis and D. Albrecht [editors] *What Makes Education Environmental?* Data Courier, Inc. Louisville, Ky., and Environmental Educators, Inc., Washington, D.C. p. 4-20.

32. U.S. Department of Health, Education, and Welfare, Federal Interagency Committee on Education, Subcommittee on Environmental Education. 1977. *Toward an action plan: A report of the Tbilisi Conference on Environmental Education.* G.P.O. 017-080-01838-1, Washington, D.C. 33 pp.

33. Wade, N. 1980. *For the 1980s, beware all expert predictions.* Science 207(4,428): 287-290.

34. Walsh, J. 1979. *Advisory group says DOE slights education for PR.* Science 203 (4,379): 422.

35. Weinberg, G. M. 1975. *An introduction to general systems thinking.* J. Wiley and Sons, New York, New York. 279 pp.

36. Wilson, T. L. 1979. *Formation of the Southern Regional Environmental Education Council (SREEC).* In A. B. Sacks and C. B. Davis [editors] *Current Issues V: The Yearbook of Environmental Education and Environmental Studies, Selected Papers from the Eighth Annual Conference of the National Association for Environmental Education.* ERIC/ SMEAC, Columbus, Ohio. pp. 289-293.

29

Getting Ready for Tomorrow: Educating the Resources Manager

Barbara B. Clark

Office of Dependent Schools, U.S. Department of Defense
Washington, D.C.

Since the passage of the National Environmental Policy Act (NEPA) in 1969, life in this nation has changed for everyone. I need not recount those changes; it is sufficient to say that NEPA and all subsequent environmental legislation has altered significantly the way this nation does its business in both the public and the private sectors. The questions may now be asked fairly: Were we then and are we now prepared for the changes that have occurred and surely will continue to occur throughout our lifetime as environmental/conservation issues, coupled with energy scarcities, continue to hold the nation at bay? Do we know where we are headed as the impacts of what had been perceived as desirable laws sum and take hold out there in our future? Do we now, as a result of these new laws and regulations, have a sense of any national environmental goals that can provide us with clear guidance and direction as we face a future of vastly increased pressures on our resources—pressures that demand, in turn, particularly astute management of those resources?

As with many laws designed to change behavior through the regulation of procedures, environmental law has created a nation of dutiful compliers, but few true believers. Compliance alone cannot foster an understanding of the issues, which is needed now to more effectively and efficiently manage our environmental/resource problems. Somewhere between our initial en-

260

thusiasm for environmental quality and sanity and the promulgation and implementation of the complex regulations, Americans lost sight of the need to prepare to use the new tools that legislatures provided. Neither institutions nor professionals could have anticipated the impacts of new responsibilities that require so much: sophisticated information synthesis; attention to resource values; a team approach to problem identification and solution; considerably more sensitivity to the public; much more inter-institutional cooperation; broader, more holistic perspectives on the issues; and greatly modified organizational patterns that could accommodate the above requirements. I believe that many of us have recognized that new ways of doing business were in order, but we have been slow to react to the need. We now need to seek the means for retooling our organizations, our people, and our procedures to meet the challenges presented by our complex environmental problems and our equally complex regulatory remedies.

William H. Matthews, writing in *Resource Materials for Environmental Management and Education* has given us a strategy for change that would go a long way toward achieving more effective management of our resources. That strategy includes the following three elements: "A reorganization of our extensive substantive knowledge, the development of new functions and roles in the public and private sectors, and the creation of new educational programs and institutions to meet the critical needs of a wide variety of persons who analyze environmental problems or who make decisions concerning the environment" (2). These strategies are interwoven, one with the other. My objective, however, is to discuss two of the elements, recognizing that the third must also be addressed with equal emphasis. In fact, I will touch upon it later in this paper. But the elements of the strategy I wish to stress here are the development of new roles and functions and the creation of educational programs.

Department of Interior study

My thoughts are based on a recently completed study conducted by the Department of the Interior's National Park Service, titled "Resource Management: A Study of Selected Problems and Solutions."

As the nation's largest natural resources manager, the Department of the Interior had an interest in exploring the issues discussed in my opening remarks. The competing demands and expectations of the many publics served by the department had greatly complicated its relationship with those publics, particularly since the passage of NEPA. The result was that unprecedented pressures were and are placed on the expertise of its staff. As with other resource management agencies, life changed drastically for the department and its staff after 1969.

In late 1977 the department was requested to look at the general issue of the adequacy of education and training in the resources management profession. The initial request focused almost exclusively on discovering how public and private policies in resources management could be made more coherent using education of the resources manager as the common denominator, out of which could spring some common national goals and provide staff with more rational guidance. Lester Brown of the World Watch Institute, believing that the environmental crisis was at least equal in importance to national defense, proposed a national academy of resources defense that would raise the image, stature, and prestige of resource managers to that enjoyed by graduates of our military academies. Brown's paper was presumably one of the inspirations for the educational explorations that were initiated within the department.

As discussions proceeded and as people outside the department became involved, the focus shifted toward developing theoretical models of institutions that could accomplish several things, including delivery of a new kind of education to resource managers. The feasibility of those models would be tested against predetermined criteria, such as cost, political safeness, and public/private support. A final model would be selected that presumably would be evaluated by various concerned groups. Then, final recommendations would be transmitted to the secretary of the interior for action.

It was necessary at the outset of the study to define resource management and to conceptualize the typical manager's roles and functions within an institutional setting, be it public or private. The actual research would then seek for coincidence between what managers actually do and what they are prepared, through their education, to do. Should gaps be identified, the contractor would make recommendations for closing them. These recommendations would be formulated into the aforementioned institutional models and subjected to certain tests of feasibility and the impartial scrutiny of an outside panel of experts representing a cross-section of concern in this field.

The study, which took 16 weeks to complete, identified and examined, by survey, four selected topic areas that had been identified in the study proposal request and validated through subsequent literature searches. The four topics included resources management in the private sector; resources management in the government sector; education, training, and research practices and trends; and current and future job markets.

Results of the surveys were analyzed to form the models for change as described above. Given the time constraints and Office of Management and Budget regulations governing the survey process, almost all information developed in the first two categories was collected by telephone. Each survey took the form of a structured interview lasting from 30 to 90 minutes. Interviewees were selected at random from lists provided to the contractor by various government and private sources. A small number of in-person interviews were conducted with Washington area people.

Interviews were designed to elicit data about current job functions, role, and scope of responsibility; preparation, education, and training; years in employed capacity; relationship to management; job purpose; effectiveness of prior education and training; major barriers to job performance; recommendations for graduate and undergraduate education and training programs; and operating environmental ethics in the workplace.

Information about education and training was solicited from selected institutions. Job market data was obtained from a variety of occupational outlook resources.

Over 55 surveys were conducted in the governmental sector, including 18 agencies, Congress, and the White House. Thirty-five people, representing 25 industries or related professional groups, were contacted in the private sector. In addition, 26 members of the academic community and 9 people representing environmental interest groups took part in the survey.

Study results

The nature of the surveys did not permit quantification of the results. As a check on the contractor's interpretation of primarily subjective information, an advisory committee reviewed the results and made comments on the interpretation.

The outcome was the formulation of two theoretical institutional models. Before reviewing those models, let me acquaint you briefly with some of the important results of the surveys by topic area.

Private sector. Respondents indicated that although they themselves and/or their employees possessed the basic skills for good management, the institutional factors with which they dealt often constrained the application of those skills. Those constraints or barriers to effective management found in the private sector included:

• Environmental managers in the private sector are faced with a complex political, technical, and administrative milieu that makes it difficult for them to take decisive actions.

Environmental managers' activities are constrained by governmental requirements and fragmentation, legal considerations, political pressures, unproven management strategies, scientific uncertainty, lack of corporate support, and economic considerations.

The use of a litigation model for environmental dispute resolution coupled with business' suspicion of environmental objectives encourages lawyers and administrators, rather than technically trained scientists, to develop policies and solutions. The result is that the problem-solving and decision-making authority of most environmental resource managers is highly constrained.

• The lack of shared, comprehensive understanding of the goals of resource management obstructs successful job performance.

Industry's traditional use of profit indicators to measure employee performance prohibits the development of more appropriate performance indicators for resource managers.

Resource managers receive little recognition or reward for making positive environmental contributions, and as a result move into other corporate activities to further their careers.

In sum, with the exception of a number of the youngest employees, there is no sense of common purpose that binds business resource managers other than loyalty to the company and loyalty to a particular technical discipline. We did not discover an independent environmental ethic among these people or a sense of collegiality with other professionals working to resolve environmental problems. Indeed, in two instances environmental coordinators had no idea of how similar issues were handled within other divisions of their own companies.

Public sector. Turning to the public sector, the barriers, in order of priority, included:
- Political and philosophical.
- Bureaucratic, administrative, and time related.
- Personnel management problems.
- Knowledge and education.
- Research and development.

I believe it is significant that in both the public and private sectors, institutional barriers constitute the number one constraint on resource management effectiveness, according to the managers. Furthermore, knowledge and education constraints either did not exist, as in the case of the private sector, or were lower in priority, in the case of the public sector. We, however, could categorize each of the constraints mentioned as educational ones, should we be looking for causitive phenomena.

What is important to note in the study is the overwhelming criticism of the institution, the agency, the bureau. Over 50 percent of all interviewees expressed this. Is this an excuse, a whitewash? Are the managers making the institution whipping boys for when, in reality, we are dealing with a manager's failure? I think not. One has to be in government for but a short period to know that the system more often than not has difficulty accomplishing its business. This personal observation is stated more precisely in a fact sheet prepared by the White House Press Office explaining justifications for the proposed Department of Natural Resources.

"Government institutions have failed to keep pace with this need to make important and complex natural resources policy decisions. These institutions were established one-by-one to meet particular needs. They lack the ability to make the comprehensive natural resource decisions that are now needed" (3).

I cite these perceived institutional failings because they exist and because they detract strongly from the manager's ability to do the job irrespective of training and education.

Educational constraints

Turning to the educational constraints mentioned by the managers, two issues surfaced. First, the politicization of resource decisions demands managers who possess strong capabilities in people management. Second, effective managers must possess a sound knowledge of systems management methodologies. The study specifically reports:

"Individual resource managers are expected to possess an extremely wide range of skills and knowledge. In order to perform the broad spectrum of duties that resource management entails, resource managers must be managers, planners, problem solvers, politicians, and researchers. The enormous demands on the resource manager's skills and knowledge are compounded by the rapid rate of change that occurs in the field. New legislation and regulations are constantly being created, new scientific discoveries are made, and social and political crises occur—all of which affect the resource manager's job. The very fact that our knowledge of the ecosystem increases rapidly each year will, ironically, always be a constraint on the resource manager because he or she will always lack complete knowledge of the consequences of our interactions with natural systems. The following quote catches the essence of this point eloquently:

"'The more we unravel the ecosystem, the more we see the limits of our foundation of knowledge. Actions thought benign are found to have second- and third-level effects never contemplated. This is a critical issue because the whole business of resource management is respectable because it's a righteous activity—trying to live harmoniously with nature and accept some deprivation. These insidious effects crop up to put the resource manager on a very shaky fulcrum. He's hardly the Errol Flynn of the show when he's found to be human and error-prone.'

"Several of the respondents went on to say that it does not matter that this knowledge problem really besets all scientists. What is critical is the time it takes to transfer new knowledge into practice.

"Some made the point that nonscientific knowledge transfer is equally important. Many resource managers come into their job with scientific or technical backgrounds. As they assume positions of greater responsibility, they need additional skills in personnel management and supervision, finance planning, and other general administrative areas. For instance, weaknesses in written and oral skills were the deficiencies most frequently cited by the federal employees we contacted. These skills are becoming increasingly important as resource managers interact much more frequently with the public. Similarly, several respondents said there is a great need to teach resource managers human resource management as an integral part of their overall curriculum, whether an undergraduate, a graduate, or a continuing education program. One national park superintendent expressed this point, saying it applies to virtually all resource managers, not just park rangers:

"'There is a big gap in knowledge of human motivations and interactions in natural resource settings. Ninety percent of a ranger's work is people work, yet ninety percent of their knowledge is in more technical resource management related areas. Few rangers are trained in motivation, attitudes, and behavior, and more research and training needs to be authorized to correct this situation.'"

Lending credence to this observation, Daniel Henning (1), writing in *In-*

terdisciplinary Environmental Approaches, states that resources managers "must recognize that the majority of their problems are basically human ones, and solutions, therefore, are more in the realm of social science than in a particular biological discipline. Decisions are basically concerned with management of people's behavior to natural resources, rather than the natural resources per se." In his remarks is a clear signal to our institutions— one they would do well to heed.

Survey findings based upon interviews with academicians and examination of selected programs reveal that:

• Because of the many different roles that resource managers have to fulfill, there is no one specific ideal academic preparation for jobs in resource management. A number of programs can adequately prepare students for jobs in this field.

• There is no agreement among universities about which areas of study should be included in the core curriculum of resource management education programs. There is also no consensus on approaches and methodologies for teaching and learning about resource management.

• Universities are searching for new ways to satisfy the national need for better trained people to enter resource management jobs.

• Education and training programs will need to be improved and must respond to future trends.

There are numerous educational and training opportunities available to people who will be entering or who now hold positions in resource management. The educational content and philosophy of these programs range from highly specialized technical training, such as mining engineering, geology, biology, and chemistry, to broad-based interdisciplinary programs, such as environmental science and natural resource management.

The lack of a consensus as to the ideal academic preparation for resource managers is a reflection of the diverse nature of the roles and responsibilities of resource managers. Some argue that the flexibility of interdisciplinary programs is an asset. Others, however, argue that there is a clear need for more rigid requirements.

Some people distinguish between the role of an undergraduate versus a graduate degree in resource management. Undergraduate degrees, according to some educators, should not be career oriented, but should educate the student in the true sense of liberal arts. Moreover, universities have traditionally taken a dim view of undergraduate courses that primarily teach techniques.

Some people maintain that an ideal academic preparation must provide a sufficient grounding in ethics. They view ethics as an essential part of education because of the important role values play in making decisions about the lives of future generations.

Because of the diffuse and broad nature of environmental resource management, there is controversy as to the subject areas that should be included in a resource management educational program. The general subject areas most frequently mentioned include: values and ethics, ecology, environmental effects, environmental indicators, environmental impact assessment methodology, modeling, monitoring, growth and its implications for the future, economics of the environment, environmental law, administrative processes, and actor/role interactions (2).

Many educators believe that these subjects will prepare students adequately for careers in resource management and enable them to effectively interact with scientists and technologists, policy makers, and the public. Others feel that an ideal academic preparation must develop the interpersonal/human/public relations skills of resource managers. Moreover, as one study respondent explained: "Resource managers need to learn how to understand and cope with uncertainties and how this can be translated into policy that is not destructive to the economy."

Matthews (2) observes:

"Perhaps the greatest challenge of professional education in environmental management is to develop the generalizable contexts along knowledge, cultural, decision, and role categorizations. These must be broad enough to be useful for more than one specific environmental problem. On the other hand, the contexts cannot be so broad that the amount of time and energy required to obtain the needed knowledge and insights would be prohibitive for any given person or that the coverage would necessarily be so superficial that it would be of little practical value to a manager" (2).

Many contend that interdisciplinary training is lost on people who are not firmly grounded in at least one technical area. Faculty and administrators claimed that there are inherent weaknesses in interdisciplinary programs; for example, students do not develop a sufficient depth of understanding in any one area. As one respondent remarked: "The environmental science programs currently offered are 'chop suey.' Students are not learning in depth, nor are they learning how to be circumspect. The programs do not provide the student with sufficient expertise in at least one discipline. In certain instances, students have too much latitude in the choice of courses and independent study."

In other words, academic preparation has become too general, while the trend in resource management has become more dependent upon teams of specialists. This reinforces the need for specialist training. Furthermore, the complexity of resource management issues demands that more technical expertise be developed in a wide range of areas.

Regardless of the approach or the techniques currently used to train resource managers, many people recognize that changes and improvements need to be made for universities to keep pace with the national resource management manpower needs of the 1980s.

Educational trends

In the future, resource management education will be required to address the following trends:

- The need for a futures perspective.

• The increased importance of citizen participation in the decision-making process.

• The increased controversy over resource management decisions.

• The necessity for a broad approach to problem resolution.

Respondents emphasized the increasing significance that these trends will play in the careers of resource managers. For instance, one professor noted: "The current system does not adequately consider the long-term implications. The time perspective needs to be expanded. Students need a 'futures education' that gives them a sense of the earth's resources and the ethical and moral responsibility to the future."

There is a growing demand for resource managers to learn more economics, modeling, and other quantitative techniques and conflict resolution. Students need to learn how to work in an interdisciplinary framework. One respondent addressed this question with a comment about the fact that not enough students are trained to integrate information and to interact with other disciplines: "There's a need to think about working on an interdependent system. Right now, in interdisciplinary education the parts are episodic. They don't appear connected."

One respondent explained that the system has not encouraged the development of integrative capacities because: "Persons who perform roles within conventional disciplines have not defined roles the way they really exist."

According to several respondents, there is a need to place more emphasis on the role of ethics, vis a vis environmental decisions. Too many programs neglect the human dimension of environmental decisions and ignore the demand that society account for the significance and implications of its actions.

Citizen participation will make the resource manager's job more problematic. Many respondents in government said that there continues to be many more active constituencies that resource managers must respond to. More decisions are being made on a collective and, in many cases, more localized basis. Resource managers need to learn how to listen to and eventually relate to the public. As one respondent said: "There will be a lot of citizen participation that is irritating to managers. We are in a period of citizen activism. Managers will have to listen to the public."

Many respondents also believe that resource management will become more controversial. One respondent asserted: "There will be more controversies. Increasing demands will be placed on diminishing or inaccessible resources. Some major decisions, though, will have to be made at all levels of government."

There will also be demands for greater efficiency, cost effectiveness and practicality. At present, too much time and resources are expended on tasks indirectly or remotely directed to the issues at hand. The proliferation of the bureaucracy in both public and private sectors at the expense of the on-the-ground field force attests to this.

The foregoing is a quick description of the major findings of the Department of the Interior study. Let me sum up the surveys by saying that managers and academia are concerned about preparedness. They are cognizant that things have changed, that new approaches and skills are demanded, and that the entire resource management community must catch up and catch up quickly. The most efficient means for doing this will be in-service or mid-career training. Private and public enterprise must place a very high priority on this activity seeking to retool current management personnel with all due haste.

Accordingly, both institutional models proposed in the study contain a professional development component. Remember that while the impetus for this study was perceived educational needs, one of the two models addresses other needs identified in the surveys and/or in the literature. Professional development then turns out to be but one component in this model.

The components of model number one, which I shall call the institute model, follow:

An institute model

Professional development support. To explore the core knowledge areas, professional values, and ethics that need to be developed for the field of resource management; to support the development of innovative curricula designs and training programs at all academic levels and career stages; and to provide opportunities for academicians and representatives of industry and government to explore, formally and informally, the trends, opportunities, and needs for trained resource managers.

Policy analysis and research. To contribute to the development of regional and national ecological models useful for political decision making; to assist the development of regional planning models; to conduct inquiry into a range of public policy issues not yet comprehensively addressed due to the lack of an effective mechanism; and to assess the national resource and environmental implications of developments that are currently resolved only in terms of local or regional impacts.

National information access system. To provide a uniform catalog, access, and referral system to information relevant to making resource management decisions, such as federal reports, research studies, ecological and environmental data, and statistics.

Environmental planning and conflict resolution. To develop, and to support the development elsewhere, of planning, negotiating, and mediating techniques that can resolve environmental conflicts efficiently and optimally and to provide a forum for joint planning among competing interests and for the resolution of conflicts.

In support of these four functions, the institute would also undertake a fifth major activity:

Technical support and assistance consisting of a limited amount of scientific, economic, and environmental/resource planning assistance to localities, industries, states, and regional groups who wish objective information and technical help in arriving at resource development alternatives that satisfy a broad community of interests. Projects would be undertaken to further the understanding of resource management and environmental principles, provide case study data and other material useful for professional development, and understand the uses and limits of various conflict resolution techniques.

To achieve the level of support and prestige necessary for such an institution to succeed, its development and structure must be carefully planned. The major organizational features that were recommended include:

• Charter—by act of Congress, as a private, nonprofit organization.

• Funding support—federal seed money, plus continual matching grants and special grants, private endowments, corporate donations, and membership dues.

• Board of governors/directors—drawn equally from academia, the business community, environmental groups, and government.

• Staff—a relatively small, permanent core staff supplemented by a fellows program drawing on business, academia, and the scientific and governmental communities. Special groups of associates—academic deans, business and environmental leaders, scientists, and others—to convene for the purpose of providing direction to and work on specific issues such as professional development and training. Regional Associate staff members would work on technical projects carried out locally.

The growth of the institute must be cautiously phased over a suitable period of time. Two functions appear particularly appropriate for initial concentrated effort: professional development support, which serves as a basis for all other functions, and the environmental planning and conflict function.

A professional development model

The second model, which I will call the professional development model, has as its major function the training and career development of in-service resources managers. As envisioned, it would:

• Have an interagency focus.

• Stress collaborative planning and team-building techniques.

• Use actual governmental case studies for analysis.

• Emphasize the strategic aspects of natural resource planning.

• Present and evaluate the latest techniques used to clarify options and quantify trade-offs.

• Permit supervised independent study.

• Examine future trends in the government's role in natural resources management.

• Promote intergovernmental cooperation in resource management, for

example, state and local personnel would be admitted to the program.
- Promote international cooperation in resource management.

The program should not, and need not, be grandiose. While this service could eventually offer a range of programs, the cornerstone would be an extended (eight weeks or more) residential program that provides a course of study of sufficient depth to allow for personal growth and the completion of independent study work if desired. The core program content should be targeted to meet the needs of personnel at the threshhold of assuming their first significant managerial post. Personnel at other career stages would not be excluded, however.

The study seems to have concluded that preservice education and training for the resource manager is necessarily vital to the effective functioning of the manager. At the same time it also says that when the actual duties, responsibilities, and functions of the manager are taken into account, an inservice career component will better suit the needs of the manager and prepare him or her for the real world. That this real world is probably less resource managerial and scientific than would be expected is a discovery of this study. That it is juggling public opinion, political expedience, interagency territoriality, career opportunity, and regulatory mandates is the real world. No college or university can be expected to deal with these real world facts.

At the same time, colleges and universities do have a responsibility to prepare the graduate for this real world in these suggested ways:
- Examine what you are teaching. Does it make a contribution to the operational functioning of the resource manager? The orientation is more often than not toward the environmental assessment. And with this comes a need to have a sense of operational, societal values.
- Examine the focus of the entire program. Is there a realistic focus on the politics of the job?
- Are you inculcating an environmental ethic in which the bottom line is the protection, management, and wise use of ecosystems so that graduates have at least a benchmark? When it comes to critical decisions, does the ecosystem get fair treatment?
- Is your approved methodology and program spirit reflective of an interdisciplinary view of the world, in which human actions and natural systems are in fact a continuum of responses to diverse stimuli?

These questions and thoughts should provide initial guidance for preservice program review. More effective would be to include an operational resource manager from business and industry and from government on your curriculum review committee. They can "tell it how it is" and give you more guidance and support than can academia at a time when events are moving rapidly. Ultimately, the goal is to produce a professional cadre of people with special knowledge uniquely suited to manage our natural systems in harmony with our human needs. We are at the threshold of recognizing this. Now we need to put the guidance into practice. A concerted effort among affected parties can accomplish this goal.

REFERENCES

1. Henning, Daniel H. 1974. *Interdisciplinary environmental approaches.* Educational Media Press, Costa Misa, California.
2. Matthews, William H. 1976. *Resource materials for environmental management and education.* The MIT Press, Cambridge, Massachusetts.
3. Office of the White House Press Secretary. 1979. *Fact sheet on reorganization proposals, March 1, 1979.* Washington, D.C.

30

Environmental Education for the 1980s

C. Richard Tillis

Director, Office of Environmental Education
Florida Department of Education, Tallahassee

We live in a world that is doubling its population every 37 years.

We live in a world that is doubling the size of its industrial complex every 10 years.

We live in a nation that is doubling its consumption of oil every 9 years.

We live in a nation whose national objective is to double our use of coal every 14 years.

We live in a state that is doubling its consumption of electricity every 8 years.

Reflect for a moment on those five statements. Each contains a doubling time, a mathematical fact, a result of exponential growth.

The first statement says that within the next 37 years, by 2017, we will add as many people to this earth as have been added in the entire history of mankind. Are we ready?

The second statement says we will add as much industry between now and 1990 as have been developed throughout earth's history. Are we ready?

The third statement says we will increase our use and dependence on oil between now and 1989 as much as we did from the beginning of the history of man until today. Are we ready?

The fourth statement says we will increase our coal use between today and 1994 by as much as we have increased it in history. Are we ready?

The fifth statement of fact says that Floridians, the citizens of one state, will increase their electrical consumption between today and 1988 by as much as they have since its discovery. Are we ready?

We all know, particularly our friends in the business world, that an investment of $1,000 at 5 percent will total $2,000 in 14 years. Yet we hesitate to recognize the fact that a 5 percent increase in consumption of oil, coal, or any resource will double the consumption in 14 years. This principle, which was so well described by University of Colorado Professor Al Bartlett and which is almost an essential for the survival of our society, is still almost unknown to the average citizen.

It seems obvious that the American public is not ready to deal with the many powerful impacts that a dwindling resource base will have on our lifestyle, our security, and even our democratic system of government.

If this be the case, why are we faced by what seems to be a declining interest and support for environmental education?

What is environmental education?

To approach this problem, we must first define environmental education. For 50 years or more, wise people of many nations have struggled to teach each new generation attitudes and skills that would result in a sustained yield of earth's natural resources. The term that described that effort was conservation education. During the late 1950s and 1960s, as we began space exploration and our cities exploded in size, many educators, while recognizing a growing need for "wise-use" education, felt that the word "conservation" implied a concern about agricultural soils, woods, and wildlife. In essence they said "conservation" was an insufficient word for this age of urbanization and spaceship earth awareness.

The term environmental education was coined in a noble effort to describe wise-use education that dealt with all of man's environments—inner city, suburbia, the industrial arena, the farm, as well as all of our recreation areas and wilderness. Environmentalists were to be persons who cared about rivers they would never fish, trails they would never hike, and cities they would never call home.

Environmental education offered an excellent opportunity for the members of a community to become involved in education. The professional educator sought the wisdom of farmers, businessmen, sportsmen, housewives, doctors, and others in an effort to develop wise-use attitudes and skills among his students.

Most people would agree that ours is a rather wasteful society. So, wise use often suggested a curtailment of our "more and bigger is better" philosophy. This, of course, angered some who stood to profit from our hang-up on growth. They became enemies of environmental education.

Many environmental groups, reacting to problems around them, soon were seen as proponents not of wise use but of nonuse.

With considerable support from government, these organizations became increasingly stronger and more and more identified as antibusiness and anti-development.

As we enter into the 1980s, we find ourselves in an era of economic decline and unfairly tagged with a reputation as proponents of nonuse of America's natural resources.

Looking back to 1970 and the origin of Florida's presently well-staffed well-financed, and extremely successful environmental education program, one thing rings clear. A key task for the program's administrator for 10 years has been a continuing explanation of environmental education and, equally important, what it was not.

Certainly, we live in a time when education for wise use is essential to the survival of our culture and our nation. The young people who have benefited from our efforts have not yet achieved the political power to override the critics of environmental education and set our nation on a wise-use trail.

What we must do is consciously operate our programs to defend them against opponents, make our wise use objectives so obvious that they cannot be ignored, and accentuate positive environmental cases. This is really a linguistics and philosophical issue. But perhaps a few concrete examples of programs and content will help.

Some examples from Florida

Value of livestock wastes. In Florida there is a very large beef-producing company that, on only 18 acres, feeds, fattens, and processes over 20,000 head of cattle at a time— each year processing over 250,000 head.

As Florida's rigid water quality laws and regulations developed, this company encountered very serious problems. Faced with strict environmental laws, what could they do with the wastes from 250,000 cattle a year?

Dealing with cattle wastes at this company, an age-old environmental problem, has developed into a total nutrient recycling system—a model for the world (Figure 1). Wastes are collected, washed, and processed to separate fibrous solids and liquids. The solids are treated and then go back, as roughage, into the cattle's feed. The remaining liquids and plant wastes flow to a lagoon system where fermentation and algae growth occur. In a final lagoon the algae are consumed by fish; then the fish are harvested and marketed; and the water is used for cattle drinking and irrigation of feed crops.

Another by-product is methane, which is fermented from the waste liquor. Enough methane gas, a natural gas substitute, can be produced to run the plant and supply a nearby town. Also, another by-product, carbon dioxide, can provide much of Florida's dry ice.

Every part of this upbeat story offers opportunities to teach science, social studies, mathematics, in fact, almost any academic discipline. The difference is that it is a success story—not the mind-boggling mass of unsolvable problems that are too often the center of environmental education content.

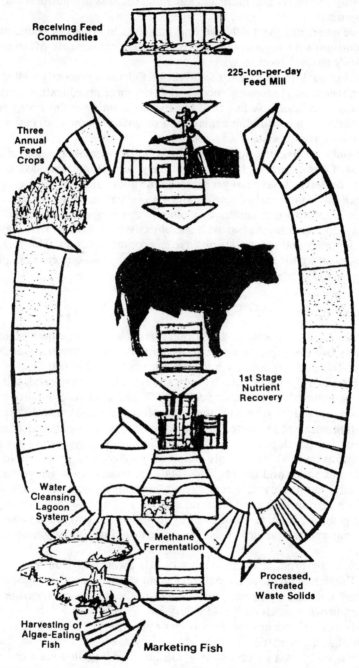

Figure 1. Closed-loop nurient cycle used by a Florida beef-producing company to deal with wastes.

A lesson on energy rates. Any electric power company that is in a growth posture, faced with the need for capital investment and new generating facilities, is a valuable energy conservation ally for the educator. Florida utilities have long been friendly supporters of environmental education. The extent of cooperation and trust can be seen in the fact that the 1979 legislature appropriated funds for developing an energy conservation program by a consortium of Florida utility companies. The Florida Office of Environmental Education administers the program, but the utilities are doing the job.

This program now has school teachers under contract to develop science and mathematics lessons geared to Florida's competency evaluation program. The units are academically solid, tied to a serious national issue, and student interest is high.

One example follows. The cost to burn a 60-watt light bulb for a day is 6 cents. This seems insignificant and not worth the hassle of turning lights off and on. Six cents is slightly more than the cost of 1 kilowatt hour of electricity. One Florida utility company serves more than 2.5 million customers. Two and a half-million bulbs equals 2.5 million kilowatt hours. The capital investment to build generating facilities for producing this current could cost $500,000. The student recognizes that by this simple conservation action, one could possibly eliminate the need for a $500,000 investment. Because utility companies can raise money only through increasing their rates to consumers, the benefits are obvious. The environmental problems and costs are also high.

The education program consists of an in-class curriculum and a three-dimensional display of appliance loads driving an actual electric meter. The meter is tied to a digital display that shows how much any or all of the appliance loads cost in "dollars-per-day." By flicking a switch, the student can easily tell how much it costs to operate, individually or collectively, an air conditioner or heater, hot water heater, range, refrigerator, or electric lights for a typical family of four. Moving the switch allows the student to compare the costs of maintaining a home at 75 °F in the summer as compared to 78° recommended by President Carter. Also, the energy units and dollar costs for heating a home at 70° and 65° are visually displayed.

The curriculum activities emphasize math and science skills as they relate to energy concepts. These skills are tied to the basic skills identified in the Florida Student Assessment Program.

Students can plug a hair dryer or any electrical device into the "blue box" and determine the cost-per-day for operating the device at different settings. Justification for turning off one light is obvious. The mathematics and science for understanding the example are essential citizen skills for this decade.

An environmental assessment exercise. Endangered species laws are under constant threat by those who misunderstand them or stand to lose financially by their enforcement. An environmental education program in Lee

County, Florida, offers another example for environmental education in the 1980s.

A class of high school juniors and seniors interested in studying endangered species settled on the Florida manatee as their topic. This animal is seriously threatened, has no overt financial benefit to man, and is in jeopardy because of unintentional human actions. Habitat alteration and injury from boat propellers are principal threats to the manatee.

The high school class initiated a community-wide survey of manatee sightings. Soon, communty members and students were phoning in manatee sightings. Color-coded pins were used to identify their location. A system was implemented so that the class could recognize the number, concentration, and patterns of movement of the animals.

During the second year of the student research project, the Environmental Protection Agency (EPA) filed an injunction to require Florida Power and Light (FPL) to stop or substantially reduce their thermal discharge into the Orange River because they were creating a thermal block, top-to-bottom and shore-to-shore, thus violating EPA estuarine discharge of thermally enriched waters policies and regulations.

FPL estimated that to change their discharge canal system would cost rate payers $6 to $8 million and would not be a worthwhile solution because the plant has only another 10- to 15-year life expectancy.

Knowing of the students' work on the Florida manatee in the power plant vicinity, FPL officials asked the environmental education seminar class if there was any interest in supporting the FPL position that the new canal was not necessary.

As is policy in the seminar class, the class: (a) visited the site and became thoroughly familiar with the proposal; (b) visited and heard officials of FPL state their case; (c) heard officials of the Department of Environmental Regulation and EPA state their case; and (d) reviewed the power plant's original impact publication and consultant reports sponsored by FPL.

Upon accomplishing their background homework on the issue, students took the following positions:

1. The EPA policy and regulation were excellent.

2. The Orange River had been so altered by upstream development that it was no longer of significant nursery value or reproductive habitat for the species of concern the EPA had identified.

3. Changing the thermal discharge significantly directly into the Caloosahatchee River would cause the Florida manatee population of 300 + animals to move from the protected Orange River and power plant canal cold weather gathering site to the Caloosahatchee River channel, which is part of the heavily traveled intercoastal waterway. Thus the manatee would be more vulnerable to injury by boat propellers.

4. Students carried out a public information campaign on the issue and joined in the request for the EPA to hold a public hearing on the issue in Ft. Myers.

5. Students testifying at the hearing took the position that: (a) The EPA

policy was a good one; however, in this case, there were extenuating circumstances. (b) The Orange River estuarine character had been substantially altered by land development, making it of marginal value for the estuarine species with which EPA was concerned. (c) The economic, social, and environmental benefits to the public were only marginal. (d) The watering manatee population would be severely threatened by boat traffic if the new canal were to discharge into the Caloosahatchee River Intercoastal Waterway. The students also pointed out that in light of these facts, the EPA would be violating the Marine Mammals Protection Act and the Endangered Species Act, both of which indicate the federal government cannot take any action that would further endanger an endangered species; therefore, the requirement as proposed would not be legal.

The result was that EPA waived the injunction within very specific guidelines that FPL agreed to operate within. A strong coalition of business, government, organizations, and citizens has formed for the protection of the manatee.

The Florida utility company is quick to admit that the environmental education students' concern for the manatee, expertise at research, and objectivity led to a savings of from $6 to $8 million for Florida consumers. Students from this same school district have headed up a successful effort to pass a bond issue to purchase a large tract of cypress swamp for their area. They have also conducted research and testified effectively against environmentally deterimental projects. But, this example is one almost never publicized, one in which the corporation, the environment, and the Florida electric consumer all benefited from a high school environmental studies class.

The potential in energy education

The next examples are in an area of environmental education that I believe holds enormous potential for teaching wise use in a field that will create broad public support. This is the field of energy education as it relates to the community and directly to the school system.

Looking back to the early days of environmental education, you will recall that there was a problem of attempting to teach wise use in a system that wasted paper, food, electricity, space, and many other resources. Gradually, environmental educators' efforts have borne fruit to the extent that it is now considered out of taste and style to waste paper and food.

Now is the time for those interested in environmental education to seek out the building and utilities managers and get involved in the preparation of school and school district energy management plans. To emphasize the creation of an energy-efficient environment for energy education, simple, nontechnical actions, such as turning various furnace, air conditioners, and lights off and on at a regular efficient time, can save a school thousands of dollars. This is something taxpayers and school board members appreciate.

When educators are involved in such planning and can add their knowledge of such actions to their teaching, the school can become a cooperative system targeted toward wise use of the most publicized resource of our times—energy.

Such school energy management plans have resulted in enormous savings of energy and money. One plan saved $2.5 million in two years for one school district in one state. Another plan saved $1.75 million in two years. Small school districts with small budgets are saving $50,000 and $100,000 a year.

These savings are used in several ways—to hire teachers, to provide incentive awards to school budgets, to encourage more savings, and to help the schools survive the pressure of soaring energy costs. The effort, of course, is important to prevent waste, but it is also an outstanding opportunity to teach students that planning, cooperation, and a sense of purpose can help one deal with a resource shortage.

Fossil fuels are a finite resource. So long as we depend on them for the energy to operate our systems, we will face an increasing energy problem. This is the time to prepare students to deal with future problems while exposing them to our efforts to handle them today.

An upbeat effort in the eighties

These examples illustrate the upbeat environmental education activities that merit emphasis in the 1980s.

The core content of environmental education remains what I call the "economics of nature," a study of the cycles that produce the remarkable life-support system here on planet earth. We still have the enormous task of preparing people to consider the economics of nature along with those of man before they make a decision that could be detrimental to their environment.

We also need to emphasize the fact that environmental education concerns itself with multiple environments. We cannot let the urban student think we are concerned only about natural areas or let the outdoorsman or farmer think we are concerned only about the problems of the cities.

If we are to prevail in the 1980s, we must return to our previous stress on wise-use education, emphasize our concern for the immediate environment of the learner, and seek the upbeat, positive environmental education examples around us. And, we must prevail if our society is to survive; the need for environmental, wise-use education is, in resource terms, as necessary as the air we breathe, as right as the rain that waters our crops and provides us with drink, and as real as the rocks on which our nation and our society stand.

VIII. Restoring and Maintaining Living Space

31

Trade-offs in Use of Resources for Recreation

Daniel D. Badger
Professor, Department of Agricultural Economics
Oklahoma State University, Stillwater

The concepts of economics, ethics, and ecology have various meanings to different individuals and groups in society. A financier or president of an industrial firm with $1 million in annual tax-sheltered income has a different perspective of economics than a blue collar worker who receives $20,000 in annual wages. The perception of what are good ethics may be different for these two individuals also. Certainly the concept of ecology is different for them, based on the contacts they have with their man-made and natural surroundings.

Similarly, the theme of restoring and maintaining living space has varying connotations for different groups in our society. To me the topic means taking care of what we have, that is, improving the qualitative aspect of our natural environment. It is in this context that I address trade-offs in the use of natural resources for recreation.

When I was younger and more idealistic, issues were black and white, and I took firm positions on one side of land use issues. Note I do not use the phrase "land use problems" because "problems" connote unsolvable issues to many environmentalists. The idea of problems leads to an either/or proposition, a taking of sides.

I perceive trade-offs not as exclusives but as compromises. Natural resource issues, including those involving recreation as a single-purpose or or multiple-purpose use, become matters for reason and arbitration.

A discussion of trade-offs in the use of natural resources for recreation involves an analysis of such specific questions or issues as these:

1. What are our natural resource development and use policies?
2. What are some ways to increase the quality of recreational experience?
3. What are some of the trade-off issues between recreation and other uses of the resource, for example, camping in the forest versus timber harvest?
4. What are some of the trade-off issues between recreational quantity and quality regarding both the resource and the experience if we overuse and abuse the resource?
5. What impacts do management policies have on seasonal recreation use, and how can these policies be changed to spread use out?
6. Should natural resources be set aside just for the sake of preservation, that is, for use by future generations? Or should we weigh the short- and long-run benefits and costs of such a policy before making such a decision?

Natural resource development and use policies

A dichotomy exists in policies concerning use of natural resources for recreation. On one hand we have governmental officials bemoaning the loss of prime agricultural lands to other uses. A recent report of the National Agricultural Land Study (6) reemphasized the horror story told by the secretary of agriculture, Council on Environmental Quality (CEQ) officials, and other policy-making officials. The report said the nation is losing 1 million acres of prime farmland each year. Straight-line projections to the year 2000 showed all this land shifting to nonagricultural uses.

I am not belittling the concern about such trends. Certainly, as an agricultural economist at a major land grant university, I see agricultural land conversion problems developing in highly populated and highly industrialized areas, but it is unrealistic to expect such trends to continue at the same pace in the future. Population growth has slowed to a trickle except for immigration. Higher energy prices are reversing the flight to the suburbs. Restrictive zoning regulations, requirements for environmental impact statements, and lawsuits by environmental and conservation groups are slowing further encroachment of nonagricultural uses onto prime agricultural lands.

Generally, in physical terms, agricultural production has not suffered from previous shifts in agricultural land use. Farmers have become better managers. They have better tools. Yields on class II and III land are higher today than were yields on class I land 20 or 30 years ago. Better conservation and tillage practices, as well as increased use of pesticides and fertilizers, share credit for increased productivity.

As an agricultural economist, I am concerned about the profitability of farming in general. More specifically, I am also concerned about the survival of the family farm. I can provide you with examples that show that overproduction and market surpluses have done more damage to the family farm than have shortages of crops and higher prices. Do governmental agencies or other policy makers have the moral right to tell U.S. farmers to produce more, when producers must often sell their products at a price below the cost of production?

There is a delicate balance among abundance of prime agricultural lands, market prices of agricultural lands, market prices of agricultural products, and profitability of farming. Hypothesizing that 15 to 20 million acres of prime agricultural lands lost from production between 1960 and 1980 came back into production, would this mean that farmers would not produce crops on the 30 to 40 million acres of class II and III lands that were in extensive use 20 years ago? Does it mean that farmers voluntarily would use fewer pesticides and less fertilizer on more marginal lands? Or does it mean that the resulting production from this "restored" prime farmland would be greater, driving prices lower and requiring the government to intensify its price support and crop storage operations?

There are no easy answers. It is evident that technological improvements in farming, including irrigation, allow us to produce on land today that would not produce crops or livestock 20 to 30 years ago. If prime agricultural lands had not been lost to recreation and other urban uses, does this imply that such technologies would not have been developed? Does it imply that these technologies would not have been used to bring lower quality lands into intensive agricultural production? I think not!

On the other hand, conservation and environmental groups lobby for the transfer of lands from private ownership to public ownership for wildlife refuges, wilderness areas, parks, and other recreational areas. Also, public lands that have agricultural production potential are being incorporated into nondevelopment uses. Almost every year since the early 1960s, hundreds of thousands of acres of privately owned lands have shifted from open uses to restricted uses, or have been purchased outright for recreational and/or wilderness uses. For example, the National Park and Recreation Act of 1978 created eight new wilderness areas covering about 2 million acres. Pending are other proposals (5) to designate 15 million acres of roadless national forest lands as wilderness, and being debated is a bill to reserve 100 million acres of land in Alaska for permanent federal protection and management. Additions to the Wildlife Refuge System through 1978 (5) increased the number of refuges to 392, covering 46 million acres, an area larger than Oklahoma.

Some of this acreage is classified as prime agricultural land—the old axiom, to have your cake and eat it, too, applies to environmental groups as well as to any other special-interest group.

Many U.S. Department of Agriculture (USDA) and CEQ publications allude to urban sprawl as if it were a kind of social disease caused by invaders from another planet. Yet, by and large, these invaders are our relatives, friends, and other fellow Americans looking for a better, more convenient life. Who is to say that they cannot buy a piece of land for its amenity? Who made the ground rule that all prime agricultural land should be used only for producing more wheat, cotton, or corn so that we can export those crops to reduce our foreign earnings deficit caused by importing too much oil and too many televisions, stereos, watches, and cars? All of us use these products, not just invaders who usurp our prime agricultural lands.

We need to realize why a lot of our prime agricultural land has been covered over by water, concrete, and blacktop. Often, federal programs have stimulated these land transfers, as in the case of interstate highways, flood control programs, and rural water, sewer, and housing programs.

Enhancing the recreational experience

Everyone who wants to see a first-run movie or stage play cannot attend on opening night. These events have a limited capacity. The same is true for hotels, restaurants, and other such facilities designed for entertainment. Generally, reservations are required so those who do visit any of these facilities on a given day will not be overcrowded and will have a higher quality experience.

Yet when it comes to use of our public and private resources for an outdoor recreational experience, the law of the jungle seems to prevail. The herd instinct, with its attendant trampling and abuse of the natural environment, takes over. On a summer weekend, the mass media proclaim open season and encourage everyone to head for the lake or the woods. Consequently, in Oklahoma, 60 to 75 percent of the use of recreational facilities around Corps of Engineer and Water and Power Resources Service (Bureau of Reclamation) lakes occurs during the period between Memorial Day and Labor Day.

Certainly we can find ways to ameliorate this situation. For example, we need to educate industry leaders who schedule production cycles. Rather than close all automobile plants in June and July to change over for the new model year, why not introduce 1981 model cars in December 1980, January 1981, or even March or April 1981? Or if the psychological need to get a new model car is so great, why not begin selling 1982 model cars in the spring of 1981? My point is that if the automobile industry would shift its new model year introductions and close for vacation in April or October, we might have better luck in encouraging more people to use outdoor recreation resources in slack periods of use. The quality of the recreational experience would undoubtedly improve, as would the ability of vegetation to recuperate.

I could cite other examples. However, my point is that public and private outdoor recreation managers do not properly manage their facilities and resources.

A 1975 Council for Agricultural Science and Technology (CAST) report (*4*) stated: "Management of recreation only recently has been recognized as a major responsibility of land-management agencies which sometimes still treat the activities and problems with tolerance rather than with enthusiasm."

Too often I have heard public agency representatives say something to the effect of "let all the city slickers come in June, July, and August and get their fill and leave us alone after Labor Day. Then we can get a rest."

Such an attitude leads not only to abuse of the natural resource base, but also to mismanagement of human resources. More part-time employees are hired in the summer or peak months, while permanent employees rest on their laurels and in many cases do not pull their weight during the off-season. They may be required to repair damage caused by vandalism or they may need to revegetate denuded areas. But the off-season work is slow. And insofar as visitors to the recreational area are spread over a longer period, there probably would be less vandalism to repair and fewer denuded areas to revegetate!

Water quality in rural areas often is a function of land use management, combining soil type, topography, and rainfall with cultural practices and conservation or land treatment practices. In considering land treatment practices, perhaps we should refer to the newest moniker, best management practices (BMPs). BMPs focus primarily on holding soil in place, reducing soil erosion losses, and improving water quality. Hence, BMPs may overlook wildlife habitat and recreational values, such as hunting. Although we may be working toward a goal of "fishable and swimmable waters" by 1983, and toward "zero discharge of pollutants into any navigable stream by 1985," we still may be trading off one form of recreation for another. Trade-offs exist not only between recreation and other uses of natural resources, but among different recreational uses as well.

Management policy effects on seasonality of use

We need to do a better job of managing natural resources designated for recreational uses. Also, we can better manage many other acres of land, both public and private, to provide high quality recreational experience without competing with other uses. This concept of quality of experience is the key issue in the use of resources for recreation.

For too many years we have promoted quantity—more acres, more campsites, and more picnic tables. There is no national law or policy stating that public agencies are required to provide a certain number of facilities for peak-season use. We should promote a policy of high-quality experiences, even if such a policy entails assigned camping, reservations, user fees, or a combination of these forms of rationing.

In previous recreational studies, I discussed the trade-offs between quantity and quality, as these parameters relate to peak-season versus off-season recreational use of natural resources. Suggestions (1, 2) have been made on ways to reduce visual pollution, water pollution, physical degradation of the environment, and vandalism and ways to extend the seasonal use periods.

In a recent study (3) on the use of state parks and recreational areas in Oklahoma, we interviewed 1,636 persons at recreational sites. Forty-five percent of the respondents indicated they recreated at their particular site because it was an attractive area; 44 percent of those interviewed indicated they had visited the area before and returned because they liked the quality of the recreational experience on previous visits. Only 7 percent of those interviewed came to the area for multiple visits throughout the year because the area had year-round attractions, and 6 percent of the respondents liked the area because it was patrolled by rangers. Regarding seasonality of use, our study showed that 63 percent of the annual visitor use occurred in June, July, and August. Only 5 percent of visitor use occurred in April and 3 percent in October, two excellent months in Oklahoma for foliage colors and excellent camping weather (3). We also observed that 70 percent of those surveyed indicated they would be willing to pay an entrance or admission fee of $1 per day or $10 per year to use Oklahoma parks and recreational areas if the funds were used for site maintenance and improvement of facilities. (Oklahoma currently does not have an admission fee for use of its parks.)

Where do we go from here?

The 1975 CAST report (4) pointed out that "multiple-use planning and management of public lands attempt to optimize the production of goods and services for all people of the United States." Included in the grouping of goods and services were recreational opportunities, water, aesthetics, and wildlife. The report also pinpointed conflicts in the multiple use of public lands: recreation versus timber harvesting or livestock grazing, livestock versus wildlife, and destruction of sparse habitat by off-road vehicles.

Certainly, conflicts exist among uses of natural resources. However many of these conflicts could be resolved or at least minimized if groups representing diverse views worked together rather than against each other. Too many Americans have lost the ability to compromise. Too many of us see every competitive situation involving recreation and other uses of natural resources as an either-or situation; too many of us are not givers, but takers; and too many of us want policy changes implemented immediately. Of course, we also want someone else to pay for providing and maintaining the natural resources for recreational, wildlife, and other leisure-time pursuits, rather than paying our share of these costs. Unfortunately, too many of us do not respect others' property rights, including the right to privacy by other recreationists and property owners. The United States probably has the highest rate of vandalism and littering within recreational areas of any country in the world. Millions of dollars are required annually to clean up and repair these areas.

These conflicts need to be addressed. And we need to decide how much land we are going to set aside for recreation or wilderness. The mass media and public education will participate in these decisions. Educational television and radio programs, press coverage, and public education are beginning to have an effect on the thinking and attitudes of younger generations.

Using more public funds for rangers and other park employees to patrol and maintain security of the areas is a better use of our tax dollars than attending to litter and toilet repair. More stringent enforcement of our park rules and regulations, including fines and jail sentences, presumably would sound the alert that Americans no longer tolerate littering and vandalism of natural resources and recreational facilities.

As a researcher at a land grant university, I recommend more research on issues that involve the quantity and quality of recreational resources. Furthermore, we must find better techniques to measure values of quantity and quality recreation.

Professonal agricultural and natural resource organizations must develop programs emphasizing more effective management techniques for our existing resource base, including ways to encourage multiple-purpose uses while minimizing or avoiding conflicts among uses. We cannot avoid trade-offs or all conflicts. However, with proper planning and continued development of educational programs concerning the need to give equal consideration to quality of resources and recreational experiences, we will begin to eliminate some of these conflicts.

REFERENCES

1. Badger, D. D., and W. M. Harper. 1975. *Assessment of pool elevation effects on recreation visitation and concession operations at Tenkiller Ferry Lake.* AE 7503. Department of Agricultural Economics, Oklahoma State University, Stillwater.
2. Badger, D. D., D. F. Schreiner, and R. W. Presley. 1977. *Analysis of expenditures for outdoor recreation at the McClellan-Kerr Arkansas River Navigation System.* IWR Contract Report 77-4. Department of Agricultural Economics, Oklahoma State University, Stillwater.
3. Badger, D. D. L. L. Parks, C. A. Quinlan, and V. K. Lenard. 1980. *Impact of travel related leisure time activities in Oklahoma, 1977 Survey Data.* AE 8005. Department of Agricultural Economics, Oklahoma State University, Stillwater.
4. Council for Agricultural Science and Technology. 1975. *Multiple use of public lands in the seventeen western states.* Report 45. Iowa State University, Ames.
5. Council on Environmental Quality. 1979. *Environmental quality, the tenth annual report of the Council on Environmental Quality.* Washington, D.C.
6. Fields, S. F. 1980. *Where have the farm lands gone?* National Agricultural Lands Study, Council on Environmental Quality and U.S. Department of Agriculture, Washington, D.C.

32

The Great Lakes Basin: What Costs Environmental Quality?

Lee Botts
Chairman, Great Lakes Basin Commission
Ann Arbor, Michigan

The environmental revolution of the past decade ended with agreement that environmental protection must be considered in all development decisions and in the way we live. Now that environmental impact analysis is a fact of life, the issue is how to protect the environment, not whether it is desirable or necessary. Once an environmental problem and alternative protective measures are defined, the question becomes a matter of which alternatives should be applied. Cost is usually a major consideration.

Forging a regional approach

The Great Lakes Basin Commission staff has developed a method of evaluating costs of pollution control alternatives. The method was developed through the cooperation of water chemists, soil scientists, biologists, engineers, and environmentalists in Canada and the United States. Although the method was developed for making decisions about control of water pollution in the Great Lakes, the U.S. Environmental Protection Agency (EPA) now intends to apply it nationally. Originally applied to phosphorus pollution from point and nonpoint sources, the approach may be useful in controlling other forms of pollution as well.

Several years ago, the urgency became clear that we needed to determine how much pollution of the Great lakes is caused by pollution from land runoff. At that time, under the Clean Water Act, regulations and programs were underway to control point-source pollution, such as wastes from municipal sewage treatment plants and industry. There was considerable concern about whether point-source control would be enough. There was general agreement that nonpoint-source control would be necessary. But if it was possible, what would it cost?

It is often argued that environmental protection is an uneconomic burden. This view assumes that the money spent is nonproductive. Environmentalists point to the intangible benefits and contend that short-term costs produce incalcuable long-term benefits. As an editorial in the *Los Angeles Times* stated: "Profits can no longer remain the sole criterion for decisions. Price, love and joy, as well as the future of humanity itself, have no price tags." This is good rhetoric, but we must still consider the price tag. In our work in the Great Lakes Basin, we are finding that it is possible to demonstrate that good environmental protection is also good economics.

There is no question about the value of the Great Lakes Basin as a resource. The basin contains one-fifth of the world's fresh surface water, drained from 75 million acres of land, 32 million acres of which are in agricultural use. One-seventh of the U.S. population and one-half of Canada's population live in the basin. A large proportion of these people reside in the area's many cities—Toronto, Cleveland, Chicago, Buffalo, Toledo, Duluth, and others.

Great Lakes problems are complex, as is the institutional structure for dealing with them. However, the success of our effort demonstrates that it is possible to surmount institutional and political complications when there is determination and good will.

Our effort was international, involving a network of federal, state, and provincial agencies, plus 15 citizen advisory panels. The overall sponsoring agency was the International Joint Commission (IJC), an agency independent of both the U.S. and Canadian governments but responsible to them. The IJC worked through the government requests that specific problems be addressed.

In a 1971 Great Lakes water quality agreement, the United States and Canada agreed to meet specific water quality objectives. The agreement called for a 1-milligram-per-liter effluent limit for phosphorus and a reduction in phosphorus loadings by other means as necessary. Thus the IJC established the Pollution from Land Use Activities Reference Group (PLUARG) to address the issue of pollution from land runoff. PLUARG was to answer three questions: How much pollution of the Great Lakes is caused by land runoff? Where does pollution happen? What needs to be done about it?

In the United States water quality of the Great Lakes is regulated both by states and the federal government. Though the Great Lakes are recognized as the fourth seacoast in federal legislation, the jurisdictions are not the same as for the oceans. The federal government retains jurisdiction over the navigable waters, but the bottoms of the lakes are owned by the states. Each lake is divided legally by state boundaries, but, of course, neither the fish nor the waters conform to such borders. Regional coordination of state and federal planning for the future of the lakes is charged to the Great Lakes Basin Commission. The commission has no regulatory authority.

Fortunately, as I indicated, the fine points and complexities of jurisdictional authority were transcended in the PLUARG effort. After five years of effort, involving hundreds of officials, scientists, and citizens, substantial agreement was reached for answers to all three of the key questions. The massive PLUARG report was submitted to the IJC in the summer of 1978. Its information and resulting policy development are having a pervasive influence on Great Lakes' management. We are still functioning under what is called a post-PLUARG project, which aims to assess new developments and implement recommendations.

In answer to the question about the extent of land runoff, we concluded that land runoff does not contribute enough to pollution of the Great Lakes to justify an expensive, basinwide program of structural control. Land runoff is one, but not the major source, of Great Lakes' pollution.

Finding the sources of pollution

To answer the second question of where pollution occurs, we identified specific areas where nonpoint controls are likely to be beneficial. These areas included rural land in the Lake Erie basin and parts of the Lake Ontario, southern Lake Huron, and southern Lake Michigan basin. However, we also recognized that within these areas, individual watershed or sub-watersheds must be examined more closely to identify so-called "hydrologically active areas." Such areas, because of their specific characteristics and location within the watershed, may contribute a large portion of the nonpoint load. However, they may occupy only a small portion of the total area considered. If controls can be directed at these areas, nonpoint-source reductions can be achieved most efficiently and, it is hoped, inexpensively.

Unfortunately, while identifying the hydrologically active area is a good concept, we really do not know how to apply it practically. There are no known techniques or criteria that allow one to identify a hydrologically active area. Remote sensing offers some promise. However, our best approach at this time is to assess such areas in the field, using the best judgment of local expertise.

The PLUARG report makes clear that land use is not the only factor affecting nonpoint pollution. Certain land characteristics, notably soil texture, were identified as particularly important factors.

Overview modeling: Estimating costs of pollution control

I want to concentrate on the methodology used to answer the third question, that of what action is necessary to prevent pollution. We have found that this methodology has a wide application in determining costs of environmental protection. The method employs "overview modeling," a technique used to determine the cost-effectiveness of obtaining the level of control needed for a given situation, such as in the case of a watershed.

A detailed estimation of pollutant loads from each source in a drainage area is the first step of the process. To do this, we first determined land characteristics and land use intensities. PLUARG satellite photographs of the United States, taken from Landsat, were used to quantify relative amounts of farmlands, forest, wetlands, urban land, and so forth. We used other data, such as the comprehensive inventory of land cover that the basin commission had made for its Great Lakes Basin Framework Study.

We collected land-form data, such as soil texture and slope information. Then we factored in the presence or absence of a sewer system and the degree of sewage treatment provided. All of this data collection was made more feasible by the Section 208 planning program under the Clean Water Act. For the Great lakes, we used data from all 29 areawide water quality or 208 plans. We used a computer modeling process to simplify accounting for all the different inputs. The computer also permitted rapid assessment of social changes, such as potential population changes or urbanizaton of rural areas.

As the PLUARG report states, the real value of the review modeling process became clear when information about alternative pollution control measures were introduced. The results of various possible remedial programs could be tested in different combinations.

Because phosphorus control is so important for the Great Lakes, overview modeling was used to compare the costs and results of maintaining the effluent limit for sewage treatment plants at the 1-milligram-per-liter level required, or to a more stringent 0.5-milligram-per-liter level. For urban runoff we made an analysis of simple actions, such as cleaning the streets more often, to more complex measures, such as treating stormwater and combined sewer overflows.

Controlling urban runoff is not the best way to reduce phosphorus loads, but it will decrease loadings of heavy metals. The lack of a comparable bonus for municipal point-source control and rural runoff must be considered in analyzing the total picture.

We analyzed three increasingly expensive programs for agriculture. The least expensive would be voluntary "good stewardship" on all agricultural land. The most expensive level included the first two management levels, as well as such measures as drainage improvements and gradient terracing, which are fairly structural in nature. As experiments have proceeded with management practices, such as no-till measures in the Lake Erie basin, we have found direct benefits for the farmer as well as reduced phosphorus runoff to the waterways. Thus, if farmers turn to no-till management to save labor, the bonus may be more protection for the Great Lakes.

Cost-effectiveness, as used in the modeling process, means the ratio of the annual cost of a control program to the reduction in pollutant loading to receiving waters. The ratio can be determined for an entire watershed, part of it, or even a specific sewage treatment plant or individual farm.

A cautious approach

For the Great Lakes, the commission recommends that all municipal treatment plants discharging 1 million gallons of effluent a day or more reduce phosphorus concentrations to 1 milligram per liter and that all non-point-source control measures be implemented that are possible at relatively low cost. Our analysis has convinced our member agencies that stricter controls are not justified at this time. Nor have we found justification for proceeding with expensive nonpoint control programs for land runoff. Rather, we urge continued monitoring of water quality to detect any trends that might dictate reconsideration of control programs, a cautious approach made viable by the flexibility of overview modeling.

Our policy on phosphorus control is consistent with the goal of protecting the Great lakes from degradation, and if fully implemented, the policy will result in further improvements in water quality. This approach of using cost-effectiveness as a criterion avoids unjustified expenditures, therefore making more resources potentially available for dealing with other Great Lakes' problems, such as toxic contamination.

The Great Lakes have served as an early warning system for the world. The discoveries that DDT and PCBs had contaminated the food chain of Lake Michigan initially were not recognized as a signal that these chemicals were contaminating the environment everywhere on earth.

The Great lakes are beyond price. Saving them is an obligation that must be fulfilled for future generations. Still, the commitment to do so does not justify unnecessary expenditures. At the Basin Commission we are proud to have contributed to the PLUARG effort and are convinced that the method for weighing cost-effectiveness represents another contribution to the cause of environmental protection.

33

Protecting Our
Natural Heritage

Frank Jones

Regional Director
Heritage Conservation and Recreation Service
Ann Arbor, Michigan

The natural heritage issue is being surrounded by increasing concern—as we in the Heritage and Recreation Service think it should be.

A hundred years ago, though, the concept of natural heritage was no doubt a moot point. The bulk of the nation's land mass probably fit a present definition of natural heritage. But neither Congress nor the general public recognized that our natural resources were neither infinite nor invincible until they began to disappear. Laws encouraged the exploitation of these natural resources until their depletion caused a shift in policy.

By 1865, railroads were using 6.5 million cords of wood a year; as much as another 25 million acres of forest were being destroyed by fire. In 1889 the last roundup of wild bison took place—89 survivors of a population that was once 60 million on the prairies. Of a population that once numbered perhaps 5 billion, the last passenger pigeon on earth died September 1, 1914.

In the 50 miles or so I commute from Ann Arbor to Detroit, there are no visible remains of the natural heritage of southeastern Michigan—of the old-growth beech-maple forests, wetlands, native prairies, and large swamp forests of elm, ash, oak, and hickory. Even the River Rouge, where the freeway crosses, has been unable to hold out. It is now channelized and paved.

We live in a world of economic reality that has little room for unproductive spaces. But by virtue of their increasing rarity, the last remnants of our natural heritage are becoming more valuable. Just how rare these remnants are becoming has been dramatically illustrated by a survey of the entire state of Illinois that revealed that a mere .07 percent of the state remains in a relatively undisturbed, natural condition. Some elements of the state's natural heritage have completely disappeared. For those to whom the value of the preservation of our natural heritage is not self-evident, I would like to offer a few pragmatic reasons.

Preservation's practical benefits

Preservation of our natural heritage creates a system of "genetic diversity preserves" that are valuable in a number of ways. As we continue to mold the natural environment to suit our economic needs, we simplify it, sometimes snuffing out complex genetic information that has accumulated over hundreds of millions of years. Protected species preserve this information and may be called upon for use in reclaiming environmentally devastated landscapes that are either human-induced or naturally occurring, such as the Mount St. Helens area. The species within these preserves may hold the secret for a cure for cancer or may produce compounds with yet undiscovered medicinal and industrial uses.

By selection and interbreeding of domestic species with wild ones, these gene pools may also be tapped to develop new strains of domestic plants. To quote a study (1) done for the U.S. Department of the Interior: "By setting aside selected areas of the natural landscape representing the full range of communities with their component species, we can create a resource bank of incalculable value which is sure to yield critical, irreplaceable and, therefore, priceless resources to meet unanticipated future needs."

There are a couple of other immediate uses for the remnants of our natural heritage. These natural areas serve as environmental monitoring stations, or "ecological baselines." They preserve a diversity of species, which gives them a greater likelihood of possessing species that are sensitive to certain substances. These indicator species reflect changes in the environment. For example, some lichens wither if exposed to low concentrations of nitrous oxides.

Natural areas are also outdoor classrooms, where young children can first sense the complexity and balance of nature. They also serve as laboratories where scientists can test evolutionary or ecological theories.

The pragmatic reasons are not alone in illustrating why our natural heritage should be preserved—there are equally important aesthetic reasons. One is the intrinsic value of something rare—the largest, the oldest, the last. Human beings value these natural things, and to most persons it is self-evident that the remnants of our natural heritage should be preserved.

Another reason is the inspirational value a natural area holds for the visitor. An example is an area in Illinois called Giant City, which contains a hill that is capped by a layer of sandstone and underlain by softer material.

As this softer material erodes and undercuts the sandstone layer above, great sandstone slabs break off and slowly slide down the hill. Slowly, indeed. Over generations there is no appreciable change. But as one stands on the hill and views the massive blocks at the hilltop that grade to smaller, more eroded blocks that have slowly slid farther down, one is imbued with a sense of the immense time scale of geological forces working slowly upon this hilltop. Or alternately, one glimpses in perspective the fleeting instant in which a human lifetime occurs.

Finally, for some, preservation of our natural heritage is a question of morality, that as stewards of this planet mankind has the duty to protect it. We have no right to allow a species to disappear simply because it seems to serve no immediate purpose.

How do we protect our natural heritage? A two-pronged approach is required. The first step is gathering information to identify those best examples of the various elements of national diversity that are in most need of attention. The second step, implementing a wide range of protection techniques, can then be focused on the exemplary representatives of our natural heritage.

Exemplary programs

Information gathering is a cooperative effort involving federal, state, and local levels of government, universities, and private organizations. At the center of this effort are what we generally term the state heritage programs. Most states have some form of program that identifies and dedicates natural areas and locates endangered species and their habitats. The number of states with such programs grows each year.

Two types of state heritage programs illustrate what programs are possible, the Ohio Natural Heritage Program and the Illinois Natural Areas Inventory. These are just two of many excellent heritage programs. We are fortunate that in my region, the Lake Central Region, all six of our states have active, effective natural heritage programs.

The Ohio Natural Heritage Program is representative of the most common type of natural heritage program, typical of the design pioneered by The Nature Conservancy, a national nonprofit organization dedicated to the preservation of natural diversity. I believe that more than 24 states have adopted this type of program to date.

The key feature of the program is an "element approach." In this approach a detailed classification of the state's biological and geological environment is first devised. In Ohio, 888 elements emerged from this system: 575 special plants, 183 special animals, 87 plant communities, 42 geologic features, and one in a catch-all category, "other natural features." Together these elements create a cross section of the state's natural heritage.

The program then seeks to pinpoint where these elements appear in the state, relying on secondary sources, such as museum and herbarium data, to build a rich bank of information. The information is then augmented and verified by field surveys. This scrutiny of Ohio revealed that most of these 888 elements have less than five occurrences statewide. Many elements had one or no known occurrences.

The natural heritage program process must be an ongoing process so that the program can accurately gauge the changing character of Ohio's natural landscape. The computerized data that the program generates already contains more biological data pertaining to the state's natural diversity than is available anywhere else in the state, making the program the center for determining the existence and quality of elements of Ohio's natural heritage.

The Illinois Natural Areas Inventory employs a similar, though modified, approach. While relying on secondary information sources, it emphasizes primary field surveys to identify the few remaining undisturbed natural areas in the state. This approach includes examining maps and aerial photographs and conducting aerial and on-the-ground surveys. The actual form of the survey, whether through literature or primary field work, depends upon what is being surveyed: undisturbed natural communities; railroad or cemetery prairies; habitats with rare, threatened, endangered, or relic species; geologic areas; unique natural areas; nature study areas; or aquatic areas. In the search for undisturbed native prairies alone, 11,000 miles of railroad and 3,923 cemeteries in the prairie region of the state were surveyed.

The product of the first survey cycle included a list of 1,089 areas, each with a corresponding computerized bank of information detailing the areas' natural characteristics, ownership, use, management, protection status, and boundary. Sixty-one percent of the high-quality natural communities identified by the inventory were previously unknown to the Department of Conservation.

State heritage programs such as these are the foundation upon which a national program to inventory our national natural heritage is built. The National Natural Landmarks Program is administered by the Heritage Conservation and Recreation Service. It seeks to identify areas that best illustrate the full range of ecological and geological features constituting the nation's natural history—its terrestrial and aquatic communities, geological materials and processes, fossil evidence of the development of life on earth, and habitats of rare or restricted plant and animal species.

We do this by conducting multistate regional studies, relying heavily on data generated by state heritage programs, but comparing areas among states to select those that truly best represent our natural heritage in the physiographic region. By directing our efforts nationally, we determine significance on a national level. We have contracted scientists to further study most potential national natural landmarks on-site to determine this significance and to flesh out details of the areas. Currently, there are 511 designated national natural landmarks. These occur on both public and private property.

As you can see, information gathering is well underway and will be a continuing process. The next step is to protect those resources that have been identified. The Ohio Natural Heritage Program, for example, found that approximately 70 percent of the identified element occurrences are on unprotected land. For publicly owned or administered areas, or for areas that might be affected by publicly funded or licensed projects, information on the significance of the particular resource is itself a tool for protection. The public owner or administrator is in a much better position to make resource-use decisions, knowing the level of significance of an area and its relative quality. Of course, in some cases a decision must be made that preservation of a particular area is preempted by other considerations. But in many other cases, projects can be modified to protect natural values. Or it may be found that protection of the resource is consistent with the agency's mission. At least resources will not as likely be lost accidentally through ignorance.

Where the private sector profits

The protection of our natural heritage should not be considered just another piece of red tape that the public land manager must wrestle with. The existence of a good natural heritage inventory has a two-fold benefit for public land managers and, we have found, for some of their counterparts in private industry. The inventory provides detailed information about the natural characteristics of a particular area at the earliest stage of the planning process. The inventory also indicates where critical natural heritage resources probably do not exist. Environmental concern then can be focused on this "lean list" of the best representatives of our natural heritage.

An example drawn from the private sector, the electric utility companies, illustrates this benefit. A company embarking on a transmission corridor development project can obtain natural heritage data at the outset of the planning process, thereby avoiding environmentally sensitive areas. The nation's natural heritage is protected. And the utility company saves money by avoiding problems that might have otherwise surfaced later in the planning process when changes would have been more costly. This advantage has stimulated public utility companies in at least two states in the Lake Central Region to make substantial financial contributions to natural heritage programs.

Land protection techniques

A complex array of protection tools is available to the individual private owner. The most simple and least expensive tool is owner notification. Many states have undertaken this program as the next logical step to a natural heritage inventory. We perform this function in our National Natural Landmark Program. In these programs owners of outstanding resources are identified and notified of the significance of their property. Some notification programs also have a registration provision whereby the owner can enter into a legally nonbinding agreement indicating intent to protect the resource voluntarily. Frequently, this awareness is all that is necessary to protect a piece of our natural heritage.

For the owner with a stronger personal commitment to natural heritage protection, formal dedication of an area or granting of a conservation easement on the property allows the property to remain in private ownership, but protects its natural qualities. If the easement is donated, the owner enjoys a tax deduction for the gift. Conservation easements (sometimes also known as scenic or preservation easements) in effect are transfers of certain development rights from the property owner to another party, the easement holder. The easement holder, usually a public agency or private conservation organization, is then able to prevent future development of the property. This is generally the limit of the easement holder's rights. Very few conservation easements also provide for other rights, such as public access, although these other rights are options that the landowner might desire to have written into the easement.

Some owners are confident they can protect the area during their lifetime, but are uncertain what will happen to their property after their death. For these persons, a bequest may be desirable and save estate taxes. Selling or donating property with a reserved life estate is another option. It transfers property to another party, but reserves the right for the owner and perhaps a spouse and children to remain on and use the property for their lifetimes. A donation of a life estate may save both estate and income taxes.

Then, of course, there are those who because of personal conviction and/or financial security choose to make an outright full or partial donation of property to a public agency or public organization that will protect and manage the property. This is done usually because the owner wants to see the area protected. A by-product is the tax deduction the donor may gain. Even if the owner has neither the ability nor the interest in making some form of donation, a public agency or private organization may be interested in making an offer to purchase the property outright, especially if the area ranks high on the list of priority resources.

A rather sophisticated body of land protection techniques has developed as the result of the desire of public and private agencies and organizations to protect our ever-dwindling natural heritage. The techniques already mentioned are the most simple. A complex transaction may involve any of a number of different approaches, including leases, sale-leasebacks, undivided interest in property, installment transactions, use of an intermediary land-holding organization, and use of the threat of condemnation to defer capital gains taxes for the seller. Representatives of federal, state, and private organizations are continually working with private owners of outstanding examples of our natural heritage to minimize the financial or personal hardship heritage conservation might cause them. Usually, something can be worked out.

All forms of natural heritage protection, whether for publicly or privately owned heritage resources, are predicated on communication, two-way communication. Communication informs the resource owners of the quality of their property. It can indicate when there is a change in ownership or a pending threat to a heritage resource. It also assists landowners interested in taking steps to protect their property.

The National Heritage Policy Act

Interest in natural heritage protection has been snowballing with the growing environmental awareness of the 1960s and 1970s. Now, in the 1980s this awareness has culminated in legislation currently before the Senate Subcommittee on Parks, Recreation, and Renewable Resources—the National Heritage Policy Act. In his 1977 environmental message, President Carter called for the creation of a National Heritage Program in response to the critical need to preserve special places, including those of natural and scientific value, which give this nation a sense of history and continuity. The National Heritage Policy Act would achieve this goal by a number of means, including (a) the establishment of a national policy and central source of direction for public and private efforts in heritage conservation; (b) creation of a comprehensive and consistent system for compiling information on important heritage resources; (c) protection of heritage resources from adverse federal actions; and (d) establishment of a National Register of Natural Areas to include resources of national, state, and local significance. This type of legislation is timely and necessary.

We are excited about natural heritage protection in my agency. And we are gratified to see the same interest and enthusiasm spreading through state governments, other federal agencies, and the public. It is becoming apparent that heritage conservation is not a hindrance to economic progress and to our standard of living. It is, in fact, part of that standard of living, a part we cannot afford to ignore.

Aldo Leopold once said, "The first prerequisite of intelligent tinkering is to save all the pieces." Protection of our natural heritage saves the pieces of our environmental tinkering. In the flow of our everyday lives, we are leaving, as a nation, a few tiny islands untouched, islands that remind us of the past and perhaps serve as a yardstick with which to measure the future.

REFERENCE

1. The Nature Conservancy. 1975. *The preservation of natural diversity: A survey and recommendations.* Contract No. CX 0001-5-01110. U.S. Department of the Interior, Washington, D.C.

34

Agricultural Policies for Fish and Wildlife in the Future

Glen Loomis
*Associate Deputy Chief for Technology Development
Application, Soil Conservation Service, Washington, D.C.*

Three basic premises underlie my discussion on the future of fish and wildlife policies. The first is that to achieve a robust yet stable economy we must consider all the effects of land and water use and management. The second is that conservation policies and fish and wildlife policies have compatible objectives. And the third is that sometimes we can significantly enhance fish and wildlife habitat improvements.

The production of cultivated crops and wood products is accomplished only through great effort, constant attention to the land, and intensive use. For fish and wildlife habitat to continue to occupy a significant position in this scheme, we first must temper our use of the land and water with sound soil and water conservation decisions and then superimpose applicable habitat management.

Future policies must first consider the interrelationships of primary land use with wildlife habitat. This is evident in the growing need for production of food, feed, fiber, wood products, and oilseed crops. More than ever, we must strive to maintain a reasonable balance between natural communities or ecosystems and land use and management. Monoculture, especially if supported with heavy applications of herbicides, limits wildlife species. Providing even small areas of critical habitat can often result in maintaining certain species that would not otherwise exist. Many times critical habitat can be obtained at minimal cost if such provisions for preservation are included early in planning.

A historical problem compounded

Landowners and the public face steadily increasing problems concerning fish and wildlife habitat and how this nation is going to use its land. In facing this challenge, history can help us predict the future. Theodore Roosevelt was not a scientist, but his dynamic dedication proved to be among the most decisive of factors encouraging conservation of America's wildlife, scenic areas, and renewable resources. At a time well before natural resource shortages, as we know them now, Roosevelt instituted a national policy of natural resource stewardship.

In 1920 only half of the people in the United States lived in towns and cities; the other half lived on farms. People worked long hours and had relatively little money to spend. The demand for recreation was minor. Today the situation is totally different. Our population has grown, most of us live in cities. Leisure time is a major component of our daily life. We work fewer hours, we have more money to spend, and we play more. There is an increasing demand for outdoor recreation and availability of natural areas. It appears likely that this supply and demand problem will become worse as our society grows more affluent. Unlike hypothetical widgets, however, we cannot easily mass produce more natural areas—at least not without extreme cost and commitment.

Residences, factories, shopping centers, and roads are absorbing land at an increasing rate. From 1958 to 1967, about 10 million acres of rural land were converted to urban, development, and transportation uses. In the decade that followed about 29 million acres of rural land were converted to nonagricultural uses. We are presently losing more than 1 million acres per year of our prime farmlands to development.

Defining future policy

Future fish and wildlife policies need to address two major questions. How can we get private landowners to maintain, restore, and manage wildlife and fish habitat for present and future generations? How can those private landowners be convinced to welcome hunters and fishermen onto their properties?

Farm programs influence fish and wildlife habitats—be it purposely good or bad, or largely accidental. The landowner is a producer of wildlife. His use and management of the soil and water resources control habitat quality. The public is the consumer of fish, wildlife, and related recreational opportunity and therefore must share responsibility relative to wildlife abundance and outdoor recreation opportunities. A recent report (1) outlines a new model act of access, liability, and trespass that specifically deals with private lands.

Recent agricultural policy action

The U.S. Department of Agriculture (USDA) recently took steps to address these concerns. Secretary's Memorandum No. 2019, dated July 8, 1980, specified USDA policy on both USDA-administered lands as well as private land receiving USDA assistance. According to the memorandum, fish and wildlife policy has as its goal "to develop and implement authorized program policies and actions that will support the economic, esthetic, ecological, recreational, and scientific values of fish and wildlife, improve their habitats, and insure the presence of viable, diverse, naturally occurring wildlife populations, while fully considering other department missions, resources, and services. This will be accomplished through: (1) management actions on lands administered by the department; (2) educational, technical, and financial assistance programs for private and other nonfederal lands; (3) programs to improve the status of threatened and endangered species; (4) alleviating economic losses to agricultural crops, livestock, and forest and range resources caused by vertebrate animals (birds, rodents, predators, and other mammals); (5) support and encouragement of biological controls to regulate insects, diseases, and pest vegetation; and (6) research providing the necessary technology to accomplish the foregoing."

In addition, the policy calls for each agency to review its programs within 12 months and prepare an analysis of its role in fish and wildlife habitat management. Moreover, the policy is to develop specific recommendations on any changes needed to encourage the protection and improvement of fish and wildlife habitats consistent with the stated policy.

To address these concerns, we are taking a hard look at fish and wildlife opportunities in implementing the Soil and Water Resources Conservation Act (RCA). Seven resource areas have been identified that we are addressing as we look at USDA's soil and water conservation program—34 programs in all. In the fish and wildlife program we are specifically looking at options that include the following features: (a) activities designed to reduce the loss of wetlands caused by agricultural pursuits; (b) improvement of wildlife food and cover conditions on intensively cultivated land; and (c) application of good grazing management on rangelands.

Under the new USDA fish and wildlife policy, agencies are to review pertinent legislation on regulations, policies, and directives and then make specific recommendations that encourage the protection and improvement of fish and wildlife habitat by private landowners. Obviously, some existing USDA policies and programs directly or indirectly affect alteration or loss of wetlands. Identifying and reviewing these policies and programs will begin to improve coordination among agencies to help reduce loss of wetlands as a result of agricultural conversions. This effort will strengthen our implementation of the fish and wildlife resource area of RCA.

Wildlife habitat associated with cropland can be improved by modifying or applying soil conservation prctices. For example, RCA data show that during 1975 in the conterminous United States residue was removed from more than 51 percent of the harvested cropland. On the other hand, new tillage systems, such as no-till cropping, minimum tillage, and stubble mulching, are more beneficial to wildlife than conventional tillage practices.

To help identify and establish fish and wildlife policies for the future, the Soil Conservation Service and the Fish and Wildlife Service have initiated a cooperative agreement with the National Academy of Sciences to study the impact of emerging agricultural trends on fish and wildlife habitat. The results of this study will provide valuable guidelines for redirecting existing programs and establishing new programs within USDA, which meet our food and fiber needs and yet are sensitive to opportunities for improving habitat.

Future policies may need to provide more economic incentives for private landowners. Incidental wildlife habitat benefits accompany most types of agricultural and forest operations. However, incidental habitat losses can also occur. Greater and more predictable benefits result in cases when land managers deliberately plan their activities to enhance habitat. This usually will occur only when there is an incentive, especially an economic incentive. Private property and concern about public access still play major roles in the way private landowners view wildlife habitat.

Aldo Leopold, renowned for having raised wildlife management to the level of a science, may actually come to be honored more for his philosophy of conservation. In 1932, Leopold wrote, "Effective conservation requires, in addition to public sentiment and laws, a deliberate and purposeful manipulation of the environment. This manipulation can be accomplished only by the landowner, and the private landowner must be given some kind of an incentive for undertaking it." Leopold's statement is just as valid today. Many landowners are anxious to improve habitat and to increase species numbers and diversity only to find that too often the public refuses to honor private property rights. The incentive for private landowners to act in a manner benefiting the public is lacking—and vice-versa.

USDA programs will continue to be designed to meet the specific needs of the day. I suspect we will have crop set-aside programs again in the future. I believe we will make special efforts to convert rapidly eroding cropland to land with permanent vegetation. Working together, we can have programs that include special provisions to benefit fish and wildlife and at the same time meet such major objectives as stabilizing agricultural production or reducing soil erosion.

We should take a hard look at the potential of dedicating certain lands specifically to fish and wildlife use. For example, the nation is conducting a major national effort to control development of floodplains and wetlands. Some of our best opportunities to benefit fish and wildlife occur in these areas. I see significant opportunities in the future to ensure that our programs promote proper land use and provide critical habitat. The future will likely bring more monoculture systems, in which case we will need to give even more attention to how we use our floodplains and wetlands to offset losses of habitat in intensively cropped areas.

A national land trust

There is another approach that needs comprehensive review. Some have suggested that we need to establish a national trust system; landowners could enroll their lands in this national land bank in exchange for signs designating their lands as "National Trust Lands." They would also receive technical and financial assistance aimed at erosion control and the improvement of wildlife habitat. Constraints on public use of the enrolled land could be negotiated as a condition of enrollment. This system could help bring down the barrier between landowners and consumer. Members of the public using National Trust Lands might be more likely to respect the conditions of use specified by the landowner if a sign says "National Trust Lands" instead of "No Trespassing." A number of organizations have been looking at various ways that such a system could be developed.

In summary, I believe that future fish and wildlife policies must continue to address land stewardship, education, voluntary soil conservation, economic incentives, and last—and least in my opinion—some regulation.

Future policies will be influenced by several major factors:

1. The supply of land with potential for food and fiber production. We estimate there are 128 million acres with medium to high potential for conversion to cropland. About 25 million of these acres are wet soils.

2. National policies for agricultural exports. Will the United States try to play a major role in feeding the world in the future?

3. Opposition to federal involvement in land use regulation.

4. Costly energy supplies.

5. Rate of agricultural technology development. Technology has increased output by about 1.5 percent per year. Recent increases appear to be more like 1.1 percent per year. What should we expect by the year 2000?

6. Public interest and support.

These six factors and others will have a lot to do with shaping the social attitudes about resource use and stewardship.

Privately owned farms, ranches, and forests, which make up more than half of America's land resources, provide habitat for much of the nation's fish and wildlife. On farmlands, food and fiber production is and will continue to be of primary importance, but many acres used for crops, range, or forestry also offer ideal habitat for wildlife. Still, many acres can be improved for habitat value. Let's take full advantage of the opportunity of government programs, farmer interest and concern, and public support to improve this important national resource.

REFERENCE

1. Church, W. L. 1980. *Private lands and public recreation: A report and proposed new model act on access, liability and trespass.* School of Law, University of Wisconsin, Madison.

35

Retaining Environmental Values in Channel Work

David L. Herbst
Great Lakes Regional Executive
National Wildlife Federation
Rochester, Indiana

When Congress passed the Watershed Protection and Flood Prevention Act (Public Law 566) in 1954, conservationists hailed it as being a dream come true. Finally, we had the means to attack many of the nation's natural resource ills on a watershed basis, a sensible, logical approach then that remains valid today.

Many areas and individuals accepted and implemented the watershed planning concept. However, probably more times than not, "watershed" work consisted mainly of improvements to move water off the land more quickly and efficiently. Streams were gouged and straightened. Native vegetation was replaced with grasses. It was painfully obvious that some resources were being developed at the expense of others, as there was little or no input from the environmental community. And once again we were haunted by the words of Aldo Leopold (*1*): "Nearby is the graceful loop of an old dry creek bed. The new creek bed is ditched straight as a ruler; it has been 'uncurled' by the county engineer to hurry the runoff. On the hill in the background are contoured strip-crops; they have been 'curled' by the erosion engineer to retard the runoff. The water must be confused by so much advice."

A challenge to channelization

Many early supporters of Public Law 566, particularly those in the fish and wildlife field, became rapidly disenchanted with the on-the-ground implementation of the program. Consequently, battle lines were drawn throughout the nation's agricultural regions.

Indiana was no exception. Agricultural interests argued that improved drainage was necessary for the state to maintain its important agricultural production role in the Corn Belt. Fish and wildlife conservationists stressed repeatedly that streams and their immediate environs (a) were extremely important to a great variety of wildlife and associated forms of recreation, such as hunting, trapping, fishing, and boating; (b) served as outdoor educational and scientific laboratories; and (c) provided pleasing aesthetic corridors in an otherwise monotonous rural monoculture. The environmental arguments, I might add, were almost always after the fact; there was little opportunity to participate in the early planning stages. Ensuing confrontations were dramatic, but little was accomplished.

Toward an understanding

By the late 1960s, attitudes were changing, however. Leaders from both sides of the watershed controversy began to recognize and accept the other side's problems and agreed that reasonable people ought to be able to reason together to resolve their differences. An informal agreement was struck among the U.S. Soil Conservation Service, Indiana Division of Fish and Wildlife (IDFW) and U.S. Fish and Wildlife Service. The agreement called for an interdisciplinary, multiagency approach to Public Law 566 planning. This agreement was formalized in 1973 as a joint memorandum of understanding and is thought to have played a key role in the development of the present national channel modification guidelines adhered to by the U.S. Departments of Agriculture and Interior.

Under the memorandum of understanding, representatives from the three agencies conduct field investigations to survey fish and wildlife resources and to evaluate riparian habitat, including wetlands, for possible acquisition and other areas critical to the survival of endangered species, such as the Indiana bat. Also as part of the process, the multiagency biology team is given the opportunity to comment on specific design details for project features that provide for protection and/or mitigation of fish, wildlife, and riparian habitat losses. To date, some 30 miles of channels in Indiana have been modified using this approach.

A watershed plan ideally calls for minimum disturbance to a channel, whereby fallen and hazardous trees, stumps, drifts, and other debris are removed manually or by carefully maneuvering special machinery. The endproduct is an aesthetically pleasing and efficient channel with relatively undisturbed banks and associated habitat.

Evidence of success

Other projects may call primarily for simple modificaton of landowner operations. Such was the case on a portion of Buck Creek in east-central Indiana. An agreement was reached with a feedlot owner to fence his livestock out of the stream, except for a small stretch that was to be used for watering. Only minor alteration of the streambed took place, and the banks were revegetated. Field inspections one year later indicated success. Vegetation was established and growing well. And there was an obvious improvement in water quality (2).

On those projects where major channel modifications were determined to be in order, such as on Rock Creek in Wells County, Rock Creek in Cass County, and, again, on a portion of Buck Creek in Henry County, work was done only from one side, with woody and shrubby vegetation on the opposite side saved for its shade, cover, and filtering qualities. Fish deflectors, consisting of stone dams and fishways providing a pool and riffle effect, were constructed, and streambanks between cropland or pasture were either permanently marked with posts anchored in concrete or fenced and then planted with herbaceous and woody vegetation.

Five growing seasons later, vegetation was luxuriant and provided food and cover for wildlife. Deflectors and fishways were functioning, and pools had stabilized at a depth of 3 to 4 feet.

In addition, subsequent fishery surveys were most heartening. By electro-sampling, five years after construction, IDFW biologists found in Buck Creek 18 species of fish, compared to 11 species 1 year prior to construction. And in Rock Creek, 25 species of fish were identified in the man-made fishway. Included were a number of smallmouth bass ranging in size from 3 inches to 20 inches. It would appear, then, that mitigation had not only been successful in these projects, but also that a certain degree of enhancement had occurred.

Times change, people change, and ideas change. Likewise, methods of problem solving change. In Indiana, on some Public Law 566 small watershed projects, we were able to attain our goals through cooperation and coordination and, above all, by listening to one another. Not only did we achieve improved agricultural drainage, but we also were able to save a place for wildlife and preserve a bit of America's heartland.

REFERENCES

1. Leopold, Aldo. 1966. *A Sand County almanac. With essays on conservation from Round River*. Sierra Club/Ballantine Books. New York, New York. 295 pp.
2. McCall, James D., Robin F. Knox. 1978. *Riparian habitat in channelization projects*. In Proceedings, National Symposium on Strategies for Protection and Management of Floodplain Wetlands and Other Riparian Ecosystems. Callaway Gardens, Georgia.

IX. Energy Challenges to Natural Resource Values

36

Energy Development and Use: An Environmental Quality Perspective

Mohamed T. El-Ashry
Director of Environmental Quality
Tennessee Valley Authority, Norris, Tennessee

The development and use of energy resources inescapably bring about impacts on mankind and the natural environment. Therefore, we must thoroughly explore the nature, magnitude, and distribution of these impacts in order to make balanced decisions regarding future energy development and environmental quality.

Energy will be the predominant domestic issue of the 1980s. Our challenge as natural resource managers is to move through the transition from decades of energy waste and declining fossil fuels to a future based on conservation and renewable sources of energy without destroying the hard-fought environmental gains of the 1970s. We dare not trade off environmental and energy goals. We should strive instead to meet them both.

In April 1977 President Carter announced a National Energy Plan containing specific proposals that would virtually double coal production by 1985. In 1979 President Carter's energy message resulted in major legislative proposals, including an Energy Mobilization Board to expedite energy projects and a Synthetic Fuels Corporation to expedite development of shale oil, coal gas, and other synthetic fuels. The first proposal was defeated by the House in June 1980 and sent back to conference committee. The second proposal passed Congress and was signed into law in July 1980. Another major piece of legislation concerning coal is the utility "oil back-out"

313

bill that would mandate the conversion of 107 coal-capable plants at 50 generating stations. This action would boost coal use by 40 million tons per year by 1985.

A perilous reliance on coal

As we increase our coal use and embark on oil shale and other synthetic fuel development, we must not abandon our commitment to continued environmental improvement. Increased reliance on coal presents a number of real hazards. The list of hazards related to its extraction, preparation, transportation, and use is long and challenging. Some of the major problems include sulfur oxides and sulfates in the air, acid in the air, acid drainage in the water, trace elements and radioactivity in the air and water, disruption of water sources, scarring of the earth by surface mining, health and safety in deep mines, subsidence over deep mines, disposal of boiler ash and sludge from scrubbing, and atmospheric warming from carbon dioxide. Many of these problems are also associated with the extraction and processing of oil shale.

In surface coal mining the topography is modified by the elimination of old landforms and the creation of new ones as well as by increased slope angles. The process accelerates soil erosion, and sediments may choke streams and increase the flood hazard. Moisture-catching depressions and pits increase the potential of acid mine drainage in the East and may cause surface accumulation of salt in the West.

"Reclaiming the West," a new report by the nonprofit research organization INFORM, concluded that at 6 of the 15 surface mines studied in the western states "the arid climate makes it doubtful that reclamation can ever be successful, even with the best practices." Although federal law prohibits strip mining where the land cannot be reclaimed, the study further reported that mines have been opened in many areas where there is lack of sufficient rainfall to support revegetation.

In the room and pillar method of underground coal mining, failure of one or more roof supports and failure due to overburden loading on broad roof spans between supporting columns can cause the collapse of the overlying strata and surface subsidence, which may result in excessive damage in highly developed urban areas.

Deterioration of water quality from eastern coal mining activities is caused mainly by acid mine drainage, which increases the cost of water treatment, destroys aquatic life, inhibits the use of waterways for recreation, and decreases aesthetic values. In areas where acid is no problem, surface coal still can pollute streams with chemicals. In Kentucky calcium, magnesium, and sulfate were the elements showing greatest increases following mining.

Disruption of groundwater systems and flow patterns by surface mining are of particular concern in the semiarid western region. This is due to the importance of groundwater to irrigated agriculture and livestock in the region. Mining activity can drain shallow and coal-seam aquifers, causing the temporary or permanent loss of existing wells near the mined area.

The impact of surface mining on alluvial valley floors has brought growing concern. These areas are composed of unconsolidated, highly permeable material and have shallow water tables. In the West the alluvial aquifers are an important source of irrigation water. In addition, shallow alluvial aquifers serve to buffer seasonal fluctuations in surface runoff and reduce flood peaks through bank storage.

Air pollution is the most serious environmental problem associated with the conventional burning of coal. At present, nearly two-thirds of the sulfur oxides and one-third of the particulate matter emitted into the atmosphere are from burning coal for electric power generation. Major increases in electricity generation from conventional coal combustion could have great adverse air quality impacts in the absence of improved combustion and pollution control technologies. In this regard, the National Energy Plan proposes that best available control technologies be required on all new coal-fired facilities.

The same provision has been included in the Clean Air Act Amendments of 1977. Yet sulfur oxides are projected to be higher in 1985 and 2000 than in 1975. In the year 2000 sulfur oxides are projected to be about 12 percent higher than in 1975. In addition, with planned and proposed increases in coal use, increasing amounts of sludges and spent ashes may present a solid waste disposal problem. It is projected that in 2000 noncombustible solid wastes from coal burning will increase to 2.7 times the 1975 level and sludges will increase to 8.5 times the 1975 levels.

Acid rain: A problem presently escaping control

As a result of the combustion of huge quantities of fossil fuels, the United States annually discharges about 50 million tons of sulfur and nitrogen oxides into the atmosphere. Through a series of complex chemical reactions, these pollutants can be converted into acids, which may return to earth as acid precipitation or acid rain. Acid rain has long been recognized as an environmental problem in Japan and in northern Europe. In recent years research has suggested that this particular form of air pollution also is a serious problem in northeastern North America and California and may be affecting the Rocky Mountains and the Smokies as well.

Records from measurements of the acidity of rain and snow, while not complete, have suggested to many researchers a trend toward more widespread and strongly acidic rain. In one extreme example, a rain shower in Kane, Pennsylvania, in 1978 had a pH of 2.3.

Although sulfur and nitrogen oxides accounted for 26 percent of the total air pollution in the United States in 1977, they are considered the major contributors to the acid rain problem. Estimates place man's present contribution to the total sulfur in the air at about 60 percent. Despite existing regulations, total emissions are expected to increase due to increased coal use.

Unlike most other environmental and health issues, acid rain typically originates in one state and comes down and brings about impacts on another. In recent years taller and taller smoke stacks have been built in an effort to reduce ground-level concentrations that might endanger health or the local environment. As a result, emissions are transported for hundreds of kilometers downwind from these power plants. This problem of long-range transport is not addressed in the Clean Air Act.

Acid rain may have severe ecological impacts on widespread areas of the environment. Because of their acidic condition, more than 90 lakes in the Adirondacks of New York State can no longer support fish life. Recent data indicate that other areas of the United States, such as northern Minnesota and Wisconsin, may be vulnerable to similar adverse impacts. Although many of the aquatic effects of acid rain have been well documented, data related to possible terrestrial impacts are just beginning to be developed. In addition, acid rain is contributing to the destruction of stone monuments and man-made objects throughout the world. The 2,500-year-old Parthenon and other classical buildings on the Acropolis in Athens, Greece, have shown much more rapid decay in this century as a result of the city's high air pollution levels.

Acid rain poses a challenge to the increased use of coal and other fossil fuels. However, insufficient knowledge exists about its explicit causes and specific effects. But we should not wait until every last unknown is investigated and risk irreparable damage to fragile environments. The prospect suggests a more vigorous exploration of ways to reduce the release of both sulfur and nitrogen oxides into the atmosphere.

The Tennessee Valley Authority (TVA) is conducting research into the cause and effects of acid rain through monitoring; studies on atmospheric movement and chemical reaction of pollutants; and laboratory and field studies of vegetation, soil, and surface waters. In addition, sulfur dioxide emissions from TVA power plants are undergoing drastic reductions, about 50 percent, at a cost approaching $1 billion. TVA does not have all the answers, though, and its studies cannot provide all the information needed for a national approach to this interregional problem. The president's 1979 environmental message to Congress thus called for a $10-million-per-year research program to be conducted over the next 10 years. Congress provided funding for acid rain research in the newly enacted Synthetic Fuels Bill.

As I said earlier, the list of environmental problems related to coal is long and challenging. However, the nation has developed reasonable answers to many of these concerns. Some are technological, and others are regulatory in nature. Industry continues to attack many of these laws and regulations, and I believe that we have a good mine safety law and a good strip mine law.

We have better mining methods and are learning more about controlling sulfur oxide emissions and particulates. We also are developing advanced systems for direct clean burning of coal, such as fluidized bed combustion, and for producing cleaner coal-based fuels. What we lack is a national commitment to meet energy and environmental goals simultaneously.

The fundamental mechanisms and institutions were developed in the 1970s. Now we must focus on their implementation in the 1980s. Environmental standards and regulations should not be made the scapegoat for our failure to achieve energy independence. The key to increased production and use of coal and other domestic energy sources is not in relaxing environmental standards but in a genuine commitment to extract them and use them without harming everything in sight.

Alternative energy sources

Cheaper, less disruptive, and more effective alternatives to the present energy program exist. These alternatives are demonstrated in recent reports by authorities as diverse as the Harvard Business School, Resources for the Future (*Energy in America's Future*), the National Academy of Sciences (NAS), and the President's Council on Environmental Quality (CEQ).

The six-year Harvard Business School study (*Energy Future*) concluded that the centerpieces of any rational and workable energy policy for the future must be solar energy and conservation. The study found that with governmental support and without any dramatic technological breakthroughs a conservative estimate of energy supply from solar sources by the late 1980s is the equivalent of 4 million barrels daily of oil. This is 60 percent more than the present, highly optimistic 2.5 million-barrel goal for synfuels.

Proponents of continued reliance on conventional, nonrenewable energy sources, which inevitably increase in price as supplies diminish, have sought for some time to characterize solar energy as a high-technology source that cannot make a significant contribution until the next century. The facts simply do not support this picture. Solar technology is available today, and with even minimal government support it can significantly contribute to our energy supply. For example, a 55 percent tax credit enacted in California for solar installations created a boom in that state's solar industry.

Its opponents often equate conservation with sacrifice, but again the facts run to the contrary. America now uses much more energy per capita and per unit of gross national product than other industrialized countries enjoying equally high standards of living.

A recent NAS report (*Alternative Energy Demand Futures*) concluded that by the year 2010 we could achieve a 20 percent reduction in energy use, with continued economic and population growth. In fact the report showed that the same standard of living could be achieved with a 20 percent reduction in consumption as can be achieved with a doubling of energy consumption. Clearly, there is tremendous flexibility in reducing energy demand. A CEQ study (*The Good News About Energy*) reached similar conclusions.

These significant reductions in demand, then, can be achieved without major changes in lifestyle or standard of living. We must remember that conservation is itself a source of energy; a 20 percent reduction in demand means a 20 percent increase in supply. Efforts such as increased heating, cooling, and lighting efficiency in commercial and residential buildings; energy-efficient modes of transportation; and cogeneration can dramatically improve our energy supply picture. A 1979 Office of Technology Assessment report (*Residential Energy Conservation*) concluded that we can achieve a 50 percent reduction in residential and commercial energy use with little, if any, change in lifestyle.

Appropriate governmental incentives are necessary if we are to realize the full potential benefits of conservation and solar energy. The cost, both economically and environmentally, would be significantly less than conventional energy sources and a fraction of the synfuels program's price tag.

However, we now have an energy program based on coal and oil shale. In pursuing the program, conflicts with environmental values will arise. We can minimize these conflicts and make balanced decisions only if we address environmental concerns early on in plant siting and in project planning and design.

This is the objective of our environmental quality program at TVA. An example is the proposed commercial-scale coal gasification demonstration plant to be constructed by TVA in northern Alabama. The objective of the project is to demonstrate that coal gasification is an economically feasible and environmentally acceptable energy source. We are addressing environmental and health concerns up front in project planning, and safeguards are being incorporated into plant design. In addition, TVA is working closely with the Environmental Protection Agency in formulating regulator guidance and developing more detailed data for coal gasification processes and synthetic fuels. As this regulatory guidance is developed, it is factored into the coal gasification plant design.

Our environmental efforts in the United States thus far have been geared largely to correcting previous excesses and oversights or mistakes. With increased understanding of new energy technologies and with a strong commitment to environmental quality, we can now avoid or at least minimize environmental damage before it occurs.

37

Environmental Quality: An Energy Development Perspective

Charles W. Margolf

Director of Western Coal Operations, Mining Division, W. R. Grace & Co., Denver, Colorado

While I am a graduate engineer by training and a lawyer by profession, and while I have been directly and closely involved with the coal industry in the West for a quarter of a century, I claim several other credentials.

I am an *environmentalist*. As an environmentalist, I am convinced that the greatest threat to our nation's environment, both physical and economic, comes from those individuals in our society masquerading as environmentalists but who are in reality no-growth or antitechnology advocates. They use the "environment" as their weapon, not against pollution but against economic growth and, more specifically, against freedom of enterprise economic growth. The logical conclusion of the no-growth advocates program, whether achieved by accident or design, will change our political and economic system. Freedom will be the loser, both political and economic, because freedom is indivisible.

I am a *conservationist*. As a conservationist, I hold that true conservation means the wise use of resources, that is, using our resources as efficiently and as frugally as our levels of technology will economically permit.

I am a *consumer*. As a consumer, I am alarmed by the ever-increasing governmental control of the production and distribution of goods and services—a definition, incidentally, of socialism. I am alarmed by the ever-increasing costs of goods and services resulting from the political, legislative, and judicial "successes" of the so-called "consumer activists," who are, in reality, anticonsumer for those very reasons.

I am a member of the *public*. The public, on nearly every occasion on which it has had the opportunity to record its position on issues placed on the ballot by the so-called public interest groups, has repudiated the positions of these so-called public interest groups. Those groups, therefore, should more properly be classified as special interest, antipublic interest groups.

I am also a *citizen* of this nation. I hold firm the conviction that this nation, for all of its flaws and imperfections, is freedom's last, best hope on earth. Therefore, for all of these reasons, I am a concerned citizen.

The energy decade

The 1980s is the decade during which the American people will finally become aware that energy is a great deal more than gasoline for cars. This is the decade during which the American people will learn the hard way that energy is:

• Food—planting, harvesting, processing, preserving, and delivering food.

• Jobs—not only new job opportunities, though these are certainly needed, but existing jobs in lighted, heated, and operating plants that receive raw materials and component parts and process, manufacure, and fabricate those parts into products to be delivered to other plants, retail stores, and consumers.

• National security—not the preservation of a lifestyle or even our survival as a nation, but most certainly our survival as a free nation.

Energy is a subject holding enormous implications for every citizen— whether or not every citizen knows it or whether or not every citizen cares. Energy also holds enormous implications for our country, and because of the critical role of our nation in defending freedom, energy holds enormous implications for the entire world.

The energy situation is extremely grave. The gravity of the situation deepens with each new dispatch that reaches our shores from abroad. The gravity also deepens with each day our society puts off the hard decisions demanded by the real world in favor of continuing the dialogue so dear to those in the political world.

Our leaders seem paralyzed, unwilling or afraid to make decisions. There comes a time, inevitably, when if decisions are not made, events will have made the decisons for us. Therefore, some perspective seems very much in order—perspective both as to context and as to scale.

The perspective of context

America was not built, nor has it been preserved, by people who were afraid of freedom. Quite the contrary. America was built by men and women for whom freedom was their faith, not their fear.

As a contemporary English observer of events in America recently pointed out: There was no government agency to issue a Certificate of Seaworthiness to the Mayflower when she set sail from familiar shores to cross an uncharted sea. And those who boarded that frail, leaking vessel for the voyage, and nearly all those who have made the crossing since, did not find the gangplank blocked by protestors objecting to the insanity involved in an undertaking posing such fearful risks.

Nor did those who came to these shores come seeking security or life in a risk-free society. They came, all of them, seeking freedom. Freedom, by meaningful definition, is risk. Freedom, by meaningful definition, is opportunity. Risk includes the chance of failing as well as succeeding. Opportunity includes failure as well as success.

I do not know if there was a no-growth, no-risk, philosophy being preached and peddled east of the Blue Ridge Mountains a century ago. I do know that if there was, the elected representatives of a free people in our nation's capital were not buying it.

The western migration was not held up to make an environmental assessment of the Oregon Trail. On the contrary, Congress passed the homestead laws, and those who were willing to take the risks seized the opportunities those laws afforded.

The climate in America then was a climate of freedom. As always in such a climate, both the depths and the heights of man's spirit were manifested, for the challenge was a challenge to man's spirit.

As America looks ahead to the 1980s, all would agree that the challenges we face are just as real and formidable as when America set its face west a century ago. Today, as then, the challenge is to man's spirit.

A century ago man's spirit met that challenge. What then is different in America today? I suggest the difference in America today is that America is responding to the voices and counsel of those to whom freedom is their fear, not their faith.

Our leaders, responding to the fearmongers, seem to feel we must identify, quantify, and eliminate all risks before we do anything.

For the fearmongers, and the antigrowth and antitechnology bogymen in our society, let me quote from *The Congressional Record* of 1875:

"Stores of gasoline in the hands of the people interested primarily in profit...would constitute a fire and explosive hazard of the first rank. Horseless carriages propelled by gasoline engines might attain speeds of 14 or even 20 miles per hour....The development of this new power may displace the use of horses, which would wreck our agriculture....The discovery with which we are dealing involves forces of a nature too dangerous to fit into any of our usual concepts."

Knowledgeable people know our nation has problems.

In the arena of economics, problems of unemployment, inflation, productivity, balance of trade, and erosion of currency come to mind.

In the arena of environment, problems of air and water quality, land use and misuse, and health and safety come immediately to mind.

At the heart of these economic and environmental problems is energy.

Knowledgeable people know energy is the dynamo that drives our nation's economy. Knowledgeable people know that the lifeblood of our nation's energy requirements, both now and for decades to come, is oil. Knowledgeable people know our nation's economy is being kept alive today on a 50 percent transfusion of its "blood" supply—oil. And, knowledgeable people know our nation controls neither that supply nor its price.

Knowledgeable people also know these problems are not only critical, but complex. First, then, a few words about knowledge:

To know that you know or to know that you do not know is
     one thing.

It is quite another to not know that you do not know.

Worse by far is to think you know when, indeed, you do not.

America has no shortage of energy fuels today. Nor will it have a shortage of fuels for centuries to come. America is facing, and soon, a scarcity of energy. The scarcity is caused not by a shortage of resources but by a shortage of spirit. America's greatest energy resource is the genius of its people. But that genius can only manifest itself in a climate of freedom.

Laws and regulations, though printed on paper, are nevertheless controls on the freedom of individuals and of enterprise. They are just as real and just as confining as chains forged of steel.

When government dictates not only the goal, but prescribes in infinite detail how we must get there, its reason for doing so is to try to prevent socially undesirable conduct by irresponsible individuals and enterprises. The result, however, is to stifle initiative, imagination, ingenuity, and enthusiasm; the result is to destroy incentive and to smother man's spirit.

In speaking about the energy resource I am most familiar with, let me begin by talking about solar energy and about waste, dead vegetation, and recycling waste. The solar energy I am talking about does not have to await development of new technologies to recycle wastes or to store energy on sunny days for use in the dark. The recycling of this massive waste and the storing of this form of solar energy was done for us eons ago. This form of solar energy is now a solid and was made from huge masses of decayed vegetation. It is spelled C-O-A-L.

Coal is a solid hydrocarbon. In its solid form it can be burned under boilers to generate electricity and used in furnaces and fireplaces to provide heat. Coal can be made into a liquid—synthetic crude oil. Coal can also be made into a gas—synthetic natural gas.

Coal has been a primary source of energy for several centuries and can continue so for centuries to come.

The perspective of scale

In addition to providing some perspective as to context, let me suggest some Useless Bits of Information (UBIs) on perspective as to scale.

• This nation's coal reserves, on a BTU equivalent basis, exceed all the known oil reserves of the entire Mideast. Measured in the hundreds of billions of tons, we know where the coal is, we know how to mine it, process it, convert it, transport it, and use it. In short, our nation's coal reserves are so massive that there will be no shortage of energy fuels in this century, the next, or the next.

• One ton of coal used as boiler fuel can replace at least 4 barrels of oil. While our oil imports increase (and our exportation of dollars to buy the oil also increases), coal mines are shutting down (while coal accumulates in stockpiles unsold) and the industry has more than 100 million tons of idle capacity and miners (more than 20,000 now) are laid off while we import steam coal from Poland and South Africa and import coking coal from Europe and Australia.

The fearmongers and antigrowth, antitechnology bogymen, with such credentials as "actress," "pediatrician," and "Pentagon analyst," look forward with fear and warn of carcinogens, greenhouse effects, climate changes producing coastal inundation, and other catastrophes. There is no need to speculate about these dire predictions of future risks from using coal. A long record of coal use already exists by which to measure these "fears."

In 1918 the coal industry produced about 678 million tons, a record not broken until sixty years later. As we contemplate using more coal, one of the concerns or fears we read about is acid rain. Liquids are either acid, neutral, or base. If we eliminated all acid rain, we would have to eliminate all rain because all rain is acid. Natural rain has a ph of about 5.3. The problem is not acid rain. The problem is the increasing acidity in rain. Keep in mind that back in 1918 when we used more than 600 million tons of coal in this country, coal was not burned using best available control technology. There were no controls of any kind on homes, factories, or locomotives. Who was scaring people with talk of acid rain in 1918?

• The Amory Lovins and Clubs of Rome warn of finite mineral resources and insist we must change our way of life. Granted that all mineral resources naturally occuring are finite, and granted that we must become less wasteful and more efficient, and granted that our nation uses minerals in prodigious quantities; can anyone name even one single mineral (finite though they all may be) that has become extinct?

• We in the mining business, hear much these days about the surface disturbance our industry causes. But did you know that the entire mining industry in 200 years of disturbing the surface to produce all the minerals that have been produced in this nation (including Alaska) has disturbed a total of less than 6 million acres of surface land. And one-third of that 6 million acres has already been reclaimed by man or healed by nature. By contrast, this nation has more than 30 million acres of land in rights-of-way for highways, airports, and railroads. Furthermore, every year more than 300 million acres of surface are disturbed by the agricultural industry in producing food and fiber. No one has yet found a way to plow without creating fugitive dust. Furthermore, a recent U.S. Department of Agriculture (USDA) report states that agricultural lands are being converted to nonagricultural uses at the rate of nearly 3 million acres per year. Thus, every 2 years, population land uses take over, that is, permanently disturb as much surface land as the entire minerals industry has disturbed producing all the minerals that have been produced in this nation in 200 years. USDA has also calculated that each year our river systems carry away more than 2 billion tons of our nation's soils.

By way of perspective, it should also be noted that agriculture, not industry, is the largest polluter of our nation's water, and motor vehicles, not industry, are the largest polluter of our nation's air.

A wise man said: "The facts are what they are and the consequences will be what they will be."

Recognizing the infallible truth of that statement, the logical response is to ask: Why, then, should we deceive ourselves? There is really no reason why we should deceive ourselves. But the problem, unfortunately, is that facts really are not important today. Rather it is the public's perception of the facts that is critical.

The reason the public's perception of the facts has become of critical importance is because most of the decisions being made, or not being made, with respect to energy, the economy, and the environment, are being made, or not being made, by government. Government is political and therefore responds to the public whether or not the public's perception of the facts conforms to the facts.

Some central realities

What, then, are some of the central realities of the real world?

One is that 4 percent of our nation's population produces all the food that feeds the remainder of our population as well as millions of people in other countries. American agriculture cannot continue to perform this productive miracle without energy, not only electric energy to run irrigation pumps, but fluid fuels for tractors and petroleum feedstocks for fertilizer, pesticides, and insecticides.

Another central reality is that our nation's transportation system is almost entirely dependent upon the fluid fuel forms of energy. Every truck, car, bus, train, or plane, and nearly all ships, use oil or petroleum products to move.

For both our agricultural industry and our transportation industry there is no substitute for oil now or for decades to come.

Another central reality is that nearly 175 million Americans are locked into urban life. For all practical purposes this enormous number of people is totally dependent upon energy for warmth, for light, for transportation, and for food. For these 175 million Americans, the central reality is that there is no fall-back position in the event of an energy shortage.

These are certainly some of the central realities, and energy is the key element as to each of them. When our political leaders finally contemplate these central realities, I suggest there is one very major and most significant impact on the human environment that should be addressed as the overriding concern. The impact on the human environment to which I refer is, in my judgment, the greatest of all polluters of the human environment—poverty. I submit, as a postulate, that if our nation fails to provide adequate supplies of energy to insure a strong, healthy, productive, creative, and growing economy, the results of such failure will be such massive social evils as starvation, epidemics, joblessness, hopelessness, and finally anger that could lead to riots, war, or revolution. Time is not our ally.

In considering the environment there are some immutable postulates that are so basic and so simple that we may overlook their importance:

• We must produce and use minerals to survive. I am not talking about maintaining a lifestyle, I am talking about survival.

• Minerals can only be found where they are! No amount of research, studies, investigations, or wishful thinking can change the location of a single ounce of mineral deposit from where it is to where the public might like it to be.

• Whatever the costs imposed by our society to mine, process, and use the minerals require, the full cost must be paid. And the full cost will be paid in higher taxes and/or higher costs of the products produced from such minerals. Most of us are taxpayers. All of us are consumers.

• Nobody gets it when there ain't any!

• Political pronouncements do not produce energy any more than legislation produces bread. Laws do not create wealth; labor does.

Finally, as the public grapples with energy, the economy, and enviromental concerns, and as our politicians respond to the public's perception of the facts, I hope the public will soon address the most important of all endangered species. The endangered species to which I refer is free men—not Homo sapiens the species—but free men!

If we do not, the epitaph on our nation's tombstone, as Richard Barnett has suggested, might well read as follows:

"Here lies the only civilization that perished at the peak of its power, with its power unused.

"Here lies a decent people who wanted love, not empire, and got neither—who tried to trade power for popularity and lost both.

"Here lies a nation of advertisers who knew how to change consumer tastes in cigarettes but were themselves manipulated on all the issues that really mattered to their salvation and survival.

"Here died a sort of Lancelot in the Court of Nations who, granting all his grievous flaws, was still somehow the noblest knight of all; except this Lancelot, crippled with an undeserved guilt complex, let his weapons and ideals fall unused—and so condemned all mankind to the thousand-year night of the Russian Bear and the Chinese Dragon."

38

Energy: New Kinds of Competition for Land

R. Neil Sampson
Executive Vice-president, National Association of
Conservation Districts, Washington, D.C.

Competition for the use of land is not new; it has been a feature of the human struggle for millenia. But seldom has such a totally new set of competitive forces been unleashed on the land as those that appear on the horizon in the declining decades of the petroleum era. As America, and the world search for new sources of industrial materials and fuels to replace increasingly expensive, scarce, or unreliable sources of the past, major attention has been focused on agriculture.

New types of farm-grown energy, liquid fuels, and industrial materials are technically possible, politically attractive, and increasingly economically feasible. For the first time in history, farm-grown industrial products appear to offer serious economic competition for the use of available farmland and water. Whether or not these new competitive forces are manageable, in terms of the market economies and land use traditions of North America, is a serious question. If they pit fuel against food, with the result that prices rise and poor people lose access to the necessities of survival, we face critical decisions.

Competent observers forecast a worrisome burden on the land and water resources, not only of the United States, but of all the world (4). On the other hand, some construct a rosier view of the future, one that holds little but opportunities (14). With no reliable crystal ball, though, the most prudent course seems to be one that prepares for a difficult and demanding situation. If that future turns out to be better than expected, and our public policies and private actions turn out, in retrospect, to have been too prudent, the worst that can be said is that some economic opportunity may have been missed.

On the other hand, policies that proceed today as though there were no potential problems in the future lead us down a very risky course. If wrong, our policies could strand us on technological paths that lead nowhere. They could cut future options by prolonging waste and delaying needed conservation efforts. And they could necessitate harsh governmental intervention in place of gentler strategies that might have been pursued if started soon enough.

We need to look at new energy proposals, the technologies they entail, and the sources of fuel they use, in terms of their total potential effect on the land. We can't talk about gasohol as if it were the only strategy being considered; neither can we focus all of our attention on surface-mined coal. A new energy era is liable to see some development of each of these sources, along with many other strategies as well. It is important that we try to see the situation as a whole and deduce what it may mean.

In so doing, we must avoid the trap of constructing scenarios that bespeak impending disaster, but bear no more scientific credibility than those that forecast sunshine and roses. Forecasts must be couched in humble terms, particularly those that pretend to guess how the vast and complex market system in the United States will use and manage land and water resources in response to a given set of circumstances.

The indications for future pressures on the land are troubling and call for immediate policy attention. But the straight-line projections of current trends will not continue. The reason is simple. The courses we are now taking, in terms of energy, land, and water use are simply untenable in the future. And the future is not very far away. But that should not be interpreted to mean that we will "run out of land." We won't. What appears more likely is a period of intense and difficult competition for land and water resources. The required economic, environmental, and social adjustments that will be required will be both significant and, for many, traumatic. The question, for both public and private decision making, is how we will prepare to make these adjustments with the least possible pain.

If we don't face that question, and face it soon, we will lose a great deal of land, in both quantitative and qualitative terms. Once that land is lost, it cannot be easily reclaimed, if it can be reclaimed at all. We will forego options in soil and water conservation, and in energy technology, that will not be open again. Most significantly, we will risk losing a large measure of personal freedom as a result of governmental intervention in matters of land use and conservation.

Let's not delude ourselves. Americans are not going to "starve in the dark," despite what many catchy doomsday slogans say. Neither are others in the world, if they can help it. Fuel to power our devices and our lifestyle is important, but if it begins to compete with food for our land and water, a new calculus must emerge, and new priorities must be set.

I do not intend to address this new calculus or set of priorities here. Instead I want to discuss the new level of competition for land and water resources, and the factors that point to the likely timing and severity of this competition. Then, from the basis of this kind of discussion, we need to proceed hastily to a consideration of the required new policies, priorities, research, technology development, and conservation strategies.

The land available for agricultural production

To evaluate the current and possible future trends in agricultural land availability, we start with the concept of a resource pool. According to estimates by the National Resource Inventories (NRI) carried out by the Soil Conservation Service (SCS) (31) in 1977, the cropland pool consists of 343 million acres of planted cropland plus 70 million acres of cropland slack, for a total of 413 million acres of cropland. There are an additional 127 million acres of high and medium potential cropland, making a 1977 cropland resource pool of 540 million acres.

Two factors must be recognized about this resource pool. First, it is a fair

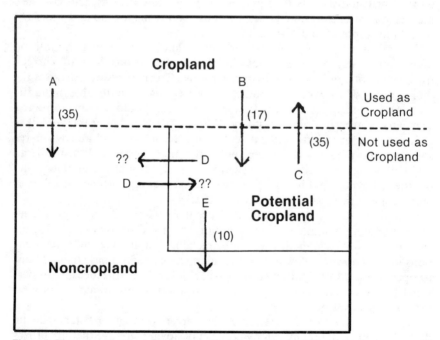

Figure 1. Elements of land use change that affect the land in the U.S. cropland resource pool, with estimates of the 1967-1977 acreage change in millions of acres.

Table 1. Estimates of land use shifts within the cropland resource pool, by decades, assuming a continuation of 1967-1977 trends.

Type of Shift	1967-1977	1977-1990	1990-2000	2000-2030	77-30 Total
	millions of acres				
A. Cropland to noncropland	35	45	35	105	185
B. Cropland to potential cropland	17	22	17	51	90*
C. Potential cropland to cropland	34	44	34	102	180*
D. Potential cropland to noncropland	?				?
D. Noncropland to potential cropland	?				?
E. Potential cropland to noncrop uses	10	13	10	30	53
Total loss from cropland pool	45	58	45	135	238

*These estimates cannot be used to calculate the size of the cropland resource pool, as they indicate the shift of marginal cropland in and out of crop use. The same acre may shift two to three times in 50 years.

estimate of the amount of arable land in the nation as viewed in the economic and environmental context of 1977. As economic situations change, so does our view of the kinds of land we can afford to farm. Second, land use shifts constantly affect the arable land of the nation. Land is constantly being removed from the pool, sometimes permanently, and the size and nature of those shifts are vital elements in evaluating the agricultural productivity and future potential of the nation's land and water resources.

Figure 1 illustrates how private land users shift land between cropland and other types of use. The arrows indicate the direction land is shifted within the resource pool, and the numbers in parentheses give estimates of the amount of change that was experienced between 1967 and 1977.

Table 1 shows what may occur if these land use shifts continue into the future. In order to construct this table, some data adjustments were required. The 1975 Potential Cropland Study (PCS) (35) estimated the acreage that had moved from one use to another between 1967 and 1975. At the same time, it recorded the capability of the land and the potential for its future cropland use.

The 1977 NRI measured the total amount of land in each use, but did not identify which type of land had changed in use since 1967. Thus, while both surveys could be used to estimate the net shift in use over a period of years, they must be combined in order to determine the internal characteristics of the changes in the cropland resource pool.

The size of the cropland resource pool under this set of projections would be 437 million acres in 2000 and 302 million acres in 2030. Shrinkage at such rates, of course, would result in a serious problem in the view of U.S. Department of Agriculture (USDA) estimates of future cropland needs. One major unknown lies in the set of shifts labelled "D" in figure 1 and table 1. Land that was potential cropland under 1977 prices and conditions may not be so feasible in 1985. Or, conversely, it could be more feasible. A great deal of land outside the cropland resource pool is arable, given enough economic

incentive and technological skill. For now, the 1977 figure is the most logical figure. Future estimates can be adjusted to changing conditions.

Changing our assumptions about future trends

Projecting the rate of today's land use change into the future, especially
for 50 years, is a very uncertain exercise, particularly when it appears logical
that economic competition will force a slowdown in cropland conversion. A
slowdown could be caused by many factors, but most likely it would be
caused by a rise in farm prices relative to other aspects of the economy.
Such a price rise would dampen agricultural land conversions.

Another possibility would be effective action at local, state, and national
levels to protect farmland from conversion to other uses. Although there is
no indication today that such action is immediately forthcoming, the resource competition currently forecast may hasten farmland protection.

Table 2 is based on the assumptions that the rate of cropland loss experienced in 1967-1977 will remain essentially the same through the decade of
the 1980s, and that by the end of the decade rising pressures will slow the
rate of change so that each successive decade will see only one-half of the
conversion experienced in the previous decade. Such an assumption would
mean that the current loss of cropland to noncrop uses would be essentially
halted by 2030.

These assumptions give a more sanguine picture of the land that might be
available for cropping in the future, indicating that the resource pool might
be in the range of 458 million acres in 2000 and 436 million acres in 2030.

Brewer and Boxley[1] point out that the current rate of conversion of rural

---

[1]Brewer, Michael, and Robert Boxley. 1980. "The Potential Supply of Cropland." Paper presented at Resources for the Future symposium on the Adequacy of Agricultural Land, Washington, D.C.

Table 2. Estimates of land use shifts within the cropland resource pool, by decades, assuming a
slowdown of land use conversion trends in the future.

Type of Shift	1967-1977	1977-1990	1990-2000	2000-2030	77-30 Total
	millions of acres				
A. Cropland to noncropland	35	45	20	17	82
B. Cropland to potential cropland	17	22	9	8	39
C. Potential cropland to cropland	34	44	34	102	180*
D. Potential cropland to noncropland	?				
D. Noncropland to potential cropland	?				
E. Potential cropland to noncrop uses	10	13	5	4	22
Total loss from cropland resource pool	45	58	23	20	104

*See footnote in table 1.

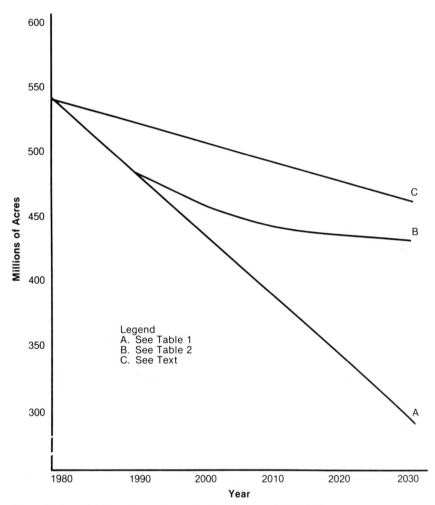

Figure 2. Potential losses from the cropland resource pool 1977-2030.

land to urban, built-up, rural transportation, and water is about 2.9 million acres annually, up substantially from the trends observed in the 1958-1967 period. Not all this conversion comes from cropland, of course. They estimate that in the 1967-1977 period, about 700,000 acres per year of cropland were converted to these uses. A portion of the remaining 2.2 million acres per year comes from pasture, range, woodland, and other lands that also have a high and medium potential for conversion to cropland. To the extent that such land is lost to nonagricultural use, the nation has suffered a loss from its total cropland resource pool. Just how to evaluate that loss and reconcile it with the estimates shown in tables 1 and 2 has been the focus of concentrated study in USDA.

The estimate published in the RCA Act draft documents was for a loss from the cropland resource pool of 48 million acres over the next 50 years, but that figure had demonstrable deficiencies that were quickly pointed out by many analysts.

Discussions between the staff of the National Agricultural Lands Study (NALS) and USDA should result in an agreed-upon level of projections that can be used in both the NALS and the RCA reports. Line C is included in figure 2 to illustrate that we expect USDA to be slightly more conservative than the estimates developed in tables 1 and 2. It is not an official USDA estimate.

The land needed for food and fiber production

In carrying out the appraisal called for in RCA, USDA (37) used a computer model developed cooperatively with Iowa State University. The model provides estimates of the amount of acres needed to produce the nation's major crops on the basis of the least-cost methods and lands available. Future commodity needs were projected on the basis of predicted population, per capita disposable income, and export levels. When the number of bushels or tons of the basic commodity needs was known, the model provided estimates of the number of crop acres needed for production.

There are two ways of gaining the crop production needed in the future: We can increase the number of acres of land cropped and increase the yields per acre of crops. Since the amount of land that can be cropped is limited by rising costs of conversion as we move toward more marginal lands, the amount by which yields can be increased is a critical factor. There is some difference of opinion today as to the prospect for future yield increases. Many observers feel that although yields will continue to increase, the rate will be much slower than in the past few decades (2). Their reasons include an uncertain climate; the continuing effects of soil erosion and other forms of land degradation; rising air pollution; and the continued prospect of increased prices for fertilizer, pesticides, and irrigation water.

In explaining its forecasts of future yields, USDA (37) pointed out: "Ovver the past 50 years, agricultural productivity has grown at the rate of 1.6 percent per year. The increase in productivity was about 2.1 percent annually between 1939 and 1965, but the rate of growth has recently declined to about 1.7 percent annually. Lu and Quance (1979) predict that without significant technological breakthroughs, the rate of growth in productivity will continue to decline. The agricultural productivity growth curve under the "science power" era is now entering the stages of declining growth rates."

Pierre Crosson (7) of Resources for the Future agrees with this assessment: "My reading of the evidence indicates that since 1972 the trend in yields did in fact diminish relative to the pre-1972 period. Given the projected increase in real prices of yield-increasing inputs, the implication is that

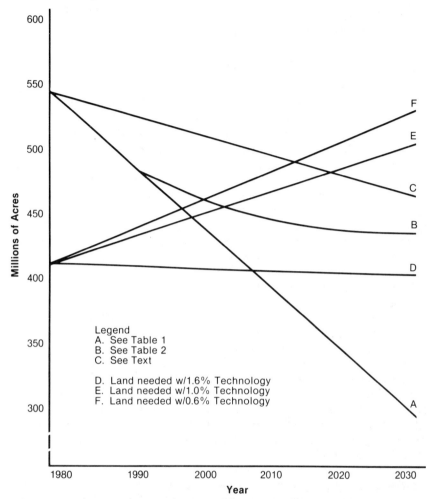

Figure 3. Potential losses from the cropland resource pool 1977-2030, compared with the land likely to be needed for food and fiber under three different levels of future technology and yield increase.

the slower rate of increase in yields experienced since 1972 will continue.''

On this basis, the USDA-CARD linear programming model has recently been used to estimate the effects that three reasonably expectable rates of technology (and yield increase) might have on future land needs. The three levels tested were 0.6, 1.0, and 1.6 percent per year. The results are shown in figure 3. By the year 2030, the difference in acres planted under the three assumptions would be about 119 million acres, or almost 30 percent of the average acreage forecast. That is, if nothing else, a fair measure of the nation's current reliance on a technical "fix." If we get it, our productive capability looks strong in relationship to foreseeable demands. If not, serious problems are imminent.

Adding energy issues to the land demand equation

From the foregoing assessment, it is clear that future pressures on the cropland base could be fairly severe even without added competition created by the energy situation. But, at the same time, there will be some new pressures created by the rising prices of petroleum-based energy, and it is important that we have some idea of what those might be.

Because of the methods used to evaluate future farmland conversions in this paper, all of the energy-related pressures cannot be treated as new demands on the land. For instance, the demand for cropland as a result of surface mining, electrical generation, and competition for water are not new. They have been part of the past conversion trends, and make up much of the pressure that would cause a continuation of those trends. Whether these kinds of land conversions will increase in the future or not, of course, is open to speculation.

New demands, however, will be felt if large-scale production of biomass for energy is initiated. One of the most important of these demands could be the production of ethanol fuel as a means of stretching or replacing gasoline and diesel supplies. Another, less well-recognized demand could come from the production of agricultural crops to be used as industrial feedstocks. These types of agricultural production have not been a factor in the past and thus will become important new additions to future trends.

In addition, we need to remember that there will be energy conservation issues as well. If increasing prices of farm fuels and other inputs (largely fertilizer) cause farmers to shift toward a more land-extensive type of farming pattern, future acreage demands could be still higher than predicted in the preceding section (7).

Mineral extraction, transportation, and processing. Surface mining, largely for coal, has taken an increasing amount of agricultural land in recent years. An estimated 3.2 million acres were disturbed by surface mining for all minerals in the United States prior to 1965. Since that time, disturbed land has increased to 4.0 million acres in 1972, 4.4 million acres in 1974, and 5.7 million acres in 1977 (30).

SCS estimates that the current rate of land disturbance due to surface mining now averages about 400,000 acres per year (8). About half of this land is cropland, a particular concern in states such as Illinois where more than half of the acreage for which strip mining permits issued between 1972 and 1977 was former cropland (11). Much of this land is prime farmland as well, particularly in the west central and northern parts of Illinois (9).

Theoretically, cropland used for surface mining for coal is to be restored to its former productivity upon the completion of the mining process, under the terms of the Surface Mining Control and Reclamation Act of 1977. This act contains strong language requiring the restoration of prime farmlands in particular. But there is still some skepticism as to the ability of reclamation efforts to restore land to its former productivity. J. Dixon Esseks (9) points out that some soil scientists in Illinois have cautioned that reclaimed land "tends to suffer from inferior soil structure and excessive compaction," which may permanently impair productivity.

In addition, surface mining for phosphates in Florida, North Carolina, and Idaho; oil shale in Colorado; and uranium in several states will add to the toll. Surface mine reclamation standards for these minerals are not yet established by federal law, so the question of post-mining agricultural productivity is more problematic than that for coal.

Surface mining creates additional problems for agriculture, and not all of them are confined to the mined land. Again, to quote Esseks (9):

"The potential damaging impacts on agriculture from strip mining include the excavation of farmland under which coal lies (as far down as 75 to 100 feet) and the bulldozing and/or filling of half again as many acres for haul roads, storage areas, and other mining purposes. Stripping may also disrupt drainage on adjoining land, and it can pollute surface or ground water used by livestock and farm families. In the mid-1970s, coal surface mines produced an estimated 6,000 tons of sulfuric acid daily, which found its way into about 13,000 miles of streams."

While there are many factors that may affect the rate of future surface mining, coal companies currently plan to mine another 312,000 acres between now and 1985. This would require an additional 120,000 acres to provide for storage areas, haul roads, etc. Approximately one-fourth of this acreage lies in states with major prime farmland regions (19).

The conversion of coal to liquid fuel also must be considered. President Carter proposed an Energy Security Corporation that would foster development of a 1-million to 1.5-million-barrel-per-day synthetic fuels industry by 1990.[2] The Department of Energy (DOE) has identified 41 counties in 8 states—including 10 in Montana, 8 in Illinois, 7 in North Dakota, 6 in Wyoming, and 5 in West Virginia—that might be logical locations for synfuel plants (40).

But as Wendell Fletcher[3] has pointed out, the DOE analysis explicitly excluded consideration of prime agricultural lands, problems with water transfers, and the "cumulative impacts of large-scale facilities"—all crucial factors for assessing the impacts that such a program might have on agriculture and agricultural land.

In terms of direct acreage impact, surface mining for coal thus will probably disturb somewhere in the range of 100,000 to 250,000 acres per year in the foreseeable future. Added to this will be the impact of noncoal surface mining and the off-site problems that can accompany surface mining opera-

---

[2]Fletcher, W. Wendell. 1980. "Farmland and Energy: A Conflict in the Making." Unpublished manuscript submitted to the National Agricultural Land Study. American Land Forum, Washington, D.C.
[3]Ibid.

tions. This acreage, particularly if much of it can be returned to productive use following the mining operation will not in itself impose a serious burden on agricultural land at the national level. At the local level, however, serious dislocations seem likely. One study pointed out that "as of 1976, 202,422 acres in 40 Illinois counties have been affected by surface and deep mining" (*28*).

Acid precipitation. It is not always easily or well recognized, but the pressures on agricultural land, and agricultural productivity, can come from across the fence, so to speak. A case in point is acid precipitation stemming from air pollution, which is largely the result of both the form and amount of fossil fuel energy being used. Acid precipitation is beginning to affect crop production and forest yields, although the extent of the nationwide damage is not yet known with any accuracy (*32*). A recent increase in the acidity of rain and snowfall, particularly in the Northeast, has now spread so that it extends from Illinois eastward (*42*). While the effect on crop yields and therefore on the amount of land that must be added to the cropland inventory to offset lost production is unknown, there have been estimates that it may be as high as 1 percent (*32*). This would be roughly equivalent to the annual loss of production from 3.5 million acres of farmland.

That acid rain is a serious problem is not in question; that it will grow more serious is equally certain. A recently published DOE report estimates that sulfur dioxide emissions from coal-fired utility boilers could grow by 15 percent by 1990 even if Federal Clean Air Act requirements are maintained. The effects of coal conversion by other industries could bring an increase of 149 percent when 1990 is compared to 1975 (*39*). If efforts to relax the emission standards under the Clean Air Act are successful, the impacts of acid rain, of course, will rise accordingly.

Electrical generation and transmission. No small amount of land is used in the generation and transmission of electricity, and forecasts for the future circulated by the electric power industry suggest that additional demands will be significant, as well. In 1978, with existing generating capacity somewhere in the range of 579,000 megawatts, the industry projected that some 308,000 megawatts of added capacity would be in operation by 1987 (*28*). Power plants, whether coal or nuclear, need land: 2,000 acres or more is common. One nuclear plant in the Chicago area took 4,480 acres, most of which had once been farmland (*13*).

In estimating the amount of land liable to be required in the near future, Fletcher[4] estimates "well over 100,000 acres" before 1987, and Esseks (*9*) estimates that "new coal and nuclear power plants may result in the permanent conversion of yet another 1.5 million to 2 million acres."

Although difficult to compare their land requirements with those of other types of power generating facilities, hydroelectric power plants are also im-

---

[4]Ibid.

portant land users. Reservoir sizes of 1,000 to 25,000 acres are common, and much of this land is valley bottomland that qualifies as prime farmland. But hydroelectric reservoirs also serve a variety of other purposes, such as flood control, irrigation, and recreation, so they are difficult to compare with other forms of electrical generation facilities. In addition, the hydro plant contains its own "fuel" source within the acreage taken for the reservoir. This is in contrast to a coal-fired plant that might only take 2,000 acres of land, but require thousands of acres of strip-mined land to provide fuel over the life of the facility.

In addition, we have about 4 million acres dedicated to rights of way for transmission (9), with the estimates of future needs ranging from 1.5 million to 3 million additional acres before the year 2000.[5]

The importance of these estimates does not lie in the acreage within the transmission line rights-of-way. This acreage is part of the loss that we would expect if current trends continue (Figure 2). The issues that may prove most difficult are those concerning the effect of new extra-high-voltage transmission lines on surrounding land use, crops, livestock, and human health. Research in the United States on this problem has been sketchy at best.[6] However, enough controversy has been generated to suggest that agricultural users next to transmission lines may soon face restrictions in the use of extra-high-voltage rights-of-way (47). Even without these kinds of problems, farmers face disruptions and added costs in their operations if power line structures are placed in fields (29).

New competition for agricultural water. Water is an ordinary but amazing compound. It covers nearly three-fourths of the earth's surface, but less than 3 percent of that total is fresh water. Oceans, ice caps, and glaciers contain some 99.35 percent of the world's 326 million cubic miles of water It is from the remaining two-thirds of 1 percent that man finds the usable fresh water to supply his needs (18).

More water is used for agriculture than for any other use. Almost half of the fresh water withdrawn from surface or groundwater supplies is for irrigation, and more than 80 percent of the water consumed in the nation (that is, not returned to streams or ground water reservoirs) is consumed in this manner (36). But agriculture's grip on the nation's water supply is largely in terms of law and tradition, not economics. As Don Paarlberg notes, "Compared with its rivals, agriculture is not an efficient user of water." Nonfarm users such as municipalities, mining interests (especially coal and potentially oil shale), industrial users and developers have the advantage in that "economics is on their side in overwhelming measure" (22).

Of the nation's cropland in 1977, about 14 percent was irrigated, up from some 8 percent in 1958 (36). Every state but Rhode Island and New Hampshire reported some irrigation in 1977, but the major acreage occurs in the

---

[5]Ibid.
[6]Ibid.

17 western states. There the competition for water is fierce, and the impacts of increased energy production promise to make irrigation still more difficult. USDA predicts that "the areas where there will be great concern over water used for energy will be in the Missouri, Ohio, and Upper Colorado regions where there are large coal and oil shale deposits" (36).

The Colorado River already serves 15 million people, with considerable conflict in regard to both quantity and quality of the available water, and because it is one of the largest storehouses of energy resources in the United States—including coal, oil, natural gas, uranium, tar sands, and oil shale deposits, new development means serious water disputes between farmers and energy producers (34).

To make matters worse, the available water supply is shrinking fastest in some of the same areas where new energy-related uses will be most demanding. The most serious areas of groundwater overdraft and declining water tables are southern Nebraska, western Kansas, western Oklahoma, western Texas, eastern New Mexico, eastern Colorado, central Arizona, and the San Joaquin Valley of California (45).

In the Texas High Plains, the annual overdraft from the Ogallala Aquifer is 14 million acre-feet (45). As natural gas prices have gone up, more and more irrigation has been discontinued, put out of business by the rising cost of energy and the increasing work needed to lift water from the declining water table. Net farm income in the region is expected to fall 40 percent by the year 2000 as 3.5 million irrigated acres revert to dryland (48).

Because of the existence of similar problems throughout much of the region, a High Plains Aquifer Study is being conducted by the U.S. Department of Commerce, in cooperation with the High Plains Council. This look at both the economic and social impacts of declining water supplies in the region will map out the terrain for what seems certain to be a difficult battle for available water.[7]

In that battle, the outcome is virtually preordained. Again, to quote Paarlberg (22):

"That water use in the West will be a major public policy issue in the decade ahead is a certainty. And that agriculture will lose relative to non-farm users also seems certain....Only if agriculture is willing to accept some modification of tradition and received doctrine, or if the West settles for no growth, can collision be avoided. And if collision does come it seems likely to me that agriculture will be the loser."

Thus far we have evaluated the agricultural land situation and the resulting conflicts that may ensue as a result of energy issues largely in terms of the continuation of past trends and technologies. Surface mining, electrical generation, coal gasification, oil shale production, coal slurry pipelines, and many other competitors for agricultural land and water may be the result of

---

[7]Boone, Shelden G. 1980. "Agriculture's Use of Groundwater: Needs and Concerns." Unpublished paper presented at a U.S. Environmental Protection Agency conference on developing strategy in the regulation of groundwater, Arlington, Virginia.

new energy technologies or economic conditions. But competition for the land is much the same as has been experienced in the United States over the past two decades. In large measure, we have already factored it into our assessment of the future of agricultural land, insofar as we base that assessment on the continuation of current trends.

But there are new factors that are not a continuation of the past, and therein lies the basis for a new urgency in the energy/food production issue.

Biomass as a fuel source. Burning biomass from current plant stocks (as opposed to burning the fossilized remains of prehistoric plants) is one way to replace the energy provided by burning increasingly expensive petroleum supplies. Generating industrial power by woodburning is nothing new, of course. It was a feature of many early energy attempts, such as the wood-burning locomotive that carried its own wood supply, or the sawmill that burned waste products to generate steam to run the mill. Now, with prices of other fuel sources going up, wood has been rediscovered.

But what has happened to date may be dwarfed by what could happen in the future. The new Energy Security Act of 1980, recently signed by President Carter, contains $1.45 billion through fiscal year 1982 for financial assistance to synthetic fuel projects using biomass energy sources (21). The increase in biomass production likely to result will be a new pressure on the land. Many woody plants can be grown on land that is not high quality cropland, and such biomass production will not compete immediately with food production. Using this land for biomass production, however, may preclude its use for crops in the future.

A great deal of added pressure could fall on the current cropland base however, if plans for utilizing crop residues as an energy source are not carefully implemented. It is estimated that the nine leading crops produce about 363 million metric tons of residues yearly (15). If burned for energy, this crop residue would provide about 5 percent of the nation's energy use. But such a removal would lead to disastrous soil erosion levels, and thus cannot be seriously considered. What can be considered, however, is the use of from 10 to 80 percent of the residues, depending on crop, location, and soil type.[8]

This calculation was based solely on the value of the residues in preventing soil erosion and did not account for the value of the residues in providing plant nutrients or contributing to soil tilth and structure. Also ignored is the importance of plant residues as a primary source of energy for soil microbial activity, a value that might best be assessed by conducting an energy analysis of the soil system (26). Soil scientists[9] do not agree on the amount of crop residues that can be safely removed without adverse effects on soil

[8]Larson, W. E., and F. J. Pierce. 1980. "Crop Residues: Availability for Removal and Requirements for Erosion Control." Unpublished paper presented at Bio-Mass World Congress and Exposition, Atlanta, Georgia.
[9]Ibid.

productivity. Clearly, the most prudent course appears to be that which does not depend too greatly on crop residues for energy protection.

Currently, it is estimated that biomass energy provides less than 1.5 percent of the nation's total energy consumption, with some forecasters predicting that this amount could be tripled by the end of the century and doubled again by 2020.[10]

Judging the land effects of such an increase in biomass energy utilization is no simple matter. In addition to questions about the type of biomass to be used, and the manner and locations in which it is to be grown, lies a significant technological question. If small-scale biomass technology is used, in which the energy is produced largely for on-farm or home use, the implications for the land will be far less threatening than if biomass energy is produced on large-scale, commercial operations.

Small-scale uses have risen rapidly in recent years. For example, the number of wood-burning stoves has been estimated to have increased from 1 million in 1974 to 5 million in 1976.[11] Farmers are lining up by the hundreds for noncommercial fuel alcohol permits at the U.S. Bureau of Alcohol, Tobacco and Firearms. Fletcher[12] points out that "At the end of 1978, there were only 18 such permits in effect. By October 1979, over 700 permits had been issued, and 3,000 applications—most of them from farmers—had been received."

Since the energy demands of American farm production are only about 2 percent of total national consumption, farmers may find it both possible and advantageous to develop additional on-farm sources of liquid fuel. Even though several studies have shown that the economics of such production are marginal at best, farmers may feel that the advantages of being somewhat more energy self-sufficient on the farm make it worthwhile (3). If integrated into a crop rotation that includes ample soil-building crops and appropriate use of crop residues, the adverse effects on the land of such a strategy seem minor (6).

Even so, some critics point out that agriculture could not hope to become fully self-sufficient in fuel production without some major readjustments. To produce the gasoline and diesel needed to run America's farms, it is estimated that 133 million acres of corn would need to be devoted to alcohol production (12). This estimate, which appears to be based on the net energy that can be produced from an acre of corn, without accounting for the energy benefit in the distillers grain by-product, is substantially higher than the estimates of the amount of land that would be required simply to produce the feedstock for the alcohol fuel process (49).

Going further, the notion of growing crops to provide fuels for large-scale commercial strategy make the numbers sound even larger. USDA estimates that it would take about 300 million acres of corn to produce just 10

[10]Fletcher. "Farmland and Energy."
[11]Ibid.
[12]Ibid.

percent of the nation's current energy usage (49). This is about triple the acreage currently in corn production, and 75 percent of the total cropland in use in the nation today. Such a production level from cropland is clearly impossible, simply on the basis of land constraints. Whether there are offsetting methods of production that could be used to lower those land needs is still a matter of some contention.

In addition to cropland, there are about 740 million acres of forest land in the nation, part of which could be devoted to the production of biomass for energy. In its Resources Planning Act (RPA) report, the U.S. Forest Service estimated that some 488 million acres of this land are capable of commercial timber production. The current inventory is estimated at 800 billion cubic feet, not counting the tops, limbs, bark, and other portions not usable in ordinary wood products production (43).

Wood products can be used for energy by direct burning, through the production of methanol, or through "gasification." Most biomass-derived energy is currently obtained by direct burning, but the development of improved technology for converting cellulosic materials into alcohol seems likely. Many experts feel this will be the source of the majority of the biomass used for energy, at least in the near future. Crosson[13] notes that "at a meeting of the Bio-Energy World Congress and Exposition, held in Atlanta in April 1980, most speakers agreed wood rather than grain is the most economical source of biomass for energy production."

This forecast portends greater pressure on forest lands, pressure which will add to the needs created by the growing demand for wood products in building and fiber uses as well as the pressure for conversion of some forest lands to cropland. One estimate (56) is that 70 to 83 million acres of forest plantations would be required to produce just 10 percent of the nation's 1980 energy use.

Gasohol: Panacea or problem? Among the major elements of the debate surrounding a national gasohol program have been the questions of competition between food and fuel and the issue of whether a net positive energy balance can be achieved if the energy consumed in crop production is included in the calculation.

The energy balance question, though unresolved, is generating less concern among policy makers in light of new technology, and the issue has focused on whether or not a net liquid fuel balance can be achieved. If a net liquid fuel balance is realized, gasohol may be said to have converted a type of energy—solar—that is not scarce to a type—gas or diesel—that is. DOE estimates that new distilleries (designed especially to produce fuel-grade alcohol) could result in a positive liquid fuel ratio approaching 4:1 (41).

The food vs. fuel debate is unsettled and less likely to be resolved through technology. Even though the distillers grain remaining after fermentation

---

[13]Crosson, Pierre. 1980. "Future Economic and Environmental Costs of Agricultural Land." To be published by Resources for the Future, Washington, D.C.

contains all the original protein of the grain and can be used as a livestock feed, this does not, in itself, resolve the question.

There may be a limit to the amount of distillers grain that can be used as a feedstuff. Producing 2 billion gallons of ethanol from corn would yield 17 times as much distillers grain as was consumed in 1976 (5). Because distiller grain is a less desirable feed supplement than soybean meal, it is doubtful that this much can be absorbed by the current animal industry according to testimony by the secretary of agriculture before the House Committee on Science and Technology, May 4, 1979. The net effect on food supplies that will result from shifting cattle from soybean meal to distillers grain, and soybean land to corn for ethanol is not subject to a simple calculation, even if the shift is technically feasible.

Another element of the debate concerning a national gasohol program that has received less attention is the impact of such a program on the land base. If marginal lands were brought into production as a result of new demands and higher prices for farm crops, more soil erosion problems are certain. The National Association of Conservation Districts (NACD) expressed concern about this problem in testimony before the House Agriculture Committee in 1979 (44).

The Office of Technology Assessment (20) has also expressed concern about the implications of a national gasohol program on land and food:

"A commitment to produce enough gasohol to supply most U.S. automotive requirements could involve putting approximately 30-70 million additional acres into intensive crop production. Assuming the acreage was actually available, this new crop production would accelerate erosion and sedimentation, increase pesticide and fertilizer use, replace unmanaged with managed ecosystems, and aggravate other environmental damages associated with American agriculture.

"A combination of ethanol subsidies and rising crude oil prices could drive up the price of farm commodities and ultimately the price of food. The extent to which this will happen depends critically upon how much additional cropland can be brought into production in response to rising food prices and, eventually, on the cost of producing ethanol from cellulosic feedstocks. These and other major uncertainties, such as future weather and crop yields, make it impossible to predict the full economic impact of a large fuel ethanol program."

Even DOE (41), trying to demonstrate both the viability of and the need for a national program to encourage ethanol production, could not refrain from noting that major problems might be created for both agriculture and the land:

"From our analysis, it appears that an upper limit of approximately 4.7 billion gallons per year of ethanol could be produced from raw material supplies using existing technologies, if conversion capacity capable of processing these feedstocks existed. This limit could be achieved by bringing into production all existing grain land and by supplementing food processing wastes with sugar surpluses and fermentable municipal solid waste. Achieving this limit would be expensive, and would reduce the flexibility of U.S. agricultural land and restrict options for food production."

Wes Jackson (12) brings the problem down to a more human dimension, arguing that the issue is primarily one of ethics:

"Keep in mind that the energy in the alcohol required to meet the demands of an average U.S. car for one year could alternately be used as food to feed 23½ people for an entire year. From our point of view, the issue is not whether the alcohol is there, but that massive alcohol production from our farms is an immoral use of our soils since it rapidly promotes their wasting away. We must save these soils for an oil-less future."

Prior to 1979, USDA expressed serious reservations about the impact of a national gasohol program and the ability of the land to absorb the added demand. Since then, however, the department's position has become more favorably disposed toward the production of gasohol. In describing the department's new program to Congress in 1980, Deputy Secretary Jim Williams noted:

"This alcohol fuels program represents a basic policy change. The USDA is now including production of farm commodities for alcohol feedstocks as a major objective of agricultural policy—alongside the production of food, feed, and fiber. Grain reserve targets, commodity price supports, acreage diversion and other related agricultural policies are being managed to include the grain requirements for alcohol equally with other consumers of grain."

In January 1980, President Carter set a national goal of producing 500 million gallons of ethanol by the end of 1981. And before the U.S. National Alcohol Fuels Commission in June 1980, Secretary Bergland estimated that the goal could be reached by a 4 percent increase in the land devoted to corn (or a 4 percent increase in average national corn yields). He also noted that "distillation capacity, not agricultural feedstocks, is currently the restraining factor on fuel alcohol production."

Gasohol is clearly not a cost-free solution to our energy dilemma. Whether it is panacea or problem probably awaits an answer. One thing is certain—that answer is likely on its way. With the enthusiastic support of farm groups, who see a new market that might give farm prices a much-needed boost, and Congress, which has been looking for something (anything?) to make farmers happier, the passage of the Energy Security Act of 1980 signals a major political commitment to this effort.

That ethanol production is attractive to oil companies is in little doubt. In June 1980, Martin Abel[14] told a Resources for the Future Conference:

"Only recently, Ashland Oil and Publicker announced plans for a 60 million gallon plant at South Point, Ohio, and American Maize Products and Cities Service Corporation announced a 50-million-gallon plant at Ham-

---

[14]Abel, Martin E. 1980. "Growth in Demand for U.S. Crop and Animal Production by 2005." Paper presented at Resources for the Future conference on the adequacy of agricultural land, Washington, D.C.

mond, Indiana. Furthermore, an Iowa cooperative is considering building a 50-million-gallon plant. We believe, therefore, that beginning in 1982, production capacity will rise rapidly, reaching 1.1 to 1.3 billion gallons by 1985-1986 and 1.5 to 2.0 billion gallons by 1990-1991. Thus, if U.S. and world energy prices evolve in the way we and others anticipate, there may be no shortage of incentives for investment in facilities to produce ethanol from grain.''

If Abel is correct in his assessment for the future and USDA was correct in predicting that such major investments in plant capacity would tend to lock the nation into the allocation of grain for fuel production up to plant capacity once conversion plants are constructed and operational, it seems that the die is cast (5). The challenge for conservationists will be to help farmers and ranchers find ways to integrate energy production into their land and water management systems in such a way that we do not permanently damage our basic resources in the experiment.

Industrial feedstocks from the land. In addition to the petrochemicals that are imported to provide a wide range of industrial feedstocks, the United States also imports a wide variety of agricultural materials. Included in the list are natural rubber, waxes, resins newsprint, and adhesives. Many of these materials can be produced within the country, and this is an option that is beginning to look more and more attractive to policy makers. Economically, the stakes are large. The United States currently imports agriculturally produced industrial materials at the rate of an estimated $27.3

Table 3. Products that might be grown agriculturally in the United States to replace current imports.*

Product Imported or Manufactured from Petro-chemicals	Percent Imported	Plant Species Used to Replace Imports	Land Needed Year Full Production Could Be Achieved	For Full Production (million/a)
Natural rubber	100	Guayule	1995	1.2
Synthetic rubber	50	Guayule and milkweed	2000	12.0
Plastics	50	Many oilseed crops	1990	50.0
Rubber and plastic additives	50	Same as above	1990	(with above)
Coatings and printing inks	60	Flax, caster, soybean, cottonseed, safflower	1985	4.0
Adhesives	50	Stokes' aster	1995	1.0
Lubricants	60	Jojoba, crambe	1995	20.0
Detergents, etc.	60	Cuphea	2000	1.0
Newsprint, paper	?	Kenaf	1998	0.9
Synthetic and natural fibers	50	Cellulose from trees, cotton, flax	1990	1.0
Waxes	50-100	Jojoba, crambe	1990	0.2

*Table prepared from data developed by Dr L. H. Princen and staff scientists at the USDA/SEA North Central Regional Research Laboratory, Peoria, Illinois, March 1980.

billion per year. In addition, another $8 billion is spent for petroleum products to be used as industrial feedstocks (Table 3).

Recent political instability in many of the countries where this material is obtained has caused a rising interest in the potential for domestic agricultural production. Interest in the Congress, the Defense Department, and the industrial community has centered on the possibility of achieving more self-reliance, at least in the case of those products that are felt to be either "strategic" (critical to defense) or "essential" (required by industry to continue normal operations).

In assessing the situation, Howard Tankersley, director of land use for SCS, wrote to me in 1980:

"Sufficient technological research has been done that we could commercialize the agricultural commodities that produce the substitutes for these imports within 5 to 20 years, if that were to become a national goal. However, achievement of total domestic production of these products would require the use of about 55 million acres of land. This acreage is equal to about 22 percent of our current cropland base or about 17 percent of our crop and pasture land base (SCS figures). While it is technologically possible to produce all these essential materials domestically, studies need to be undertaken to determine the optimum level of production to meet the objectives of this program, given the constraints of our land base and foreign trade commitments."

Not all the land for these new crops would need to come from the current cropland base. Jojoba, for example, is a desert shrub that can be grown in the southwestern deserts under conditions where little, if any, other agricultural production is possible. Jojoba seeds contain 45 to 60 percent of an unsaturated liquid wax similar in composition to sperm whale oil (10). Commercial production of jojoba could not only make the nation more self-sufficient in a strategic material (sperm oil), but also reduce the demand for whales, which might help prevent their extinction.

Jojoba can be planted in hot, low deserts where freezing is not a hazard. With small catch basins around each plant to concentrate rainwater, it can be grown with natural rainfall or limited supplemental irrigation. It takes five to seven years for the plants to mature and produce an economic yield, but a 60-year-old plant can yield up to 30 pounds of seed per year (17).

Guayule is another desert shrub that is currently undergoing intensive research. It produces rubber of a quality nearly identical to that of the Hevea rubber tree, with the foliage containing up to 20 percent rubber by weight (46). Harvesting the entire plant is possible every two to five years, after which the plant will regenerate from its perennial rootstock. Nabhan reports yields of 200 to 1,000 pounds per year, with researchers testing varieties that will have better, more dependable yields (17).

Two other crops, buffalo gourd and devil's claw, also show promise for semiarid agriculture in the Southwest. Buffalo gourd grows well on disturbed soils and can survive with as little as 10 inches of rain annually. It yields up to 3,000 pounds of seed per acre. The seeds contain more than

1,000 pounds of vegetable oil and 1,000 pounds of protein meal. In addition, the roots can be harvested for starch, yielding up to 6 to 7 tons of starch per acre (*1*). Devil's claw seeds contain up to 40 percent oil and 27 percent protein, with the oil similar to safflower. The plant is adapted to both dryland and irrigated farming. Work to collect and improve seed stocks is now underway (*17*).

These crops offer a potential cropping alternative to land that could not be cropped otherwise, and also offer a possible agricultural future for land in the Southwest that is being threatened by loss of irrigation water. Also, there are crops that could become competitors for agricultural land in the more humid climates. Among these are crambe, an oilseed crop that contains 30 to 40 percent oil, of which up to 60 percent is erucic acid. According to Princen, crambe oil "has been evaluated successfully for the manufacture of lubricants, plasticizers, nylon, and other applications" (*24*).

Crambe has been successfully grown from North Dakota to Texas, and from California to Connecticut, with yields of 600 to 4,000 pounds per acre. Typical yields are 2,000 pounds per acre under normal management and conditions (*23*). Agricultural researchers are fairly confident that the basic information needed to successfully grow crambe is available. The crop is said to be competitive with all traditional crops except corn at a sales price of 8 cents per pound.

Kenaf is another crop that can compete for agricultural land, particularly in the warm, humid zone. It has produced yields of 5 to 10 tons of dry harvested matter per acre, about twice the production that can be obtained from normal tree farming operations (*23*). As a source of cellulose for newsprint or other paper products, kenaf appears very promising.

Princen (*25*) has demonstrated in several papers that growing domestic crops to replace imported materials is indeed a feasible option, but not without its problems, however. One major problem is the need for coordination and timing of all facets of the research and development program. When the knowledge is available for growing the crop, the industrial capacity to use it must also be ready. A problem is created when one segment of production gets ahead of the other. With most of the crop research in USDA and most of the utilization research in industry, timing is made more difficult. In addition, American industry has always found it easier to buy imports than deal with the necessary problems of domestic production. In this way, they have left "the worries of production, processing, and by-product use to the countries of origin" (*25*). A domestic production strategy will make us address those problems directly, and some will not be easily resolved.

Regardless of the problems, the nation's interest in using these products to achieve self-reliance, in reducing consumption of petroleum by an estimated 640,000 barrels per day, and in reducing our import bill by an estimated $37 billion per year, is likely to lead to more research, testing, and production. These new crops could become an important part of the agricultural picture in the future.

Estimating the land requirements of industrial crops. The "new" energy-related demands on land apparently might result in a significant addition to the current agricultural land use situation. Gasohol, for example, could add from 8 to 30 million acres of effective demand in the next two decades if, as Martin Abel predicts, the new industrial capacity is built on the basis of using corn as the major feedstock.

The production of industrial feedstocks could add up to 55 million more acres of industrial crops, but it appears that well over half of those acres would come from lands not now in cropland or considered to be potential cropland for ordinary crops. Without a great deal of data to rely on, it might be reasonable to estimate that the new demand for cropland could be in the range of 10 to 20 million acres by the year 2000, with the remainder of the production coming from semiarid or desert lands.

The low-range estimate I would make of the total demand on U.S. cropland for industrial products by 2000 is 18 million acres. The high range would be on the order of 50 million. These would be acres in addition to those needed for food, feed, and fiber production as we now know it, allowing for some substitution and double usage, such as a gasohol cattle feed or double cropping involving an energy crop with a food crop.

These numbers are not, by themselves, very startling. It has been estimated that 50 million acres of idle cropland was brought back into production in response to the Russian grain purchase and the bad weather experienced in the period from 1972-1974 (*16*). We have estimated that some 34 million acres of potential cropland was converted to cropland in the decade between 1967 and 1977 (Table 1). Assuming that the land is available, adding that many acres again the next 2 decades does not sound unreasonable.

What makes this added pressure sound ominous, however, is the concurrent need, shown by the Resource Conservation Act (RCA) study, to have from 407 to 520 million acres of cropland still available in 2030 to meet growing needs for food and fiber at home and abroad. Coupled with the demand for industrial crops, this adds up to a low estimated requirement of 425 million acres and a high estimate of 570 million. Figure 4 shows how these demands might develop in the future.

Scenarios for the future

Admittedly, any forecast of future land use in the United States must necessarily be based on data that are inadequate. The best data at hand are being assembled by USDA as part of the RCA study and by the National Agricultural Lands Study (NALS). Both studies are quick to point out the data deficiencies. Brewer and Boxley[15] ascribe this, in part, to the fact that federal agency budget constraints have resulted in very different levels of statisti-

[15]Brewer, Michael, and Robert Boxley. 1980. "The Potential Supply of Cropland." Paper presented at Resources for the Future symposium on the adequacy of agricultural land, Washington, D.C.

cal reliability in the various inventories that have been made in recent years.

A more serious question to the forecaster, however, is how well these past trends can be used to predict future trends. In looking at current data relating to the use of agricultural lands, we face a quandary. The trends of the recent past cannot continue much longer; we are losing too much land, and too much topsoil to erosion, too rapidly. Logic dictates that these losses must be slowed. The problem comes in looking for evidence that erosion is slowing down, or that political or economic forces are slowing down the loss of farmland productivity. Currently, there appears to be none.

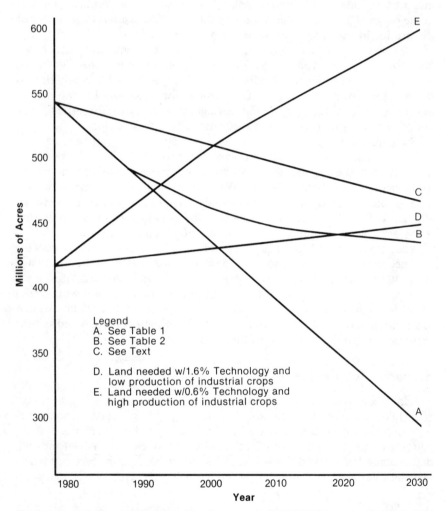

Figure 4. Potential losses from the cropland resource pool 1977-2030, compared with the land likely to be needed for food, fiber and industrial crop production under two different levels of future technology and yield increase.

Thus we are forced into the dichotomous position of saying that, although we believe that the past trends cannot be allowed to continue, it seems likely that they will, at least in the short term.

Figure 4 predicts a range of situations in which economically disruptive competition for agricultural lands may fall between 1990 and the end of the century. Even the most optimistic forecasts predict resource shortages by 2020. Some of the most serious, and imminent, problems are those that are indicated by the short-term (less than a decade) continuation of current trends. Clearly, we must pay immediate and serious policy attention to the cropland resources of the nation. The most optimistic case would still require the conversion of millions of acres of land into crops, land that is now in pasture, range, or forest, and its conversion will both cost money and cause the loss of other values.

Some new croplands may result in the draining of wetlands, adding another dimension of environmental loss and concern. If energy prices continue to climb in real terms, the conversion of this land will cause the average costs of production to be somewhat higher.

Soil erosion will be accelerated by this shift because cropland is more prone to erosion than less intensive agricultural uses and the potential cropland is, on the whole, more erosion-prone than the land currently cropped. Recent experience indicates that not only does new land have higher soil erosion potential, but the high cost of conversion tends to discourage the added investment in soil-conserving practices (33).

The conservative case, of course, means far more competition for land and far more intensive problems with conversion costs, soil erosion, environmental degradation, and supply management. It would require the rediscovery of many acres currently thought to be uneconomic to farm. Many of those acres will be in small, isolated tracts and will require a different farming style than today's large machinery will allow. Does this mean that small farms would once more be possible in some parts of the country? If so, many persons would count that as a positive effect.

The important thing to remember about the crossing of the "supply" and "demand" lines in figure 4 is that it will not happen. There is no such thing as a "negative acre." We won't run a deficit; we will simply not be able to produce some commodities for some markets. As a result, food prices will rise. But that is foreordained if energy prices continue to rise at a 2 percent real rate each year. We are talking about the degree to which these effects will be felt.

The most critical factor is the almost total loss of flexibility to respond to normal fluctuations in climate. USDA has pointed out that concern in relation to the gasohol question, but the problem is acute whether we enter the gasohol market or not. As they note, "the volatility of farm production levels is increased by intensive agricultural practices. For example, heavy use of nitrogen fertilizer to increase corn yields has also increased the amplitude of fluctuations in corn yields due to weather variations, since positive yield response to nitrogen is dependent upon favorable weather conditions" (5).

The United States has used its tremendous land resource, its constantly growing technology, huge amounts of capital, and favorable weather conditions to build up an intensive, high-producing agricultural plant. With technological development seeming at the moment to have plateaued, with growing competition for available capital in all parts of the economy, and with the weather hinting that it will be less certain, the attention turns to the land base. If the yield-increasing investments and technologies don't prove to be adequate on the existing, shrinking cropland base, is the land reservoir adequate to cope with all foreseeable demands? The answer, it appears, is no, not any longer.

America needs a new strategy of wise land use, conservation management, and planned reinvestment in the productive land base more than at any time in the nation's history. Without such a strategy, market forces are going to hasten the destruction of productive lands that will be sorely needed before the century draws to a close. Competition between industrial crops and food crops is going to increase, with the end result all but preordained. Food costs are going to rise, and low-income people will suffer first and worst. The time spent in pointless arguments over whether agricultural land protection is needed in the national interest is a luxury the nation can no longer afford (27).

REFERENCES

1. Bemis, W. P., James W. Berry, and Charles W. Weber. 1979. *The buffalo gourd: A potential arid land crop.* In Gary A. Ritchie [editor] *New Agricultural Crops.* AAAS Selected Symposia Series. Westview Press, Boulder, Colorado.
2. Bertrand, Anson R. 1980. *Overdrawing the nation's research accounts.* Journal of Soil and Water Conservation 35(3): 109-111.
3. Blobaum, Roger. 1979. *Energy alternatives for agriculture.* In *Resource-Constrained Economies: The North American Dilemma.* Soil Conservation Society of America, Ankeny, Iowa.
4. Brown, Lester R. 1980. *Choosing food or fuel.* Journal of Soil and Water Conservation 35(3): 146.
5. Brown, Lester R. 1980. *Food or fuel: New competition for the world's cropland.* Worldwatch Paper 35. Worldwatch Institute, Washington, D.C.
6. Commoner, Barry. 1979. *The politics of energy.* Alfred A. Knopf, New York, New York.
7. Crosson, Pierre. 1979. *Agricultural land use: A technological and energy perspective.* In Max Schnepf [editor] *Farmland, Food and the Future.* Soil Conservation Society of America, Ankeny, Iowa.
8. Dideriksen, R. I., A. R. Hidlebaugh, and K. O. Schmude. 1979. *Trends in agricultural land use.* In Max Schnepf [editor] *Farmland, Food and the Future.* Soil Conservation Society of America, Ankeny, Iowa.
9. Esseks, J. Dixon. 1979. *Nonurban competition for farmland* In Max Schnepf [editor] *Farmland, Food and the Future.* Soil Conservation Society of America, Ankeny, Iowa.
10. Hogan, Lemoyne. 1979. *Jojoba: A new crop for arid regions.* In Gary A. Ritchie [editor] *New Agricultural Crops.* AAAS Selected Symposia Series. Westview Press, Boulder, Colorado.
11. Illinois Department of Mines and Minerals. 1978. *1977 annual coal, oil and gas report.* Springfield.
12. Jackson, Wes, Mari Peterson, and Charles Washburn. 1980. *Impacts on the land in the new age of limits.* The Land Report, No. 9. The Land Institute, Salina, Kansas.
13. Jacobsen, Sally. 1973. *Land use dispute in Illinois: Nuclear power vs. crops.* Bulletin of the Atomic Scientists 29.
14. Kahn, Herman, William Brown, and Leon Martel. 1976. *The next 200 years: A scenario for America and the world.* William Morrow & Co., New York.
15. Larson, W. E., R. F. Holt, and C. W. Carlson. 1978. *Residues for soil conservation.* In W. R. Oschwald [editor] *Crop Residue Management Systems.* Special Publicaton 31. American Society of Agronomy, Madison, Wisconsin.

16. Little, Charles E., editor. *Land and food: The preservation of U.S. farmland*. American Land Forum, Washington, D.C.
17. Nabhan, Gary. 1979. *New crops for desert farming*. The New Farm 1(3).
18. National Association of Conservation Districts. 1979. *Tuesday Letter*. NACD, Washington, D.C.
19. Office of Surface Mining Reclamation and Enforcement. 1979. *Final environmental impact statement. Section 501(b) regulations*. U.S. Department of the Interior, Washington, D.C.
20. Office of Technology Assessment. 1979. *Gasohol: A technical memorandum*. U.S. Congress, Washington, D.C.
21. Office of the White House Press Secretary 1980. *Fact sheet: S. 932, the Energy Security Act*. Public Law 96-294. Washington, D.C.
22. Paarlberg, Don. 1980. *Farm and food policy: Issues of the 1980s*. University of Nebraska Press, Lincoln.
23. Princen, L. H. 1977. *Potential wealth in new crops: Research and development*. In *Crop Resources*. Academic Press, New York, New York.
24. Princen, L. H. 1979. *New crop developments for industrial oils*. Journal of the American Oil Chemists' Society 56(9): 845
25. Princen, L. H. 1980. *Alternate industrial feedstocks from agriculture*. Northern Regional Research Center, Science and Education Administration—Agricultural Research, U.S. Department of Agriculture, Illinois; 1977. *Need for renewable coatings raw materials and what could be available today*. Journal of Coatings Technology 49(635): 88-93.
26. Sampson, R. Neil. 1976. *Energy analysis as a tool in conservation planning*. In *Critical Conservation Choices: A Bicentennial Look*. Proceedings of the 31st annual meeting, Soil Conservation Society of America, Ankeny, Iowa.
27. Sampson, R. Neil. 1979. *The ethical dimension of farmland protection*. In Max Schnepf [editor] *Farmland, Food and the Future*. Soil Conservation Society of America, Ankeny, Iowa.
28.. Smith, Janet M., David Ostendorf, and Mike Schechtman. 1978. *Who's mining the farm?* Illinois South Project, Herrin, Illinois.
29. Smith, Thomas W., et al. 1977. *Transmission lines: Environmental and public policy considerations*. University of Wisconsin Institute of Environmental Studies, Madison.
30. Soil Conservation Service. 1979. *Basic statistics: Status of land disturbed by surface mining in the United States, as of July 1, 1977*. U.S. Department of Agriculture, Washington, D.C.
31. Soil Conservation Service. 1979. *SCS national resource inventories, 1977: Final estimates*. U.S. Department of Agriculture, Washington, D.C.
32. Subcommittee on Natural Resources and Environment, Committee on Science and Technology and Subcommittee on Conservation and Credit. 1979. *Agricultural and environmental relationships: Issues and priorities*. Committee on Agriculture, U.S. House of Representatives, Washington, D.C.
33. Timmons, John F. 1979. *Agriculture's natural resource base: Demand and supply interactions, problems, and remedies*. In Max Schnepf [editor] *Soil Conservation Policies: An Assessment*. Soil Conservation Society of America, Ankeny, Iowa.
34. Tombargo, Francisco, and Robert Young. 1978. *The Colorado River salinity problem in Mexico*. Journal of Natural Resources, January 1978.
35. U.S. Department of Agriculture. 1977. *Potential cropland study*. Statistical Bulletin 578. Washington, D.C.
36. U.S. Department of Agriculture. 1979. *Appraisal 1980: Review draft, part I*. Washington, D.C.
37. U.S. Department of Agriculture. 1980. *Appraisal 1980: Review draft, part II*. Washington, D.C.
38. U.S. Department of Energy. 1978. *Additions to generating capacity: 1978-1987*. Washington, D.C.
39. U.S. Department of Energy. 1979. *An assessment of the national consequences of increased coal utilization*. Washington, D.C.
40. U.S. Department of Energy. 1979. *Environmental analysis of synthetic liquid fuils*. Washington, D.C.
41. U.S. Department of Energy. 1979. *The report of the alcohol fuels policy review*. DOE/PE-0012. Washington, D.C.
42. U.S. Environmental Protection Agency. 1978. *Environmental effects of increased coal utilization: Ecological effects of gaseous emissions from coal combustion*. EPA-600/7-8-108. Washington, D.C.
43. U.S. Forest Service. 1976. *The nation's renewable resources—an assessment, 1975*. U.S. Department of Agriculture, Washington, D.C.
44. U.S. House of Representatives. 1979. *National fuel alcohol and farm commodity produc-

tion act of 1979. Hearings before Subcommittees of the Committee on Agriculture on H.R. 3905. Washington, D.C.

45. U.S. Water Resources Council. 1978. *The nation's water resources: 1975-2000.* The Second National Water Assessment. U.S. Government Printing Office, Washington, D.C.

46. Vietmeyer, Noel D. 1979. *Guayule: Domestic rubber rediscovered.* In Gary A. Ritchie [editor] *New Agricultural Crops.* AAAS Selected Symposia Series. Westview Press. Boulder, Colorado.

47. Young, Louise B. 1973. *Power over people.* Oxford University Press, New York, New York.

48. Young, Robert. 1978. *Impact of increases in natural gas prices on irrigation in the Texas high plains.* In *25th Annual Proceedings of the Mid-Continent Research and Development Council.* Colorado State University, Fort Collins.

49. Zeimetz, Kathryn A. 1979. *Growing energy: Land for biomass farms.* Agricultural Economic Report 425. U.S. Department of Agriculture, Washington, D.C.

39

Energy Production and Natural Resource Trade-offs

Folke Dovring
Professor of Land Economics
University of Illinois, Urbana-Champaign

Natural resource trade-offs are an essential part of America's energy problem. At the core of this problem is one of capital formation. Resources and technology will not allow us to produce all the energy we now use because of high capital requirements. At present we are "living off the capital." Because oil and gas have low requirements in man-made capital, they function as if we had already invested heavily in more expensive sources, and thus the need for replacement investments is less than apparent to most people. Oil is imported at costs that are now the equivalent of large domestic capital expenditures, a fact but dimly perceived. The dwindling of both petroleum and natural gas supplies threatens to leave us in a void where capital should have been formed over a long stretch of years. Parts of that investment bill are long overdue, and we are groping for a new energy investment strategy.

Whatever choices are made eventually, capital costs to replace energy sources are so high that we cannot and should not expect to fill the entire energy bill for the medium-term future in ways in which demand is usually projected. Reducing final energy demand must be a large part of the answer. This should be kept in mind to underline the severity of the constraints under which we will exercise our options. The future trade-off in land use for food and fuel points to the same difficulty. When it is at all possible to think of withdrawing land from food production to obtain more fuel, then the reasons ought to be compelling and exclude frivolous or avoidably wasteful uses of energy.

Extraction versus biomass: snowballing requirements

The main alternatives for energy production to replace oil and gas in the United States in the medium term are either extractive—fossil, nuclear—or solar—collector panels, biomass. The latter are obviously more space-using. If land scarcity were the only important consideration, extractive sources would prevail.

When we look at capital requirements, the picture is different. It is not just that capital requirements are high; they are higher in nearly all alternatives with the possible exception of wood. Capital-intensive industries, in turn, draw indirectly on natural resources by their materials requirements.

Detailed comparisons of capital intensity are difficult because every day we receive new estimates based on new technology or new computations or both. At best, we can discuss magnitudes and directions. In one important respect, however, we can compare extractive and solar alternatives and trace a consistent difference. This is in the way cost estimates and real resource claims may change with rising volume of activity. The extractive alternatives tend to have their capital and their indirect energy requirements "snowball" as volume of activity goes up. Solar alternatives have much less of this.

An explanation of snowballing requires detailed input-output analysis of energy (*1, 2, 8, 12, 15*), but in its most simple form it is this: All energy production also consumes energy, both directly and indirectly, through capital goods and other manufactured inputs used in the energy industries. What is disturbing is that energy requirements for energy production now tend to become larger, whether we turn to new energy sources or to varieties of the old sources that were previously regarded as too expensive. A frequently overlooked fact is that as the more energy-expensive sources take on more scope in our energy system they begin to draw on their own output, or its equivalent, from other new and energy-expensive sources, as inputs in their production process. Thus the total requirement, direct and indirect, for energy in energy production grows at a faster rate than does the direct requirement alone.

This snowballing is larger the higher the direct requirement is as a percentage of the gross energy output. For instance, a direct energy input requirement that is 10 percent of the gross energy output rises to 11 percent when the indirect, indirect-indirect, and so on requirements are included. But 20 percent grows to 26.5 percent, 30 percent becomes 43 percent, 40 percent becomes 66.5 percent, and 50 percent of gross output energy as direct energy input snowballs to nearly 100 percent of the gross energy output when all the indirect requirements are included and are drawn from sources of the same energy input intensity as the output energy in the case.

At present this problem is obscured by our use of yesterday's cheap energy as input to produce tomorrow's expensive energy. When the latter becomes its own input, as it must eventually, the arithmetic of snowballing will catch up with us. Then some energy sources that once appeared manageable will reveal themselves as crushingly expensive.

With the energy requirements, capital requirements will also snowball, in fact even faster. Rising capital requirements will become a rising proportion of the gradually smaller net energy output—that part of gross energy output delivered to the rest of the economy and not retained in the energy sector. This can be especially embarrassing if capital has to be built up over a short period, as seems likely when the oil crunch comes. We can then no longer "live off the capital." However, new capital formation is being delayed by the current reliance on imported oil.

Examples of snowballing

We can expect more snowballing of energy and capital costs in extractive energy sources than in solar energy sources. One reason is in the rising costs of extraction, another in the mounting bills for waste disposal and environmental protection.

Costs of extraction at a constant technology are bound to go up when finite resources are exploited farther toward their margins. "Tertiary" oil (petroleum at great depth, lodged in sand or decomposing rock) is a good example. Cost of drilling increases exponentially; drill three times as deep and it costs nine times as much. The need and the cost of injecting steam or chemical solvent also increases with depth. Tertiary oil is plentiful, but most of it is recognized as unreachable by any known technology (13). Before we get that far, "heavy" oil close to the surface costs more than light oil, not only in money but in oil. Recently, a heavy-oil field in California was reported to burn one-third of its own output just to generate steam for extraction. Energy input into building the steam boiler was not included in this estimate of higher energy input into energy, and neither were the refinery costs that also are higher for heavy oil.

Uranium mining has a variant on the same theme; the farther one goes into mining ores with lower content of the target metal, the more energy and capital it takes to obtain 1 ton of uranium (14). Going to greater depth also adds costs.

Coal may appear to present less of this kind of rising costs, but this is true in appearance only. Coal companies take on the least costly fields first. Statistics from some nations show coal seams that are too deep for economical mining at present costs and prices. Energy costs of mining coal are lower than in other extractive energy sources, so maybe snowballing of energy input will never come to the fore in the coal mines. But there is so much more of snowballing environmental costs in the use of coal, as I will later describe.

All of these cost situations may be improved by new technology. Oil drilling already has been improved greatly in recent decades, probably leaving less room for future improvement. Uranium mining may go over to leaching techniques, assumed to cost less in energy and capital than extraction and crushing of rocks. At each level of technology, however, there will still be diminishing marginal rates of return, meaning rising and snowballing expenses in energy and capital. And some types of costs show little tendency to yield to technology. This is above all true with extraction at greater depth because it includes an element of vertical transportation.

There is less of this type of snowballing cost in solar energy sources. There is no equivalent of deep drilling. The distance factor in assembling energy feedstocks from vast areas has a trade-off in smaller processing plants and decentralized delivery systems. Solar panels are area using, but the only margin concept is in going from sunny to cloudy climates.

Environmental costs are most easily perceived in the burning and processing of coal. To agree on some type of smoke "scrubber" deemed efficient under present circumstances is insufficient. The more coal we use, the more efficient the scrubbing techniques must be, meaning more indirect energy and more capital per unit of energy delivered to the rest of the economy outside the energy complex.

We have not found remedies to some environment problems. Release of sulfuric acid into the groundwater, which is serious in mining of high-sulfur coal in humid areas, will increase in proportion to the volume of coal mined. If any remedy is found, it is likely also to have snowballing costs. Release of carbon dioxide into the atmosphere from fossil fuels risks producing a "greenhouse effect" of as yet unknown consequences, for which a remedy is also unknown. This effect will accelerate in proportion to the rate of use of fossil hydrocarbons. Heating of the atmosphere and withdrawal of free oxygen from the atmospheric treasury are other hazards from abundant use of fossil fuels, again for which no remedy is in sight.

Fission energy entails the still unresolved problem of long-term storage of fission fragments. The technical side of this is hard to visualize. Whatever the method eventually adopted, we can probably expect that costs of storage will rise faster than the volume of material to be stored, snowballing to huge proportions if the fission-energy industry were to grow to a large part of our energy system. There is no merit in belittling this future problem. The lesson from chemical dumps should not be lost on us. Love Canal is the model case of a cost bill coming due long after the goods have been used and their leftovers discarded. The true cost of those chemical products was in fact higher than the prices paid at the time, and the deferred cost is now higher than if it had been paid at the time.

Fission fragments apart, a fission-energy industry based on plutonium also would entail snowballing costs for security protection. The larger the volume of activity, the more expensive it would be to watch over every plant and every shipment—thieves and saboteurs are sure to take advantage of the least-protected ones.

Environmental costs from solar energy sources are much less serious than from extractive ones. Capturing and transforming sunshine introduces no new heat or radiation. Green plants merely recycle carbon already part of the biosphere. There are some environmental repercussions from using hardware in the building and maintenance of solar installations.

Alcohol distilleries and other factories for the processing of biomass generate some environmental problems, particularly in the use of water and the disposal of effluents. These are in part the same as in the processing of coal, oil shale, and tar sands into liquid fuels. However, biomass plants are able to mitigate these problems by decentralizing to form smaller plants, which offsets the dispersed nature of the feedstock sources. Conversely, fossil-fuel plants tend toward large, centralized operations.

Such differences between fossil and solar sources tend to remain obscure as long as data come from experiment-scale applications, as in current efforts to extract oil from shale and tar sands.

Extractive versus solar sources in land use

Given the problems of extractive sources of energy in their present experimental stages, new energy sources must include a full gamut of solar applications so that both extractive and solar sources can be better understood as to the costs and the logistic problems they entail.

Extractive sources compete only moderately with other activities for the use of land. Uranium, thorium, oil shale, and tar sands occur mostly in places that are little suited to other intensive uses of the land. Coal mines are somewhat more space using and sometimes ruin valuable farmland. Even so, loss of farmland to strip mining is moderate and can at least in part be remedied by reclamation, which is done most economically immediately after mining. Subsidence of old underground mines is also space destructive, and the solution is less clear.

Trade-offs in the use of water are more important as regards some of the extractive energy sources. Conversion of coal into liquid fuels requires large amounts of water, and so does extraction of shale oil by the techniques mostly tried to date; "in-situ" recovery promises to deliver the oil without drawing on scarce water supplies but may yet be problematic when pursued deep inside the mountains.

Solar sources are obviously much more space using. Solar panels for heat and hot water in dwellings can, on the whole, draw on the space already taken by buildings and surrounding sites in the spacious layout of American cities. Central-station electricity generation from photo-voltaic cells will take large land areas whenever such activity becomes important, which will be some time into the future.

In between, there beckons a futuristic technology dubbed "cell-free agriculture," a factory technique to synthesize hydrocarbons from air and sunshine by aid of artificial chlorophylls. Such technology will be more space-using than most extractive sources, but less so than conventional agriculture. As an economic reality, it is extremely futuristic.

Meantime, we look to green plants as possibly a substantial source of energy, especially liquid fuels for vehicles. Depending on what the other trade-offs are, the use of land for fuel could become large. For the use of present and prospective cropland, we only discuss liquid fuel (ethanol or methanol), plus some use of crop residues as boiler fuel in distilleries. For forest land or areas suitable for tree planting, both of these liquid fuels are candidates for land use, as is the use of wood as solid fuel for boilers and space heating.

Alcohol from crops

The current wave of interest in biomass fuel centers on the concept of "gasohol"—a blend of 10 percent 200-proof ethyl alcohol and 90 percent gasoline, as yet but a tiny fraction of all motor fuel in this country.

Grain alcohol needs some accounting convention for the relation between grain used and alcohol produced. The ratio usually given is 2.6 gallons of alcohol from a bushel of corn (*11*). Alcohol production uses up 70 percent of the corn, leaving the rest as food or feed. A bushel of grain starch thus serves as feedstock for 3.7 gallons of alcohol (*6*).

High-protein residues from the distilleries, such as distillers' dry grain or other less dehydrated forms, will displace soybeans from the feed market. This displacement will cause some increase in the use of nitrogen fertilizer, a high-energy input.

The prospect of fuel from grain can be pursued at four alternative levels: for price support, for on-farm fuel, for supplying 10 percent of all gasoline used in the country, or for supplying some larger fraction of all transportation fuel now used in the country.

Price support. The medium-term past has seen large areas of cropland "set aside," idled to ensure support price levels for crops. Growing grain for alcohol production might be a more productive use of such land. From past experience, the surplus capacity appears to be in the range of 1 to 1.5 billion bushels corn equivalent (25-37.5 million metric tons) a year (*4*). Fuel production from set-aside land could add from 3.7 to 5.5 billion gallons of ethanol. Depending on how it is used, this fuel could replace the same number of gallons of gasoline (in gasohol) or, when used unblended, two-thirds of the same number of gallons of diesel fuel.

Price supports have recently taken a new twist because of the now very high prices of imported petroleum and the rather low export prices of grain. At these proportions we should not export any grain (except as disaster relief), because the proceeds of the grain exports will buy less energy (in petroleum) than we can obtain by distilling the grain (*6*).

The trouble with price-support alcohol production is twofold. For one thing, we do not now have enough distillery capacity for alcohol production to make much impact on grain prices. This may be remedied in a year or two, as investment plans are abundant. But once built, the distillery capacity needs to be used in full for economic production. A distillery industry may not be flexible enough to meet the year-to-year varying demands of price support, unless supports are a minor fringe on a large distillery industry.

Fuel for farms. Farms are vulnerable to supply interruptions, and many farmers therefore want to build their own small-scale distilleries. In the central Corn Belt grain alcohol could supply the fuel for farming by drawing on corn production from 5 percent of the cropland. When unblended alcohol is used, the farmers' rule of thumb for farming need is 15 gallons per acre (1.5 gallons of alcohol for each gallon of diesel fuel).

To replace the fuel used in farm tractors, harvesting machines, and farm trucks in U.S. agriculture would require about 9 billion gallons of ethyl alcohol. This would draw on 2.4 billion bushels (corn equivalent) or some 60 million metric tons of cereal grains, close to one-fourth of the annual harvest. This represents more land than could be set aside and would conflict either with existing market demands for grain or with soil conservation needs. In the central grain areas of the Corn Belt and Great Plains, the replacement fuel might be obtained by drawing on surplus potential only.

To supply 10 percent of U.S. road motor fuel under the gasohol scheme would require in excess of 10 billion gallons of alcohol, thus reducing feed grain supplies by 2.7 billion bushels, or more than our entire export of cereal grains. Displacements within the agricultural system would be severe.

To supply more than 10 percent of U.S. road fuel consumption of recent years would necessitate even larger displacements in the existing agricultural system. If substitution of high-protein vegetable foods for animal products were widely accepted, some 100 million tons of grains (or their equivalent in other crops) could be released for fuel production. Adding 50 million tons of export grains, we could produce in the range of 20 to 25 billion gallons of ethyl alcohol—still far from replacing the bulk of present motor fuel consumption in the United States.

Crops other than grains could yield more fuel per acre than grains and at less expense of input energy, possibly also with less strain on erodible land. Sweet sorghum, root crops, and several silage crops have been proposed. Not all of these alternatives would yield a by-product usable as food or feed. Some might yield more boiler fuel than others. The details of these alternatives are not well explored as yet. Some of them would improve soil conservation by permitting conversion of cropland to permanent vegetation, as in the case of the Jerusalem artichoke, the Kansas sunflower.

All field and permanent crops require energy embodied in farming costs: tillage (fuel and machines), chemicals for plant food and protection, and farm overheads. Farming costs use up about one-fifth to one-third of the fuel obtained from grains as alcohol. Most of these inputs are high-grade fuels, oil and gas. Irrigated grain crops often take even more energy, sometimes in excess of what is recovered by alcohol distillation. But even without irrigation the input energy into crops intended for conversion to fuel needs monitoring because these inputs eventually will come from more expensive sources, subject to snowballing, which will make these inputs a larger fraction of output energy than now.

Wood-based fuels. Trees generally fix more energy per area unit per year than do annual crops on the same kind of land and in the same climate (*10*), largely because trees cover the ground for a larger part of the season. Trees also require less input energy than crops (*3*).

When wood is to be used to produce liquid fuel, methanol is preferred over ethanol (ethyl alcohol) because of higher conversion rates (*9, 16*). Not all of the alternative processes have been tested in commercial production.

For mediocre farmland, "silvicultural energy farms" have been proposed and will probably be established in considerable quantity. Their output, plus various quantities of wood and bark refuse, leftover wood from both commercial and noncommercial forests, plus municipal sewage wastes, could produce methanol in a quantity that would exceed half of the current use of motor fuel. Ethanol would then remain a minor component of the alcohol fuel supply. Of course, alcohol fuels can be used for more purposes than to propel vehicles. Total alcohol fuel supply could rise to 10 quads or more, more than one-eighth of the present U.S. energy budget.

Use of farmland for forest production must be planned on more indications than just wood production potential. Forests affect microclimates and thus have potential impact on crop growth in interspersed cropland areas. Corn Belt farmers often show distrust of wooded areas because of shade effect and wind turbulence.

Inventory of nondescript farmland with little or no current use may turn up more potential woodland (or land for permanent herbaceous fuel crops) than would be deduced from available statistics. Shelterbelts along farm fields have effects that are different from those of solid woodlots—they are more directly beneficial to crop growth and yields, and their wood production might be obtained at no land cost. Research is needed to determine the possible payoffs and trade-offs.

In addition to supplying feedstock for liquid fuels, trees also supply solid fuel to fire distilleries to heat rural homes. The relation between feedstock and boiler fuel needs special attention.

There is little possible snowballing of capital or energy costs because energy input into wood production is much smaller than into field crops. Some permanent crops for hay and silage may be intermediary in this. When we begin to fertilize woodlots, the input energy into tree production will rise somewhat. Some trees, such as locusts and alders, are nitrogen-fixers and so may help keep down fertilizer inputs.

Capital invested in processing plants will have the same snowballing effects as are found in all industrial investment, but the effect is no more apparent in alcohol distilleries than in conventional oil refineries, for instance.

Boiler fuels: Biomass versus coal. At present, most alcohol distilleries use natural gas or propane, an oil refinery product, as boiler fuel. A large alcohol-distilling industry cannot use such fuel, for then it would fail to add much high-grade fuel to the energy budget of the economy.

The alternatives for future boiler fuels are generally coal and biomass. The choice is thus because biomass—crop and tree refuse—may be converted into alcohol, but so may coal. The relative merit of coal and wood as methanol feedstock do not at present appear well explored. Looking at the transportation overheads from source to distillery, it appears more logical to use biomass also as boiler fuel in alcohol production, at least in small distilleries. Coal conversion into alcohol could better take place in large establishments located near coal mines and drawing their fuel from the same concentrated source.

Crop residue is not altogether easy to fit into either use, as feedstock or as boiler fuel. Corn stover, for example, presents high costs of both collection and storage and also is a possible risk in storage. At best, corn stover could be thought of as a seasonal component in a system using several sources. Corn cobs, a much smaller source, may be somewhat more favorable as a fuel, if ear corn is harvested and stored unshelled.

Crop residues may also provide boiler fuel in small distilleries by anaerobic digestion, either of some crop residues as they are, or of manure that in part comes from feeding distillery residue to nearby livestock, or possibly of distillery residue from crops other than grain.

Compared with crop residues, wood residues are easier to visualize as fuel no less than feedstock. Collection and storage conditions are about the same for both uses. To the extent that wood is used for process heat, the output of alcohol from a ton of wood is less, but the input of fossil fuel is also less and so the proportion of fossil to renewable fuel is improved.

Such alternatives are worth keeping in mind because future perspectives of both production and consumption of liquid fuels are as yet highly flexible. If, as appears necessary because of capital costs, consumption of liquid motor fuel can be reduced considerably, say to half its present volume in this country, then the likelihood increases that all liquid fuel may be produced from biomass, using crop and wood residues as process fuel.

Capital intensities and land use

Capital intensity in energy production is important for several reasons. It is generally high; the need to make large investments over a short period of the near- and medium-term future threatens to burden the economy beyond its capacity; and the perspective of snowballing through rising energy costs of investment makes both of the previous points even more serious.

An attractive feature of producing alcohol from crops is that investment costs in starch-derived ethanol distilleries appear moderate, considerably lower than in most energy systems. To the investment costs in distilleries one should add farming costs, which are moderate too. When this is applied to about 70 percent of a distillery's output value, the total capital cost remains lower than in most of the energy complex. In the short run, agriculture is a going concern with its investments in place. To the extent that feed-stock for distilleries (and some of the fuels) can be obtained by relocations within the farming and food systems, net additions to investment may remain small in the medium term. This will be even more true when feedstock comes from crops with permanent growth habits rather than those planted annually.

Wood as feedstock has higher investment costs in alcohol plants than those for ethanol from starch but lower costs for the production of feedstock. The composite capital requirement, for both methanol and ethanol from wood, may be higher than for ethanol from grain, but they are almost certain to remain lower than for several other enterprises in the energy system.

Biomass fuel will thus draw less on renewable capital but more on land. If land is included in agricultural capital, farming becomes one of the most capital-intensive industries when comparing stock to output, but this would still have no effect on depreciation as conventionally reported. Analytically we treat land as a gift of nature, supplying a permanent flow of services. Neither is quite correct, for the productivity of farmland depends critically on land clearing and past melioration and on maintenance through continuous use in biological production. This is written off as part of the annual costs of producing crops and trees. The value of land reflects its opportunity cost in production, and this in turn is affected by the production system that is in place and the market demands it is designed to satisfy.

When approaching the philosophical and ethical questions about the use of land to grow fuel, we should realize that it has been done in the past and still is done in many places through the feeding of draft animals, which, like the biomass fuels, uses up some part of the annual flow of biomass growth from farmland. And wood still is a leading source of household fuel in large parts of the world. Without cooking, raw food is of less value, and without draft power, not all farmland could be used to grow crops. Fuel equals food; we are now "eating oil" (7) but cannot go on doing so for long. By all accounts, biomass alcohol in America will deliver the draft power cheaper than could be done by horses or mules.

Looking at the alternatives, we must also realize that dangers to the environment from other sources, such as very large use of coal, may turn out to be no less vital than food. It is also clear that an over-large drain on capital to build up energy supplies based on extractive sources could hamper food production (as well as other production) no less than is the case by diverting land from food to fuel. Rather than regarding land for food farming as a mystical entity of incomparable value, we must look at the entire economic system and decide how total resource use best serves the national and world economy. Not even food for the poor countries need finally present any demand on America's land, for in most cases poor countries would be better served if we exported to them the fertilizers rather than the grain, which is more easily done if we use less fertilizer in growing biomass for fuel.

Stripped of its mystique, farmland is a resource to use for best economic result, now and in the long run. Biomass fuel may prove to mean more complete and more balanced land use, with better protection against erosion. This should be yet another advantage for biomass over extractive energy sources when the total balance is struck between the alternative energy systems.

The jury is still out, but we cannot wait much longer.

REFERENCES

1. Beller, M., editor. *Energy Systems Studies Programs*, Annual Report. Brookhaven National Laboratory, Upton, New York.
2. Bullard, Clark W., Peter S. Penner, and David A. Pilati. 1976. *Net energy analysis: Handbook for combining process and input-output analysis.* Document 214. Center for Advanced Computation, University of Illinois, Urbana-Champaign.
3. Department of Energy. 1979. *Report of the alcohol fuels policy review.* DOE/PE-12. Washington, D.C.
4. Dovring, Folke. 1979. *Cropland reserve for fuel production.* A report for the Alcohol Biomass Task Study. U.S. Department of Energy, Washington, D.C.
5. Dovring, Folke. 1979. *Energy doubling by year 2000? Critique of a growth perspective.* Congressional Record (December 6, 1977): S19354-S19356.
6. Dovring, Folke. 1980. *Export or burn? American grain and the energy equations.* Illinois Business Review 37(4): 9-12.
7. Green, Maurice B. 1978. *Eating oil: Energy use in food production.* Westview Press, Boulder, Colorado.
8. Griffin, J. M. 1976. *Energy input-output modeling: Problems and prospects.* Center for Energy Systems, General Electric Co., Washington, D.C.
9. Hannon, Bruce, and Horacio Perez Blanco. 1979. *Ethanol and methanol as industrial feedstocks.* Document No. 268. Energy Research Group, University of Illinois, Urbana-Champaign.
10. Lieth, H. 1972. *Modelling the primary productivity of the world.* Nature and Resources 8(2): 5-10.
11. Miller, Dwight L. 1980. *Starch-based fermentation ethyl alcohol.* In Proceedings of the First Inter-American Conference on Renewable Sources of Energy, New Orleans, Louisiana. pp. 152-154.
12. Odum, H. T., and J. Alexander. 1977. *Energy analysis models of the United States.* Florida State University, Gainesville.
13. Penner, Peter S., and Donna Amado. 1977. *Net energy effects and resource depletion: An all-oil economy.* Document No. 231. Center for Advanced Computation, University of Illinois, Urbana-Champaign.
14. Penner, Peter S., Clark W. Bullard, and Donna L. Amado. 1977. *Net energy effects and resource depletion: An all-nuclear economy.* Document No. 238. Center for Advanced Computation, University of Illinois, Urbana-Champaign.
15. Reister, D. B. 1977. *Energy embodied in goods.* Institute for Energy Analysis, Oak Ridge, Tennessee.
16. Spano, Leo, et al. 1980. *Enzymatic hydrolysis of cellulose to fermentable sugar for production of ethanol.* In Proceedings of the First Inter-American Conference on Renewable Sources of Energy. New Orleans, Louisiana.

X. Protecting a Finite Land Base

40

Farmland Retention: Efficiency versus Equity

Richard W. Dunford
Assistant professor
Department of Agricultural Economics
Washington State University, Pullman

In recent decades much of the urban growth in the United States has occurred on nearby agricultural lands. The interstate highway system has contributed significantly to urban sprawl and itself has consumed farmland. In addition to the farmland actually converted to urban uses, a large amount of farmland is often idled prematurely in anticipation of conversion. Hobby farms, large-lot rural homesteads, and recreational parcels have also contributed to the loss of farmland in recent years.

The conversion of agricultural lands to more intensive issues has concerned many people for a variety of reasons.[1] A commonly expressed concern involves the adequacy of our ability to meet future food and fiber requirements, nationally and internationally. In broad terms, this concern is not confined solely to nutritional needs. Increasing demands for local produce, a varied commodity mix, and biomass crops are also involved. Addi-

---

[1]Some authors argue that one's concerns will vary depending upon whether one takes a national, state, or local perspective. See, for example, (*1*) and Colette, W. Arden. 1978. "Preservation of Prime and Unique Agricultural Lands in the Perspective of National Goals and Policies." Paper presented at the American Agricultural Economics Association annual meeting, Blacksburg, Virginia. For the purposes of this paper, the origin of concerns with respect to farmland retention is not particularly important.

tionally, concern has been expressed over the cost and availability of the water and energy resources that will be needed to bring poorer quality farmland into production to meet future demands. Because of the uncertainty of future food needs and the relatively irreversible nature of many farmland conversions, some people have advocated the retention of farmland as insurance against unexpected economic or environmental problems.

Apart from concerns related to food and fiber needs, several other concerns have resulted from the loss of farmland to nonfarm uses. In an isolated geographic area, the widespread conversion of farmland to more intensive uses could lead to the disappearance of local agricultural input and output businesses, resulting in a further loss of farmland. Consequently, farmland conversions have led to a concern about the potential loss of the economic benefits associated with a viable agricultural support industry. Another concern involves the problems that result from residential developments being scattered throughout the farmland surrounding urban centers. One of the most common of these problems is the high public service costs associated with discontiguous urban sprawl. And, finally, some persons (3, 6) are concerned about the losses of open space and environmental amenities that occur as farmland near an urbanizing area is converted to more intensive uses.[2]

These concerns have led many people to advocate and support government intervention in an effort to preserve farmland. From an economic perspective, government (or public) intervention in the farmland market can only be justified (a) to correct or mitigate inefficiencies in the market or (b) to "improve" the allocation resulting from an efficient market. The first justification is known as the efficiency basis for collective action, and the second justification is known as the equity basis for collective action (9).

Rationale for government intervention

Efficiency. If the private market system is to function efficiently, the following requirements must be met: (a) perfect competition in all factor and commodity markets, (b) increasing costs in all industries, (c) no technological external effects, (d) no collective goods, and (e) no market failure due to uncertainty (6, 9, 10).

Perfect competition is the first requirement for private markets to efficiently allocate commodities. Under this requirement, each factor and commodity market must operate freely; no external control of market forces, including governmental intervention, can be present. There must be large numbers of small buyers so that no economic agent can exert any control over the prices of goods and services being exchanged. The commodities being sold must be identical or homogeneous so that buyers are indifferent as to the seller from which they purchase the commodities. All resources and

---

[2]See also: Wood, William W. J. 1979. "Agricultural Land Conversion: An Overview." Paper presented at the National Agricultural Lands Study workshop, Vancouver, Washington.

firms must be perfectly mobile, yielding free entry and exit of firms into and out of industries. And, finally, perfect competition requires perfect knowledge on the part of consumers, producers, and resource owners. This requirement includes complete knowledge of future as well as present conditions (5).

Given these requirements, it is obvious that the theoretical ideal of a perfect market does not exist. Some agricultural markets meet most of the requirements, but the perfect knowledge requirement can never be met. Nevertheless, the theoretical construct of a perfectly competitive market is important for economic analysis. Since no theoretical model can perfectly describe a real-world phenomenon, the abstraction of a perfectly competitive market enhances the generality of economic research. Models based on perfectly competitive markets have also led to fairly accurate explanations and predictions of real-world phenomena. Furthermore, this theoretical construct can be used to analyze the effects of public policies that change the economic incentives facing consumers and producers (5).

The perfect competition requirement for market efficiency implies that as any firm grows larger, "there is some output level at which his costs per unit begin to rise....If increasing costs did not exist, the first producer of a commodity would find that his costs continually fell as he grew larger....In such a situation there would tend to be only one producer of a commodity. By definition, this means the absence of perfect competition" (9).

In order for market prices to efficiently allocate commodities to competing uses, there can be no technological external effects. Also known as spillover effects or externalities, such effects arise if "one agent's decisions directly affect the utility or output of other agents, over and above any indirect effects they may have through their effects on relative prices. If there are such direct effects, the decision maker is not fully charged for any costs his actions impose on other people nor rewarded for any benefits he may confer" (10). In summary, if technological external effects are present, market prices are faulty and not efficient in allocating goods and services.

Private markets do not provide the efficient amount of collective goods. Collective goods can be simultaneously consumed by more than one individual, yet one person's consumption does not diminish the quantity of the good consumed by others (4). Many collective goods also exhibit a lack of excludability, and once they are provided, nobody can be excluded from their use. A lighthouse is the quintessential collective good. Once operable, any boats in proximity to the lighthouse can use its services without diminishing its services for other boats, with no possibility of exclusion. As explained by Gardner (6), the market will not supply the optimal amount of a collective good because the efficient supply price for such goods is zero.

The final requirement for the efficient allocation of commodities by the private market involves the absence of any market failure associated with uncertainty. Basically, uncertainty stems from a violation of the perfect knowledge criterion for perfect competition. However, market failures associated with uncertainty are considered separately because it is possible for a free-market allocation to be efficient despite uncertainty (*10*). In general, if any one of the five requirements noted in this section are not met, the free market will not efficiently allocate commodities among competing uses. (The presence of inefficiencies in the private market, however, does not necessarily mean that public intervention will result in improvement. This will be dealt with in the concluding section.)

Equity.   As indicated previously, "The economic welfare of society depends upon satisfying efficiency conditions and meeting social goals with respect to the distribution of goods and services among individuals" (*4*).

Society may thus reject the distribution of commodities resulting from the operation of efficient markets. This justification is based upon ethical judgments rather than market failure. Markets are particularly suited to allocating large quantities of goods and services among large numbers of consumers and producers. However, the ultimate allocation of these goods and services depends upon the underlying distribution of income. An efficient allocation of commodities based upon ability to pay therefore may not produce a result that coincides with social objectives.

"It can be shown that under certain conditions moving from an efficient to an inefficient allocation may be socially preferable on the basis of society's distributive preferences" (*4*). Of course, distributional preferences and perceived equity generally vary from individual to individual. So agreement on social goals and what constitutes an improvement of equity can be difficult to obtain. Nevertheless, the "equity motivation for governmental action is fully as potent in rationalizing governmental action as the pure efficiency arguments. Some would argue that as our society grows more affluent and can afford more inefficiency and waste, the equity rationale will (and should) become even more prominent" (*9*).

At this point, it is appropriate to ask: Why is it important to determine whether social intervention is being justified on the basis of efficiency or equity? The distinction is important because the former justification signifies a technical breakdown in the operation of the market system, while the latter justification is based on value judgments and social goals. The efficiency basis of collective action is more objective, while the equity basis of collective action is more subjective. For a given distribution of income, improvements in the efficiency of resource allocation results in unambiguous improvements in net social benefits. Alternatively, whether a change in the distribution of income is an improvement in equity is a matter of distributive preferences and social goals, which usually vary among members of society. By separating efficiency and equity justifications, it is hoped that the issues with respect to farmland retention will be clarified.

Farmland and the farmland market

Farmland (and land in general) is a unique commodity. It is immovable, nonreproducible, unstandardized, and heterogeneous (*7*). Farmland yields two distinct types of services (*12*). First, it provides a service as simply space. Its location, topography, and climate are a unique aspect of its service as space. "This service flow is indestructible, unchangeable over time, and independent of the actual economic activity to which the land is allocated" (*12*).

Second, farmland provides a flow of production/consumption services that vary among and within various uses of a parcel. The nature of productive/consumptive service flows available from farmland in the future are often altered by changes in use, for example, changes from agricultural to urban use. Furthermore, productive/consumptive service flows may be depleted in future periods by current consumption within certain types of land use. For example, farming techniques that lead to soil erosion may reduce future yields on farmland. And, finally, some tracts of farmland are more dependent upon interactions with other resources like water and energy for crop production than are other tracts of farmland.[3] Climate, topography, and soil characteristics are the primary determinants of the dependency on these other resources. Farmland with a low dependency on interactions with water and energy resources is referred to as prime farmland.

The market for farmland also exhibits some unique characteristics that bear examination.[4] Although there are many potential buyers and sellers of farmland, most people are infrequent market participants. The uses of the farmland being exchanged are often subject to regulatory policies involving building criteria, sanitation, and other environmental factors. The property is subject to *ad valorem* taxation, capital gains taxes, inheritance taxes, and the income from productive uses of the property is taxed. On the other hand, agricultural support policies subsidize various farm uses of agricultural land. The actual exchange of farmland must conform with various transfer and sale policies involving the filing of legal documents, procedural matters, and the payment of excise taxes. Special conditions, such as those concerning deed restrictions, easements, minimum lot sizes, and setback requirements, often restrict the use of rural real estate. Moreover, some public policies actually encourage or create incentives for certain types of land use. For example, Internal Revenue Service provisions have encouraged the acquisition of farmland as an investment (*6*). Alternatively, Raup (*13*) outlined a myriad of public policies that have directly or indirectly stimulated urban sprawl. These policies include the methods used to finance highways, housing, and public services; the promotion of fragmentary local governments; and the structure of the property tax system.

Farmland as a commodity and farmland markets fall far short of the requirements for perfect competition. Specifically, the heterogeneity of farmland and the numerous public policies that influence the use of farmland

---

[3]Ibid.

[4]For an institutional view of the land market see: Mulkey, David. 1978. "Agricultural Land Preservation: Understanding the Policy Issues." Paper presented at the American Agricultural Economics Association meeting, Blacksburg, Virginia.

violate the homogeneous product and free-market criteria. Regarding the impact of existing public policies, Wood[5] poses the following question: Is the land market allocation system inefficient or is the market not allowed to allocate land efficiently due to the pervasive effects of existing public policies? Social intervention may be necessary to correct market inefficiencies brought about by existing public policies.

Economic analysis of farmland retention concerns

Food and fiber. From the broadest perspective, the impact of the conversion of agricultural land on the production of food and fiber takes many forms. The most basic concern is focused on whether the farmland base will be adequate to meet the nutritional requirements of a growing population. Recent U.S. Department of Agriculture studies (*8*) indicate that the U.S. agricultural land base is more than adequate to meet domestic needs. But what would happen if there were a shortage? As Gardner (*6*) pointed out, the food and fiber sectors are relatively competitive. Any food and fiber shortages will rapidly raise market prices. Producers will respond by expanding their use of other inputs, like fertilizer and machinery, on the available farmland to increase yields, and/or they may convert previously unfarmed land into productive farmland through drainage, clearing, terracing, or the application of water. In general, the greater the demand facing producers, the greater the profitability of food and fiber production and the more competitive agriculture is with other land uses in acquiring and retaining farmland (*6*). (To the extent that existing public policies prevent this anticipated response to rising food and fiber costs inefficiencies may occur, however.)

The same reasoning can be applied to concerns involving the increasing demands for local produce, a varied commodity mix, and biomass energy crops. As preferences become stronger for locally grown produce or specialty crops, prices rise, which in turn elicits the progression of events just described. Similarly, a dramatic increase in the demand for biomass energy crops would boost food and fiber prices, which would eventually enhance the value of farmland for farming relative to other uses of the farmland.

Supply of food and fiber will meet demand for food and fiber. The only unknown involves prices, the real concern that underlies the conditions just discussed. Will we have sufficient food and fiber supplies to meet our nutritional needs at reasonable prices? Can we meet the increasing demand for local produce and specialty crops at reasonable prices? Since food and fiber are among our most basic needs, for poor and rich people alike, society has advocated a "cheap food" policy. Price—not quantity—is the real issue. Therefore, these concerns involve equity not efficiency.

Given certain assumptions regarding population growth, relative prices, and income levels, researchers can estimate the future demand for food and fiber. Similarly, the future supply of food and fiber can be approximated

---

[5]Wood, "Agricultural Land Conversion." p. 1.

for various scenarios involving farmland conversion trends, input prices, rates of technological change, and environmental parameters. With information on anticipated demand and supply, future food and fiber prices can be estimated. However, researchers cannot determine what prices are reasonable. This must be a social judgment. If society determines that future food and fiber prices are projected to be too high, farmland retention policies can be examined as a way of controlling future food and fiber prices.

Gardner (6) noted that there are some technological externalities associated with food and fiber production. The application of chemicals to farmland does lead to some environmental quality problems. Prime agricultural land generally uses fewer chemicals and produces less sediment runoff and erosion than nonprime agricultural land, but the market value of prime land will not "fully reflect the social benefits of generating lower environmental costs" (7). If environmental quality considerations become more important in the future, prime land will be even further underpriced relative to nonprime land. The retention and use of more prime farmland versus nonprime farmland to produce a given quantity of food and fiber would lower external environmental costs and improve efficiency.

Two food and fiber concerns must still be addressed: concerns about our ability to feed starving people in other nations and the future cost and availability of the water and energy resources needed to maintain or increase food and fiber production. First, the goal of trying to help feed the starving people in other countries is clearly tied to humanitarian considerations. Because of their lack of ability to pay, these deprived people cannot enter the marketplace as normal consumers. Nevertheless, their needs are real and compelling. The issue thus is one of equity. Even if the future farmland base is sufficient to meet domestic needs for food and fiber at "reasonable" prices, the needs of other countries might increase demand enough to raise prices significantly. Of course, the amount of food and fiber this country provides to other nations is a matter of social choice.

The final food and fiber issue involves the future cost and availability of water and energy resources. Food and fiber production requires the interaction of land and other resources. Water is a crucial input in most of the West and in other scattered areas in the United States. Energy resources are used to make farm chemicals, power farm machinery, move water, and get crops to consumers. Insofar as water and energy resources become more scarce, an upward pressure on food and fiber prices will occur. The equity implications of this price rise have already been highlighted. The retention of farmland would allow the substitution of land for these increasingly scarce resources, thereby dampening food and fiber price increases.

Apart from the equity issue, the use of water and energy resources in food and fiber production gives rise to a technological externality. Irrigation water, particularly in the West, is usually provided to farmers at less than its full social cost. The prices of many energy resources, particularly petroleum, have been kept artificially low through various regulations and tax policies. In both cases producers tend to use more of these inputs than they would if charged the full social cost. Efficiency thus would be improved by altering the public policies that create underpriced water and energy resources. The farmland requiring the fewest of these resources for production—prime farmland—would rise in value, enhancing its value for farming as opposed to its value for competing uses. Of course, the effect on food and fiber prices could still violate the social goal of keeping these prices low.

Irreversibility and uncertainty. Nothing has yet been mentioned about the uncertainty associated with forecasting future demand and supply. It was assumed that any anticipated or unanticipated future shortages could be offset by intensifying production on existing farmland and/or by bringing idle or poorer quality lands into production. This assumption may not be very realistic for major changes in economic or environmental parameters. The importance of this uncertainty is magnified by the relative irreversibility of the conversion of agricultural land to urban uses. While urban land uses can theoretically be returned to agricultural uses, "the capital and reclamation costs are so high as to make this reversal effectively unfeasible" (*12*).

While the current rate of conversion of farmland may be appropriate, considering present conditions and anticipated future conditions, unexpected environmental problems, for example, may require more farmland than what is available. Thus, a type of intertemporal technological externality is involved (*12*). The allocation of land uses in the present generation directly affects the utility or output of the future generation, and the present generation is not fully charged for any costs imposed on the future generation in the way of foregone benefits. In summary, uncertainty and the effective irreversibility of land use conversions result jointly in a market failure—an efficiency problem.

Ciriacy-Wantrup (*2*) has argued that the interaction of uncertainty and irreversibility necessitate a reformulation of the objectives of land policy. Rather than trying to maximize the gains associated with the most efficient allocation of land use, society should strive for an allocation of land use that minimizes the future chances of maximum possible losses possibly resulting from unexpected economic or environmental problems. This policy objective of trying to avoid maximum possible future losses is known as the "safe minimum standard." Ciriacy-Wantrup has argued that the safe minimum standard is a valid and relevant policy objective when the costs of such a policy are low relative to the greatest possible losses.

As an example of the type of environmental or economic problems that could lead to maximum possible losses, Wood[6] has noted the uncertainty of future climatic trends:

"Either cooling or heating on a global basis can shift significantly the amount of arable land available for certain commodities. However, our informational base is very limited. Not only do we not know what actual

---

[6]Ibid. p. 7.

trend in global weather to expect, we do not know to what extent resources may potentially substitute for each other in commodity production."

Maintenance of viable agricultural industry. From a local, short-run perspective, the number of acres in cultivation is closely related to the use of agricultural inputs and the quantity of agricultural outputs. "Farm processors, farm suppliers, transporters, financial firms, university professors in agricultural fields, and government agency personnel have obvious stakes in a viable and stable industry" (6). As farmland is converted to more intensive uses, these interrelated economic activities will decline. However, these effects are primarily pecuniary—they arise as the market adjusts to changing conditions. There is no market failure in this chain of events. [As the farmland base shrinks, some excess capacity and underemployment may result in related businesses that have some indivisible inputs. Thus, some inefficiencies may be present in the process of transition (4).]

It has been argued that once farmland conversions proceed beyond a certain point in isolated geographic areas, agriculturally related businesses may go bankrupt. The closure of these businesses may force many remaining farmers to quit farming. From an equity standpoint, society may want to stabilize the farmland base so that farmers who want to farm may continue to do so. This is strictly a matter of equity, however, not one of efficiency.

It should be noted further that a diversified economy may be maintained by fostering a viable agricultural industry through a farmland retention program. The resulting collective good might be the security and stability associated with knowing that a downturn in one sector of the national economy (like automobile manufacturing) will not seriously disrupt the diversified local economy. This argument is rather tenuous, however.

Managing urban growth. Scattered or leapfrog developments are common near many urban areas. For a given increase in population, this pattern of development results in much greater public service costs than a more compact, contiguous pattern of growth. The extra costs of providing public services to a distant subdivision as opposed to a close-in subdivision are not a problem per se. The residents in the distant subdivision may realize benefits from "country living" that exceed the additional public service costs. The problem is that residents of the distant subdivision do not pay the full costs of the public services they receive. The additional costs of the public services for the distant subdivision are shared by all users of the public services. If the full costs of providing the public services were charged to distant subdivisions, fewer distant subdivisions would be built, or at least the subdivisions might not be so distant. As Ervin and associates (4) noted, "Inefficiencies are likely to be associated with a pricing system which divorces payment by the beneficiary from the costs of providing the service."

In summary, there is a clear technological externality attributable to the pricing of public services for new developments, resulting in too much urban sprawl. A farmland retention policy does not necessarily eliminate this market failure, however. As Gardner (6) explained, if development on farmland is restricted, it will occur on other parcels:

"Whether the result is a more or less efficient urban development is far from clear, however. It depends on where these parcels are, how efficient they are in producing urban amenities, what the costs are of bringing public utilities and transport to these parcels, etc. It is not obvious in principle that urban 'leapfrogging' will be reduced over what the free market would have produced."

It would seem more efficient to modify public service pricing policies to eliminate the subsidy for urban sprawl or to use a growth management policy to accommodate future development efficiently and orderly.

Apart from problems with the pricing of public services, urban sprawl creates other efficiency problems. For example, land uses on adjoining parcels often impose technological externalities on one another. These effects are commonly referred to as nuisance problems. Adjacent urban and farmland uses often result in nuisance problems. The spraying of chemicals, odors from manure, dust, night harvesting, etc., impose an uncompensated, external cost on an adjacent subdivision. Conversely, vandalism and trespassing impose an uncompensated, external cost on the farmer. These nuisance problems could be eliminated or at least minimized by restricting development in farming areas.

As urban sprawl proceeds, many farmers in the rural-urban fringe form an expectation of eventually selling their land to a developer at a price above the agricultural value of the parcel. These farmers typically do not make investments that would maintain their competitiveness and increase productivity. Hence, efficiency suffers.

"Chances for future development, no matter how remote, can affect the farmer's willingness to invest in the business. Far more land is affected by the possibility of development than can actually ever be used. The [frequent] result is that much land is prematurely pulled out of farming by unspecified development potential when land allocation relies entirely on a land market replete with misinformation" (11). Uncertainty or a lack of perfect information is the source of this market failure.

Urban sprawl sometimes progresses to the point where farmland is confined to relatively small, discontiguous parcels scattered throughout the urban fringe. As Gibson (7) noted, "Fragmented parcels of land may not be as productive as land in which ownership is not fragmented," other things being equal. Even if farmers are willing to invest in new capital, the parcel may be so small that farming is inefficient. This is an example of a technological externality that the pattern of development imposes on remaining farmland.

Open space amenities. Farmland used for agriculture in proximity to urban areas provides open space and other environmental amenities. These amenities clearly meet the criteria for collective goods. A technological externality is also involved. Take, for example, a large wheat field surrounded by subdivisions. The aesthetics of this open space can be consumed simultaneously by many people without any one individual's consumption diminishing consumption by others. Thus, the aesthetic benefits provided by the wheat field are a type of collective good. Additionally, the benefits provided by this open space to the subdivision residents cannot be captured by the owner of the wheat field. The wheat field imposes a technological external benefit on the neighboring subdivisions. Because of the presence of these two types of market failure, "the market will not provide the optimal quantity of these amenities" (6).

Two caveats need to be introduced at this point. First, open space only has value when it is a scarce commodity. The amenity value of open space "would be much higher in Los Angeles County in California than in central Wyoming" (6). Farmland retention as a means of providing open space could clearly be supported on efficiency grounds in the former case, but this support would be more tenuous in the latter case. Second, open space amenities are not necessarily correlated positively with the acreage of prime farmland.

"Commercial agriculture is becoming less attractive esthetically; hence, noncommercial agriculture provides more benefit to the nonfarm public in terms of esthetic values than does commercial agriculture" (7). Thus, it is not clear that retaining farmland—particularly prime farmland—is the best way of correcting the misallocation of open space and other environmental amenities on the rural-urban fringe.

Conclusions and policy implications

The controversy concerning the justification for social intervention in the land market is multidimensional and quite complex. Prior to analyzing concerns involving farmland retention policies, it was noted that the efficient operation of the land market may be precluded by the effect of existing public policies on the exchange, ownership, use, and value of farmland. The analysis of some of the concerns also supported the contention that "many of the factors responsible for the divergence between the private and socially optimal rates of land conversion are policy variables" (4). Thus, it should be possible to correct some of the inefficiencies in the land market by modifying or amending existing policies. For example, public service pricing policies could be changed to eliminate the subsidization of urban sprawl.

Market failures are associated with technological externalities, collective goods, and uncertainty in the farmland market. However, efficiency problems do not necessarily mean that social intervention will result in an improvement. Social intervention on efficiency grounds is only justified when the social benefits of correcting the efficiency problems exceed the costs of governmental intervention.

The costs of farmland retention programs are comprised of two components: opportunity costs and administrative costs. The opportunity-cost component equals the social benefit foregone by keeping the land in farming rather than allowing the farmland to be converted to an alternative use. The administrative-cost component equals the governmental cost of implementing the particular farmland retention program. In conclusion, the effectiveness of various farmland retention policies for correcting efficiency problems must be compared with the costs of implementing these policies.

As discussed previously, society may reject the distribution of commodities resulting from the operation of efficient markets on the basis of equity. Despite the subjective nature of society's distributive preferences and goals, this rationalization of social intervention is as strong as the efficiency justification. Most of the food and fiber concerns with respect to farmland conversion trends have an equity foundation—the promotion of a cheap food policy. If the collective will of society dictates such a goal, then farmland retention policies can be examined as one approach toward reaching this goal.

Despite the importance of societal preferences in equity matters, researchers have an important role to play. They need to provide the information necessary for members of society to make informed choices. Supply and demand models need to be formulated so that future prices can be estimated. Only then can society decide if future prices will be "too high." It should also be remembered that "public policies tend always to redistribute who gains and who loses."[7] Thus, society needs to be aware of the equity implications of social intervention.

As a final point, one misconception must be exposed. Many people have assumed that social intervention implies the complete abandonment of the land market for some government-directed, nonmarket alternative. Obviously, markets are particularly suited to coordinating and communicating information from a large number of people about the relative value of various competing uses of a commodity. Markets should not be abandoned. Rather "policy efforts should concentrate on institutional changes to alter market outcomes to be more in line with the goals of society without destroying the unique abilities of the market system to handle the day-to-day allocation of resources."[8] In other words, the challenge is to devise public policies that alter economic incentives in the market in such a way that improvements in efficiency and/or equity can be realized.

---

[7]Ibid. p. 8.

[8]Mulkey, "Agricultural Land Preservation." p. 10.

REFERENCES

1. Anderson, William D., Gregory C. Gustafson, and Robert F Boxley. 1975. *Perspectives on agricultural land policy.* Journal of Soil and Water Conservation 30(1): 36-43.
2. Ciriacy-Wantrup, S. V. 1964. *The "new" competition for land and some implications for public policy.* Natural Resources Journal 4(2): 252-267.
3. Dunford, Richard W. 1980. *A survey of property tax relief programs for the retention of agricultural and open space lands.* Gonzaga Law Review 15(3): 675-699.
4. Ervin, David E., James B. Fitch, R. Kenneth Godwin, W. Bruce Shepard, and Herbert H. Stoevener. 1977. *Land use control: Evaluating economic and political effects.* Ballinger Publishing Company, Cambridge, Massachusetts.

5. Ferguson, C. E., and S. Charles Maurice. 1978. *Economic analysis: Theory and application* (third edition). Richard D. Irwin, Inc., Homewood, Illinois.
6. Gardner, B. Delworth. 1977. *The economics of agricultural land preservation.* American Journal of Agricultural Economics 59(5): 1,027-1,036.
7. Gibson, James A. 1977. *On the allocation of prime agricultural land.* Journal of Soil and Water Conservation 32(6): 271-275.
8. Gustafson, Gregory C. 1979. *Land use policy and farmland retention: The United States experience.* Working Paper No. 28. Economic Research Service, U.S. Department of Agriculture, Corvallis, Oregon.
9. Haveman, Robert H. 1976. *The economics of the public sector* (second edition). John Wiley and Sons, New York, New York.
10. Layard, P.R.G., and A. A. Walters. 1978. *Microeconomic theory.* McGraw-Hill, New York, New York.
11. Libby, Lawrence W. 1974. *Land use policy: Implications for commercial agriculture.* American Journal of Agricultural Economics 56(5): 1,143-1,152.
12. McInerney, John. 1976. *The simple analytics of natural resource economics.* Journal of Agricultural Economics 27(1): 31-52.
13. Raup, Philip M. 1975. *Urban threats to rural lands: Background and beginnings.* Staff Paper P74-23. Department of Agriculture and Applied Economics, University of Minnesota, St. Paul. pp. 4-9.

41

Open Space Protection Through Land Use Controls: A Review of Methods with California Examples

Robert A. Johnston[1]
Associate Professor, Division of Environmental Studies
University of California, Davis

Recent, widespread concern about the protection of open space has resulted in many proposals for preserving land from development. Land protection proposals include such measures as tax incentives, restrictive zoning, government purchase, and nonprovision of utilities. Because of the variety of resource types requiring protection, the various state tax and land use statutes and court decisions, and the differing political climates across the United States, there is a lack of consensus about which mechanisms to use to prevent urbanization of productive lands.

The University of California, Davis, undertook a comprehensive study (*3*) to identify open space protection devices and their applicability to various natural resource problem areas, including agriculture, forestry, watershed management (steep slopes, riparian areas), floodplain management, water recreation, and sewage system efficiency. The unique study examined such protective measures as taxation devices and urban service policies as well as regulatory and purchase schemes. Moreover, the research went beyond a determination of these measures' effectiveness in various resource management situations to estimate the legal and political feasibility of adopting each of the mechanisms.

[1]The author's research on which this chapter is based was funded by the University of California Water Resources Center, project UCAL-WRC-W-487.

In all, we examined 17 specific land protection devices, some of which have never been tried. After identifying the measures, we examined the basic legal differences among them. Then we looked at the types of resource management problems to which the various protection devices apply. Finally, we evaluated the effectiveness of the measures and their legal and political feasibility.

A review of preservation methods

Compensable land use controls. The first group of measures are the compensable land use controls under which landowners are paid for restrictions imposed upon them. Full-fee acquisition involves the acquisition of full title to a parcel through voluntary sale or condemnation. Local and state bodies are limited in the purposes for which they can buy lands and are quite restricted in the reasons for which they can condemn lands. Although full-fee acquisition is expensive, costs can be reduced through leasing or resale of the lands with conditions on use.

Less-than-fee acquisition attempts to reduce costs by purchasing only the development rights to a parcel or securing limited occupancy rights for recreation in certain areas or seasons. This measure is expensive, too.

Compensable zoning has never been tried. This plan would down-zone a parcel to lower value uses than presently permitted and pay the owner the difference in land value. This also is a costly alternative.

Transfer of development rights (TDR) is a recently proposed device whereby lands are down-zoned in a preserve area, and the owners are given coupons—development rights—for the number of unbuilt dwellings no longer permitted on their parcels. A nearby area, suitable for development, is up-zoned to higher densities than before, but owners in this area may build the extra units only if they possess the necessary number of coupons. So the down-zoned people sell their coupons to the up-zoned people. This scheme compensates the "losers" by letting them sell their lost development rights. The device is legally uncertain and inflexible in the way that nonexistent development rights are created.

All four compensable controls are generally designed to get around the political problems of straight down-zoning, an unpopular device in the past.

Zoning mechanisms. There are various zoning mechanisms that restrict development but do not compensate the landowner. In interim zoning, which is permitted in most states, local governments may adopt a development moratorium or low-density zoning so as to study a particular area. Interim zoning is useful when resource conflicts are severe and development imminent. Most state courts permit total denial of development for short periods if good cause is shown.

In conditional or contract zoning, which also has been used throughout the United States, local governments agree to permit certain uses and landowners agree to certain restrictions. Zoning contracts are legally fuzzy and appear to be nonbinding on subsequent local legislatures. Therefore, they are risky for developers.

Cluster zoning, or planned unit development (PUD) zoning, permits the landowner to depart from traditional lot-and-block development and place dwellings on very small parcels, often with shared parking areas. The open spaces and parking lots are owned in common. Cluster development, which is now widely used, reduces development and service costs and provides small open spaces.

Phased zoning is also coming into common use in developing jurisdictons. Instead of zoning the entire city for its eventual land use pattern, only lands needed for development in the next few years are zoned for urban uses. The lands beyond the urban boundary are kept in low-density zones to prevent leapfrog development. Phased zoning reduces public service costs, protects resource lands, and reduces private transport costs, air pollution, and energy consumption.

Agricultural and resource zoning is widely used to keep resource lands in production. Generally, state courts permit widespread use of resource zoning, which permits only one dwelling per 80 or 160 acres or more, as long as the lands are economically viable for forestry or farming.

Public health and safety zoning can be used only when a definite threat to health or safety can be shown, as in a floodplain. Many state courts will allow complete deprivation of use in these situations. It is yet to be seen how far courts will go in permitting open space zoning based on preventing less direct threats to health, such as soil erosion from steep lands or air pollution from remote developments.

Subdivision controls are similar to zoning, but instead of regulating development densities they regulate the parceling and improvement processes. Subdivision regulations usually permit great flexibility on the part of the local government staff, which deals with developers on a case-by-case basis. Because many state courts hold that there is no right to subdivide, this is a powerful mechanism for protecting open space. Subdivision gives local governments the power to require open space dedications, certain grading practices, and cluster development.

Nonprovision of utilities. The third major category of devices, nonprovision of utilities, is similar to zoning in many ways. Many local governments recently have adopted phased sewer policies, often in conjunction with phased zoning to prevent sprawl and reduce service costs. Although private utilities (generally water companies) must seek increased supplies and cannot deny service in California, cities and counties may refuse sewer service to certain parcels and need not seek expanded capacity. Laws vary from state to state, but generally local governments may provide services in a manner that supports their general plan.

Tax measures. While the preceding zoning and servicing devices are site-specific, affecting certain parcels with their restrictions, the following taxation devices apply to whole states, counties, or parts of counties. Therefore, they are a less direct form of land use control. In general, local government taxation authority is limited, and most of these tax measures require state operation or state-enabling legislation. Because landowners respond to tax measures in a variety of ways, it is difficult to estimate landowner responses to these devices.

The realty transfer tax has been suggested as a way to reduce speculation and turnover of lands at the urban fringe. It is imprecise because it taxes total land value. To raise revenue, several states have transfer taxes at very low rates.

The capital gains realty tax is applied to the capital gain at time of sale and is intended to reduce speculative land holding. Vermont's tax is higher for shorter holding times to reduce turnover and land value increases. The tax bite is offset by the federal deduction permitted for state and local taxes, however. This measure is unselective, weak at the rates used, and extremely unpopular.

A land value increment tax has never been tried in the United States. This tax, applied at time of sale, is levied on the increase in land value due to development in the area or to government investment nearby. It is intended to reduce windfall profit accruing to landowners from such projects as freeways and dams built near their properties. It was tried twice in England, but not for long enough to see how it worked. Not only is the method legally difficult, it would be very unpopular as well.

Site value taxation is an idea popularized by Henry George. This plan taxes land only, not improvements. The idea is to create more centralized development in urban areas and cause less vacant urban land and less sprawl. Our economic analysis shows that site value taxation could be counterproductive, causing sprawl at the urban fringe. The administration would be complex. State constitutional amendments would be needed.

Preferential taxation is used in many states. After signing a contract preventing development of resource lands for a certain period of years, a landowner is assessed at a lower value, usually as a proportion of the use value of the particular parcel involved. Generally, landowners can break the contract if the back tax difference or some proportion of it is paid. These programs are generally voluntary for the landowners and so are not very effective.

Legal distinctions

As a way of analyzing land preservation measures, let us outline some of the basic legal distinctions among them. If wishing to occupy the lands, subdivision controls (to require a dedication of open space to the city or county), full-fee acquisition, or less-than-fee acquisition (with limited occupancy rights) must be used.

To control the location of uses, rather than changing the permitted uses, cluster zoning and agricultural and resource zoning or public health and safety zoning on part of a parcel may be applied.

Land uses can be changed directly or indirectly. The tax measures all control land uses indirectly. Direct control of land uses can be accomplished temporarily through phased zoning and interim zoning.

Landowners affected by direct and permanent controls over land use can be compensated with compensable zoning and TDR or not compensated. If not compensated, agricultural and resource zoning must leave some "reasonable" use. Preferential taxation can help here. Only public health and safety zoning can be used if no use of the land is permitted, and only if persuasive studies document the need for such zoning.

Application to resource problems

Another useful way to analyze land protection measures is to place them where they fit in the landscape (Figure 1). On steep slopes, public health and safety zoning prevents development on hazardous lands; agricultural and resource zoning protects grazing lands and watershed lands; and cluster zoning and subdivision controls keep developments off steep areas within certain parcels.

Urban sprawl could be reduced indirectly with tax measures, temporarily with phased and interim zoning, and permanently through agricultural and resource zoning and nonprovision of utilities.

To keep development away from riparian areas, planners could use cluster zoning and subdivision controls, agricultural and resource zoning on parts of parcels, and perhaps public health and safety zoning for whole parcels.

Water recreation could be accomplished through subdivision controls where small open space areas are exacted from the developer of a large parcel. Otherwise, full-fee and less-than-fee acquisition must be used.

Our last case, floodplain protection, can be accomplished through the expensive acquisition schemes or public health and safety zoning.

Evaluation of land protection methods

Because laws vary from state to state, we restricted our legal analysis to California. However, we do have knowledge of the laws in most other states (1). For our political feasibility analysis we used all available published case studies, the theoretical literature, and personal experience. We also performed four case studies.

In the study we quickly assessed all of the land protection measures and then evaluated the six most promising mechanisms in more detail. We studied the economics of each measure, which permitted us to estimate generally the impacts of the measures on various interest groups, such as owners of vacant land and farmers. Then we estimated the political feasibility of adopting each measure (from the predicted responses and importance of the groups). In the final analysis we estimated the effectiveness of each

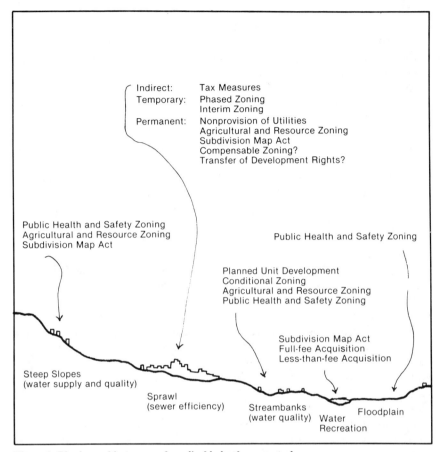

Indirect: Tax Measures
Temporary: Phased Zoning
Interim Zoning
Permanent: Nonprovision of Utilities
Agricultural and Resource Zoning
Subdivision Map Act
Compensable Zoning?
Transfer of Development Rights?

Public Health and Safety Zoning
Agricultural and Resource Zoning
Subdivision Map Act

Public Health and Safety Zoning

Planned Unit Development
Conditional Zoning
Agricultural and Resource Zoning
Public Health and Safety Zoning

Subdivision Map Act
Full-fee Acquisition
Less-than-fee Acquisition

Steep Slopes
(water supply and quality)

Sprawl
(sewer efficiency)

Streambanks
(water quality)

Water
Recreation

Floodplain

Figure 1. Physiographic types and applicable land use controls.

measure in terms of its usefulness in resource management and its political, legal, and administrative feasibility.

Our results are indicative. For political or legal reasons they will not apply in many areas. We do believe that our results are generally useful for resource managers and land use planners, however, and that our evaluation procedure can be used by others to reach conclusions about their own areas.

The acquisition methods are too expensive to be used, except for certain parcels of special importance. We feel that compensable zoning and TDR are legally difficult, potentially expensive, and inflexible because they create rights to development.

The capital gains and realty transfer taxation devices are indirect in their effects and weak. A land value increment tax might reduce speculation but is politically impossible. The site value tax is unwieldy to administer, politically improbable, and probably counterproductive in its effects on sprawl.

Being voluntary, preferential taxation appears to be ineffective in California. Without agricultural and resource zoning to first protect the valuable lands, preferential taxation becomes merely a tax break for farmers.

Interim zoning is valuable as a temporary device to stop development while studying resource problems. Cluster zoning is useful for protecting small land areas, on steep slopes or near streams, for example. Phased zoning is useful for reducing sprawl and temporarily protecting open space near cities. All of these forms of zoning are generally accepted and are being used more frequently.

Agricultural and resource zoning involves potentially by far the largest land areas in all but the most highly urbanized counties. The device is effective and legal, and its political feasibility is moderate, variable, and increasing. Public health and safety zoning is legal in many states and untested in many others. Although it is effective, the method's political feasibility is low, variable, and increasing. As the public becomes aware of the social costs of land mismanagement, the political feasibility of both of these types of zoning will increase.

Nonprovision of utilities is legal in some states and untested in many others. It is effective and becoming politically acceptable.

To summarize, phased zoning and nonprovision of utilities are the best bet at the urban fringe to keep development compact and to temporarily protect resource lands. For rural lands, agricultural and resource zoning is effective, with preferential taxation to increase political feasibility. For hazardous lands, public health and safety zoning will be used increasingly. Our results, of course, coincide with actual trends. Phased zoning and exclusive agricultural zoning are steadily gaining acceptance all over the United States.

Because of the effectiveness of these devices—phased zoning/nonprovision of utilities for growth management at the urban edge and agricultural and resource zoning/preferential taxation in rural areas—we studied them further, hoping to gain insight into the politics of their adoption.

Case studies of open space protection measures

In the early 1970s many California counties adopted agricultural zoning accompanied by preferential taxation and nonprovision of utilities for their open space areas. Phased zoning was adopted for land on the urban fringe. Because of the effectiveness of these protection devices, we will briefly examine the politics leading to their adoption (2).

Marin County water supply restriction.   Marin County, immediately north of San Francisco, is a stunningly beautiful region of wooded hills facing the Pacific to the west and San Francisco Bay to the east and south. Its population was about 290,000 in 1970. The southern and eastern portions of the county are urbanized along the U.S. Highway 101 corridor. The northern half of the county is largely grazing land for dairies.

In 1971 the directors of the county's largest water agency, the Marin Municipal Water District, sought state legislation to permit them to commit $22 million to an intercounty aqueduct without a vote of the people. Citizen groups and the county supervisors strongly denounced this action because a year earlier the water board had publicly promised to submit all aqueduct bonds to votes. The bill was withdrawn.

Later the same year, the water board put a bond issue for $35 million to a vote. It was defeated 31,708 to 3,732. The cost—$35 million plus interest—was one reason. Many people believed the cost would be much higher. Second, the credibility of the district board was poor. Third, opponents said that alternative means of supply should be examined, such as recycling, reclamation, and development of local watersheds. Fourth, because the area's growth was constrained by lack of water supplies, the aqueduct would have allowed the water district's population to grow from 166,000 to 355,000. In the opinion of the district manager at the time, the growth issue was the most important.

In the following two years three conservationists were elected to the board by campaigning for explicit growth limitation. Marin County experienced a dry year in 1972. Fearing water shortages, the new board placed a moratorium on new water line extensions, effectively stopping all major new projects. The water district board was displeased by the lack of growth rate controls in the county and decided to put some "teeth" into the county general plan. The county supervisors, after heated exchanges with the water board, requested that the water district build aqueduct facilities sufficient for the 1990 population projected in the county general plan, in effect, requesting a scaled-down intercounty aqueduct. Although a majority of the water district board felt that breaking the project into stages was not completely honest to the voters, it placed a $7.5 million measure on the ballot, which was to be followed a few months later with another bond vote. The board also declared that this pipeline must be large enough to carry the full supply of water turned down in 1971. Subsequent votes were to have decided the issue of adding pumps. To further tie the aqueduct bond vote to county growth control in general, the board announced that it would lift the hookup moratorium if the measure passed. Finally, the board refused to endorse its own bond proposal.

In an effort to stem the pro-growth control vote, the county supervisors circulated a draft growth control ordinance that would allocate building permits in the various portions of the county. The supervisors endorsed the bond measure, as did the building industry and real estate interests. The proponent groups basically argued that the bond was needed to serve existing residents and so avoid rationing.

Opposition came from the many environmental organizations in Marin County. They argued that water must be limited until the county supervisors enforced the county general plan adopted in 1972 that supposedly limited growth to 2 percent per year. Opponents also maintained that the water board could go around the voters with rate increases and augment the water supply beyond that authorized by the bond after the full-sized aqueduct was built. Taxpayer groups also opposed the bond issue.

The 1973 bond issue lost 30,905 to 16,932, mainly because of the desires of the voters to protect open space and limit taxes. In Marin County there is a strong desire to protect the scenic hills from further development. Many feared that once the aqueduct was built the water agency would increase supplies without referenda.

Sacramento County urban limit line. Sacramento County lies in the heart of the Central Valley of California. With a population of 634,000 in 1970, the county consists of rich agricultural lands in the western half and rolling hills to the east. About half the population lives in Sacramento, the capitol of the state, and the rest of the population resides in adjacent unincorporated areas. The urbanizing area is surrounded by prime agricultural lands on the north and south.

During the 1950s, the county's population grew at an average rate of 6 percent per year. In the 1960s the rate slowed to 2½ percent. In this 20-year period much prime agricultural land was urbanized. The county permitted a large amount of noncontiguous development, and service problems due to the low densities began to worsen in outlying areas by the late 1950s. Then, in 1968, a supervisor was elected on a growth management/rational planning platform.

In late 1970, census figures for Sacramento County showed that recent population growth was considerably slower than had been expected. However, the county planning staff became convinced that sprawl would worsen because of the perceived overcommitment of lands to development in the 1965 county general plan. In early 1971 the area's Council of Governments (COG) adopted an advisory regional plan endorsed by the county supervisor that showed a substantial reduction in the lands designated for development in the county. To promote service efficiency, the regional plan also introduced the concepts of phased land use classifications to reserve agricultural land and an urban limit line beyond which no services would be provided.

The county planning staff decided to reformulate the county general plan using the basic idea of growth phasing. An urban area would be designated for 880,000 people, the 1990 population projected by the 1970 census. Designated urban reserve areas would be kept in agricultural uses until needed for urban growth. Finally, certain lands would be classified as agricultural preserve for permanent agriculture. This plan, the staff hoped, would lower farmers' taxes and make urban services more efficient.

It was decided that the urban area would not have to be larger than the existing urbanized area because more than 50 percent of that land area was vacant. After designating the urban limit line and reserve land use areas, the staff circulated the policies and map to the major environmental and building industry groups for comment. The staff then recommended the plan to the county planning commission. The plan would redesignate from urban to nonurban classifications more than 140,000 acres, or more than 25 percent of the undeveloped land in the county. The urban limit line itself was included as a means of promoting an understanding of the policy distinction between those areas that would and would not be serviced. Also, subsequent plan amendments would be made more difficult because the conceptually important line would have to be moved to allow development.

In early 1972 the county planning commission held hearings on the proposed general plan. More than 1,000 persons came to one of the hearings. Representatives of dozens of major interest groups presented their views. Opponents argued that land values in the urban area would rise, taxes would shift away from remote lands, and unemployment would grow. Environmentalists countered by saying that growth would not be slowed, only channeled locationally, and that the high percentage of vacant land would prevent large land value increases for many years. Three economic consultants verified this view at the hearings. The planning staff subsequently prepared an economic study showing that the phasing plan would lower service costs and not drive up land values significantly. Opponents also charged that those landowners whose lands would be redesignated from urban to nonurban uses would suffer losses in land values. The planning staff could not counter these claims and reasoned that protecting the agricultural economy required these losses. Lawsuits were filed by one developer and petitions to fire the planning director were circulated. Neither of these efforts were successful. The director dropped the limit line from the plan, but retained the phasing policies. The planning commission voted not to adopt the plan.

After the 1970 and 1972 elections, conservationists gained control of the board of supervisors. The supervisors held their own hearings in the fall of 1972 and adopted the plan (without the urban limit line) in February 1973. Basically, the supervisors agreed with the planning staff: Too much land was designated for urban development and growth had to be directed to serviceable lands. Significant factors explaining the adoption of the growth-phasing plan were (a) the general environmental and growth control sentiment in the county reflected in the supervisorial elections, (b) the aggressive and environmentally committed planning staff, (c) the dramatic downturn in population expectations, (d) the advisory regional plan of 1971, and (e) rising service costs. Apparently, service efficiency (tax minimization) and agricultural protection (for economic and environmental reasons) were the chief motivations of the staff and the decision makers.

Modesto sewer phasing. Modesto is a thriving agricultural service center 80 miles south of Sacramento in the Central Valley of California. Food processing, packing, and distribution are its dominant industries. The city's population in 1974 was 84,000, double that of 1960. In 1973 the Modesto area contained more than half the population of Stanislaus County (210,000).

Some decision makers became worried about the conversion of prime agricultural lands in the Modesto area during the late 1960s. Many farmers were worried that the area would become another Santa Clara Valley, where San Jose and other cities had gobbled up prime orchard and croplands in the 1940s and 1950s. In 1970 the agricultural extension director for the county held a workshop on soils and land use planning. This conference stimulated thinking in Modesto and the county about agricultural land conversion. Similar conferences followed in 1971 and 1972.

In 1972 the COG staff for the county prepared an advisory land use plan that proposed steering future urban development away from prime agricultural lands. Specifically, the staff recommended that Modesto restrict growth to its existing phase-I sewer area (37 square miles). The COG board rejected the plan.

Meanwhile, an environmentalist newcomer proposed to the Modesto City Council that it adopt an advisory policy statement seeking to limit growth to the phase-I sewer service area. The council treated the person rudely. This shocked some long-time citizens, who then joined forces to place the policy statement on the 1973 ballot. The measure merely required written findings before any agency could approve development on prime agricultural lands. The council unanimously opposed the measure, as did the labor, building, and real estate interests. The League of Women Voters supported the proposition. The initiative lost 7,165 to 5,046. Despite the proposition's failure, however, a strong supporter was elected to the council, which was badly shaken by the move.

The council declared a moratorium on trunk sewer line extensions until its capital improvements committee could study land availability. This committee visited other cities having growth problems, held many public meetings, and toured Modesto to look at developable land parcels. The committee's deliberations and reports changed the opinions of the council members and of most opponents. After meetings with the city planning commission, the city council adopted the 1974 urban growth policy without substantial debate.

The resolution directs urban growth to already serviced areas in a contiguous fashion. Any trunk extensions beyond the phase-I area require a general plan amendment and hearings. The planning staff is directed to prepare an annual review of the effects of this policy on land availability and prices.

Also in 1974 the county replaced its 1-acre agricultural zoning with 10-acre zoning, discouraging hobby farms and protecting commercial agriculture. The county also decided to prohibit subdivisions on septic tanks and not to provide further urban services. These policies greatly enhanced the city's ability to prevent leapfrog development.

In Modesto the motivation for growth phasing appears to have been the preservation of prime agricultural lands. The conservative Farm Bureau supported the city and county growth phasing policies. The growth control policies, so violently opposed at first, were accepted placidly after they went through channels and were supported by political insiders. The city council rapidly accommodated itself to the new sentiments for agricultural land protection.

Summary of cases. It is primarily in urban counties where large-scale open space protection has taken place in California. The motives in the above cases and in others appear to be (a) service efficiency and tax minimization; (b) protection of scenic, often agricultural, open space; (c) agricultural protection per se for economic reasons; and (d) general concern for environmental quality, meaning riparian lands, steep lands, wildlife, air quality, and energy consumption. Even the rural counties in California are now becoming concerned about uncontrolled growth, primarily for tax reasons, and the old laissez-faire land use policies are giving way to exclusive resource zoning in nonurbanized areas.

Urban growth control and open space preservation

The three cases presented represent the progressive end of the spectrum of open space politics in California. There are counties with stronger programs, however. For example, Yolo County has for several years had agricultural and resource zoning for nearly all of its nonurban lands. Significant growth is confined to the four existing urban areas. Lot splitting, even for agricultural sale, is generally prohibited. More than 90 percent of the potentially qualifying agricultural lands in the county are enrolled in the state's preferential taxation program. The cities all employ phased zoning and service limitation policies.

As these cases illustrate, open space preservation is tied closely to urban growth management. If resource lands are to be protected, counties and cities must cooperate. The counties must take the lead by adopting agricultural and resource zoning that provides lot-size minimums large enough to support commercial agriculture and eliminate hobby farmers. Phased zoning in urban fringe areas must be implemented jointly by the county and its cities. Finally, the cities must adopt service limitations to complement phased zoning.

Because of concern for service efficiency and for open space protection, Americans are increasingly pushing for growth management in their cities. This new political movement in the cities complements the older movement for open space protection in county politics headed by public and private resource managers. It appears that the new combination of rural conservationists and urban growth management advocates is making headway in many urbanizing counties.

REFERENCES

1. Delafons, John. 1969. *Land use controls in the United States.* MIT Press, Cambridge, Massachusetts.
2. Johnston, Robert A. 1980. *The politics of local growth control.* Policy Studies Journal (December).
3. Schwartz, S. I., R. A. Johnston, J. R. Blackmarr, and D. E. Hansen. 1979. *Controlling land use for water management and urban growth management: A policy analysis.* Contribution No. 180. California Water Resources Center, University of California, Davis. 79 pp.

42

A Values Dilemma: Standards for Soil Quality Tomorrow

D. E. McCormack
Leader, Soil Technology Staff, Soil Conservation Service
Washington, D.C.
and
W. E. Larson
Soil Scientist, Science and Education Administration—
Agricultural Research, St. Paul, Minnesota

Maintaining the productivity of our soil resources is a widely shared national goal. The public opinion surveys recently completed as a part of the Soil and Water Resources Conservation Act of 1977 (RCA) showed that 85 percent of the respondents rated soil and water conservation among the most important national issues. Protecting soil resources is certainly a major goal of the U.S. Department of Agriculture (USDA), and this objective will become increasingly more important to many farmers.

Lowdermilk (8) made a survey of land use and soil degradation in areas of ancient civilizations and concluded that "in the last reckoning, all things are purchased with food." He reaffirms the fact that food buys the division of labor that begets civilization.

In the ancient accounts of Columella (4), written at about the time of Christ, one is impressed with the extent of knowledge about soil husbandry and erosion control. Much of Columella's knowledge came from earlier writings salvaged when Carthage was destroyed in 146 B.C. (8). Despite this knowledge, however, soil erosion destroyed extensive areas of productive soils and the cities and nations they sustained.

Now we have much more information. We know there are alternative approaches to soil erosion control. We know that their effectiveness depends upon the kind of soil. We know that to get widespread application of erosion control practices the public must share the cost with farmers.

But there is still much that we do not know. A key question is what rate of soil erosion is acceptable? We readily agree that the answer cannot be zero. Can we agree so readily that our goal is a rate that allows maintenance of soil productivity in perpetuity?

What we know

Farmers and scientists, sharing a strong conviction that erosion was destroying soil productivity, helped spawn a major new federal initiative in soil conservation in the mid-1930s. They regarded the truth of their conviction to be self-evident from their own observations and experiences. Scientific proof was not demanded. Most early research addressed ways to effectively control erosion.

We did not know whether or not farmers could afford erosion control. We had not yet proved that federal assistance could substantially contribute to reducing soil erosion. Most importantly, research data on the precise impact of erosion on soil productivity were not available. Still everyone knew that erosion control was necessary.

Erosion rates. The rate of soil erosion in 1977 exceeded 5 tons per acre (11.2 metric tons/hectare) on nearly 100 million acres (40 million hectares) of cropland. On an additional 41 million acres (17 million hectares) of cropland, erosion exceeded 10 tons per acre (22.5 metric tons/hectare). Because the soil loss tolerance (T-value) is 5 tons per acre per year (11.2 metric tons/hectare/year) on about two-thirds of the nation's cropland, we estimate that erosion currently exceeds the established T-value on 160 million acres (64 million hectares) or 40 percent of our cropland.

In the early 1950s, erosion rates were estimated to exceed the T-values (then assumed to equal the rate of soil formation) on more than 300 million acres (120 million hectares) of cropland (8). The average rates of erosion by land capability class and subclass in 1977 are shown in table 1.

Yield reductions. Yield reductions caused by soil erosion have been summarized by Hagen and Dyke (6) using estimated yields of uneroded sloping soils and their eroded counterparts from about 1,100 published soil surveys. Their general estimate for all soils in the Corn Belt is that for each inch of A horizon lost corn yields are reduced 3 bushels per acre per year (1 centimeter of soil loss reduces yields by 188 kilograms per hectare).

The yield estimates in soil surveys are developed in each of the survey areas (mostly counties) by a team consisting of the Soil Conservation Service (SCS) district conservationist, the county extension agent, soil scientists in the soil survey party, and other knowledgeable persons. Over the course of the survey, normally 4 to 6 years, this team discusses crop yields and soils with many farmers. One or more of the team members commonly has many years of experience in the county.

A recent USDA study in Iowa showed that as soil erodes and changes from the slightly eroded to the severely eroded class yields are reduced 23 bushels per acre (1,450 kilograms/hectare) for corn, 8 bushels per acre (538 kilograms/hectare) for soybeans, 13 bushels per acre (403 kilograms/hectare) for oats, and 1.1 tons per acre (2.46 metric tons/hectare) for hay (*21*). These reductions are substantially lower than those in many parts of the nation where soils are thinner or otherwise less productive.

In Illinois the rate of decline in productivity for a similar change in erosion class is estimated at 10 to 12 percent for soils with favorable subsoils and 20 to 25 percent for soils with unfavorable subsoils (*5*). The larger yield reductions apply to the more sloping soils. A high level of management is assumed; for lower levels, even greater yield reductions are projected.

The Iowa study also showed that in 1974 slightly less than 10 percent of the 2.1 million acres (0.88 million hectares) of harvested cropland in the study area was severely eroded. The study predicted that 41 percent of the area will be severely eroded by 2020.

Predictions of soil erosion rates using the universal soil loss equation (USLE) are accurate enough to guide conservation planning (*24*). For most of the nation, use of the equation has been validated for identifying the

Table 1. Estimated average annual sheet and rill erosion for cropland in the United States (excluding Alaska) in 1977, by land capability class and subclass.*

Class and Subclass	Percent of Total Cropland*	Sheet and Rill Erosion		Percent of Total Cropland Erosion†
		Average Rate		
		(t/a)	(mt/ha)	
I	7.6	2.8	(6.3)	4.5
IIe	21.4	4.9	(11.0)	22.7
IIw	14.7	2.8	(6.3)	8.7
IIs	4.5	2.5	(5.6)	2.4
IIc	4.8	1.5	(3.3)	1.5
All II	45.4	3.6	(8.0)	35.4
IIIe	19.3	6.9	(15.5)	28.7
IIIw	8.2	2.8	(6.3)	4.8
IIIs	2.9	1.9	(4.3)	1.2
IIIc	1.5	1.4	(3.1)	0.5
All III	31.9	5.2	(11.7)	35.2
IVe	7.1	8.8	(19.7)	13.4
IVw	1.6	1.9	(4.2)	0.7
IVs	1.7	2.2	(4.9)	0.8
IVc	0.2	1.3	(2.9)	0.1
All IV	10.6	6.6	(14.8)	14.9
V	0.6	1.8	(4.0)	0.2
All VI	3.1	11.2	(25.0)	7.5
All VII	0.7	14.2	(31.8)	2.2
Total	99.9	4.7	(10.5)	99.9
Total subclass e	50.4	6.8	(15.2)	73.8

*Dideriksen, R. I. 1980. "Resource Inventory—Sheet, Rill, and Wind Erosion." Unpublished paper, presented at the American Society of Agricultural Engineers annual meeting in San Antonio, Texas.
†Percentages do not total 100 because of rounding.

main options available for conservation farming and the general consequences of each option. The USLE is especially valuable in showing the erosion control benefits of conservation farming systems compared with other systems.

What we don't know

Based on a recently intensified review of information on soil loss tolerances, it is clear that we need more information about the soil erosion issue. At the special Soil Science Society of America symposium at Fort Collins, Colorado, in 1979 and at the Conservation '80 Symposium in Silsoe, England, in July 1980, this point was affirmed repeatedly. USDA agencies are now giving new emphasis to seeking the required data.

Rates of soil formation. Soils require an extremely long time to form, and accurate data on the rates of soil formation are limited. However, it is impossible to outline soil conservation objectives and policies properly without making some important assumptions about the rates of soil formation.

We will consider the rate of formation of A horizons separate from the slower and ultimately more important formation of rooting depth. Deducing the rate of formation of the soil's rooting depth must be based on assumptions about soil weathering over thousands, even millions of years. It cannot be determined from base-level measurements covering periods as short as a few hundred years. Recent measurements can help us estimate the rate of formation of the A horizon.

The A horizon. From sketchy data it is estimated that in permeable, medium-textured soil material in well-managed cropland an A horizon can form at the rate of 1 inch (2.5 centimeters) in 30 years (*1*). This rate—assuming that over 1 acre, 1 inch of soil weighs 150 tons (1 centimeter/hectare weighs 408 metric tons)—is equivalent to the formation of 5 tons per acre (11.2 metric tons/hectare) of new topsoil each year. This is the single most important reason that the maximum T-value has been established at that level.

Recent studies indicate annual rates of A-horizon formation exceeding 5 tons per acre per year (11.2 metric tons/hectare/year) in soils of medium to moderately coarse texture.[1] Rates are likely to be much slower in soils of finer texture.

Rooting depth. The weathering of parent rock or deeper soil horizons to favorable root-zone material is a distinctly different phenomenon from the

---

[1] Hall, G. F., R. B. Daniels, and J. E. Foss. "Soil Formation and Renewal Rates in the United States." Paper presented at the Soil Science Society of America annual meeting, Ft. Collins, Colorado, August 1979.

formation of the A horizon. In most soils it proceeds much more slowly. Knowing the rate of root-zone formation is vital to predicting the long-term effects of erosion.

Data on this rate are not yet conclusive; however, numerous reviews have been made of reports on the rate of rock weathering (*13, 18*) and dust deposition (*14*). A renewal rate of 0.5 ton per acre per year (1.1 metric tons/hectare/year) is thought to be a useful average for most unconsolidated materials with the possible exception of alluvium. For most consolidated (rock) materials, rates are much lower.

Keying the T-value to the rate of soil renewal would ensure that soil thickness is maintained. On most cropland, however, it would be extremely difficult, if not impossible, to limit erosion to 0.5 ton per acre per year without major reductions in production.

In figure 1, two sets of T-values and a soil renewal rate of 0.5 ton per acre per year are used to project the reduction in root-zone thickness over several thousand years (*26*). It is assumed that the rate of erosion equals the T-value and that the T-value is reduced as the thickness of the root zone decreases. In figure 1, the initial T-value is 5 tons per acre per year (11.2 metric tons/hectare/year), which is reduced when depth of favorable root zone is 40 inches (100 centimeters). In figure 2, the initial T-value of 10 tons per acre per year (22.5 metric tons/hectare/year) is reduced stepwise with the loss of each 10 inches (25 centimeters) of soil.

According to figure 1, a cropland soil with 60 inches (150 centimeters) favorable for plant growth would decrease to 40 inches in 660 years; a soil 90 inches (225 centimeters) thick would decrease to 40 inches in 1,800 years.

In figure 2, a soil with a 60-inch root zone would decrease to 40 inches in about 400 years. A soil with a 90-inch root zone would decrease to 40 inches in about 1,050 years.

There is little question that the 40-inch soil would be less productive for most crops than the 60- or 90-inch soil. Data are inadequate, however, to show conclusively the extent of soil productivity decline over several centuries.

Erosion and its impacts in the United States

Monoculture, the use of large farm machinery, a growing population, conversion of cropland to urban uses, and high prices for crops are increasing the demands on soils. In several parts of the United States, there exists no economically feasible approach to the production of cultivated crops that can keep erosion within the soil loss tolerance. Many farmers simply will not apply conservation practices if they lose money in the process.

As part of the early work needed for a major restudy of both soil loss tolerance and soil conservation objectives, we need to assign rates of soil formation to all soil series. This would provide a basis for answering some basic questions. For example, how much cropland has rates of soil formation of less than 0.5 ton per acre per year (1.1 metric tons/hectare/year)? Of

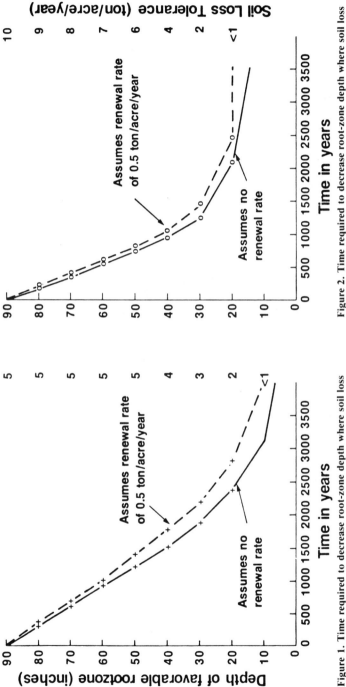

Figure 2. Time required to decrease root-zone depth where soil loss tolerance is 10 tons per acre per year (22.5 metric tons/hectare/year) initially and declines as indicated.

Figure 1. Time required to decrease root-zone depth where soil loss tolerance is 5 tons per acre per year (11.2 metric tons/hectare/year) initially and declines as indicated.

this cropland, how much has a favorable root zone more than 60 inches (150 centimeters) thick?

At the other extreme, how much cropland has rates of A-horizon formation of 5 tons per acre per year (11.2 metric tons/hectare/year) or more? And how much of this has favorable rooting depths of less than 40 inches (100 centimeters)?

We also need to acquire information about the impact of soil erosion on crop yields. Estimates of crop yield reductions by erosion from soil surveys (6) are helpful, but they are judgments and lack thorough scientific validation. These data, however, should help the agricultural community convince others that the prevention of soil degradation is an important public responsibility.

Eroded soils are delineated in detailed soil surveys if, compared with their uneroded counterparts, they are less productive, require different management, or differ notably in appearance. Thus, the degree of erosion on most soils is identified. However, because soil surveys are completed on only about two-thirds of the nation's cropland, we do not know how much is severely eroded already.

It would be possible to use completed soil surveys to develop estimates of the proportion of eroded cropland in each major land resource area (17) and derive a national estimate. This we should do. Also, we do not know how much cultivated land has been ruined by erosion and allowed to revert to pasture or woodland. Thirty years ago it was estimated that there were 50 million acres (20 million hectares) of such land (8). Obviously there is more than that now, but we do not know how much more.

In an effort to better understand the impact of soil erosion on crop yields, we have attempted to develop simplified soil productivity index models based on the physical characteristics of each soil horizon. The characteristics used are soil texture, coarse fragments, bulk density, and organic matter content. These characteristics were used to develop an index and then were integrated over a 60-inch (150-centimeter) profile depth.

We correlated our index with corn yields in the central Corn Belt. Corn yield estimates were taken from the SCS-SOILS-5 sheets. Our objective was to estimate corn yields after various amounts of A horizon were removed.

However, we found that corn yield and productivity index were only moderately related. We also discovered that our soil productivity model needs improvement and that documented soil and crop yield data were difficult to find. If we are to make progress in relating soil erosion to crop productivity over wide areas, we must have more reliable and better coordinated data banks.

We do not fully understand the mechanisms that cause yield reductions from erosion for all soils. To gain these insights, we need a new set of soil groupings for national analyses, one that would distinguish between deep soils and shallow ones, between stony soils and nonstony ones, etc. Without such groups, much of the value of collected data is lost.

A related void in the data base results from the improved technology for using sloping land for crop production. For example, no-till systems make it possible to grow row crops on land where conventional methods do not work. Large acreages of soils in classes VI and VII have deep root zones that are favorable for crop production. Many acres of class VI soils have much more favorable root zones for corn production than those of some class II soils. These class VI soils are mapped in detailed soil surveys, but crop yields generally are not given. Some people assume erroneously that class II soils will always produce a higher yield of corn than class VI soils. Such an assumption violates a basic tenet of the land capability classification system (16).

We need a new approach to estimating yield probabilities. The commonly observed variaton in crop yields within fields, especially in dry seasons, is not properly reflected in the estimated yields in published soil surveys. An uneroded soil commonly withstands drought better and has a much narrower yield fluctuation between a normal season and a dry season than an eroded soil. We strongly recommend the sequential testing approach to measuring yields within a given field (9).

A good understanding of the mechanisms that result in yield reduction would permit the accurate prediction of crop yields through simulation models. When properly developed, such models will prove valuable in analyzing options for conservation policies, objectives, and programs.

Finally, we do not know the extent to which we have reached biological limits for the production of any major crops. If these limits are two to three times greater than current world record yields of individual crops, as indicated by Wittwer (25), then the need to preserve cultivated land may not be so pressing. Ultimately, though, the same conservation objectives must be established regardless of the biological limits.

Irreversibility of soil damage

We have no conclusive evidence that a decline in production caused by soil erosion is recoverable under continued cultivation. For the sake of discussion, let us assume that the loss in a given year continues year after year into the future.

Rapidly improving technology has tended to mask the loss in productivity. Fragmentary data (21) suggest that production decreases average 1.5 bushels per acre (90 kilograms/hectare) of corn per 0.4 inch (1 centimeter) of topsoil lost. The production losses are much greater on some soils than on others having the same amount of erosion. Limited data on Swygert soils in Illinois indicate a curvilinear relationship on that soil. The rate of loss in production per inch of topsoil lost increases as the A horizon becomes thinner. However, even on soils with a nearly impervious, clayey B horizon, such as Swygert, improved technology may reduce yield reductions.

To illustrate such an idealized relationship, figure 3 shows that if erosion had not occurred yields would currently be substantially greater than they are now. It is postulated that the nonrecoverable impact of soil erosion reduces yields of all crops. Those crops most sensitive to moisture stress would likely have the greatest yield reduction because loss of available moisture is the most serious impact of soil erosion on most crops. Our improving technology, though, has tended to offset the other impacts of erosion on production.

Pimentel (10) calculated the total energy output per acre of several crops. For corn in the United States, he calculated 71.5 million British thermal units (Btus) (17.9 million kilocalories); for cassava in Africa, 76.8 million Btus (19.2 million kilocalories); for rice in the Phillipines, 23.9 million Btus (6.0 million kilocalories); for rice in the United States, 83.9 million Btus (21.0 million kilocalories); for potatoes in the U.S., 80.8 million Btus (20.2 million kilocalories); for wheat in the U.S., 30.1 million Btus (7.5 million kilocalories); and for tame hay in the United States, 34.3 million Btus (8.6 million kilocalories). Based on these figures, an average energy production equivalent (EPE) of 24 million Btus per acre (15 kilocalories/hectare) has been assumed for cropland in the United States.

Assuming that 3.8 bushels (104 kilograms) of corn production is lost per 150 tons (137 metric tons) of topsoil loss, about 3 percent of the production is lost at the 125-bushels-per-acre (7,840-kilograms/hectare) yield level. This rate appears to be a reasonable average based on limited evidence. A production loss of 0.03 bushels per acre (1.74 kilograms/hectare) of corn is thus calculated for each ton of soil loss. Therefore, about 0.02 percent of the total production is lost per ton of soil loss. Applying this percentage to the average EPE, we find that 13,094 Btus are lost per ton of soil loss (3,000 kilocalories/metric ton). Although this represents less than 3 percent of the energy in a gallon of diesel fuel, the total effect is large.

The current annual rate of soil erosion from cropland in the United States is estimated at 1.97 billion tons (1.73 billion metric tons), an average of 4.7 tons per acre (10.8 metric tons/hectare). Thus, the loss in one year from this erosion is 20.6 trillion Btus (5.2 trillion kilocalories). This represents less than 0.1 percent of the total energy used annually on U.S. farms and ranches, but when we extend this loss over 100 years under the assumption that the erosion losses are not recoverable, the total losses are very large. The loss sustained in the first year is also sustained in each following year so that the total EPE loss in the 100-year period would amount to 104.3 quads or 104.3 quadrillion Btus (26.3 quadrillion kilocalories). Furthermore, the annual loss in 1980 as a result of the erosion of the last century is about 1.96 quads (500 trillion kilocalories), or about 85 percent of the total energy currently used annually on the nation's farms and ranches.

This loss will also occur in the next 100 years if erosion is permitted to continue at the current rate. From this perspective, erosion can be viewed as an energy tariff on future generations, who may be less able to pay than we are today because of higher energy prices or lower net productivity. At the current value of energy in gasoline—per $1 per 99,000 Btus (25,000 kilocalories)—this annual loss amounts to around $20 billion. At $100 per cord or $1 per 230,100 Btus (58,000 kilocalories) for firewood, the annual loss

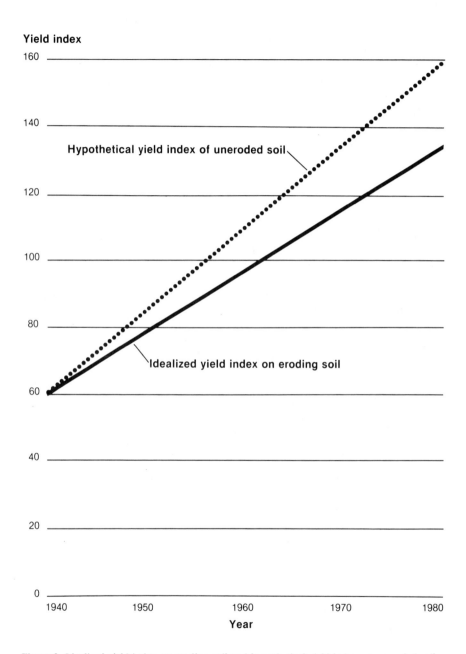

Figure 3. Idealized yield index on eroding soil and hypothetical yield index on uneroded soil.

amounts to around $8.6 billion. Expressed as equivalents of corn production loss at the rate of 3.8 bushels (238-kilocalories) lost per 150 tons (137 tons) of topsoil loss, an annual loss of $12 billion is estimated.

Because some soils in medium- to coarse-textured materials form at rates of well over 1.0 ton per acre per year (2.2 metric tons/hectare/year), the losses in production due to erosion can be recalculated to allow for a partial recovery from the erosion loss. The recovery in productivity is assumed to be proportional to the difference in total thickness of soil available, that is, the erosion rate minus the soil formation rate equals the net soil loss or gain.

Based on this assumption, accumulated over 100 years, this loss totals 83.0 quads or 83.0 quadrillion Btus (20.9 quadrillion kilocalories). At the value of unrefined energy in firewood, the annual loss after 100 years would be $7.0 billion.

Other losses due to erosion

In addition to crop production losses, soil erosion creates other costs. These include the fertilizer value of eroded topsoil, the cost of dredging harbors and channels, costs resulting from loss of reservoir capacity, and costs resulting from impaired water quality.

The value of plant nutrients in a metric ton of fertile eroded topsoil is estimated at $6.80. At the current average annual erosion rate, the value of these nutrients is nearly $13 billion. A portion of these nutrients is deposited on lower slopes near the eroding soils; however, at least half is lost entirely from cropland. These nutrients either contribute to water pollution or are deposited with sediment in floodplains not used for cropland.

Dredging to keep waterways and harbors open to navigation to a large extent results from soil erosion in the watersheds upstream. In 1972 the annual cost of this activity was estimated at $120 million (22). Because at least one-half the total sediment probably came from cropland, a cost of $60 million (1972 dollars) can be assigned to cropland erosion. In 1979 dollars the cost is $119 million.

The estimated cost of construction of U.S. reservoirs, excluding some municipal reservoirs, is estimated at $214 billion (1975 dollars). This total is derived from an estimate of 55.5×10 billion cubic meters (450×10 million acre-feet) of storage and a construction cost of $385 per 1,000 cubic meters ($476 per acre-foot) (22). Overall, the SCS water resources staff estimates that, on the average, the reservoirs will fill with sediment in 100 years. The annual loss in capacity is thus valued at $2.14 billion (1975 dollars). Erosion from cropland probably accounts for at least half this loss.

Soil conservation objectives

The criteria that we currently use to derive T-values were established to ensure preservation of the long-term productive capacity of soils. We need to make it clear that the best evidence indicates that these criteria do not assure preservation of most soils in the United States[2] or in other parts of the world (*19*). The fact that they do not do so may not mean that the criteria are improper, however. Instead, the objectives of conservation planning on most sloping soils may need to be restated to allow a gradual decline of soil productivity over many years. If our objective is to maintain soil productivity in perpetuity, then the criteria and the T-values themselves will need to be changed.

To date, the question of soil loss tolerance has been approached primarily as a technical issue. The maintenance of soil productivity, the prevention of gullies, and the control of off-site sediment damage have been studied, as have the results of failure to manage soils to meet these needs.

How much erosion can be tolerated? Social and ethical as well as technical issues are involved[3] (*23*). A definitive answer is difficult because the future demands on soil resources are unknown.

Ideally, we would know the rate of formation of a favorable root zone for each soil. We would use tillage methods and other agricultural practices that allow the production of needed food and fiber while ensuring that soil erosion does not exceed the rate of formation of a favorable root zone. In this ideal world, we would fully control all cultural aspects of crop production. We would know the carrying capacity of the land and the consequences of alternative uses and management.

Unfortunately, our evidence suggests that soil erosion on most cultivated sloping soils in the United States today exceeds the rate of formation of a favorable root zone. Given this fact, how should erosion control objectives be stated so that they are reasonable for both the present and the future? We need a new land use ethic and a new reverence for the land (*2*).

It is possible that T-values could be set on the basis of technical factors alone; soil conservation objectives could be set by political and social institutions to reflect ethical, economic, and social concerns.

Limited to a purely technical activity, T-values would be free from implications about land use restrictions that in the past may have prevented a fully objective evaluation of the impact of erosion on productivity in setting conservation objectives. With this liberty, T-values could be assigned that do not result in the decline in productive capacity indicated by the curves in figures 1 and 2.

Conservation objectives could then be based on a social consensus about the need for maintaining the productive capacity of land susceptible to erosion. When the objectives would result in erosion at a rate greater than the soil loss tolerance, scientists must explain the long-term impacts on productivity. But perhaps our political and social leaders should determine the objectives of soil conservation. To do so, they need to be informed about

---

[2]McCormack, D. E., and K. K. Young. 1980. "Technical and Societal Implications of Soil Loss Tolerance." Presented at Conservation '80 Symposium, Silsoe, England.
[3]Ibid.

the T-value but not strictly bound by it. And they must have the technical insight to defend their action properly.

Stewardship and an uncertain future

More than 25 years ago, Ciriacy-Wantrup (3) discussed safe, minimum conservation policy standards in social and economic terms. He noted that the depletion of soil resources could cause heavy social losses, that the longer resource depletion continues the more difficult it is to halt and reverse. Soil scientists must learn more about the reversibility of the impacts of soil erosion. In particular they must determine the rate at which the productivity of eroded soil can be restored and the kind of management required to restore it.

Just how reversible are the impacts of erosion? We do not know with any accuracy. Our calculations here are highly tentative and do not consider potential technological breakthroughs that might offset productivity losses. We are convinced, however, that soil should not be considered a renewable resource from the perspective of 100 to 200 years or less. Some soils might be considered renewable over a period of 1 to 10,000 years.

Sequential testing could be used to obtain accurate data on the impact of soil erosion on yields. Sequential testing uses yield data collection on two or more soils within the same field (9). Uneroded and eroded phases of the same soil series could be tested. Not enough research information exists to determine the impact on crop yield when the soil profile is severely eroded or removed.

Ciriacy-Wantrup also discussed the problem of uncertainty and its implications for conservation policy. A number of factors related to soils and erosion make the future outlook uncertain. Future demands on soils surely will exceed today's level, and it seems likely that we will reach a point within 500 years when food production will control world population. To what extent will the total population of the earth depend upon the adequacy of soil conservation? We can speculate that if soil erosion can be controlled, the earth might support twice as many inhabitants as it could if soil erosion is not controlled.

Other areas of uncertainty exist. How much should individual farmers be held responsible for preventing erosion? What will be the ability of technology to maintain soil productivity despite erosion?

If the objective is maintaining soil productivity and because the knowledge of the relationship of productivity to soil thickness is fragmentary, we need to develop a direct, logical approach to conservation objectives. Perhaps, for a relatively brief period of a generation or two, we could disregard the overall thickness of the soil and assume that soil productivity relates only to the thickness of the A horizon. In this time we must learn the rate of soil formation for each of our soils and the impact of erosion on them.

Ultimately, we must squarely face the fact that soil productivity is directly tied to the overall thickness of the rooting zone, which forms much more slowly than the A horizon in cultivated soils. Long-term soil conservation objectives must be consistent with this fact. There is no alternative. We hope that objectives derived from social considerations can be compatible with those derived from technical considerations.

Future generations will certainly benefit from current erosion control, but they cannot pay for this benefit (*12*). On the other hand, if we fail to control erosion in our time, future generations will not be able to avoid paying for our failure. We believe it is clear that to a large extent the significance of our work is to maximize the value of their heritage. Yet to the farmer it may be clear that it is possible, at little or no economic risk, to subject his soil to erosion levels that are excessive even during his own generation (*7*).

To cope with the uncertainties of soil erosion impacts, we see no alternative but to adopt a very generally stated ethic of stewardship. We must strive to protect soil and its productive capability and to "leave it as an inheritance to [our] sons forever" (Ezra 9:12).

In 1854 Chief Seattle admonished the white men who wanted to buy the land of his people. He asked them to "teach your children...so that they will respect the land,...that the earth is our mother,...that whatever befalls the earth befalls the sons of the earth" (*11*).

In the words of Lowdermilk (*8*), "A starving farmer will eat his seed grain; you will do it and I will do it, even though we know it will be fatal to next year's crop. Now is the time, while we still have much good land capable of restoration to full or greater productivity, to carry through a full program of soil and water conservation."

No doubt we will learn a great deal more in the future about the rates of formation of favorable root zone in various kinds of parent materials, about methods of tillage that will hold soil erosion to very low levels, and about restoring the productivity of severely eroded soils. Perhaps we can afford to take as long as 25 years to do so, for the soil is patient. This prospect, however, should not lead us to relax our efforts to minimize soil erosion because the possibility of irreversible depletion will remain.

REFERENCES

1. Bennett, H. H. 1939. *Soil conservation.* McGraw-Hill, Inc., New York, New York.
2. Brown, L. R. 1979. *Population, cropland and food prices.* The Phi Kappa Phi Journal 29(2): 11-16.
3. Ciriacy-Wantrup, C. V. 1952. *Resource conservation: Economics and policies.* University of California Press, Berkeley, California.
4. Columella. 1941. *Res rustica (On agriculture).* Translated by H. B. Ash. Harvard University Press, Cambridge, Massachusetts.
5. Fehrenbacher, J. B., R. A. Pope, I. J. Jansen, J. D. Alexander, and B. W. Ray. 1978. *Soil productivity in Illinois.* Circular 1156. Cooperatives Extension Service, University of Illinois, Urbana.
6. Hagen, L. L., and P. T. Dyke. 1980. *Yield-soil loss relationship.* In *Proceedings, Workshop on Influence of Soil Erosion on Soil Productivity.* Science and Education Administration—Agricultural Research, U.S. Department of Agriculture, Washington, D.C.
7. Hardin, G. 1968. *The tragedy of the commons.* Science 162: 1,243-1,248.
8. Lowdermilk, W. C. 1953. *Conquest of the land through 7,000 years.* Agriculture Information Bulletin 99. Soil Conservation Service, U.S. Department of Agriculture, Washington, D.C. 30 pp.

9. Robinette, C. E. 1975. *Corn yield study on selected Maryland soil series.* Unpublished M.S. Thesis. Agronomy Department, University of Maryland, College Park. 192 pp.
10. Pimentel, D. 1979. *Energy and agriculture.* In Biswas and Biswas [editors] *Food, Climate, and Man.* John Wiley and Sons, New York, New York. pp. 73-106.
11. Seattle, Chief. 1976. *If we sell you our land.* Fellowship 42(11): 3-7.
12. Seitz, W. D., and R. Hewitt. 1979. *Equity analysis in public policy formation.* Project Report Contract 68-03-2597. U.S. Environmental Protection Agency, Athens, Georgia.
13. Smith, R. M., and W. L. Stamey. 1965. *Determining the range of tolerable erosion.* Soil Science 100(6): 414-424.
14. Smith, R. M., P. C. Twiss, R. K. Kraus, and M. J. Brown. 1970. *Dust deposition in relation to site, season and climatic variables.* Soil Science Society of America Proceedings 34(1): 112-117.
15. Smith, R. M., and R. Yates. 1968. *Renewal, erosion, and net change functions in soil conservation science.* Ninth International Congress of Soil Science Transactions 5(77).
16. Soil Conservation Service. 1961. *Land capability classification.* Handbook 210. U.S. Department of Agriculture, Washington, D.C.
17. Soil Conservation Service. 1972. *Land resource regions and major land resource areas of the United States.* Handbook 296. U.S. Department of Agriculture, Washington, D.C.
18. Soil Conservation Service. 1980. *RCA appraisal 1980. Part II.* Washington, D.C.
19. Stocking, M. 1978. *A dilemma for soil conservation.* AREA, Institute of British Geographers 10(4): 306-308.
20. U.S. Department of Agriculture. 1978. *1977 national resource inventories.* Preliminary estimates. Washington, D.C.
21. U.S. Department of Agriculture. 1980. *Soil depletion study.* Reference Report: Southern Iowa Rivers Basin. Soil Conservation Service, Des Moines, Iowa.
22. U.S. Water Resources Council. 1977. *Appendix, erosion and sedimentation and related resource considerations. The nation's water resources.* Washington, D.C.
23. Warkentin, B. P., and H. F. Fletcher. 1977. *Soil quality for intensive agriculture.* In *Proceedings of International Seminar on Soil Environment and Fertility Management in Intensive Agriculture.* Tokyo, Japan.
24. Wischmeier, W. H., and D. D. Smith. 1979. *Predicting rainfall erosion losses—A guide to conservation planning.* Handbook 537. U.S. Department of Agriculture, Washington, D.C.
25. Wittwer, S. H. 1979. *Future technological advances in agriculture and their impact on the regulatory environment.* Bioscience 29: 603-610.
26. Young, K. K. 1978. *The impact of erosion on the productivity of soils in the United States.* In Proceedings, Workshop on Assessment of Erosion in the United States and Europe. Ghent, Belgium.

43

Cross-Compliance: Will it Work? Who Pays?

Stephen Dinehart and Lawrence Libby
Department of Agricultural Economics
Michigan State University, East Lansing

The Soil and Water Resource Conservation Act of 1977 (RCA) mandates "identification and evaluation of alternative methods for the conservation, protection, environmental improvement, and enhancement of soil and water resources." RCA is designed to improve our national soil and water conservation effort, currently a disjointed collection of 35 separate programs administered by several agencies within the U.S. Department of Agriculture (USDA). These programs have come under increasing scrutiny for their apparent lack of cost effectiveness. Both Congress and the Office of Management and Budget in Washington have pressed their demands for greater evidence of the payoff from conservation investments (8).

The present U.S. soil conservation program, which has evolved over the last 45 years, is entirely voluntary. Technical and cost-sharing assistance is made available to farmers who decide to install conservation practices. After billions of dollars in expenditures, though, the soil erosion problem is still very much with us: Voluntarism has not produced the desired conservation performance.

The RCA *Program Report, 1980 Review Draft* has proposed seven alternative strategies for program development (*12*). One of these alternatives, cross-compliance among USDA programs, requires that landowners practice soil conservation to be eligible for specified assistance programs administered by USDA. Our study concerns the likely performance of a cross-compliance policy.

The conservation dilemma

Farming has evolved from a lifestyle to a business. In the process the farmer's role as a steward of the land has come in conflict with his role as an entrepreneur. The farmer as entrepreneur is a profit maximizer, but he faces greater uncertainty in product prices and other market conditions than does his counterpart in the industrial sector. Agricultural supplies are more variable and less subject to producer control than are industrial supplies. The farmer's only choice is to maximize his production for the least possible cost, a condition that can lead to overproduction (6).

Conservation is a difficult commodity to sell. Its costs are short-run and concentrated, while its benefits are widely dispersed and realized primarily in the long-run. The cost of conservation practices is twofold. A farmer has the direct cost of installation and maintenance, plus indirect costs due to increased operation time and/or the removal of land previously in production.

Conservation reduces soil productivity losses, but quantifiying this benefit is difficult (11). When long-run conservation benefits are discounted to present value, the returns to the individual farmer are small, if not negative. Present value depends upon the discount rate selected. The lower the discount rate, the higher the present value. Benefits for erosion control are likely to be positive only with a low discount rate. Held and Clawson (5) concluded in 1965 that the value of conservation practices is not capitalized into land values. Land prices are insensitive to the state of conservation on the farm (5). Moreover, conservation reduces the short-run productivity of the land and is not valued by many purchasers.

Soil conservation is in conflict with the short-run efficiency and production incentives facing farmers. The land may be mined for its productive value, that is, soil losses may be tolerated until soil productivity is depleted. The monetary benefits of soil erosion control are seldom realized by those who pay for the practices, but by succeeding owners who may in turn be unwilling to pay for controls. As long as conservation conflicts with the profit-maximizing motives of farmers, there is no economic reason to expect voluntary, unsubsidized private investment in conservation practices.

Changing incentives for conservation

To improve the performance of soil conservaton programs, we must expect to make some institutional changes. That is, we should alter the options facing land users, thereby altering their conservation behavior. We must change the "rules of the game" to create an additional incentive for conservation.

There are several ways to alter landowners' incentives for practicing conservation. Regulation or incentive design may be used. A regulatory approach restrains an owner's use of the land and requires enforcement. Incentive design can either increase the short-run benefits of conservation or increase the short-run costs of not conserving the soil while leaving the final conservation decision with the land user. Increasing the conservation benefits has been discussed seriously in many forums. The RCA program report suggested a conservation performance bonus as one alternative strategy (12). Benbrook (1) proposed a Conservation Incentive Program, which would provide higher target and support prices to farmers who adopted low-cost soil-conserving practices. Cross-compliance raises the cost of not conserving soil resources.

Design of cross-compliance

The design of a cross-compliance policy has two major components: (1) The income or other assistance programs that are to have a cross-compliance requirement and (2) the level and measurement of conservation required on complying farms. For cross-compliance to work, programs that are to be cross-complied must provide the short-run financial incentive necessary to elicit participation in conservation programs. That is, the positive impact of the assistance program must offset the separable costs to the land user of installing soil conserving practices. Cross-compliance is particularly relevant for those programs that provide negative incentives for conservation practices. For example, credit programs encourage production expansion and may cause farmers to bring marginal lands out of conservation practices into production. Price supports and conservation also conflict (2).

The scope of programs that could be cross-complied is large. Agricultural Stabilization and Conservation Service (ASCS) commodity programs are one possibility. A major set of loan programs administered by Farmers Home Administration would include landowners other than farm owners and operators. It might be possible to include quasi-public organizations, such as the Commodity Credit Corporation, the Federal Crop Insurance Corporation, and the various organizations under the Farm Credit Administration. The larger the number of programs that are cross-complied the greater the incentive to participate in the conservation program. A drawback is that additional programs mean additional costs of administration and implementation.

The critical factor for gaining widespread participation in cross-compliance is the level of conservation required. That requirement in effect determines the cost of complying. As noted, participation will occur only when conservation costs are less than the benefits received from assistance programs. Skold has suggested a marginal approach to policy design, in which different conservation levels enable participation in different programs.[1]

[1]Skold, Melvin D. 1979. "Cross-compliance." Unpublished paper. Department of Economics, Colorado State University, Fort Collins.

Such a variable conservation requirement would allow marginal calculations on the part of participants. A policy design that equates program benefits with conservation cost will encourage maximum participation in the conservation program.

Since being discussed in RCA preliminary documents in late 1979, cross-compliance has been the most controversial of the alternative strategies. Senator John Culver of Iowa expressed the reservation of many others when he said: "One [strategy] which I personally do not like is a proposal that participation in commodity programs be made contingent upon...a good conservation plan" (3). This reaction is to be expected. Cross-compliance would alter farmers' rights in existing USDA programs. But in our judgement, such conclusions on the value of a cross-compliance policy are premature. Indications of the likely performance of such an approach are a necessary prerequisite to reasoned conclusions on the matter. Our analysis should help.

A survey of cross-compliance policy expectations

Our study was based on a sample of 400 farmers from nine farming states. We gathered data directly from farmers and from their county ASCS and Soil Conservation Service (SCS) offices. We examined only ASCS programs as the basis for cross-compliance. A full analysis of cross-compliance should examine all compliance possibilities from several agencies, however. Time and financial limitations required us to focus on ASCS programs. We divided ASCS programs into two categories: price support programs and production adjustment programs. Conservation programs were excluded because the programs are already meeting the performance criteria of conservation without any additional compliance. We averaged gross benefits accruing to the participants on an annual per acre basis over the 1977-1979 program period. We divided the sample according to program participation and the per acre level of gross benefits received.

Participation. As noted, participation in a cross-compliance program is contingent on the cost of conservation. While studies have been made of the cost of conservation in large regions, few of them have estimated average per acre cost for a farm. Padgitt (9) simulated the effect of a minimum conservation plan on income. His plan to meet a minimum requirement for conservation includes the establishment of grassed waterways, the use of contouring or strip-cropping on row crops, and no straight rows for crops planted on erosive soils.

The Padgitt data indicate that the cost of this set of practice varies from $1-$4 per acre.

For our purposes, cross-compliance was defined to include the price support and production adjustment programs of ASCS and two conservation levels. A minimum conservation plan, as defined by Padgitt, allows participation in production adjustment programs. A full conservation plan permits participation in price support and production adjustment programs.

The policy was analyzed under two alternative decision rules:

1. A farmer cross-complies with a minimum conservation plan if his annual production adjustment benefits exceed $5 per acre. He cross-complies with a full conservation plan if his annual production adjustment and price support benefits exceed $15 per acre.

2. A farmer's decision rule is the same as in rule one, except he adopts a full conservation plan only if benefits exceed $25 per acre.

The study assumed that farmers are profit maximizers. If the expected benefits from the cross-complied programs exceed the cost of the compliance requirement, then farmers would meet the compliance requirement. This behavioral assumption is expressed by the alternative decision rules. The cost of the full conservation requirement was arbitrarily chosen. The cost of the minimum conservation requirement reflected Padgitt's findings. These costs represent the expense of installation, maintenance, lost production, and increased operation time associated with a conservation plan.

We equated expected benefits with the average per acre benefits received over the 1977-1979 period. These benefits are direct ASCS payments. Commodity programs reduce risk and uncertainty. Our benefit calculation, however, does not incorporate the value of this reduction. The benefits are gross, not net, benefits. The opportunity cost of setting aside acreage was not accounted for in these benefits. Data necessary to calculate net revenue losses were not available. Average farm productivity is an inappropriate proxy for this figure because set-aside acreage is, generally, the least productive farmland.

Because cross-compliance would require a long-term agreement to ensure the continuation of conservation practices, a full analysis needs to be based on a projection of future agricultural supply conditions. For example, if a farmer expects that no set-aside will exist for five years, then this study's benefit calculations, based on one year without a set-aside and two years with a set-aside, are inappropriate for the benefit calculation in that five-year period.

Our present research is attempting to incorporate these factors. However, we feel our preliminary analysis has produced results that are indicative of the expected performance of a cross-compliance policy.

Assessing the impacts of cross-compliance options

Conservation impacts. The impacts on conservation of the two cross-compliance options are measured by the change in the number of participants and acreage covered under the conservation program. Some farmers practicing conservation prior to a cross-compliance policy would not enter the program since their incentive benefits are below the decision rule minimum. Some backlash to the added obligation under cross-compliance might occur, but we feel that most conservation farmers would not discontinue their present practices, because they perceive conservation to be in their best interest. Further, most existing conservation plans would be sufficient to qualify for cross-complied programs.

Under rule one, 16 percent of the sample would have a minimum conservation plan, 6 percent would have a full conservation plan, and 22 percent would continue their present conservation plans. Forty-four percent of the sample would have a conservation plan, an increase of 55 percent. Forty percent of all crop acres would be covered by conservation plans, an increase of 15 percent over the situation prior to cross-compliance.

Under rule two, 18 percent of the sample would have a minimum conservation plan, 1 percent would have a full conservation plan, and 22 percent would continue their present conservation plans. Forty-one percent of the sample would have a conservation plan, an increase of 46 percent. Thirty-nine percent of all crop acres would be covered by conservation plans, an increase of 14 percent over the situation prior to cross-compliance. Thus, both options show an increase in conservation performance measured by number of participants and enrolled acres.

Distributional impacts. The distributional impacts within the farm sample were analyzed with respect to (1) enterprise mix, (2) farm size, (3) land tenure, and (4) yields.

1. *Enterprise mix.* Because most ASCS programs are targeted at grains, the enrollment increase with cross-compliance came primarily from grain farms.

2. *Size.* Farms that adopt a minimum conservation plan are larger in size than the full sample mean. Farms adopting a full conservation plan are smaller in size than the full sample mean. While a larger sample is necessary to reach a firm conclusion on the structural effect of this policy, this analysis indicates that larger farms will be affected most by cross-compliance.

3. *Land tenure.* Land tenure differences present a problem in conservation policy. Land users and landowners face different opportunity sets and respond to different incentives. It is difficult to create a single program that affects both groups. The landowner is concerned with the long-term productivity of his asset and may be relatively detached from short-run production decisions. The land user is concerned with short-term production and is less concerned about long-term productivity. An effective conservation plan must have the cooperation of both the landowner and land user. If either party is not committed to the plan, it is doomed to failure.

The owner-user dichotomy is reflected in the present conservation performance of the sample. Farmers who follow a farm plan own three-fourths of their land and rent the remainder. Farmers who do not follow a plan own only 60 percent of their land and rent the rest. Cross-compliance will not solve the owner-user conflict in conservation unless programs that directly assist both groups are linked to conservation in the program. By linking short-term production incentives with long-term conservation practices, cross-compliance can significantly increase the conservation behavior of those who use land but do not own it.

The owner-user conflict may be resolved by the indirect results of cross-compliance. For example, if the landowner has a crop-share lease with the land user, the owner may receive ASCS benefits. Cross-compliance would then provide an incentive to both the landowner and land user. Alternatively, if some landowners refuse to participate in conservation programs, a rent differential may develop between land with and land without conservation practices. This may lead to a capitalization of the value of conservation into land prices, providing a conservation incentive to landowners.

4. *Yields.* The yield variation among farms affected by the policy and the rest of the sample is significant for corn farms but not for wheat farms. Corn yields are 10 to 20 percent greater on farms that would participate in the conservation program. This difference is due to ASCS programs being based on production, that is, per acre ASCS program benefits are higher on farms with higher yields. In summary, cross-compliance primarily impacts larger, farmer-owned, higher yield grain farms. This implies that smaller, rented, and marginal farms lack an incentive to participate in cross-compliance.

We conclude: (a) Cross-compliance would provide a conservation incentive for farmers who are not practicing conservation presently; (b) cross-compliance appears to be a cost-effective method for increasing conservation coverage; there is a measurable increase in conservaton activity with a minimum of federal expenditure; (c) cross-compliance will affect larger farmers, who benefit most from the ASCS support programs, more than smaller farmers; and (d) cross-compliance will increase conservation behavior of those who use land but do not own it.

Additional policy issues

Administration and implementation. An increased demand for soil conservation technical assistance would necessitate an increase in SCS personnel. Enforcement of compliance could be implemented through ASCS. Because conservation is defined by production practices, aerial photographs could be used to show whether or not compliance is being realized. Linking these programs could require even closer interaction between the two USDA agencies, perhaps a positive side effect of the whole program.

Production impacts. Macro models at the University of Illinois and Iowa State University have been used to examine the effect of mandated soil and water conservation (*4, 10*). A variable conservation requirement, such as with cross-compliance, would have effects somewhat different from those under a mandatory soil loss limit. Food prices would likely increase along with increased production costs. The effect on supply is unclear. A larger study should examine these broader impacts.

There may be conflict of purpose among programs that are cross-complied. Price-support programs are intended strictly for farmers. Production-adjustment programs, however, are intended to provide supply stability for consumers and producers. Participation in these programs may be reduced as the producers who perceive returns inadequate to cover additional conservation costs withdraw.

Equity. The public as a whole benefits from soil conservation, but it is the farmers who are causing soil erosion, and so it is farmers who would benefit in the long run from conservation. Both groups benefit from soil erosion control. Farmers might experience increased production costs from conservation, costs that could theoretically be passed on to the consumer in food prices. However, because the market is imperfect, all costs are not passed on, thus many farmers cannot afford the cost of conservation. Farmers have in effect been assigned the right to assistance programs and the right to use their soil as they wish. Is it right to alter these property rights without compensation? That is a policy judgement.

A national soil conservation policy

The question of who pays for soil conservation defines what our conservation policy is to be. A solution has been proposed in another forum recently (7). Cross-compliance has been considered an all-or-nothing policy. One program, however, cannot constitute an effective, equitable conservation policy. A program mix is needed. Everyone benefits from soil conservation, and everyone must pay. The appropriate shares of that cost are the substance of conservation policy.

Cross-compliance would provide a cost-effective conservation program. In our opinion, it is unfair to expect farmers to assume all the cost of this program. The larger public benefits and must share in the cost. The Agricultural Conservation Program must be expanded. We feel that cost sharing should be at maximum levels for any practice with which it is necessary to comply. This proposal calls for an increase in federal conservation spending. However, given limited funding, money could be targeted to areas with the most severe conservation problems. The scope of the program could expand as money becomes available. Such a policy would be equitable, effective, and viable in the face of present economic conditions. Erosion is a problem for all, and all must bear the burden of its solution.

REFERENCES

1. Benbrook, Charles. 1979. *Integrating soil conservation and commodity programs: A policy proposal.* Journal of Soil and Water Conservation 34(4): 160-167.
2. Ciriacy-Wantrup, S.V. 1952. *Resource conservation, economics and policies.* University of California Press, Berkeley.
3. Culver, John. 1979. *Soil conservation: A partial commitment is not enough.* In *Soil Conservation Policies: An Assessment.* Soil Conservation Society of America. Ankeny, Iowa.
4. Heady, Earl O., and Gary F. Vocke. *Trade-offs between erosion controls and production costs in U.S. agriculture.* Journal of Soil and Water Conservation 33(5): 227-230.
5. Held, R. Burnell, and Marion Clawson. 1965. *Soil conservation in perspective.* The Johns Hopkins Press, Baltimore, Maryland.
6. Johnson, Glenn L., and C. Leroy Quance. 1972. *The overproduction trap in U.S. agriculture.* The Johns Hopkins Press, Baltimore, Maryland.

7. Libby, Lawrence W. 1980. *Who should pay for soil and water conservation?* Journal of Soil and Water Conservation 35(4): 155-157.
8. Libby, Lawrence W., and John L. Okay. 1979. *National soil and water conservation policy: An economic perspective.* Staff Paper 79-37. Department of Agricultural Economics, Michigan State University, East Lansing.
9. Padgitt, Merritt Merrill. 1980. *An analysis of on-farm impacts for soil conservation and nonpoint source pollution abatement practices and policies on representative farms in southeast Minnesota.* Dissertation. Department of Resource Development, Michigan State University, East Lansing.
10. Seitz, Wesley D., C. Robert Taylor, Robert G.F. Spitze, Craig Osteen, and Mack C. Nelson. 1979. *Economic impacts of soil erosion control.* Land Economics 55(1): 28-42.
11. Swader, Frederick N. 1980. *Soil productivity and the future of American agriculture.* In *The Future of American Agriculture as a Strategic Resource.* The Conservation Foundation. Washington, D.C.
12. U.S. Department of Agriculture. 1980. *Soil and Water Resources Conservation Act, program report, 1980 draft review.* Washington, D.C.

XI. Water Quantity and Quality: Trends and Issues

44

Eutrophication: Who Pays?

Robert J. Sugarman
Chairman, United States Section
International Joint Commission, Washington, D.C.

The International Joint Commission (IJC) was established originally as a permanent, bilateral body to prevent disputes regarding the use of boundary waters and to settle questions arising between the United States and Canada along their common frontier. But the commission also has provided the framework for cooperation on questions relating to water and air pollution and the regulation of water levels and flows.

The commission carries out its functions with the assistance of 28 binational advisory boards, which includes scientists, engineers, and other experts from both countries. The commission frequently holds public hearings in connection with matters under its jurisdiction, often to collect comments on the findings and recommendations of its international boards.

A basis for progress

The 1978 Water Quality Agreement, which replaced the original 1972 water quality compact, was the culmination of a series of IJC reports that cited the need to enhance the water quality of the Great Lakes.

The commission's involvement with water quality began in its first year of operation, 1912. An IJC study completed in 1918 warned the two countries of developing problems in the Great Lakes that required remedial programs for handling municipal and industrial wastes.

In 1946 the Governments asked the commission to investigate water quality problems in the connecting channels of the Great Lakes. In its 1950 report the IJC recommended remedial action and established international water quality objectives. The commission's 1970 report, citing major problems in Lakes Erie and Ontario, resulted in the signing of the first Great Lakes Water Quality Agreement.

In its Great Lakes Water Quality Agreement of 1978, Canada and the United States agreed on a number of programs to minimize eutrophication problems in the Great Lakes system, including point- and nonpoint-source control possibilities. The commission also monitors the progress of programs to reduce phosphorus through treatment and nonpoint sources.

Recently, the IJC submitted two significant reports containing recommendations for measures to control eutrophication. In April 1980, the commission reported on the results of its five-year study, "Pollution from Land Use Activities in the Great Lakes Basin." In July 1980, it transmitted a task force report, "Phosphorus Management Strategies for the Great Lakes." Both reports include recommendations for addressing the complex problems of eutrophication, and both are deeply impacted by questions of cost and cost distribution.

The phosphorus problem

Before being appointed by President Carter to be co-chairman of the IJC, I was an environmental lawyer for more than 15 years. While dealing with water quality issues, I learned how diverse the theories are for controlling phosphorus inputs in our waterways. Now, after more than two years of dealing daily with water quality matters on behalf of the commission, I find the problem still complicated, but also one that can be dealt with effectively.

The commission's two recent reports are major steps toward a positive framework for dealing now with eutrophication.

Many questions, of course, remain. More research and more study are required. For example: What are the most appropriate phosphorus target loads for the Great Lakes? Have the eutrophication models produced good phosphorus loading objectives? What are the complete costs of eutrophication control, from both a technical/limnological and socio-economic perspective? What is the total picture regarding costs and benefits? How should the question of the bioavailability of phosphorus be factored into the overall phosphorus control strategy? How can we determine the proper mix of point- and nonpoint-source phosphorus control measures for the Great Lakes?

Based on what we have learned from our Pollution from Land Use Activities Reference Group (PLUARG) and Phosphorus Management Strategies Task Force studies, I believe two things are obvious. First, the costs of correcting eutrophication are almost always higher than the costs of prevention. And second, recognizing that relative cost data and knowledge of the effectiveness of proposed new technology are still incomplete, positive steps can nevertheless be taken now to control phosphorus inputs.

The commission's PLUARG report tentatively identified updated phosphorus target loads for the Great Lakes but recognized the need for additional study because uncertainty remained concerning the appropriateness of the target loads to achieve the phosphorus control goals of the 1978 Great Lakes Water Quality Agreement. This uncertainty prevented the commission from advising the governments with absolute accuracy of the present phosphorus loads and future targets. It is clear, however, that substantial reductions from present loading levels are required to assure protection of the Great Lakes from eutrophication, especially in Saginaw Bay and the lower Great Lakes of Erie and Ontario.

Because of the deadlines concerning affirmation or rejection of the target loads required in Annex 3 of the 1978 Great Lakes Water Quality Agreement, the report of the Phosphorus Management Strategies Task Force was forwarded immediately to the governments upon receipt by the commission. The commission, however, is now reviewing the report and will submit its comments to the governments in the next few months.

The task force answered many questions; however, as might be expected, it left many others unanswered. Neither PLUARG nor the task force recommend across-the-board, ultimate remedial phosphorus control measures, although both did say that further phosphorus control in the basin was needed.

Both groups also recommended that additional steps be taken to control or remove phosphorus—on a priority basis—from those areas of the lakes where severe eutrophication problems already exist, such as Saginaw Bay in Lake Huron, the western basin of Lake Erie, and the Bay of Quinte in Lake Ontario.

The task force's report included a series of specific recommendations to the commission for immediate action:

1. All municipal wastewater treatment plants discharging more than 1 million gallons per day should be designed and placed in operation as quickly as possible so that the total phosphorus concentrations in their effluents will not exceed a minimum of 1 milligram per liter.

2. Municipal wastewater treatment facilities in the lower Great Lakes Basin capable of achieving effluent concentrations below 1 milligram per liter, even though now only required to meet an effluent limit of 1 milligram per liter total phosphorus, should be operated to achieve lower effluent concentrations as soon as possible.

3. All planning for future municipal point-source discharges to the lower Great Lakes basin should consider requirements for total phosphorus removals down to concentrations of 0.1 to 0.5 milligram per liter.

4. Low-cost, nonpoint-source phosphorus control measures should be implemented where appropriate.

5. Alternative technologies, such as land application, which can reduce

loads to 0.1 milligram per liter, should be considered in all new facilities planning.

Obviously, a mix of control measures are needed to control phosphorus pollution in the Great Lakes Basin effectively. This mix will depend in large part on who pays and how much. Such factors as feasibility of specific non-point-source control measures and the operation and maintenance costs of point-source control will affect which control strategy is developed.

The promise of land treatment

It is in this context that land application presents an alternative to conventional measures. In many cases land application has a much greater phosphorus removal efficiency (down to levels below 0.1 milligram per liter on a consistent basis) and also costs less to operate and maintain.

The phosphorus task force report illustrates an encouraging increase in interest in land treatment of phosphorus-rich municipal waste water. The task force found that a growing number of studies show that land treatment can be a cost-effective and an environmentally safe technology for the treatment of municipal and industrial wastes. The task force pointed out that while this type of waste treatment system has thus far been used primarily in small communities it can, in fact, also be considered for larger communities. The technology is solidly established, not experimental.

The report noted that if all municipal wastewater treatment plants with flows less than 10 million gallons per day were converted to land treatment, the total phosphorus load discharged by municipal sources in the Lake Erie basin would be reduced by 700 metric tons per year and in the Lake Ontario basin by 500 metric tons per year. That amounts to a 5 to 10 percent reduction, or 15 to 30 percent of the needed reductions, and it applies to the type of phosphorus of most concern. The environmental impacts may be even more significant than the actual numbers suggest because this phosphorus, being from municipal sewage sources, would be primarily in a chemical form available for immediate uptake and use by algae, compared with the higher nonavailable fraction from other sources. The report did not attempt to determine what further reductions might be possible from conversion of larger plants to the land treatment method.

The report recognizes that land treatment is a very effective method for extracting phosphates from wastewaters before they flow back into waterways and lakes.

In April 1979 participants were told at the IJC-Cornell University conference on phosphorus management strategies that perhaps the only way routinely and cost-effectively to achieve phosphorus effluent concentrations of significantly less than 1.0 milligram per liter is through land treatment.

An example is the land treatment facility at Muskegon, Michigan, a 33-million-gallon-per-day facility that is regularly discharging effluent with only .07 milligram per liter of phosphorus.

Our task force report joins a lengthening list of academic, environmental, and governmental proponents who are transforming the sanitary landscape. Last year the IJC's Water Quality Board reported that a strong research data base indicates that well-designed and operated systems are clearly beneficial to the environment and that some states are in fact actively pursuing new land treatment systems as an alternative to existing treatment techniques.

Further, the IJC board stated that land treatment processes are available and viable alternatives to conventional or advanced wastewater treatment systems and should and will be considered by water quality planners in the Great Lakes Basin—if the new processes can be made cost effective and environmentally acceptable.

Costs and environmental criteria

Those who have investigated land treatment methods know how difficult it is to precisely resolve cost and environmental criteria. First, cost-effectiveness. The commission's Water Quality Board pointed out that cost comparisons between land treatment and other alternatives are extremely difficult to make on a general basis. According to the board's comparative data, both slow-rate and rapid-infiltration land treatment systems were shown to be significantly more cost-effective than conventional, advanced wastewater treatment systems using tertiary treatment, two-stage lime coagulation, and filtration at sizes up to 50 million gallons per day. The rapid-infiltration type of land treatment process proved to be cost-effective with advanced secondary treatment, such as activated sludge secondary treatment and would be even more cost-effective than activated sludge with in-plant phosphorus removal.

The board also conducted a computer model cost analysis comparing rapid-infiltration land treatment with other treatment systems. The analysis showed that construction of new rapid-infiltration land treatment facilities is substantially less costly than new secondary treatment plus coagulation facilities under both "very favorable" and "moderately favorable" conditions. The board identified numerous areas in the Great Lakes Basin where moderately to very favorable conditions exist for rapid-infiltration land treatment systems.

We know that it is extremely costly to remove phosphorus below 1 milligram per liter using conventional sewage treatment methods. Large quantities of chemicals and energy are required to remove phosphorus from wastewaters and to dispose of the resulting sludge.

Nor are other alternatives more attractive. Even a total ban on phosphorus from detergents could not be expected to lower significantly the operation and maintenance costs for municipal sewage treatment plants. Large quantities of chemicals are required to begin the process of removing phosphorus from the wastewater. At any rate, detergent phosphorus is not the source of the majority of phosphorus in municipal nonpoint wastewaters in the Great Lakes Basin.

The Muskegon facility is the best example of land treatment in the Great Lakes Basin. However, other examples of successful and long-lived land treatment systems exist in other parts of the United States and Canada, as well as in Europe and Australia.

The operators of the Muskegon facility report relatively low operating costs. Their user charges for the first five years of operation were $.17 per 1,000 gallons. With a 56 percent increase in power costs during 1977 and 1978, user costs were raised $.03 in 1979—18 percent. Costs have remained low because the system takes advantage of the natural phosphorus absorption processes in the soils at the site along with light and wind and because the sale of crops irrigated by the treated wastewater consistently offsets much of the expense involved in running and maintaining the system.

But costs or technical reliability are usually not the reasons land treatment is rejected in favor of conventional sewage treatment. Waste treatment by innovative technologies is not a popular topic. Few parents encourage their children to grow up to become sewage treatment experts. Engineers educated in traditional methods frequently resist such new and innovative technologies.

Moreover, the public has adopted an out-of-sight, out-of-mind attitude toward sewage disposal. The critic of land treatment who says the system is not environmentally sound all too often means that a proposed site is too close to his neighborhood.

In spite of its limitations we have come to the sewage treatment and discharge method. However, public confidence in this system of discharging partially treated wastewater into our lakes and rivers has been shaken by the outcry over eutrophication the past 25 years.

A convincing track record

The U.S. Environmental Protection Agency (EPA) reported in April 1979 that more than 3,000 land treatment systems—between 10 and 20 percent of all existing treatment systems—are in use in the United States. Some sites have been operating effectively for more than 50 years. EPA also said that the communities that have converted from land treatment to conventional wastewater treatment facilities have done so in most cases because of population expansion around the site, rather than because of a failure of the land treatment system itself.

The EPA report, "A History of Land Application as a Treatment Alternative," stated that the philosophy of land or soil treatment must replace the disposal concept. In addition, the report cited the urgent need for an emphasis in land-treatment methods in the education of environmental engineers, agricultural engineers, agronomists, and others who must cooperate in designing these systems.

As far as public health is concerned ample evidence exists to indicate that the risks to public health from a land-treatment system—risks that are no greater than those from a conventional sewage treatment plant—can be minimized with properly designed and managed systems. A potentially serious concern, the transmission of pathogens, including bacteria and viruses, is alleviated by a variety of proven techniques.

The health problem, then, is not major. And land treatment facilities are often found to be cost-effective when compared with standard wastewater treatment facilities.

But the question, "Who pays?" involves more than cost comparisons. It includes comprehensive ecosystem balances—a recognition of the full range of effects.

Land treatment is not new. The application of wastewater to the land began in antiquity. Land treatment began in Great Britain in the mid-1800s. EPA's 1979 report on the history of land treatment said that the method was considered to be the most effective wastewater treatment alternative in the United States from 1890 to 1905 and was used in most communities with sewage treatment. But U.S. engineers believed that the emphasis should be on sewage "disposal," not "treatment," and ignored it for the most part.

Then in the 1950s, when eutrophication of waterways became a matter of public concern, engineers and water planners started to take a fresh look at land treatment. Public pressure by concerned swimmers, fishermen, and shoreline property owners forced a revision in wastewater management thinking. The public was paying the price for water management planners' failure to recognize the problem of phosphorus and eutrophication.

As planners began to rethink their positions on water quality, a fresh look at land treatment made many aware of the system's several benefits, including, for example, the use of treated wastewater to irrigate golf courses, open spaces, and greenbelts and the use of treated wastewater in reclaiming sterile or marginal soil.

The cost of eutrophication is borne by all segments of the public, including sewage service rate payers, fishermen, landowners, and consumers. The benefits of reducing eutrophication accrues to the same groups. Correspondingly, prevention of pollution pays for itself—if we adopt methods that work with nature.

45

Implications for Water Quality on Reclaimed Lands

H. B. Pionke and A. S. Rogowski

Soil Scientists, Science and Education Administration—
Agricultural Research, U.S. Department of Agriculture
University Park, Pennsylvania

Surface coal mining in the United States will increase substantially because of the cost and scarcity of petroleum fuels, the lower extraction costs, and greater safety of surface mining compared with deep mining of coals. Moreover, substantial quantities of U.S. coal lie close enough to the land surface to be extracted by modern surface mining techniques.

There are various surface coal-mining techniques, but basically seven steps are involved: soil removal, break up of overburden, overburden removal, coal removal, overburden replacement, soil replacement, and revegetation (Figure 1). In the process, the premining vegetation and stratigraphy are destroyed and, until sufficiently revegetated, much land surface is exposed to the possibility of accelerated erosion. The surface coal mining breaks up largely continuous, slowly permeable rock strata, exposing them to air and water movement. This generally results in the generation and loss of acid, salt, and possibly trace chemical constituents to streams and groundwater, the extent of which depends upon the site characteristics and reclamation methods used.

The reclamation process designed to minimize the adverse environmental impact of surface coal mining includes effluent treatment, revegetation, topsoiling, and specific placement of overburden materials. The minimally acceptable reclamation requirements in the United States are described in

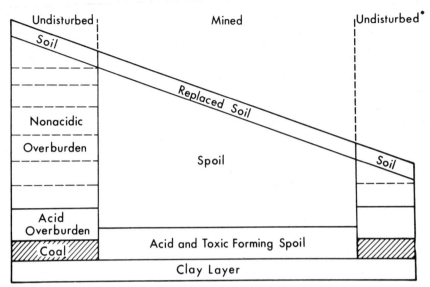

Figure 1. Schematic representation of strip mine cross-section applicable to bituminous coal-mining area in Appalachia.

Public Law 95-87, but individual states often impose stricter regulations. Public Law 95-87 sets specific surface drainage water effluent standards for total suspended solids, iron, manganese, and pH. It also requires topsoiling and covering of acid- and toxic-forming materials with at least 4 feet (1.2 meters) of the best available nontoxic and noncombustible material. Overall, the total suspended solids standards are the most difficult to achieve. There are no explicit water quality standards for groundwater. Instead the acid- and toxic-forming materials are to be handled and placed so as to minimize contamination of groundwater systems. The law provides for treatment of surface drainage or discharged effluent from the mine site to meet required water quality standards, however, the approach to controlling potential groundwater pollution is analogous to the "best management practice" concept.

There are three options for controlling water pollution resulting from surface coal-mining activities. The first and most obvious is to avoid mining. At sites where the impact is potentially very severe or extraordinary, a mechanism does exist to limit or prohibit mining. The other two options presume mining and provide for either the treatment of effluent off-site or for controls on-site.

Where water quality standards must be met, the two options may not be interchangeable. Off-site effluent treatment can reduce pollutant concentrations to meet a given water quality standard. In contrast, on-site controls attempt to minimize the loss of pollutants from the mined sites. The minimal loss may or may not meet the effluent standards. However, effluent losses may be sufficiently reduced by on-site treatment to more readily or cheaply achieve the required standards. The off-site effluent treatment is usually temporary and expensive, especially when dissolved materials need to be removed. On-site control methods usually become an integral part of the mined site, operating automatically and on a long-term basis. Aesthetically, on-site controls, which emphasize control of the soil and water losses at their origin rather than off-site recapture through treatment, which permits significant on-site losses, are preferred.

Our purpose is to identify some of the processes that control the generation and transport of sediment and chemicals from the surface coal-mined site, then to consider these processes in the context of on-site controls. We also consider some economic and aesthetic implications. The emphasis throughout is placed on those processes peculiar to strip-mined sites in the eastern United States.

Water quality problems

Suspended sediment. Mining land use resulting from surface coal mining, such as initial clearing of land, stockpiling of overburden, construction of haul roads, and even backfilling and reclamation operations, can contribute approximately ten times as much sediment as an equivalent area of cropland and 2,000 times as much as an undisturbed forest (4). Consequently, the mining of cropland and particularly forest land in Appalachia potentially can create sediment problems downstream. Should mining commence on a large scale, the potential for these problems will greatly increase.

While sediment can fill lakes and ponds and clog stream channels, it can also carry other pollutants such as plant nutrients, herbicides, insecticides, heavy metals, viruses, and bacteria. In this capacity, contamination by these other pollutants could adversely affect drinking water supplies and aquatic habitats. Although an average erosion rate from a mined watershed is approximately 70-times greater than if it remained unmined, the spoil banks and haul roads can account for 1,000- and 2,000-fold increases (3).

Federal regulations recommend that sediment yield from a mined watershed be calculated using Universal Soil Loss Equation (USLE) (24) gully erosion rates, and sediment delivery ratios. Although these procedures are adequate for computing annual runoff from agricultural fields, they are not designed for application to mined watersheds on a per storm basis. To correct for this, it has been proposed that the USLE be recalibrated for application to mined lands by using standard plot techniques previously successful for calibrating USLE to farmland. However, it may not be that simple. Extending small plot results to watersheds is not only questionable scientifically, but risky as well. Mine-soils lack structure and their texture over an area varies depending upon the materials used for topsoiling. Thus it is likely that the erodibility factor (K) in the USLE will also be variable at least until the structure of the reclaimed soil has developed and texture is consistent.

In general, slopes associated with surface coal mining in Appalachia are both steeper and longer than anything found in agricultural use, and little is known about the effects of conservation practices on reclaimed areas. In particular, there is no information on spoil settling and the resultant unfavorable effects settling has on these practices.

Acids and acidic salts. Pyrite exposed to air in the broken-up overburden oxidizes to form sulphuric acid and ferrous sulphate. The sulphuric acid can react with other minerals to form the acid salts, aluminum, additional ferrous, and manganese sulphates (20). These compounds function as weak acids and are included with the sulphuric acid in a single measurement known as total acidity, which is the titrated acidity to pH 7.3 or 8.2. The pH measures the hydrogen ion activity, which in a predominantly sulphate system is an estimate of the sulphuric acid still present. Depending upon concentrations, total acidity, iron, manganese, aluminum, pH, or the total dissolved load can adversely affect water use and rank with sediment as a major water quality problem in many eastern U.S. coal fields.

Neutral salts. The neutral salts either are produced by neutralization of sulphuric acid or are indigenous to the overburden and exist primarily as calcium and magnesium sulphates. These have been observed in the overburden at substantial concentrations (9, 11). If substantial amounts of calcium and magnesium carbonates are present, the generated acid may be neutralized to form calcium and magnesium sulfates. Usually, this effluent is still of high enough quality for many water uses.

Trace metals. The trace metals, including iron, manganese, zinc, copper, cadmium, chromium, mercury, lead, and nickel, may or may not be a problem at surface coal mine sites. We have mentioned them here because concentrations of some have been observed to exceed U.S. Environmental Protection Agency drinking-water standards in groundwater (6), and in spoil leachate (13, 16). Except for iron, manganese, and zinc, the other trace metals usually are found in very low concentrations in groundwater and in streams draining coal mine sites.

Processes controlling water quality

Suspended sediment. As in natural soils, generation and transport of large volumes of sediment on mined lands depends upon the availability of excess rain and the production of runoff. Unlike natural soils, control of infiltration and deep percolation to reduce runoff is not necessarily a viable solution on reclaimed areas. Increased percolation may be accompanied by increased acid generation and leaching if the overburden contains large amounts of acid-forming spoil. In attempting to simultaneously minimize acid generation and erosion, the distribution of percolation also needs to be selective. However, as illustrated in a following example, we might be deal-

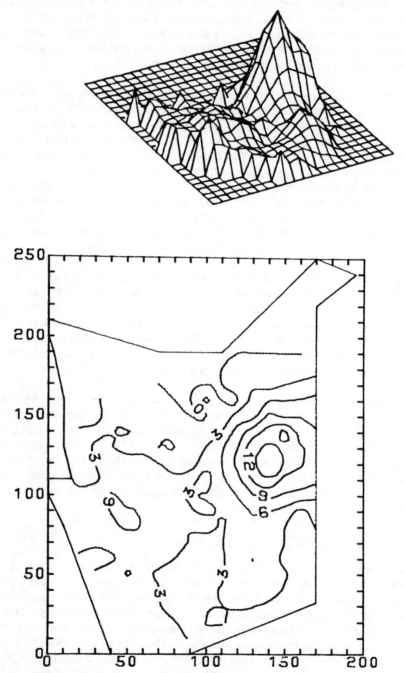

Figure 2. Kriged contour plots of infiltration at 1 minute. Contours are in millimeters. Vertical and horizontal scales are in meters.

ing here with a far more complex phenomenon than anticipated.

Figure 2 shows a distribution of infiltration (i) for t (1 minute) at our reclaimed surface coal mined experimental site based on field-determined values of sorptivity (S) and A-values in the Philip (15) infiltration equation (18):

$$i = St^{1/2} + At \qquad [1]$$

It would now seem strictly routine to compute rainfall excess and runoff for this experimental area for a known rain. Unfortunately, neither spatial (Figures 3a, b, and c) nor temporal distributions of vegetative cover, antecedent water content, and rainfall remain stable for very long. If now some experimental distribution of erodibility (K) is imposed over the site, the true complexity of the problem and uncertainty associated with prediction becomes apparent, because rain energy will also vary spatially and in time possibly as a function of slope, rain intensity, and wind pattern (21). Consequently, measurements taken on standard plots or small areas likely have little meaning for extrapolating such results to mined watersheds on a per storm basis.

How can a meaningful appraisal of erosion at a mining location be made? Compared with cropland, erosion on surface-mined land can be considerably more severe, especially on spoil banks and haul roads during and immediately following reclamation. Curtis (1) postulated that sediment yield from mined land has a six-month half-life associated with it and included formulas to compute sediment yield for any desired six-month period and a total expected sediment yield if the sediment yield for the first six months is known. Unfortunately, this approach requires a period of data gathering and does not say where the erosion is occurring or how best to prevent it.

On a mined watershed after reclamation, three processes take place simultaneously: settlement, erosion, and sedimentation. In general, overburden spoil following reclamation assumes a 25 percent greater volume than it had in natural compacted and stratified state (23). There is little information available on how fast and how much spoil settles. Spoil profiles reconstituted in 2-meter-diameter (6.6 feet), 4-meter-high (13.2 feet) caissons exhibited a 5 and 9 percent settlement on the topsoiled and nontopsoiled materials, respectively, following the initial application of water equal to about half of the normal annual precipitation at the experimental site (19). In the past, railway fills were allowed to settle under their own weight. Railway rock fills settled by about 3 percent, sandy fill materials by about 4 percent, and fill materials with considerable clay by about 8 percent of the original fill height (22). In general, therefore, we might expect less than 10 percent settlement on reclaimed areas.

The process of erosion and sedimentation on mined and reclaimed sites appears area specific. Spoil banks and haul roads register highest erosion rates, while on the flatter, low-lying areas deposition prevails. Of most interest is the net amount of sediment that could arrive at the outlet of mined area where usually a sediment pond is located. Current research programs involve several hundred 1-meter-long (3.3 feet) erosion pins, 10 millimeters in diameter (.04 inch), driven into the ground at random and in transects to

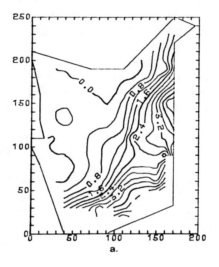

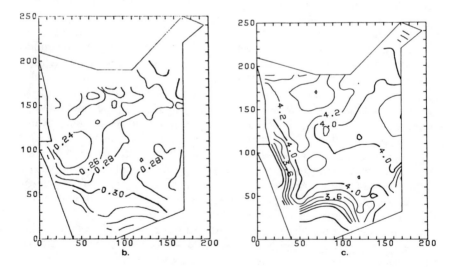

Figure 3. Vegetation density (metric tons/ha), (a) antecedent water content (m³/m³), (b) and rainfall distribution (mm), (c) on surface coal mined and reclaimed site at Kylertown, Pennsylvania. The contours are as designated, vertical, and horizontal scales are in meters.

within 100 millimeters (4.9 inches) of the top. Subsequent monitoring of their height above ground, along with the sediment concentration in runoff effluent, will provide spatially distributed erosion and deposition data input to computer contouring programs. Such programs, utilizing kriging theory and best linear unbiased estimator techniques (10), will yield contour depths of erosion and sedimentation over a site along with associated errors. Supporting evidence of rainfall depths, slopes, slope lengths, cover, and infiltration distributions will provide a sufficiently broad data base to formulate a predictive erosion and sedimentation model for mined and reclaimed watersheds, including natural parameter variability and partial area contributions.

Acid production. Acid production depends upon the type and amount of pyrite present, pH, relative humidity, temperature, oxygen content, and microbiological activity (20). The point to remember is that pyrite is insoluble, but the acid products resulting from pyrite oxidation are moderately to very soluble. The transport and loss of these acid products thus could be controlled if the conversion rate of pyrite to acid products was controlled. From the available literature it appears that overall acid production depends mostly on two factors: the availability of pyrite and the availability of oxygen. Usually only select strata localized within the unmined overburden contain most of the pyrite. During and after mining, particular attention therefore should be paid to the spoil from these strata. The extent and amount of such spoil can be estimated a priori using geostatistical techniques (10). Where oxygen is not limiting, the pyrite properties affecting acid production such as crystal form, particle size distribution, concentration, and distribution of the pyrite particles may need to be known.

At a site where predominant crystal forms, and particle size distribution are not greatly different, the acid production would be expected to correlate reasonably well with the spoil pyrite content. Where oxygen is limiting, microbiologically induced oxidation and presence of nonoxygen oxidants (ferric iron) could greatly increase acid production temporarily. However, in the long term, these systems also ultimately depend upon oxygen availability. Assuming that these conditions apply, the most obvious means of controlling acid production is to limit oxygen supply or resupply to the most pyritic spoil. The slowest process or that most potentially limiting the resupply rate of oxygen is oxygen diffusion, especially under water. The oxygen diffusion rate is 10,000 times slower in water than in air.

Transport of acid and neutral salts. Control of the acid and neutral salt concentrations in percolate and groundwater is much more difficult. Sometimes such control may be needed because part of the area to be mined was previously mined and exposed to the atmosphere, or considerable salts indigenous to the coal-bearing deposit exist, or an old abandoned mine site is to be reclaimed as in the Rural Abandoned Mines Program (RAMP). Because acid and neutral salts are moderately to very soluble, they are best controlled by controlling water flux and chemical diffusion. To clarify these processes, the spoil response will be considered separately in the unsaturated and in the saturated states.

In the unsaturated spoil, the water flux occurs primarily as short-term percolation. The salt leaching by percolating water depends upon the extent, amount, and rate of percolation, salt supply at the particle surface, and possibly the salt resupply rate to the spoil particle surface from the particle interior. The extent of percolation controls the volume of spoil leached. Newly reclaimed spoils (post-Public Law 95-87) generally have finer-textured topsoil placed over coarse-textured spoils. Others, particularly abandoned mines reclaimed under RAMP programs, may be very coarse-textured all the way to the surface. These may lead to fingering and wetting front instability (*7, 14*) or to channelized flow. The result is that incoming water percolates downward through discrete channels, thereby leaching salts from only part rather than all of the spoil volume.

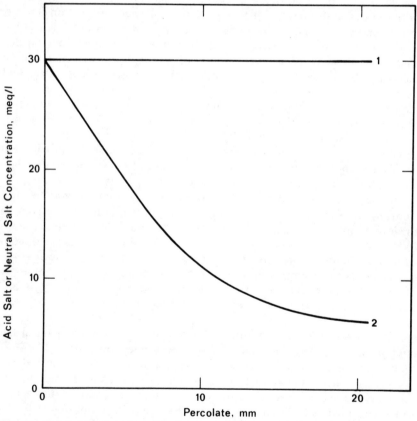

Figure 4. Relationship between acid salt or neutral salt concentration and percolate.

The amount and rate of percolation compared with salt resupply rate to the particle surface can be important depending upon the specific site (Figure 4). This simplified figure graphically represents complex relationships based on data presented in Pionke and associates (16). Assuming curve 1 depicts the relationship between salt concentration in percolate and the percolate volume, reduction in percolation could substantially reduce the amount of salt transported (transported salt load equals salt concentration times volume of percolate). In this case, the amount of percolation determines the amount of salt loss. If curve 2 depicts the relationship, the additional quantity of salt transported is much less for larger volumes of percolate. In this case, either the salt supply at the particle surface or resupply rate (through chemical diffusion to the particle surface) is transport-controlling (17). These flow-chemical quantity relationships are also expected to be highly dependent upon the percolation rate.

When the spoil is saturated and salt-containing particles are submerged either seasonally or on a year-round basis, the control of salt loss may shift from hydraulic to chemical diffusion control. Once the salt content is depleted in spoil particle surface layers, the diffusion rate of salts from the interior to the particle surface may limit salt loss to surrounding water (17). A very slowly moving or stagnant groundwater system in which salt concentrations build up enough in groundwater to suppress salt diffusion in the particle could switch a primarily chemical diffusion controlled system to a seepage flux controlled system.

Transport of trace metals. Trace metal production and transport are poorly understood. The production appears to be associated with pyrite oxidation, while the trace metals' concentrations seem related to acid salt concentrations (6, 16), to total dissolved solids (6), and to pH (6, 12).

Promising on-site reclamation approaches

Controlling loss of suspended sediment. Long-term sediment loss control can be readily accomplished on mined and reclaimed lands using standard methodology currently available. Once adequate cover is established and maintained, the threat of severe erosion is minimal. It is the severe short-term erosional losses before vegetation establishment that greatly trouble the coal industry and enforcement agencies.

There are many reasons for these severe initial losses. The spoil as a whole settles and readjusts itself after reclamation, and uneven stresses and fragment size distributions peculiar to spoil may lead to zones of weakness more susceptible to gullying, slides, and internal erosion (piping). Consequently, many conservation control practices not only become ineffective, but also may actually become detrimental. Diversion structures that break or that undergo slope increases because of settling may thus result in severe gullying. Preferential erosion of fines, which exposes coarse rock fragments, may lead to gullying, increased turbulence of runoff, and increased erosion.

Simultaneously, raindrop-caused erosion might decline because of rock pavement formation. However, such rock pavement provides a poor growth medium for vegetation. A compacted spoil surface may reduce percolation and the likelihood of acid drainage, but it also increases the potential for erosion. Thus, much that can be done to prevent sediment loss and erosion on mined and reclaimed lands needs to be viewed in the context of how such measures affect the total spoil profile. This is unlike the case with natural soil where generally only the plow layer is of interest.

When reclaiming surface-mined land, opportunities exist to modify land-forms in line with projected land use. If land is to be reclaimed for agriculture, for example, a series of level or slightly sloping terraces may be preferred to original sloping topography.

Topsoiling with selected overburden strata materials, if available, may often be more beneficial than topsoiling with the shallow, structureless, and acidic soil materials of low fertility frequently found in wooded areas of Appalachia. Some of the strata materials may weather rapidly, providing an initially erosion-resistant rock mulch that can change gradually to a good seedbed.

Internal erosion, as well as infiltration, redistribution, and availability of water to plants can be controlled by appropriate combination in layers of selected spoil fragment sizes, similar to riprap control of erosion in embankments. Zones of recharge as well as layers that can hold amounts of available water can thus be created. Acid spoil placed in a coarse gravel layer surrounded by a finer-textured medium would be bypassed by water streamlines. This type of manipulation of physical overburden properties offers a challenge and an opportunity to follow the true intent of the federal surface mining legislation.

Acid products. Limiting pyrite oxidation by controlling oxygen concentration requires that oxygen transport by air convection within the spoil mass be minor or be made minor. Whether diffusion or air convection is the controlling process depends upon site geometry, aspect, surface porosity, and internal thermal gradients. In the coal refuse piles, for example, convective transport of air can predominante. Relative to reclaimed spoil banks, these piles are usually characterized by large overall surface-to-mass ratio, wind exposure, large voids, and considerable internal thermal gradients caused by readily combustible materials.

In diffusion-controlled oxygen systems, one approach is to decrease the oxygen concentration gradient between the soil surface and the location of a pyritic layer. This may be accomplished by increasing the diffusion distance, i.e., by placing the most pyritic materials deeper in the spoil. Another way is to decrease the atmospheric concentration of oxygen in the soil by accelerating oxygen uptake by plants or by decreasing the resupply rate through the topsoiled layer. Vegetation, especially in conjunction with high soil-water status has been observed to greatly reduce oxygen content in topsoil (8). Accordingly, additions of highly degradable organic matter could potentially reduce the oxygen content of the topsoil. Increasing the topsoil depth or placing fine-textured spoil materials immediately beneath the topsoil could slow the oxygen diffusion rate.

The oxygen concentrations gradient can be greatly decreased in the zone containing the most pyritic materials by switching from an air to a water system in which underwater placement reduces the oxygen diffusion rate to .0001 of that in air. However, if submerged materials also contain substantial amounts of salts, or if the water table is not stable and fluctuates seasonally, acid production or salt loss may actually increase. Placing an air seal such as clay around the most pyritic spoil may control both pyrite oxidation and salt loss. It may be possible to manipulate the fragment sizes of the most pyritic spoils. Handling of pyritic strata during mining so as to minimize particle breakdown could increase the average particle size and thus increase the intraparticle distances for oxygen and salt diffusion. This could also minimize leaching by decreasing the wetted surface area.

Acid and neutral salts. Losses of acid or neutral salts from the unsaturated zones can be reduced by decreasing the leached spoil volume or the amount of percolation. Reducing the leached volume could be accomplished by creating localized recharge zones. The total percolation could also be reduced or seasonal percolation peaks redistributed. Topsoiling to a greater depth or with materials that can store more water in the root zone while increasing evapotranspiration losses, e.g., by planting cool weather vegetation, may reduce both the peak and total percolation amounts. Appropriate tile drainage systems could be installed to control excessive seasonal water table rise, minimizing the fluctuations.

Losses of acid or neutral salts from the saturated zone are potentially limited by increasing the diffusion pathway within the particle, i.e., larger particle sizes, or by reducing the concentration gradient from the particle to the groundwater (stagnant conditions). Most likely, the latter approach would require controlling internal water levels and limiting groundwater outflow rates.

Trace metals. Losses of trace metals may be best controlled by either controlling acid production or acid salt loss, and by dilution of groundwater before it changes to streamflow or becomes a part of the water supply. At some sites it seems that substantial dilution occurs naturally (6).

Economic and aesthetics

Before mining begins, the reclamation potential of selected sites can be considered in terms of the sites' postmining land uses (2). To do so, premining and postmining levels of physical, chemical, economic, and aesthetic properties associated with each site need to be examined. In general, a mining site's reclamation potential seems more influenced by economic and aesthetic properties than by the physical and chemical attributes (2).

Among the possible economic parameters are land property values, which are usually readily available at county courthouses or tax assessment offices. Since general land use, in this case in Pennsylvania, governs tax assessments, postmining property values can be estimated based on the projected land use. An opinion survey questionnaire sent to residents in affected areas may pose a choice between selected land use for postmining environments in an attempt to elicit input about mining and reclamation practices. From the standpoint of economics, another consideration is the effect of mining and subsequent land use on unemployment and costs associated with reclamation to a particular land use. Community acceptance of the land use selected is desirable. The size of the area mined and the subsequent degree of visual conformity of reclaimed land to the surrounding landscape seem to substantially influence the aesthetics associated with mining.

Economic factors may become particularly important if on-site selective placement of spoils to control acid mine drainage and erosion is practiced. Whether or not these considerations outweigh the price of off-site water quality control depends upon the local conditions. It is important to remember that aesthetic compatibility and local opinion should be considered on par with the premining and postmining physical, chemical, and economic attributes of a mined site.

Finally, in a system in which energy costs and technology are changing rapidly, short-term reclamation costs may need to be compared with long-term or projected benefits. What now appears farfetched—for example using reclaimed mines for heat storage from giant solar collectors—may one day be feasible economically.

Achieving reclamation objectives

Federal and state surface coal mining reclamation laws have set water quality effluent standards both explicitly and implicitly. To achieve some of these explicit standards, the emphasis is on effluent treatment. Conversely, the groundwater quality standards are not explicit, but instead require that practices or technologies be applied that minimize the degradation of groundwater quality. Essentially, this calls for the proper application of an often nonexistent technology to achieve minimum degradation. From the economic and aesthetic viewpoint, the on-site control methods often appear most attractive. If necessary, when used in conjunction with the more expensive off-site effluent treatment processes, on-site controls may help to achieve effluent standards at a substantially reduced cost.

Selecting the on-site control technology to optimize relatively long-term effluent and groundwater quality while at the same time minimizing short-term erosion may prove complex and extremely difficult. By law or necessity, these decisions and their continual updating fall to the appropriate state or federal agencies, which must designate acceptable technologies or guidelines for selecting these technologies. Part of the problem is that the processes controlling acid production and salt or trace metal losses are not sufficiently well understood on a large enough scale for adequate design of appropriate control technologies. Control methods such as those described here are based on assumptions and thus contain limitations that often make them inappropriate for a particular site. Hence there is a great need for improved understanding of the systems and for innovative application of this understanding to better and more efficiently reclaim surface coal mines.

We have described one such application to increase understanding and improve predictions of erosion and sedimentation on reclaimed coal surface mined lands. We are applying the same methodology to describe acid generation in spoil over a large area. Concentration distributions of acid-producing materials, oxygen in the profile, and of large, water-conducting voids in the spoil profile are under study. We hope that this type of research will shortly yield required answers to modern technology requirements of surface coal mine reclamation. Although it appears that aesthetic considerations promote reclamation to a premining status quo, the economic factors often outweigh most other considerations. The general challenge is to devise effective and acceptable reclamation strategies and supporting methodologies that can achieve economic, aesthetic, and pollution control objectives.

REFERENCES

1. Curtis, W. R. 1974. *Sediment yield from strip-mined watersheds in eastern Kentucky.* In *Second Research and Applied Technology Symposium on Mined Land Reclamation, Louisville, Kentucky.* National Coal Association, Washington, D.C. p. 88-100.
2. Elfstrom, R. W. 1978. *A preliminary model to estimate the strip mine reclamation potential of selected land uses.* Unpublished M.S. thesis. Pennsylvania State University, University Park, Pennsylvania.
3. Environmental Protection Agency. 1976. *Erosion and sediment control, surface mining in the eastern U.S., volume 1 (planning) and volume 2 (design).* EPA-625/3-76-006. U.S Environmental Protection Agency, Washington, D.C.
4. Environmental Protection Agency. 1973. *Methods for identifying and evaluating the nature and extent of nonpoint source of pollutants.* EPA-4030/9-73-0141 U.S. Environmental Protection Agency, Washington, D.C.
5. Federal Register. 1979. *Surface coal mining and reclamation operations, permanent regulatory program.* Book 3, Part II 44(50): 15,311-15,463. The National Archives, Washington, D.C.
6. Gang, M. W., and D. Langmuir. 1974. *Controls on heavy metals in surface and ground waters affected by coal mine drainage: Clarion River-Redbank Creek Watershed, Pennsylvania.* In *Proceedings, Fifth Symposium on Coal Mine Drainage Research, Coal and the Environment Technical Conference.* Louisville, Kentucky. p. 39-69.
7. Hill, D. E., and J. Y. Parlange. 1972. *Wetting front instability in layered soils.* Soil Science Society of America Proceedings 36(5): 697-702.
8. Hons, F. M. 1978. *Chemical and physical properties of lignite spoil material and their influence upon successful reclamation.* Unpublished Ph.D. thesis. Texas A&M University, College Station, Texas.
9. Hounslow, A., and J. Fitzpatrick. 1978. *Overburden mineralogy as related to groundwater chemical changes in coal strip mining.* EPA-600/-78-156. Interagency Energy/Environment R&D Program Report. U.S. Environmental Protection Agency, Washington, D.C. 279 pp.
10. Journel, A. G., and Ch. J. Huijbregts. 1978. *Mining geostatistics.* Academic Press, New York, New York.
11. Lovell, H. L., R. R. Parizek, D. Forsberg, M. Martin, D. Richardson, and J. Thompson. 1978. *Environmental control survey of selected Pennsylvania stripmining sites, a final report.* Submitted to Argonne National Laboratory, Contract No. 31-109-38-3497. 626 pp.
12. Massey, H. F. 1972. *pH and soluble copper, nickel and zinc in eastern Kentucky coal mine spoil materials.* Soil Science 114(3): 217-221.
13. Massey, H. F., and R. I. Barnhisel. 1972. *Copper, nickel and zinc released from acid coal mine spoil materials of eastern Kentucky.* Soil Science 113(3): 207-212.

14. Philip, J. R. 1975. *Stability analysis of infiltration.* Soil Science Society of America Proceedings 39(6): 1,042-1,049.
15. Philip, J. R. 1957. *The theory of infiltration: 4. sorptivity and algebraic infiltration equations.* Soil Science 84(3): 257-264.
16. Pionke, H. B., A. S. Rogowski, and C. A. Montgomery. 1980. *Percolate quality of stripmine spoil.* Transactions, American Society Agricultural Engineers 23(3): 621-628
17. Pionke, H. B., A. S. Rogowski, and R. J. DeAngelis. 1980. *Controlling the rate of acid loss from stripmine spoil.* Journal of Environmental Quality 9(4): 694-699.
18. Rogowski, A. S. 1980. *Hydrologic parameter distribution on a mine spoil.* Watershed Management Symposium. ASCE Irrigation and Drainage Division, Boise, Idaho. pp. 764-780.
19. Rogowski, A. S. 1977. *Acid generation within a spoil profile: preliminary experimental results.* In *Proceedings, Seventh Symposium on Coal Mine Drainage Research.* National Coal Association, Washington, D.C. p. 25-40.
20. Rogowski, A. S., H. B. Pionke, and J. G. Broyan. 1977. *Modeling the impact of strip mining and reclamation processes on quality and quantity of water in mined areas: A review.* Journal of Environmental Quality 6(3): 237-244.
21. Sharon, D. 1980. *The distribution of hydrologically effective rainfall incident on sloping ground.* Journal of Hydrology 46: 165-168.
22. Terzaghi, K., and R. B. Peck. 1960. *Soil mechanics in engineering practice.* John Wiley and Sons, Inc., New York, New York.
23. Van Voast, W. A. 1974. *Hydrologic effects of strip mining in southeastern Montana—emphasis: One year mining near Decker, Montana.* College of Mineral Science and Technology, Butte, Montana.
24. Wischmeier, W. H., and D. D. Smith. 1978. *Predicting rainfall erosion losses, a guide to conservation planning.* Agriculture Handbook 537. U.S. Government Printing Office, Washington, D.C.

46

Wetlands Versus Agricultural Lands: Perspectives on Values and Trade-Offs

Eldie W. Mustard and Glen Loomis
Soil Conservation Service
Denver, Colorado, and Washington, D.C.

Conversion of wetlands to agricultural lands has been a controversial land use issue for many years. Farmers and ranchers interested in making a living by supplying an ever-expanding population with food and fiber see excellent financial opportunities in converting wetlands to productive cropland and pastures. Those concerned with preserving natural values are alarmed by the rapidly disappearing wetlands and the loss of their rich flora, fauna, and associated values.

What are wetlands? According to the U.S. Fish and Wildlife Service's *Classification of Wetlands and Deepwater Habitats of the United States* (5), "Wetlands are lands transitional between terrestrial and aquatic systems where the water table is usually at or near the surface or the land is covered by shallow water. For purposes of this classification wetlands must have one or more of the following three attributes: (1) At least periodically, the land supports predominantly hydrophytes; (2) the substrate is predominantly undrained hydric soil; and (3) the substrate is nonsoil and is saturated with water or covered by shallow water at some time during the growing season of each year."

Many different types of wetlands fit this definition, some which may be difficult for the layman to picture as wetlands. Cattails, bulrushes, standing water, and ducks are not common to all wetlands. Wetlands may include such diverse habitats as bottomland hardwood forests and saltgrass flats.

Agricultural lands may be more easy to define. Put most simply, they are lands that produce food, fuel, and fiber to sustain our existence—but as with wetlands, there are many kinds of agricultural land, land that provides us with products ranging from wood to milk. Both wetlands and agricultural lands are important to society. They are the focus of intense competition for land use by different individuals and groups within our society.

Since European settlement of North America began, and especially in recent decades, wetlands have yielded to our appetite for more agricultural land. In a society that takes a million acres of prime agricultural land out of production each year for houses, roads, or other urban development (3), can we continue to justify replacement of these acres with remaining wetlands? Much of the land use conversion occurring on prime agricultural land could well take place on other kinds of lands that are far less valuable than wetlands or prime agricultural lands.

Precedents for draining wetlands and converting them to other uses are dated in antiquity. In the fourth century B.C., Hippocrates admonished the Athenians against locating their dwellings near wetlands or swamps because of their unwholesome, disease-causing qualities (2). This attitude prevailed in early America. Our American forefathers, including Washington and Jefferson, believed wetlands were fit only for conversion to agriculture and other uses.

It would be foolish to say that wetland drainage was not at one time a necessity to provide the rich farmland that is now the breadbasket of much of the world. It was inevitable. And it was accomplished with zest and zeal, reducing wetlands 40 percent from an estimated 130 million acres to an estimated 78 million acres currently (12, 13). Given this trend, the results of the National Wetland Inventory (5) now being conducted by the U.S. Fish and Wildlife Service will be of interest because the definition of wetlands is changing. Regardless of the outcome, can the United States continue to lose the values associated with wetlands?

The high value of wetlands was recognized in President Carter's Executive Orders 11988 (Floodplain Management) and 11990 (Wetland Preservation and Protection). These Executive Orders regard wetlands as a precious resource that should be altered or destroyed only if the trade-off is of extremely high importance and no practical alternative exists. In addition, they specify that various governmental agencies are to document how they will comply with the orders' mandates. Reducing the net loss of wetlands resulting from agricultural uses to zero by the year 2000 has been proposed by USDA in its draft program document prepared to comply with the Soil and Water Resources Conservation Act of 1977 (RCA).

Weighing the economic benefits of wetlands

Many people are asking whether the conversion of wetlands to agriculture always produces long-term net economic benefits. This is not an easy question to answer. Comparative economic judgments between wetlands and agricultural land uses are difficult to make. Agricultural products have a known value in the marketplace, while the social and environmental values of wetlands are primarily determined by nonmarket or intangible value sets. Benefits derived from wetlands are received by the general public rather than by individual landowners. Also, as with agricultural lands, all wetlands are not of equal productivity (7). Sullivan (14) noted that research compiled by the National Wildlife Federation gave a value of between $50,000 to $80,000 per acre of prime wetlands. This value represents the estimated nonmarket value to society for all the functions performed by wetlands. Some of these functions are food production, flood protection, pollution control, aquifer recharge, recreation, education, and fish and wildlife. Even though there is not total agreement on the actual economic value, there is agreement that the marketplace does not adequately reflect the total social value.

Wetlands serve to purify and take out impurities and materials that get into our rivers, lakes, and estuary systems. In many places, they are used as tertiary treatment sites for sewage disposal systems, indicating their high value in meeting the goal stated in the Clean Water Act Amendments of 1977—to make our rivers and streams "swimmable and fishable by 1985."

Agriculture's positive effects on wetlands

Not all agricultural practices have negative effects on wetlands. Even drainage, in some situations, can be beneficial. In Colorado's San Luis Valley, many areas of this irrigated valley in fact gained wildlife value because of drainage practices.

How could this be? Water from early spring runoff from snowmelt creates temporary wetlands that attract many ducks. Ducks set up housekeeping, hatch their broods, and then sometime during the rearing process, the temporary ponds dry up and the ducklings die. Ditching these areas often provides intermingled permanent open water, thus enhancing wildlife habitat and preventing a nesting situation that often ends in misfortune. This kind of drainage practice is similar in effect to level ditching, which has long been an accepted wetland habitat improvement technique for creating open water in dense herbaceous wetlands.

In the West, irrigated agriculture has created literally thousands of acres of wetlands that often attract new wildlife. Many of these wetlands, though small, are high in wildlife value. But many are in danger of being lost through irrigation system improvement, salinity control measures, and other agricultural activities (9).

On the other hand, it has been estimated that seepage from irrigation canals results in losses of up to 50 percent of the water being diverted for irrigation from some of the older, less-efficient systems. These losses are of national concern in areas short of water.

Even though irrigation creates and maintains these man-induced wetlands, they are valuable habitats, and wildlife managers will continue to promote their protection. Programs and activities that damage such wetlands should provide mitigation for these losses to the extent possible and practical. Mitigation, as used here, means avoiding or minimizing losses, replacing losses, enhancing existing wetlands, or combinations of these.

The philosophy and mitigation policies of the U.S. Department of Agriculture were stated by Assistant Secretary M. Rupert Cutler (6):

"We cannot approach this job with a blind obsession for wildlife habitat. Rather, we must see that our programs consider and balance many economic and environmental concerns or values, in an attempt to optimize them all....

"Other values of a project cannot make up for wildlife losses that may result. We must replace 'in kind,' or in a similar location; that is the USDA's policy. The net loss of 'living things' to society, even with the best mitigation we know how to provide, must be minimized."

Riparian areas: Under "attack" from all sides

Along our nation's rivers, riparian habitats, which are associated with wetlands, are being destroyed or substantially reduced every day for agricultural use. One of our local radio announcers used to say, "Land, a most precious item: they ain't makin' no more of it." The same parallel can be drawn for our riparian habitat—a most valuable part of many important ecosystems. It offers habitat for many wildlife species that must have it for their very survival. We can stand no further losses of these valuable habitats. Strict compliance with Executive Order 11988 (Floodplain Management) will help insure this.

Riparian zones are among our most valuable and productive wildlife habitat (4, 10, 11). They provide habitat essential to the survival of many wildlife species. Riparian habitats furnish valuable edge effects and offer a good wildlife food base where they transect agricultural land. The importance of these areas extends beyond their geographic boundaries. Their zone of influence may extend for 1,000 feet or more into other habitat types (4). Riparian habitats offer opportunities for many wildlife species that would otherwise not exist, and they enrich the human environment with their great diversity of plant and animal life.

Land use changes, lack of proper management, and improper grazing are destroying thousands of acres of riparian habitat each year. The casual observer may note that dominant plants, often large trees and shrubs, are still present. However, in many cases there is no reproduction because of overgrazing by livestock. With the eventual loss of the mature dominant plants, another riparian habitat will disappear.

Too often, riparian areas and other wetlands are used as livestock stomp lots, with little thought of protecting the wetland values or managing for other uses such as wildlife. Often cattails are grazed to the water level as far as the cattle can wade.

The most obvious and perhaps the easiest way to increase habitat values for the remaining riparian zones is to manage and control livestock grazing. In Colorado, Soil Conservation Service (SCS) personnel encourage land users to treat riparian habitat as a distinct ecosystem rather than to include it with upland habitat.

Many wetland types can be created with time, money, and water. This has been demonstrated by Ducks Unlimited, by the U.S. Fish and Wildlife Service, and by private land users with SCS assistance. However, riparian wetlands are virtually irreplaceable. They are a one-time opportunity now pushed to the outer limit. In many parts of the country riparian habitats have been lost to the extent that they could be classed as endangered ecosystems, facing what can be termed "extinction by increment." There are obvious reasons for these losses and they all are related to economics.

Reduced wetlands as a product of agricultural dynamism

Changing agricultural techniques, practices, and management systems sometimes reduce wildlife habitat values. In the San Luis Valley in south central Colorado, the introduction of center-pivot irrigation has reduced the amount of water flowing through drains that formerly carried away the excess water from less efficient flood irrigation methods. This results in a direct loss of wildlife habitat; the man-made drains had high wildlife value. We often have direct competition between habitat—a national concern— and water conservation—the cornerstone of the present water policy.

High erosion rates on agricultural lands cause accelerated aging or eutrophication in wetlands. Many of our natural marshes are old lakes that reached their present successional stage through eutrophication; they are now in the last stage of their lives. We can prolong the lives of these wetlands by proper land use that reduces erosion and sedimentation from our agricultural lands. For example, livestock sewage lagoons, which are increasingly coming into use, can slow the eutrophication of our rivers, lakes, reservoirs, and wetlands.

Some environmental groups are generally opposed to construction of new dams that may often cause alteration and reduction of existing critical game ranges. However, these dams store water that is used for irrigation, recreation, and power, and they do create a different type of wildlife habitat. Is it more valuable to create irrigation-induced wetlands or to protect the deer winter range? Can we trade off deer for ducks, or pheasants, or muskrats? The answers must be determined by individual cases after prudent, thorough study. Everyone will not agree with the final conclusion.

An important issue that is only now surfacing is the cumulative effect of development activities on wetland habitat. Rehabilitating irrigation systems, clearing an acre or two of riparian habitat, or installing a little drainage here or there all have cumulative effects. The effects continue to grow, and with their growth wetland habitat is lost. This is why habitat losses caused by agricultural activities need additional mitigation. Losses must be replaced, or our wetland heritage will be greatly reduced in the next few decades.

Forging a new land use ethic

Our society demands a better land use ethic. Indeed, one might say that a land use ethic still hasn't arrived in this country. Lands are still valued primarily for their economic prospects.

In considering a new land use ethic, Barnes (1) borrowed Graham Ashworth's perspective on the American land use ethic. He cited Ashworth's imperatives:

"You ought to consider land as a resource that may be yours for a time but is also held in trust for the future. Land is not a commodity that any of us can own in the ordinary sense of the word.

"You may be a trustee of the land and that will often confer private benefits on you, but you ought not to seek benefits that incur disbenefits on the community or other individuals.

"If you are presently trusted with the management of a piece of land, you ought to use it in a manner that benefits the land and does not damage it. Some land uses are abuses that have irreversible consequences, and you ought to avoid such abuses.

"You ought to accept that the use of land should be subject to public scrutiny and control and to exercise your responsibility, with others, in ensuring that no use is permitted that is damaging to society as a whole.

"You ought to ensure that the land use controls developed in your area prevent irreversible damage, avoid waste, protect your natural and cultural heritage, stimulate visual order, regulate and control the unsightly, and safeguard individual liberties (such as mobility and a choice in housing and schooling, so long as those liberties do not impede the liberties of others).

"You ought to recognize that the exercise of land use controls in the interest of the community can result in costs and benefits to individuals and be willing to see those costs and benefits equitably adjusted.

"You ought to recognize that these controls can only be exercised democratically through governmental operations. Hence, you ought to expect an extension of government to give proper expression to this new land use ethic.

"You ought to accept that the administration of the ethic must reflect local circumstances and needs so it will vary from place to place.

"You ought to be ready to give time and talents to fight for this land use control that is vital for your continued freedom.

"You ought to recognize that you may have to make some sacrifices, along with everyone else, for this control to be effective."

Aldo Leopold (8), regarded by some as the father of modern wildlife management, put it much more simply in *Sand County Almanac*:

"Conservation is a state of harmony between men and land. Despite nearly a century of propaganda, conservation still proceeds at a snail's pace in many arenas; progress still consists largely of letterhead pieties and convention oratory. On the back forty we still slip two steps backward for each forward stride....

"When one asks why no rules have been written, one is told that the community is not yet ready to support them; education must precede rules. But the education actually in progress makes no mention of obligations to land—over and above those dictated by self-interest. The net result is that we have more education but less soil, fewer healthy woods, and more flood losses than in 1937.

"The puzzling aspect of such situations is that the existence of obligations over and above self-interest is taken for granted in such rural community enterprises as the betterment of roads, schools, churches, and baseball teams. Their existence is not taken for granted, nor as yet seriously discussed, in bettering the behavior of the water that falls on the land, or in the preserving of the beauty or diversity of the farm landscape. Land use ethics are still governed wholly by economic self-interest, just as social ethics were a century ago.

"To sum up: We asked the farmer to do what he conveniently could to save his soil and he has done just that, and only that. The farmer who clears the woods off a 75 percent slope, turns his cows into the clearing, and dumps its rainfall, rocks, and soil into the community creek, is still (if otherwise decent) a respected member of society. If he puts lime on his fields and plants his crops on contour, he is still entitled to all the privileges and emoluments of his soil conservation district....Obligations have no meaning without conscience, and the problem we face is the extension of the social conscience from people to land.

"No important change in ethics was ever accomplished without an internal change in our intellectual emphasis, loyalties, affections, and convictions. The proof that conservation has not yet touched these foundations of conduct lies in the fact that philosophy and religion have not yet heard of it. In our attempt to make conservation easy, we may have made it trivial."

Unfortunately, Leopold did not live to see the 1960s and 1970s, when America had a revolution in its environmental priorities. He would have been pleased at some of our progress in conserving wetlands and agricultural lands. Some of the rules for a land use ethic have been given birth. With proper guidance and understanding, the ethic, now in adolescence, will reach maturity.

What are some of the steps society recently has taken to develop written rules for a land use ethic? A few of the more important ones would be these: National Environmental Policy Act of 1969 (NEPA); Executive Order 11988 (floodplain management), along with the published agency rules for compliance; Executive Order 11990 (protection of wetlands), along with the published agency rules for compliance; Soil and Water Resources Conservation Act of 1977 (RCA); and Secretary's Memorandum No. 1827, Revised (statement on land use policy).

We believe the nation is on its way to achieving a land use ethic based partially on social conscience, not just economic considerations. However, the nation cannot become too complacent with its recent environmental progress. Wetlands and prime agricultural land are still disappearing and will need constant support if they are to survive through the 21st century and beyond. SCS is dedicated to protecting wetlands from needless destruction and to conserving soil and water resources on agricultural lands.

In Colorado the SCS state engineer and his engineering staff call themselves "bioengineers." They consider wetlands when planning flood control, irrigation system improvement projects, and other measures that could adversely affect wetlands. Biologists and engineers together are usually able to accomplish designated agricultural goals and avoid adverse impacts of wetlands.

SCS field personnel frequently consult biologists when they have an agricultural problem on an individual's land, the solution of which may adversely affect existing wetlands. Generally the problem can be resolved to everyone's satisfaction at little or no extra cost and still maintain wetland values.

As people of good will and determination, we can work together to solve conservation problems. It should be remembered that USDA personnel work for a public larger than only those in the agricultural sector. Some also serve those who cannot speak, that constituency represented by the sora rail and the long-billed marsh wren.

Wetlands have fed the nation's demand for new agricultural land since it was founded, but there is still time to preserve some of our wetland heritage. Prime agricultural lands are still being converted to supply the demands of an urban population for space for housing, roads, and the other amenities of our way of life. Mistakes have been made in past land use decisions that will be difficult to rectify.

Carothers (4) summed up past activities and the hope for the future:

"We should not look back on the land management practices of the past with too much remorse and certainly with no blame. A summary of man's activities in and the destruction of woodlands, streams, and rivers simply reflects man's successful settlement of this arid land, allowing...us...the lifestyle we now enjoy. Land management practices of the past should, in fact, be a foundation for learning and understanding how to cautiously move forward in our interactions with the environment."

Let's stop condemning the past and join hands in protecting the nation's valuable resources for both present and future generations. NEPA requires no less!

REFERENCES

1. Barnes, Chaplin B. 1980. *A new land use ethic.* Journal of Soil and Water Conservation 35(2): 61-62.
2. Brande, Justin. 1980. *Worthless, valuable, or what? An appraisal of wetlands.* Journal of Soil and Water Conservation 35(1): 12-16.
3. Briggs, Darwin, and Enid Yurman. 1980. *Disappearing farmland: A national concern.* Soil Conservation 45(6): 4-6.

4. Carothers, Steven W. 1977. *Importance, preservation, and management of riparian habitats: An overview.* In *Importance, Preservation and Management of Riparian Habitat: A Symposium.* U.S. Department of Agriculture, Washington, D.C. pp. 2-4.
5. Cowardin, L. M., Virginia Carter, Francis C. Golet, and E. T. LaRoe. 1979. *Classification of wetlands and deepwater habitats of the United States.* Fish and Wildlife Service, U.S. Department of the Interior, Washington, D.C. 103 pp.
6. Cutler, M. Rupert. 1979. *The need to move from mitigation to multiobjective planning.* In *The Mitigation Symposium.* U.S. Department of Agriculture, Washington, D.C. pp. 54-58.
7. Foster, John H. 1978. *Measuring the social value of wetland benefits.* In *Wetland Functions and Values: The State of Our Understanding.* American Water Resources Association, Minneapolis, Minnesota. 674 pp.
8. Leopold, Aldo. 1949. *A Sand County almanac.* Sierra Club/Ballantine, New York, New York. 295 pp.
9. Mustard, Eldie W., and Claudia D. Rector. 1979. *Wetlands, irrigation and salinity control: Lower Gunnison River Basin, Colorado.* In *The Mitigation Symposium.* U.S. Department of Agriculture, Washington, D.C. pp. 310-317.
10. Pase, Charles P., and Earle F. Layser. 1977. *Classification of riparian habitat in the Southwest.* In *Importance, Preservation and Management of Riparian Habitat: A Symposium.* U.S. Department of Agriculture, Washington, D.C. pp. 5-9.
11. Rector, Claudia D., Eldie W. Mustard, and J. T. Windell. 1979. *Lower Gunnison River Basin wetland inventory and evaluation.* Soil Conservation Service, U.S. Department of Agriculture, Washington, D.C. 90 pp.
12. Reilly, William K. 1978. *Can science help save interior wetlands?* In *Wetland Functions and Values: The State of Our Understanding.* American Water Resources Association, Minneapolis, Minnesota. 674 pp.
13. Shaw, S. P., and C. G. Fredine. 1956. *Wetlands of the United States.* Circular 39. U.S. Fish and Wildlife Service, Washington, D.C. 67 pp.
14. Sullivan, Peter. 1976. *Versatile wetlands—an endangered resource.* National Wildlife Federation Conservation News 41(20): 2-5.

47

Conservation in the Palouse: An Economic Dilemma

Shiraz Vira and Harry Riehle
District conservationist and area agronomist
Soil Conservation Service, Moscow, Idaho

The economics of conservation is the single most important limiting factor preventing massive application of conservation practices on farmland in the Palouse. Farmers are caught in a cost-price squeeze—depressed prices for farm products, and increasing costs for energy, machines, fertilizers, labor, and land. Other factors limit application of long-term conservation programs in the Palouse, including limitations and conflicts within farm programs, limited conservation field personnel, and complicated in-agency conservation program application procedures.

The Palouse: Productivity and problems

The Palouse Prairie was formed from the loessal deposits originating in the glacial outwash of central Washington. A prevailing southwesterly wind brought the predominantly silt-size particles to the Palouse, covering basaltic bedrock and forming dune-like hills with gently sloping south sides and concave, steep, and short north slopes.

A unique combination of deep, fertile soils and a favorable climate make the Palouse ideal for growing winter wheat and dry pea crops. Whitman County, Washington, holds the record yield of winter wheat under dryland conditions of 132 bushels per acre and produces more wheat each year than any other county in the United States (*1*). The Washington-Idaho Palouse produces nearly 93 percent of the pea crop and 95 percent of the lentil crop in the United States.[1]

The Palouse, which has been farmed for 80 to 90 years, is one of the most highly erosive areas in the nation. Soil erosion rates exceeding 100 tons per acre have been measured frequently. Annual rates of 25 to 40 tons per acre are not uncommon. Nearly three-fourths of a ton of soil is lost for every bushel of wheat produced.[2] Average annual soil loss for the region is 14 tons per acre per year (*2*).

The Palouse erosion problem is unique because most erosion occurs in the late winter and early spring, especially after a chinook wind brings in rain and thawing temperatures. Melted snow saturates the soil surface. Beneath this saturated layer the ground remains frozen. Rainwater is unable to permeate the ice-blocked pores, causing the already saturated soil to become a paste creeping down the hillsides. If enough soil erosion occurs, the thick, deep scars of gullying appear. Soil slipping also occurs, especially on north slopes where snow has accumulated. The drifted snow adds more weight and eventually more water to the soil below the drift, causing soil slips. Blemishes of soil slippage mark the Palouse landscape in many places, even grassed critical areas.

Setting up the project

The erosion and resulting annual yield reduction of 2 to 3 bushels of wheat per acre per year per inch of topsoil lost has been masked by technological advances over the years. But because of excessive erosion of Palouse farmland and its effects on the water quality of receiving streams, the Palouse Erosion Control Project was initiated in October 1976 by the Idaho Department of Health and Water, Division of Environment, using a U.S. Environmental Protection Agency grant for a planning and demonstration project under the Idaho Clean Water Program (208). The Idaho Department of Environment contracted the Latah Soil Conservation District to carry out the project.

The Latah Soil Conservation District subcontracted specific portions of the project to various agencies, including the Science and Education Administration—Agricultural Research, the University of Idaho, and the Soil Conservation Service. The objective of the project was to evaluate Latah Soil Conservation District's five-point program, which was initiated by the district in 1978 to deal with the serious soil erosion problem of the Palouse Prairie. The five-points (best management practices) are: (1) minimum tillage, (2) divided slopes, (3) restricted summer fallow, (4) cross-slope farming, and (5) critical area treatment.

The five-point program, adopted by cooperators in the Latah Soil Con-

[1]Verbal communication, July 1980, with Idaho Pea and Lentil Association, Moscow.
[2]Kaiser, Verle G. 1939-1977. "Erosion surveys of Whitman County." Unpublished.

servation District through development and implementation of a conservation plan approved by the district, has proved effective in reducing soil erosion by as much as 75 to 90 percent. Only those district cooperators willing
to implement all points of the program applicable to their farms are accepted by the district. Currently, farmers with a total of 15,000 acres participate
in the voluntary program.

The study area selected for the Palouse Erosion Control Project lies in the
south central portion of Latah County about five miles southwest of Moscow, Idaho. The principal study area consists of the Cow Creek drainage, a
tributary of the Palouse River. The area's climate, soils, and topography
are typical of the Palouse and other nonirrigated cropland areas of Idaho,
Washington, and Oregon having similar problems. The study area encom-
passes 21,817 acres upstream of Genesee, Idaho, and involves 60 land operators.

Crops common to the areas are winter wheat, spring wheat, barley, dry
peas, lentils, grass seed, hay, and pasture. Wheat, barley, and peas are the
major crops.

The operating cost of applying the five-point program is $10 per acre per
year, voluntarily carried by the conservation farmer. Most of this cost is derived from foregone income and additional conservation practice maintenance cost.

The Latah Soil Conservation District's five-point program definitely reduces erosion when properly applied by the farm operator. It is an effective
program and has the limited support of most operators and growers. However, because of the total five-point program's cost, most operators only apply certain practices.

To achieve comprehensive land protection in the Palouse, there must be a
heavy emphasis on management practices in addition to support practices.
Management practices include crop selection, crop rotations, crop residue
use, tillage practices, and timing of the overall farm operation. Support
practices include stripcropping, divided slopes, diversions, terraces, and
grassed waterways.

Both management and support practices need to be effectively applied to
provide total protection from soil erosion, and both kinds of practices cost
the farm operator extra money for as long as he maintains the practices. For
example, changing a cropping sequence from a winter wheat/pea rotation
to annual grain provides more residue for controlling erosion. However, the
winter wheat/pea rotation is more profitable than annual grain, usually
spring barley or spring wheat and occasionally winter wheat. A rotation of
winter wheat and peas provides higher yields at less tillage and fertilizer
cost. On the other hand, annual grain may be the only practical way to control erosion in some areas. The operator thus has to absorb not only the additional direct expenses but also a reduced income every year of annual
grain cropping.

Indirect expenses of certain practices also discourage farmers. For example, with critical-area grass seeding, as much as 60 to 70 bushels of wheat

are lost per acre. This foregone income or the opportunity cost is quite substantial and can make a significant impact on landowners' decisions to seed critical areas. In addition to income foregone, operators also have increased production costs when farming critical area seedings, such as extra turns, plowing uphill, and weed control. There is the additional cost of grass seeding. Grass is the only answer for erosion control in some critical areas of the Palouse, but grass has its limits, too, and can add to the runoff control problems below it.

Support practices have both installation and maintenance costs. Installation costs occurs once and are covered adequately by cost-sharing programs. Maintenance costs, however, occur every year at the farmer's expense. For example, in Latah County no crop dusters will fly strip crops for weed control. Even if a crop duster were found to spray strip crops, herbicide selection is extremely limited because most strips are alternated with winter wheat and peas or legumes, and damage can result from herbicide drifting. Aerial application of herbicide in the spring is an essential part of effective farm management. Ground spraying is extremely limited at the critical time due to wet ground. Again, this cost is incurred annually and only to those operators who have installed strips.

To make such support practices more palatable and widespread, operators should be compensated for the high maintenance cost, which in reality is a part of the total cost of the practice.

Where needed, a complete package of best management practices should be cost-shared. Certain farmland may only require a couple of management practices for complete soil protection, whereas more severe areas need both management and support practices. When support practices are called for, they should be installed in order for operators to qualify for cost-share assistance on their management practices.

Society currently expects farm operators to control erosion and clean up our streams as dictated by our clean water legislation. But society fails to recognize the full negative economic impact of such action on farmers. Some changes that farmers are expected to make require expensive new equipment. There is no short-term economic return for farmers using conservation practices, and society is not picking up its share of the cost. Indeed, the greatest erosion control and water quality benefits are obtained from management practices that have the total cost carried by the farmer.

Re-evaluating cost-sharing policy

Cost sharing is normally limited to long-lasting structural practices. We believe it is time that we took a good look at another approach to cost sharing, one that is designed to change farmers' habits or, if you will, bring "social change." Under such a policy, cost-sharing money would be provided to farmers strictly so that they get in the habit of performing in a certain manner. Although we can expect that farmers will not accept such a policy for whatever reasons, we suggest a cost-sharing program for a total conservation program. The hope is that farmers would eventually accept the program and change their conservation habits.

From personal observation, we believe this system has performed well in the Latah Soil Conservation District. For no-till and divided slope practices, this approach can and will work. In the long-run, the system provides long-lasting benefits not provided by current approaches, which are based on continual financial assistance.

We can no longer afford to fight old problems with old methods. We have made strides with a piecemeal approach. But it is about time we combat our battles with a new tool. Cost sharing for social change is one approach. Another is through the "green ticket," or a combination of the two. We can make even greater strides with a total management systems approach.

REFERENCES

1. Berglund, S. H. 1978. *Economic evaluation of the five-point soil erosion control program in Latah County, Idaho.* Unpublished M.S. thesis. Department of Agricultural Economics, University of Idaho, Moscow.
2. Soil Conservation Service. 1978. *Palouse Cooperative River basin study.* U.S. Department of Agriculture, Washington, D.C.